GRACE & GRANDEUR

A History of Salt Lake City

Thomas G. Alexander

Published by

Heritage Media Corp.

Heritage Building

1954 Kellogg Avenue, Carlsbad, California 92008

www.heritagemedia.com

ISBN: 1-886483-60-4

Library of Congress Control Number: 2001099015

Thomas G. Alexander *Author & Photo Editor*

Charles E. Parks *CEO/Publisher*

Lori M. Parks *Editorial Director*

Stephen Hung *Executive Vice President*

Bart Barica *VP/Corporate Development*

Randall Peterson *CFO*

Design	**Editorial**
Gina Mancini *Art Director*	Betsy Baxter Blondin *Editor-in-Chief*
Robert Galmarini	Betsy Lelja *Softcover Managing Editor*
Chris Hamilton	Mary Campbell
Marianne Mackey	John Woodward
Charlie Silvia	
	Administration
	Kelly Corcoran *Human Resources Manager*
Production	Stephanie Dail
Deborah Sherwood *IT/Production Manager*	Juan Diaz
Jay Kennedy *Assistant Production Manager*	Azalea Maes
Dave Hermstad	Scott Reid
Arturo Ramirez	Vicki Verne

Client Services Aina Grant

Profile Writers

Kellene Ricks Adams

Karen Boren

Bridget Cook

G. Donald Gale

Allen Gardiner

Nora Horn

Steven Osborne

David Walden

Published in cooperation with Utah State Historical Society

Printed by Heritage Media Corp. in the United States of America

First Edition

DEDICATION

For Thomas Jade, Dominic Raphael, Joshua Webb, Adam Glen, Emma Marilyn and Benjamin Johns from a loving Grandfather

part one

Acknowledgments 7

Preface 9

chapters

The Creation of a Mormon Commonwealth 10

The Americanization of a Latter-day Saint Commonwealth 30

The Progressive City 50

Depression and War 70

Salt Lake City and its Hinterland 88

The Face of a Mature City 106

CONTENTS

part two

partners in salt lake city

Partners Table of Contents 124

Building a Greater Salt Lake City 126

Business & Finance 140

Community Commitment 150

Manufacturing & Distribution 164

Marketplace 188

Networks 210

Quality of Life 224

Technology 252

Bibliography 264

Index 268

Partners & Web Site Index 274

ACKNOWLEDGMENTS

In doing any writing an author is always beholden to others. I appreciate particularly James Allen and the crew of research assistants and secretaries, especially Kenneth Cannon, Harvard Heath, Kim James, Brian Champion, Brian Dunsmore, Bruce Lott, Bruce Van Orden, Frank Bruno, Lori Warren, Natalie Ethington, Jennifer Dean and Kyra Swain, who helped us with the research that underpinned part of this study. I appreciate also the research and books of Linda Sillitoe and John McCormick upon which I have constantly relied.

Most especially, I offer thanks to those who helped in selecting photographs. Particularly I appreciate the undying assistance of Bill Slaughter, April Williamsen, and the staff of the Archives Division of the Family and Church History Department of the Church of Jesus Christ of Latter-day Saints. Of particular help were Janell Tuttle, Susan Whetstone, Christian Hancock, Douglas Misner, Maren Jeppsen and Linda Thatcher of the Utah State Historical Society. Craig Fuller of the Historical Society also supplied photographs he had taken. Nelson Wadsworth let me reproduce copies from his extensive collection of historical photographs. Roy Webb, Lorraine Crouse and the staff of the Special Collections, Manuscripts, and Photographs Department of the J. Willard Marriott Library provided skiing photographs. Revel and LaRue Phillips furnished photographs from their family collection. Cynthia Buckingham and the staff of the Utah Humanities Council helped with photographs from their files.

I appreciate the work of others at the Utah State Historical Society. Max Evans encouraged me in this project and Stan Layton read and critiqued the finished manuscript and saved me from a number of errors.

At Heritage Media Corporation, I appreciate the assistance of Betsy Blondin, Lori Parks and Gina Mancini.

Most especially, I thank my wife, Marilyn, for her encouragement on this project.

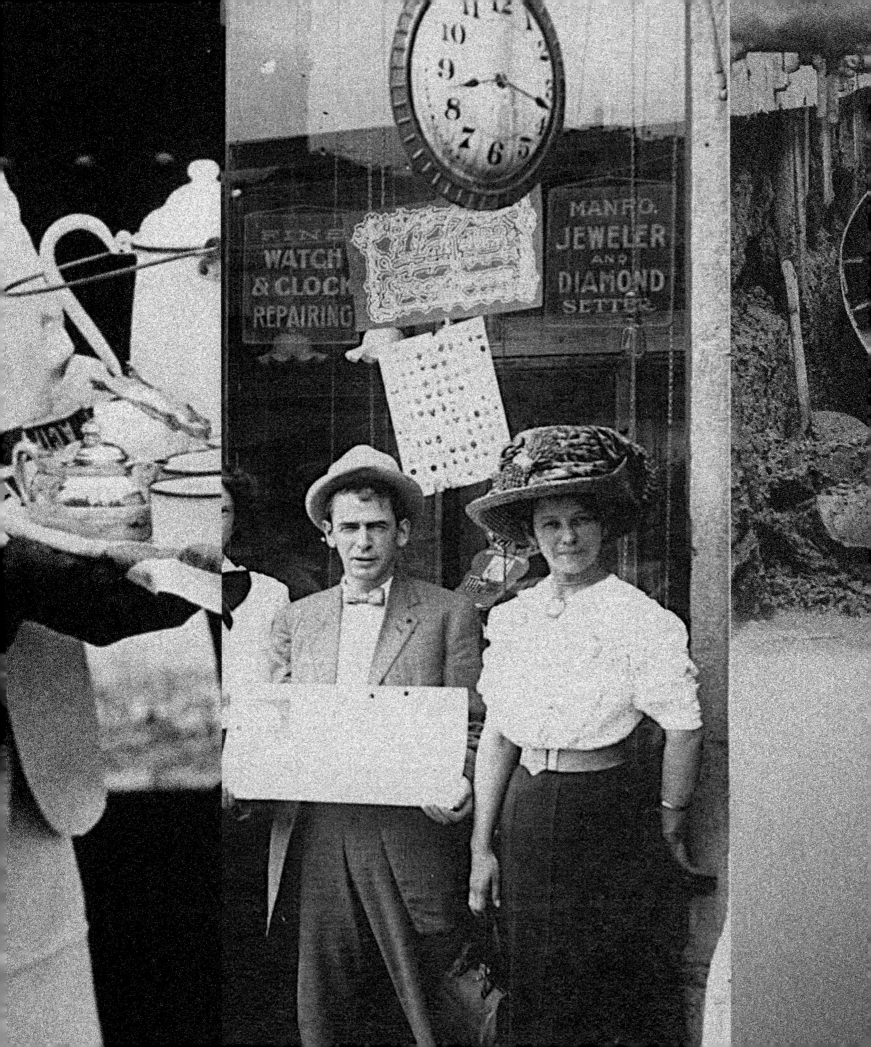

PREFACE

On September 15, 2001, Marilyn and I sat with 4,000 others in the auditorium at Cottonwood High School in Salt Lake City at the kickoff training session for a tenth of the estimated 40,000 volunteers who will serve participants and patrons for the 2002 Winter Olympics. We listened to encouragement by Mitt Romney, president of the Salt Lake Organizing Committee; Charlene Wells, a former Miss America and SLOC staff member; and others from the Team 2002 leadership. We all left invigorated at the prospect of helping host the games in Salt Lake City and at venues in nearby cities and the Wasatch Mountains.

Nevertheless, as we listened, the tragic events of September 11, 2001, weighed heavily on our minds and hearts. Many of those in attendance wore red, white and blue ribbons in remembrance of the horror of that day. This was because on September 11, teams of Islamic terrorists had hijacked four commercial airliners filled with civilian passengers. The terrorists piloted two of the planes into New York's Twin Trade Towers. The collision and subsequent collapse of the buildings killed more than 3,000 unarmed citizens and a large number of police and firefighters who had rushed to their assistance. In a coordinated attack, the terrorists rammed one of the planes into the Pentagon near Washington, D.C., destroying part of the building and killing several hundred employees and visitors.

In the wake of these horrors on September 20, 2001, a group of Salt Lake City's community and religious leaders called the "Alliance for Unity" issued a statement urging cooperation and tolerance among people of diverse religious and ethnic backgrounds. The alliance had originated in earlier conversations about the need for unity and tolerance in Salt Lake City between Mayor Ross C. "Rocky" Anderson and Jon M. Huntsman, president of Huntsman Chemical Company. In an unprecedented step, the First Presidency of the Church of Jesus Christ of Latter-day Saints, which is headquartered in Salt Lake City, instructed the bishop in each of the church's thousands of wards to read the statement in sacrament meeting on September 23, 2001. This is the first time of which I am aware that the First Presidency has endorsed a statement not written by church leaders. Signed by Huntsman and Anderson, the statement also carried the signatures of men and women who lead the city's Latino, African-American, Jewish, Baptist, Catholic, Episcopalian, Latter-day Saint, business, legal, educational and other communities.

Indeed, although the majority of Salt Lake citizens belong to the Church of Jesus Christ of Latter-day Saints, the city encompasses a broad range of peoples of diverse backgrounds and convictions. In view of the events of September 11 and the upcoming Olympic Games, never before has Salt Lake City needed more tolerance and cooperation.

Thomas G. Alexander

On the morning of July 21, 1847, Orson Pratt and Erastus Snow, members of the Quorum of Twelve Apostles of the Church of Jesus Christ of Latter-day Saints, followed the trail that the ill-fated Donner party had hacked out the year before. The two apostles passed through northern Utah's Wasatch Mountains by traveling over Big Mountain and Little Mountain and down Emigration Canyon,

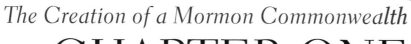

The Creation of a Mormon Commonwealth
CHAPTER ONE

Wilford Woodruff (far right),Orson Pratt (center) and Erastus Snow (right), were members of the Quorum of Twelve Apostles of the Church of Jesus Christ of Latter-day Saints and members of the advance party of Mormon Pioneers in the Salt Lake Valley *Family and Church History Department, Church of Jesus Christ of Latter-day Saints, Archives Division (LDS Church Archives)*

which opens onto the foothills east of Salt Lake City at today's 900 South. Since they shared one horse, they alternated riding and walking to the canyon summit. From that height they glimpsed the Salt Lake Valley stretching out before them for about 25 miles east to west and about 40 miles north to south. As they admired the scene, they noted the "the broad waters of the Great Salt Lake glisten[ing] in the sunbeams" at the north end.

After riding through the narrow tree- and rock-covered Wasatch canyons for days on end, they beheld the wide expanse of Salt Lake Valley scenery, and it touched their souls. "Almost involuntarily," a "shout of joy" escaped from their "lips the moment this grand and lovely scenery" stroked their senses. Tramping down to the valley floor, they made a 12-mile circuit before rejoining their companions.

Pratt and Snow led the picket line of a band of believers who sought refuge from a war of perse-cution that had driven them from their homes in Nauvoo, Illinois. Behind them a company of road builders superintended by Willard Richards and George A. Smith, also members of the Quorum of the Twelve, cleared stumps and graded the Emigration Canyon road to rough passability.

A couple of days to the rear, a smaller party accompanied their leader, Brigham Young, president of the Twelve, who rode in Apostle Wilford Woodruff's carriage. Young was gradually recuperating from "mountain fever," a disease some scholars have identified as Colorado tick fever. Behind the sick party, companies totaling nearly 1,700 men, women and children stretched out in groups across South Pass, along Wyoming's high plains, and up the

Brigham Young, President of the Church of Jesus Christ of Latter-day Saints, leader of the Pioneer Company that brought the Mormons to Utah, and Utah Territorial governor *LDS Church Archives*

Platte River trail. Most of the rest of the refugees remained tem-porarily settled along the Missouri River in Nebraska and Iowa.

On July 22, after consulting with Willard Richards and the road builders, Smith, Pratt, and seven others departed to explore the north end of the valley. Crossing Red Butte Creek at three-quarters of a mile and City Creek at two and a half miles from Emigration Creek, they discovered the hot springs located between present 800 and 900 north at about 300 West. Having traveled about 20 miles, they returned to find that Richards' party had reached the valley floor.

On July 23 at a camp near City Creek, Pratt called on God in prayer. He consecrated and dedicated the land and blessed the seed.

Then, dividing into task groups, the pioneers began transforming the wilderness into a thriving settlement. One party found a plot at what is now between 200 and 300 South and State Street and 200 East on which to plant potatoes, corn, beans, turnips, buckwheat, and sundry other crops. Mowers set out to cut down the tall grass that covered the fertile land. A herder kept the plowmen and harrowers supplied with fresh teams. After the plowing had begun, workers dammed City Creek and began digging canals and laterals to irrigate the newly planted fields.

On July 24 Brigham Young, Wilford Woodruff and the sick party crested the hill at the mouth of Emigration Canyon. Enchanted by the site that greeted them, Young looked over the valley. Then, as Woodruff remembered it, he said, "Brother Woodruff, drive on. Here is our home. This is the place God has pointed out for us to plant our feet. I have seen this place before."

Not all among the 148 people in the pioneer party saw the land's beauty. Harriet Decker Young, wife of Lorenzo Dow Young, said, "Weak and weary as I am, I would rather go a thousand miles further than to remain in such a forsaken place as this." For her and for several others, it was a land of "desolation and loneliness." Most disagreed.

Paradoxically, violent forces of nature had taken millions of years to create the grandeur that awed Pratt, Snow, Smith, Richards, Woodruff, and Brigham Young. Between 30,000 and 10,000 years ago, Lake Bonneville, the largest late Pleistocene lake in western North America, covered the Salt Lake Valley and lapped at the foothills of the Wasatch Mountains. A holocaust of subterranean volcanic activity 37 to 20 million years ago had forced igneous magma into the yielding earth to form the mountains. The magma contained minerals such as lead, copper, silver, and gold, which it deposited to the east of the valley in the Wasatch Mountains and in the Oquirrhs to the west.

Nestled between the Wasatch and Oquirrh mountains, the Salt Lake Valley lies on the eastern edge of America's Great Basin. The valley is blessed with annual precipitation of about 15 inches, which is higher than the 5 to 10 inches elsewhere in the basin because the peaks of the Wasatch Mountains to the east range between 9,000 and 11,300 feet. Most of this precipitation falls as snow. During the winter months, the mountains milk their white gold from the westerly winds blowing from the Pacific Ocean and Gulf of California.

In the mountains, precipitation is even higher and its benefits more widespread. Silver Lake near the Brighton and Solitude ski areas gets nearly 44 inches of precipitation each year. Powder snow forms because of the cold, dry climate and offers excellent skiing. As an added benefit, the spring and summer sun releases the moisture for homes, farms and businesses in the valley.

From the mountains above the Salt Lake Valley, much of the water eventually finds its way into the Great Salt Lake, a supersaturated solution of salts and minerals. Great Salt Lake is the most evident descendant of its Pleistocene ancestor. Since Lake Bonneville had covered western Utah and eastern Nevada at levels varying between 5,090 and 4,250 feet above sea level for 20,000 years, streams flowing from the nearby mountains had dropped their loads of rich alluvial soil on the lake bottom. The deposits of water-born treasure continued to deepen after Lake Bonneville had disappeared as rivers and creeks regularly deposited their bounty on the Salt Lake Valley.

This fertile soil, heavily covered with grasses, forbs, and wildlife had offered an inviting haven for numerous peoples before the first Mormons saw the Salt Lake Valley. The valley's first inhabitants, the Paleoindians, enjoyed nature's bounty as the waters of Lake Bonneville receded. Most Paleoindians subsisted on small animals as well as on since-extinct Pleistocene megafauna such as horses, camels, muskoxen, and mammoths. They hunted these animals with projectiles tipped with fluted points. In addition, the cold, damp late Pleistocene weather nurtured spruce-fir and bristlecone pine forests that may have reached to the lake's shores.

In about 6500 B.C. the Archaic culture replaced the Paleoindians. These residents remained in the Salt Lake Valley until about 300 B.C. Gathering in family-centered nomadic or sedentary hunter-gatherer communities, the Archaic Indians

(Left and below) Outline of a pit house and overview of the site of a Fremont Indian Village (below) uncovered on South Temple Street during the construction of the TRAX trolley line *Office of Public Archaeology, Brigham Young University, Provo, Utah*

subsisted to a greater degree than the Paleoindians on plants, seeds, berries and fish in addition to the animals that had fed their predecessors. The sedentary groups lived on the marshes surrounding the lakes and watercourses.

About 300 B.C. the Archaic culture yielded to the Fremont peoples. The Fremont lived in an area that stretched from southern Utah into southern Idaho, eastern Nevada, southwestern Wyoming and western Colorado. Anthropologists have identified five major Fremont subcultures. Some of the people from one of these subcultures, the Great Salt Lake Fremont, lived in the Salt Lake Valley. Some Fremont lived in pithouses, made baskets, constructed leather moccasins from the hocks of deer or mountain sheep, and molded their lovely thin-walled gray pottery.

Those who lived along the shores of the lakes and watercourses harvested the bounties of these productive environments. They ate native plants and fished with nets, harpoons, and hooks in the streams that fed Great Salt Lake and Utah Lake in the valley to the south. They cultivated corn, beans, and squash. The Fremont grew a variety of corn similar to their southern neighbors, the Anasazi, but they also cultivated a distinctive type of 14-row dent corn that matured in a shorter time, resisted drought, and fit better into the cooler climate of central and northern Utah. Fremont culture disappeared from the Salt Lake Valley, as it did from the remainder of Utah, sometime in the 13th century, probably as the result of a prolonged drought.

As the Fremont disappeared, waves of Numic or Shoshonean peoples gathered into the Great Basin from southern California. They spread throughout Utah and into the surrounding states. Displacing or assimilating the Fremont, two branches of Numic peoples, the Northern Ute and Northwestern Shoshoni, occupied the Salt Lake Valley.

Both the Ute and Shoshoni practiced sophisticated herbal medicine and maintained an elaborate animistic religion. The Utes tell of the creation of humans by Sinawaf (or Senawahv), their chief god whom they identified with the wolf. Sinawaf cut sticks and placed them in a bag where they turned into human beings. He planned to distribute people equally throughout the earth, but Coyote, a trickster god, disrupted his plans by

randomly freeing the bagged-up humans. Trying to make the best of Coyote's trickery, Sinawaf called those left in the bag the Utes, released them, and said they would be braver than any of the others.

Coyote engaged in other mischief as well. While planning the world, the animal gods and heroes argued over the length of seasons. They decided the year would include three winter months. Not satisfied with the decision and up to his usual trickery, Coyote added a fourth month — we call it March. He ordained that in March the Utes would run out of stored food. Then, they would have to subsist by stewing their grease-soaked rawhide bags. In an ultimate unkind stroke, Coyote also afflicted the people with sickness and death.

Unlike the Fremont who earned a substantial portion of their subsistence from agriculture, the Utes and Shoshonis of Salt Lake Valley fed and clothed themselves from hunting and harvesting. Situated on the western edge of the Wasatch Mountains and the eastern edge of the Great Basin, the Salt Lake Valley lay on the rim of pinyon-juniper foothills laced with serviceberries, elderberries, wild raspberries, and wild roses as well as mountain mahogany, big tooth maple, willows, cottonwood, and oakbrush. The valley west of the Jordan River hosted sagebrush flats from which they dug roots of the camas, sego lily, tule, and yucca. The entire valley also yielded grasses from which they harvested seeds.

Having invented more efficient beaters and baskets than the Fremont, the Numic people exploited the bounty of seeds more easily than their predecessors. In the mountains and nearby grasslands, the Numics hunted larger game such as deer, elk, and even some bison. In the sagebrush and grass they found eggs and small animals like rabbits and ducks. In the nearby rivers and creeks and in Utah Lake to the south, they fished by hand and with baskets, weirs, or barbed arrows. They harvested grasshoppers and crickets, and they ground these with berries to make a protein-rich cake. They made clothing from the hides of the animals, some by cutting the hides into strips they wove into a sturdy cloth.

By the 1830s Utah's Northern Utes and Northwestern Shoshonis had obtained horses, which gave them added mobility.

Many adopted the hunting culture of the plains Indians, foraging far and wide as they sought herds of large game. The Utes also rode south and west to enslave the horseless Paiutes and Gosiutes, most of whom lived as harvesters, hunters, and farmers. The Utes traded the Paiute and Gosiute captives in Santa Fe and other southwestern cities.

Just as the Utes and Shoshonis had encroached on Fremont lands, European and American explorers, trappers, and traders begun to invade the Numic domains. Spanish explorers from Santa Fe and other towns in New Mexico made the first penetrations of the Numic lands. In 1776 Franciscan Friars Francisco Atanasio Dominguez and Silvestre Velez de Escalante, seeking an overland route from New Mexico to Monterey, California, journeyed through western Colorado, the Uinta Basin, and Spanish Fork Canyon into Utah Valley. They heard of a valley and a salt lake farther to the north, but they turned southwest instead of entering it.

In the wake of the Dominguez and Escalante expedition, Mountain Men ventured into the Salt Lake region either to trade or to trap for beaver. In the early 19th century, beaver-felt hats became an international fashion rage and America's western mountain streams offered a bountiful supply of the furry animals.

The Mountain Men advanced in three waves. First, Spanish and after the revolution in 1820 Mexican settlements in northern New Mexico such as Taos and Abiquiu served as jumping-off points for those who ventured into the Uinta Basin and central and northern Utah. Second, the Lewis and Clark expedition of 1804-06 led Americans into the West in search of beaver as well. St. Louis served as the starting point for most of the American expeditions. Third, British companies led by the Northwest and Hudson's Bay companies — combined in 1821 under the name Hudson's Bay Company — had designs on northern Utah. These outfitted themselves in such northwestern posts as Fort Vancouver in southern Washington, Fort Nez Perce near the confluence of the Snake and Columbia rivers, and Flathead Post near present-day Eddy, Montana.

The first penetration of the Salt Lake Valley by Mountain Men probably took place in 1824. In late summer or early fall, French Canadians Etienne Provost and Francois Leclerc left Taos with a party to trap and trade for beaver in central and northern Utah. Settling the bulk of the party at the confluence of the White and Green rivers in the Uinta Basin, Provost took 10 men into the Salt Lake Valley, probably along the Dominguez-Escalante trail.

By October the trappers had traveled north along the Jordan River into Salt Lake Valley where they met a party of Shoshoni led by Bad Gocha or Wasatch, the chief who gave his name to the Wasatch Mountains. Anxious to ingratiate themselves with the Shoshoni, Provost and his party sat down to smoke the peace pipe with Gocha's band. The two parties seemed to enjoy each other's company until Gocha and his warriors suddenly pounced upon the unarmed trappers and killed all except Provost and one colleague, who managed to escape.

Unknown to the Taos trappers, members of a Hudson's Bay company led by Peter Skene Ogden had killed a Shoshoni chief earlier in the year. Not recognizing the difference between Provost's French-Canadians and Mexicans and Ogden's British-Canadians and Iroquois, the Shoshonis retaliated against the first trappers they met. Eight of Provost's men died as unlucky victims. The 1824 expedition probably took Provost to the site of Salt Lake City, and he may have been the first Euroamerican to see Great Salt Lake, though we are not sure because only fragmentary documentation of his route has survived. Instead, the honor of discovering Great Salt Lake generally goes to Jim Bridger who rode a bullboat down the Bear River from Cache Valley in the fall of 1824.

After Provost and Bridger had penetrated the Salt Lake Valley, trappers and traders crossed the future site of Salt Lake City during the late 1820s and the 1830s. Jedediah Strong Smith rode through the valley in his southwestern expeditions of 1826-29. Joseph R. Walker reached the valley in 1833.

Between the Dominguez-Escalante expedition and the 1840s, the Salt Lake Valley evoked a great deal of interest, in part, because of a geographical mistake. A map drawn by Don Bernardo Miera y Pacheco, cartographer for Dominguez and Escalante, led many Euroamericans to believe that a westward flowing river named the Rio Buenaventura connected the Great Salt Lake with the Pacific Ocean. Indeed, because of its saltiness, some thought the lake, itself, was an arm of the ocean.

In 1833, however, Joseph R. Walker's explorations under the direction of Capt.

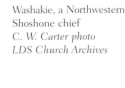

Washakie, a Northwestern Shoshone chief
C. W. Carter photo
LDS Church Archives

Benjamin L. E. Bonneville, after whom Lake Bonneville was named, erased this myth from the maps. Additional geographic knowledge ought to have deleted such stories from general consciousness, but it did not. Bonneville drew maps of the region as did William Kittson of the Hudson's Bay Company; former treasury secretary Albert Gallatin, who relied on various sources including Jedediah Smith's explorations; and Warren A. Ferris, a civil engineer and fur trader. Such myths die hard, and it was not until John C. Frémont's expedition of 1843-44 that the general public finally buried the story in its overdue grave.

After the settlers began to migrate through the Great Basin toward California in 1841, the federal government sent scientific expeditions to map, explore, and mark trails. Frémont led two expeditions into the Great Salt Lake Valley before 1847. On the 1843-44 expedition he brought Charles Preuss, an excellent cartographer, and on both expeditions, Frémont provided a systematic cataloguing of plants and animals. Frémont's 1843-44 expedition, guided by Mountain Men Thomas Fitzpatrick and Kit Carson, took the party into Cache Valley and down the Bear River gorge, which enters the Salt Lake Valley north of present-day Collinston, Utah.

*Group of Shoshones,
C. W. Carter photo
LDS Church Archives*

After exploring Frémont Island in the Great Salt Lake, the Pathmarker led his party northwestward to the Oregon Trail, the eastern Great Basin, and California. He returned to Utah by way of the Old Spanish Trail, a route from Santa Fe to Los Angeles that passed through central Utah. Leaving the Old Spanish Trail, he followed the Plateau and Wasatch fronts — the approximate route of Interstate 15 today — to Utah Lake.

Frémont's 1845 expedition took him to the Jordan River and Great Salt Lake by way of the White River and the Uinta Basin. After camping at the future site of Salt Lake City, Frémont led a party to Antelope Island. Finding the island well stocked with pronghorns, the explorers killed several for food. Returning from the island, they encountered an old Ute who claimed ownership of the game. Unwilling to argue, Frémont gave him goods in payment for the antelope. Frémont then crossed the Great Salt Lake Desert on the route later taken by the Donner party. He reached the base of Pilot Peak and the Humboldt River, both of which he named or renamed.

Crossing the Sierra Nevada to California, Frémont camped at Sutter's Fort during the winter of 1845-46. There he met a part-time fur trader and promoter named Lansford W. Hastings. Anxious to attract Americans to California, in 1845 Hastings

published the *Emigrants' Guide to Oregon and California*. The book gave short shrift to Oregon while it touted the advantages of the Golden State.

Offering emigrants an alternative to the Fort Hall-Northern Utah route previously used to reach Mexican California, Hastings suggested a cutoff. The Hastings Cutoff led from Fort Bridger down Echo and Emigration canyons, through the Salt Lake Valley, across the Great Salt Lake Desert to the base of Pilot Peak, and on to the Humboldt River, rejoining the conventional trail on the way. Frémont approved of the route, as did Jim Bridger and several others. Joseph R. Walker, who had explored and mapped the region before Frémont, thought the route an unproven risk.

The earliest emigrants in 1846 followed the usual trail by way of Fort Hall and present-day Box Elder County. By mid-July, however, four parties thought they might not succeed in crossing the Sierra Nevada before snowfall, and they decided to take the Hastings Cutoff by which they thought to save time. The first three parties managed to dig their way through the treacherous Weber River gorge that empties into the Great Salt Lake Valley near the Davis County-Weber County border. From there they traveled south to the Salt Lake Valley, took the Frémont route across the Great Salt Lake Desert, and rejoined the older trail.

The fourth party led by George and Jacob Donner and James Reed did not leave Fort Bridger until July 31. When they reached the mouth of Echo Canyon they found a note from Hastings urging them to wait for his instructions rather than trying to negotiate the Weber Canyon gorge. After waiting for several days, Reed had become troubled by the lateness of the season. He hurried west of the Oquirrh Mountains to intercept Hastings to get instructions. Hastings returned with Reed and took him to the summit of Big Mountain where he described a route from Echo Canyon through Emigration Canyon.

On August 10 Reed returned to the party's camp. Now 12 days behind the previous emigrants, the Donner-Reed party spent another 12 days hacking a trail over Big and Little mountains and into Emigration Canyon. A full two weeks behind the previous migrants when they reached the Jordan River, the Donner-Reed party followed the older tracks westward.

Planning for a two-day crossing of the Great Salt Lake Desert, they endured six days of scorching thirst-inducing salt-frosted mud. Slowed by such extravagances as Reed's double-decked rolling palace, they left the Salt Lake Desert strewn with five wagons, piles of supplies, and the bodies of dead oxen. Reaching Pilot Springs exhausted and dehydrated, they struggled on along the Humboldt route only to become snowbound in the Sierra Nevada near Donner Lake. Only 47 of the original 87 in the Donner-Reed party eventually reached Sutter's Fort. Some survived by eating the flesh of their dead associates. Some killed and ate their Indian guides.

As the Donner Party lay snowbound near Donner Lake, Brigham Young and the bulk of the Mormon pioneers had hunkered down for the winter of 1846-47 at temporary settlements along the Missouri River near present-day Florence, Nebraska, and Council Bluffs, Iowa. They called the Nebraska settlement Winter Quarters and the Iowa settlement Kanesville.

Two other parties of Mormons had already left for the West. Earlier in the year, the federal government had recruited a battalion of about 500 Mormon men to fight in the Mexican War. These soldiers marched on the southern trail to San Diego by way of Santa Fe and Arizona's Gila River Valley. Most of the Mormon Battalion members eventually rejoined the Saints in the Salt Lake Valley. In addition, a party led by Samuel Brannan had left New York in February, 1846, just as the first refugees departed from Nauvoo. They landed in San Francisco, then called Yerba Buena, where they expected to greet Brigham Young and the main body of emigrants. Some of these went on to the Salt Lake Valley, but many remained in California.

Like a number of other American religions, Mormonism originated and flourished during America's Second Great Awakening. Beginning in Connecticut in 1797, the Second Great Awakening flowed through New England towns and into the middle states, the upper South, and the Midwest. Mainline denominations like the Baptists, Methodists, Presbyterians, and Congregationalists orchestrated revivals to bring wayward souls to Christ.

Some believed they could restore primitive Christianity by adhering strictly to Biblical teachings. Such ministers as Elias Smith, Thomas and Alexander Campbell, Barton Stone, and James O'Kelly founded the Disciples or Christian Church in the expectation of restoring Christ's primitive church by carefully following the Bible. From an analysis of Biblical verses, William Miller believed that Christ would return in the 1840s.

Some came from Europe to nurture their religion on American soil. Britisher Ann Lee immigrated to America and organized the United Society of Believers in Christ's Second Coming, nicknamed the Shakers. Her followers accepted her as the reincarnation of Christ, and she taught that the faithful ought to live in celibacy. They too prospered during the Second Great Awakening.

As the awakening spread, many religiously inclined people experienced extraordinary revelations and visions as they sought to return Christianity to the New Testament model. One of these was Joseph Smith. In 1820 in the midst of this tumult of religions with varying interpretations of Christ's teachings, Smith, then 14 and living with his family at Palmyra in western New York, sought to know God's will. Praying to the Lord in a grove near his home, he experienced an extraordinarily powerful theophany in which Christ told him to join none of the churches.

In 1823 Smith recounted an angelic visitor named Moroni who told him of inscribed golden plates buried in the nearby Hill Cumorah. After retrieving and translating these plates and publishing them as the *Book of Mormon*, Smith, along with members of his family and a small body of believers, organized the Church of Christ, later renamed the Church of Jesus Christ of Latter-day Saints. Because of the *Book of Mormon*, opponents attached the nickname "Mormons" to these people. Church members sometimes referred to themselves as "Mormons" and sometimes — from the Church's name — as "Latter-day Saints" or just "Saints."

Enduring intense persecution for their beliefs and communitarian lifestyle, Joseph Smith and the Mormons sought refuge in turn in Ohio, Missouri and Illinois. Founding the city of Nauvoo on the banks of the Mississippi in western Illinois, the Latter-day Saints flourished. By 1844, however, internal dissention and external persecution led to frequent conflicts. In June 1844 the Nauvoo city authorities ordered the destruction of an opposition newspaper as a nuisance. Arrested by Hancock County authorities for authorizing the newspaper's abatement, Smith and his brother Hyrum were jailed at Carthage. On June 27, 1844, as the two men waited for a bail hearing with two of the Twelve Apostles, Willard Richards and John Taylor, a mob of local militiamen stormed the jail. The mobbers killed Joseph and Hyrum Smith, and severely wounded Taylor.

In August 1844 after a month and a half of indecision, the majority of the Mormons voted to follow the lead of Brigham Young and the Quorum of Twelve Apostles of which he was president. Renewed armed attacks on the Mormon settlers led to a decision to abandon Nauvoo and move westward. On February 4, 1846, Charles Shumway led the first party across the Mississippi to Iowa. Others followed. The last of the remaining refugees, except those like Joseph Smith's widow Emma who decided not to move, abandoned Nauvoo in September.

From Winter Quarters, Brigham Young and the pioneer company started west on April 14, 1847. As presiding officer,

Young assigned the leadership of the expedition to Stephen Markham, Albert P. Rockwood, John Pack and Frederick Roundy. Other prominent migrants included a majority of the 12 apostles in addition to farmers and craftsmen such as William Clayton, Appleton M. Harmon, Howard Egan and Charles Shumway. Three women, Clarissa Decker Young, Harriet Decker Young, and Ellen Sanders Kimball, two children

anywhere other Euroamericans had already settled as it had in Missouri and Illinois. They believed that a settlement in a region not previously occupied by Euroamericans would offer them better insurance against such conflicts. The Great Basin, occupied by Native Americans, seemed safer than California.

On July 24, 1847, members of the pioneer company reunited near City Creek in the Salt Lake Valley. On Sunday,

Ellen Sanders Kimball, Harriet Decker Young and Clarissa Decker Young, three women in the Pioneer Company to enter the Salt Lake Valley in 1847
LDS Church Archives

(Far right)
Green Flake, one of three African-Americans in the pioneer company that entered the Salt Lake Valley in 1847
Utah History Information Center, USHS

of Harriet Young, and three African American Mormons — Hark Lay, Green Flake, and Oscar Crosby — made up the remainder of the pioneer party. When they reached the Green River in Wyoming, a detachment of sick people from the Mormon Battalion and families of Saints from Mississippi joined them. These had wintered at Pueblo, Colorado.

As well prepared as their straitened circumstances allowed, the Mormons had gathered as much information about the West as they possibly could before undertaking the exodus. Frémont's reports and accounts by Mountain Men led them to decide to settle on the eastern edge of the Great Basin in what was then Mexican territory.

As they traveled, they consulted with a number of people familiar with the region including Mountain Men Jim Bridger, Moses "Black" Harris, and Thomas "Peg Leg" Smith, and a Catholic missionary, Father Pierre Jean De Smet. Samuel Brannan, who journeyed from San Francisco to meet the pioneers on the Green River, encouraged them to continue on to northern California where the remainder of the Saints who had come by sea had established a small colony called New Hope near present-day Antioch.

Young and the other leaders concluded that their religious beliefs and communitarian lifestyle would induce conflict

July 25, they held religious services. Members of the Quorum of the Twelve spoke, and those assembled took the emblems of Christ's Last Supper, which Mormons call the Sacrament.

In his talk to the assembled Saints, Brigham Young laid out his vision for an equalitarian society. He said that settlers must not buy or sell land, but that they would receive farm and city lots as inheritances from the Lord. At a later meeting he told the members that they should promote independence and self-sufficiency and not trade with Gentiles, the 19th-century nickname for non-Mormons. They planned to buy or find all the raw materials they needed, grow their own food, and manufacture their own tools, equipment and clothing.

During the next week, as part of the company continued plowing and planting near City Creek, others explored the valley to catalogue resources and to determine the best site for their capital city. On Monday, July 26, a party led by Brigham Young climbed Ensign Peak, east of the camp to survey the valley. From there they made a two-day circuit of the remainder of the countryside.

In their explorations, they visited Great Salt Lake and found that they could extract salt from the water. On the slopes of the Oquirrhs they found herds of mountain sheep, mountain goats, and antelope. Nevertheless, they found no reliable streams of water on the west side of the valley. Joseph Hancock and Lewis Barney returned from the mountains to the east to report they had found a supply of timber there.

The exploration of the valley led the leaders to conclude that Salt Lake Valley's east side, where they had begun to plant crops, promised the best site for a city. After returning from Great Salt Lake late in the afternoon of Wednesday, July 28, Brigham Young led a party north of their camp to a point between the two branches of City Creek. Waving his hands, Young said that they should reserve 40 acres at that site for a temple.

Following, in part, plans for the City of Zion devised by Joseph Smith, the settlers envisioned an expansive and comfortable garden-plot city. They agreed to lay out 10-acre blocks, to build the streets 132 feet wide and the sidewalks 20 feet wide. They also decided to plot 1.25-acre town lots of 165 by 330 feet, alternating houses so they would not face each other across the streets. Eventually they reduced the temple lot to 10 acres to match the other town blocks.

On August 3 Orson Pratt and Henry G. Sherwood began at the southeast corner of Temple Square to lay out the 10-acre city blocks according to the plan. Intending to keep larger farms outside the city south of Ninth South, the surveyors divided 5,133 acres into a "Big Field" for major agricultural operations. By 1850 the blocks and streets of Salt Lake City stretched nearly four miles north to south and three miles east to west.

The founders also made arrangements for other amenities. They agreed to preserve four blocks in the city for "playgrounds and walks" and to set aside the land in the bottoms near the Jordan River as herd grounds. Thomas Bullock and several others turned the warm springs they had discovered into a spa. Members of the Mormon Battalion sick detachment who arrived on July 29 constructed an outdoor bowery on the temple lot where the people could hold public meetings.

Before August 26 when many of those in the pioneer company left to return to the Missouri River to organize the 16,000 people waiting there for the move west, the leaders began to claim some of the city lots. Brigham Young chose lots east of the temple block, Heber C. Kimball got a lot northeast of the temple site, and Wilford Woodruff took a lot just to the southwest.

They also agreed to construct a fort at what is now Pioneer Park between Third and Fourth South and Third and Fourth West. The leaders appointed lime burners to make mortar and brick makers to mold adobe bricks from which they constructed the fort's walls. The people built log cabins and a second bowery in the fort.

The settlers also approved a temporary ecclesiastical-civil government for the city. Choosing John Smith, uncle of the prophet Joseph Smith, as president of the Salt Lake Stake (church organizational unit), they agreed to accept him, his two counselors, and a 12-man stake high council as the city government's municipal council for the next year.

Steel engraving showing Salt Lake City in 1853 from *Route from Liverpool to Great Salt Lake Valley* by Frederick Piercy, (*Liverpool and London: F. D. Richards and Latter-day Saints Book Depot, 1855*) *LDS Church Archives*

North Temple Street showing City Creek flowing westward *C.R. Savage photo from a carte de visite LDS Church Archives*

The council served as a temporary legislative, judicial, and executive authority. The councilors drafted ordinances that set penalties for such offenses as speeding horses through the settlement, adultery, violence and firing guns. Since the city had no jail, the ordinances prescribed whipping or fines for most offenses. In governing the city, the council adjudicated such matters as theft, taking irrigation water out of turn, and killing domestic animals.

By mid-September 1847 nearly 1,700 people had arrived in the valley. The municipal council continued to organize people into work details. In addition, Apostles John Taylor and Parley P. Pratt, who had returned from missions in England too late to come west with the first company, remained in the valley over the winter. They acted as super-advisors to the municipal council.

During the fall, the council divided the city into five ecclesiastical wards, each presided over by a bishop. In February 1849 the permanent city council redivided the city into 19 wards. Later, a 20th ward was added to cover the Avenues section of the city north and east of the temple. The bishops, lay leaders presiding with two counselors over each of the wards, served as neighborhood officials as well as ecclesiastical ministers.

In 1849 the people of Utah petitioned the federal government for admission to the union as the State of Deseret (a *Book of Mormon* word meaning "honeybee"). The statehood petition failed, but since the federal government did not act immediately to organize an alternative government, the State of Deseret functioned as de facto government until 1851.

In 1849 the Deseret legislature replaced the temporary council with a permanent city government in a law incorporating Salt Lake City. City government consisted of a council including a mayor, four aldermen, and nine councilors. The law gave the council both executive and legislative responsibilities. The statute also designated the mayor and aldermen as justices of the peace and as a court to hear appeals from decisions of one of their number.

The Mormons understood that these governments were temporary expedients. When the Latter-day Saints entered Salt

Lake Valley, Utah lay outside the United States on the northeastern fringes of Mexico's possessions. Though the Spanish and Mexicans had penetrated the region, they had set up no government and established no permanent settlements.

The Mexican War changed that. Nine years after Texas achieved its independence from Mexico, the United States annexed the Lone Star Republic in 1845. Fueled by President James K. Polk's expansionist ambitions, a dispute over the border between Texas and Mexico blazed into war between the two nations. In addition to Texas, Polk wanted to annex the Mexican possessions south of the 42nd parallel (the northern boundary of Utah) and to expel Great Britain from the territory jointly occupied north of the 42nd parallel.

After defeating Mexico, the United States negotiated the purchase of the territory they had conquered. The 1848 Treaty of Guadalupe Hidalgo added Utah and the remainder of the territory south of the 42nd parallel and west of the Rio Grande to United States possessions.

The political conflict between the northern and southern states over slavery delayed the organization of the new territory until 1850. In the Compromise of 1850, among other things, Congress admitted California to the union, rejected Deseret's bid for admission, and instead organized Utah as a territory.

After signing the Utah Territorial Organic Act, President Millard Fillmore appointed executive and judicial officers for the Utah Territory. Fillmore chose Brigham Young as governor and appointed Mormons to half of the positions. He appointed non-Utahns to the remainder of the offices. Except for a short period in 1855-56, the legislature designated Salt Lake City as the territorial capital.

Since a territory does not have the sovereignty rights of a state, Utahns had only a limited right to govern themselves. Under the territorial government, they could elect city and county officers, members of the legislature, and a territorial delegate who sat in the U.S. House of Representatives. The delegate could not vote on the floor of the House, but he could introduce legislation and sit on and vote in committees. Until

The Council House, formerly Salt Lake City's municipal building, is shown here with a group of Salt Lake City firemen.
The Council House stood on the southwest corner of Main Street and South Temple.
LDS Church Archives

1874 Utahns also elected a territorial attorney and marshal.

As these events unfolded, economic development and growth of Salt Lake City proceeded as well. People did not actually pay for the land in this communitarian society. They received a title from the city after the payment of $1.50 as a surveying and recording fee.

Salt Lake City, like other Mormon cities, developed its first water system through cooperative labor. Designed to irrigate home gardens and the larger farms, ditches that were dug down both sides of the streets flowed with water diverted from the various mountain streams. Bishops in each of the wards assigned men to work on the water system, and the right to use the water depended upon the contribution of labor for constructing and maintaining the irrigation works. At first, people had no guaranteed water rights, but they shared their water with one another as all contributed labor in proportion to the land they owned. Watermasters appointed by the city government regulated the distribution of water to the homes and farms.

Some people dug wells for culinary water, but others simply got their home and irrigation water from the same ditches. Although the city passed ordinances against fouling the streams, this proved virtually impossible to enforce and many Salt Lakers suffered from water-borne diseases such as typhoid. Most people used backyard privies to dispose of bodily waste, and in some cases, the refuse infiltrated the groundwater and contaminated the drinking water.

The shortage of supplies and the communitarian ideals of the society forced the territorial and city governments to regulate various economic enterprises. The legislature assigned the control of nearby canyons to prominent individuals. Acting as trustees, these men were expected to construct roads to facilitate access to timber, stone, and other resources. To pay for the expense of road construction and management, the trustees could collect tolls.

In the first year, the city government authorized and regulated certain economic enterprises. The city council authorized Charles Crismon to construct a gristmill on City Creek but in order to avoid gouging, the city limited the fees he could charge for grinding grain. The council later authorized a second flourmill,

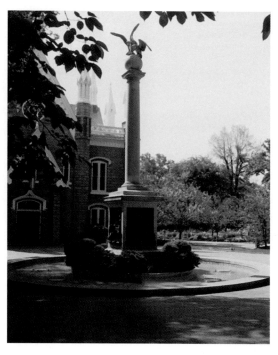

four sawmills, a carding mill, and a threshing mill. Since timber was in such short supply, city ordinances prohibited the construction of log or wood frame buildings without permission, and people could use only dead timber for fuel. As a result, the people constructed most of the earliest dwellings outside the Old Fort of adobes.

Although Salt Lakers experienced a relatively mild first winter, Coyote's curse applied to the Mormons as well as to the Utes, and as the spring of 1848 approached they faced the frightening prospect of starvation. Later in the spring, cattle and horses broke into the planted fields and destroyed everything but the potatoes. During the winter, Indians, wolves, and coyotes, harvested much of the livestock. Taking lessons from the Numics who had occupied the region for nearly a half millennium before they came, the Mormons began to subsist on native plants and animals. John Taylor and some others even tried the cakes of ground crickets and berries. The Gosiutes taught them to eat sego lily roots, and the Mormons became so thankful for this bounty that in 1911 the legislature designated the sego lily as the state flower.

In the spring of 1848 winter wheat began to emerge from the soil. A late frost killed some of these crops. Then, just as they thought that they had such dangers behind them, hordes of crickets descended upon the fields in black clouds. Some wit said that the voracious hump-backed insects looked like a cross between a spider and a buffalo. Called out to defend their livelihood, men, women and children fought the loathsome creatures with sticks, shovels, brooms, gunnysacks, and trenches filled with water.

In terror because of the prospect of starvation, the municipal council cautioned the people to keep their wagons and teams in good order against the possibility that they might have to abandon Salt Lake City. Then just as all seemed lost, seagulls flew in from Great Salt Lake and began devouring the advancing hordes. In 1955 a thankful legislature designated the California gull as the state bird.

After weathering the prospect of starvation, as trains of Mormon settlers poured into the city, events in California stoked an economic boom in Salt Lake City. In the spring of

1848, six Mormons recently discharged from the Mormon Battalion were helping James Marshall construct a mill race at Sutter's Fort near present-day Sacramento when Marshall discovered gold. Though Sutter tried to keep the discovery a secret, Sam Brannan announced the find in San Francisco, and word spread throughout the world.

Although as many as 300 Mormons were engaged in mining gold on Mormon Island near Sutter's Fort by the summer of 1848, most of these were Mormon Battalion veterans and members who had come with Brannan to California. Most in Salt Lake City agreed to follow Brigham Young's advice and remain in Utah to work in urban occupations and farming. Nevertheless, Young and several other church leaders outfitted a party of miners that they sent to California to mine gold for a time in order to provide money for the Mormon community.

In 1849 as the gold rushers poured through Salt Lake City on the way to the diggings, Mormons traded goods and services that met the miners' needs and at the same time enriched the community. In both 1849 and 1850 an estimated one-quarter to one-third of the 40,000 to 50,000 gold rushers who streamed to California passed through Salt Lake City. By the fall of 1849 as many as 6,300 people lived in the Salt Lake Valley. Of these, perhaps 500 were prospective miners bound for California who chose to remain over the winter in Salt Lake City.

Drawn by the prospect of commercial riches, a number of Protestant, Catholic and Jewish merchants set up shops in the settlement. Partners Ben Holladay and Theodore F. Warner opened a store in an adobe building on Main Street as did Charles Livingston and Charles A. Kincaid. Fanny Brooks, a Jewish emigrant, opened a millinery shop and a bakery.

Since the hard-living miners wanted a more fluid entertainment than the Mormons did, liquor began to flow quite freely. To honor the change, local wags bestowed the nickname "Whiskey Street" on Salt Lake City's Main Street.

In spite of the change in drinking habits, it seems clear that the Gold Rush of 1849 and 1850 afforded Salt Lake City a deliverance no less miraculous than the seagulls of 1848. Anxious to reach the gold fields ahead of their competitors, the miners traded unneeded goods — tired horses, mules, and oxen and heavy wagons — to the Mormons for fresh horses, vegetables and flour.

In these exchanges, Salt Lakers sold horses for $200 to migrants who had paid $25 to $30 for similar animals in the Midwest. Farmers sold vegetables and grain at comparable premium prices. By contrast, the Saints bought wagons, considered a drag on those rushing to the gold diggings, normally worth $50 to $125 for $15 to $25 and sugar and coffee previously selling for $1 a pint for 10 to 15 cents. In addition, the gold rushers paid Salt Lake City mechanics and craftsmen for services such as fixing broken harnesses, shoeing horses, repairing wagons and grinding wheat.

As the gold rushers passed through to California, the Mormons encouraged all of their members to gather in Utah. In September 1850 the Deseret Legislature incorporated the Perpetual Emigrating Company to accept donations for a revolving fund to help immigrants gather to Zion. The Utah Legislature re-enacted the Perpetual Emigrating Fund Act in 1851.

Most Mormons converts came from Europe. Most traveled from their homes to Liverpool, the 19th-century jumping off point for the journey that eventually took them to Utah. Many settled in Salt Lake City while others remained for varying lengths of time as they prepared to resettle in the towns that radiated out from the Mormon capital.

To promote economic development and the improvement of crops, fruit and animals, in January 1856 the legislature chartered the Deseret Agricultural and Manufacturing Society, headquartered in Salt Lake City. The society operated experimental farms, imported plants and animals, and sponsored a territorial fair at which Utahns received prizes for the best animals, plants, handiwork and artistic productions.

As the city grew, the people provided education for their children and youth. At their first meeting in 1851, the territorial legislature ratified the State of Deseret's incorporation of the University of Deseret. The university remained largely inactive until 1867 when it began to offer regular classes. University president, John R. Park, inaugurated a systematic college curriculum in 1869. In the 1890s it was renamed the University of Utah.

Since many of the Mormons had come from New England with its tradition of universal public education, they organized schools quite rapidly. Mary Jane Dillworth schooled the children at the Old Fort in the fall of 1847. After the organization of wards, the city council designated each of the wards as a school district assigned to provide education for the children living within their borders. Most did so by building a meeting house that doubled as a school building and community center. Until

Fanny Brooks, a Jewish businesswoman who operated shops in downtown
Utah History Information Center, USHS

Lorenzo Snow, member of the Quorum of Twelve Apostles of the Church of Jesus Christ of Latter-day Saints and leader in Salt Lake City's Polysophical Society
LDS Church Archives

(Above) Eliza R. Snow, General President of the Relief Society of the Church of Jesus Christ of Latter-day Saints and leader in Salt Lake City's Polysophical Society
LDS Church Archives

The Salt Lake Theatre in 1865 (constructed in 1862,) hosted traveling companies and housed a resident theater company.
LDS Church Archives

1891 most children paid some tuition to help fund the teacher's salary while the school trustees collected taxes to furnish supplies and maintain the building.

During the 1850s the people organized literary and cultural societies in order to provide adult education, cultural enrichment and entertainment. Voluntary organizations included the Universal Scientific Society, the Polysophical Society, the Deseret Dramatic Association, the Deseret Literary and Musical Association, the Horticultural Society and the Deseret Philharmonic Society.

The functions of all except the Universal Scientific Society and the Polysophical Society seem evident from their titles. Led by Wilford Woodruff, the Universal Scientific Society took as its purview all of human knowledge. Members met, presented lectures to one another, and discussed questions ranging from the construction of the universe to Saracen history and chopping wood. Lorenzo Snow, a member of the Quorum of Twelve Apostles, and his sister Eliza R. Snow, the most prominent of 19th-century Utah women, were prime movers in the Polysophical Society that presented plays and promoted the literary arts. In 1856, because of criticism of its activities from Jedediah M. Grant and Heber C. Kimball of the LDS First Presidency, the Polysophical Society merged with the Deseret Theological Class.

Salt Lakers also promoted the legitimate theatre. The Deseret Dramatic Association presented plays at the Social Hall, located on Social Hall Avenue between State Street and Second East. In 1862, however, church and civic authorities participated in the dedication of the lovely Greek Revival Salt Lake Theatre, constructed on the corner of First South and State streets known as the outstanding theatrical venue west of Missouri, the theatre hosted nationally renowned actors and actresses such as Julia Dean Hayne and George B. Waldron. It also housed a resident theatre company.

As these cultural and educational events unfolded and as the gold rush brought people to the West, Salt Lakers began to meet the first of a host of federal officials who came to staff the territory's executive and judicial departments. The first contingent

SAVAGE & OTTINGER

included Territorial Secretary Broughton D. Harris of Vermont and Associate Utah Supreme Court Justice Perry E. Brocchus of Alabama, both of whom arrived in 1851. Harris refused to release funds to pay for the 1850 census because Governor Brigham Young had conducted it before he arrived. The Vermonter also declined to release funds appropriated by Congress to pay the expenses of operating the territorial legislature.

In a speech at a special conference of the LDS Church, Brocchus invited Utahns to contribute a block of granite in an effort to help in constructing the Washington Monument in Washington, D.C. He cautioned, however, that they must do so in full fellowship with the remainder of the people of the nation. He then rebuked Utahns for their verbal abuse of national leaders and he called upon the people of Utah to abandon the offensive practice of polygamy. Affronted by the questioning of their patriotism and the charge that polygamy was immoral, the congregation rose to confront Brocchus. Brigham Young interceded to calm the congregation, at the same time condemning Zachary Taylor and chastising Brocchus for his bad manners for lecturing Salt Lakers on loyalty and virtue.

In the wake of the conflicts with Young and the Mormon community in the fall of 1851, Harris and Brocchus, accompanied by Territorial Supreme Court Chief Justice Lemuel G. Brandebury and Indian Agent Henry R. Day, left Utah for the United States. Professing to fear for their lives, the four sent a report to Washington condemning the people of Utah. Prior to Harris's departure, Young tried unsuccessfully to get him to release funds for the operation of the territorial government. In an attempt to counteract the bad publicity generated by the runaway officials, Jedediah M. Grant sent letters to the president and to eastern newspapers defending the people of Utah.

Grant, first counselor to Brigham Young in the First Presidency, also served as Salt Lake City's first mayor. A zealot of sorts, he initiated a religious reformation in 1856-57. Calling the Mormon people to repentance, he and Brigham Young sent waves of preachers throughout Salt Lake City and other Mormon settlements. Public charges of adultery and public

confessions became the order of the day, and members offered themselves for rebaptism. Grant died in early December 1856, and Wilford Woodruff redirected the reformation to emphasize personal integrity and brotherly love.

In early 1857, following the inauguration of President James Buchanan, reports from federal officials (especially Judge William W. Drummond,) charged Utahns with sedition, murder and other crimes. Failing to investigate the charges or to inform Young of his removal as governor, Buchanan appointed Alfred Cumming of Georgia to replace the Mormon prophet. Buchanan also ordered an army of 2,500 troops to escort Cumming to Utah and to put down the alleged rebellion against federal authority.

In July 1857 Young, who had not been notified of his removal as governor, learned that an army was marching on Utah, he declared martial law. Daniel H. Wells, commanding general of the Nauvoo Legion, (as the territorial militia was named), mobilized the troops. Sending militiamen to Echo Canyon to build fortifications to repel the invasion, Wells also ordered troops to the high plains to destroy the army's supply trains. In addition, following the pattern of Russians at the siege of Sevastopol during the 1854-55 Crimean War, the Mormons vacated Salt Lake City, sending their families, belongings and records to Provo and cities to the south. They left a small detachment to burn the city should the army initiate a conflict with them.

In a successful attempt to heal the breach between the federal government and the Latter-day Saints, Thomas L. Kane, who had developed a friendly relationship with the Mormon people as they evacuated Nauvoo, met with Buchanan, a fellow Pennsylvania Democrat.

After meeting with the Mormon leaders, he rode eastward to Camp Scott near Fort Bridger where Cumming and the army under Col. Albert Sidney Johnston had bivouacked for the winter. Kane convinced Governor Cumming to accompany him to Salt Lake City to consult with the Latter-day Saints.

Cumming agreed, and after meeting with Brigham Young and the other church leaders, he learned that far from engaging in rebellion, they were quite willing to accept him as territorial governor.

Cumming also came to understand that because of the previous attacks on their settlements and murder of their people by the militias in Missouri and Illinois, they feared a possible slaughter at the hands of Johnston's army. While at Camp Scott he had heard Johnston and others denounce the Mormon people with patent hatred, and he understood the danger of bloody conflict. Cumming agreed that instead of camping in Salt Lake City, the army would march on to some distant spot.

After learning of Kane's success in negotiating between the two antagonists, Buchanan rejected the diehard militarism of Col. Johnston and Secretary of War John Floyd. He declared an amnesty and sent a two-man commission to deliver it to the Mormons in Salt Lake City. In accordance with the Cumming-Young agreement, Johnston's army marched through a now virtually deserted Salt Lake City and established Camp Floyd in Cedar Valley, 35 miles to the southwest.

In addition to the adobe buildings, many of which have remained, the city government, the LDS Church and prominent citizens built structures in the downtown area, most of

(Far left) Photograph of Main Street looking northwest from east side of the street probably in the early 1960s. The council (right) House is in the right center. *LDS Church Archives*

Photograph of Temple Square in the 1850s. The photograph shows the old tabernacle and the bowery constructed by the Mormon battalion veterans. *LDS Church Archives*

Main Street in Salt Lake City during the late 1850s or early 1860s *LDS Church Archives*

which followed national and international architectural styles. The city, the church, and prominent citizens hired architects William H. Folsom, Truman O. Angell and William Paul to design many of the buildings. Folsom designed the Federal-Greek Revival Council House on the southwest corner of Main and South Temple, which was completed in 1849. Today a replica of that building stands south of the capitol at the head of State Street.

The Salt Lake Tabernacle of the Church of Jesus Christ of Latter-day Saints under construction c.1866
LDS Church Archives

Folsom also designed the Salt Lake Theatre, and he and Angell designed the Salt Lake Tabernacle on Temple Square, which the Saints dedicated in 1867 and which continued to host the LDS Church's semi-annual conferences until the completion of the Conference Center on the corner of Main Street and First North in 2000. Brigham Young also hired Angell as architect for the Victorian Lion House and the Greek Revival Beehive House, both of which still stand in the first block of East South Temple. Paul designed the Second Empire Devereaux House owned first by William Staines and later by William Jennings, Salt Lake City's first millionaire, which stands restored on West South Temple, a block east of the Union Pacific Depot.

During the 1860s as the city grew and the population flourished, Salt Lakers faced additional challenges. At the outbreak of the Civil War in 1861, the federal government recalled the troops from Camp Floyd. With more than a little irony, Col. Johnston, who had castigated the Mormons as traitors, accepted a commission in the Confederate Army and died at Shiloh in 1862 fighting against the United States.

Although most of the Civil War battles occurred east of the Mississippi, the federal government encountered Indian depredations on the overland mail routes in the West. To guard the routes through

Col. Patrick Edward Connor, commander of the Third Regiment of California Volunteers and founder of Fort Douglas
LDS Church Archives

northern Utah, western Wyoming and southern Idaho, President Abraham Lincoln called for the short-term services of two units from the Nauvoo Legion.

In 1862, however, he ordered units of the Third Regiment of California Volunteers under Col. Patrick Edward Connor and the Second California Cavalry Volunteers under Maj. Edward McGarry to Utah to combat the depredations. Connor, who was appointed commander of the Military Department of Utah, rejected the suggestion that he reoccupy Camp Floyd. Instead, in October 1862, he established Fort Douglas on the bench overlooking Salt Lake City. At least as intense in his hatred of the Mormon people as Johnston, Connor characterized the citizens of Salt Lake City as "a community of traitors, murderers, fanatics, and whores."

Needless to say, the Mormons viewed their relationship with the nation quite differently from Connor. In late October 1861 at about the same time that Connor established Fort Douglas, crews finished connecting the transcontinental telegraph that passed through Salt Lake City. Inaugurating the new system on October 18, Brigham Young sent a message to J. H. Wade, the telegraph company's president, affirming Utah's loyalty to the Union. In contrast to the southern states which had rushed to leave the union and form the Confederacy, Young telegraphed, "Utah has not seceded but is firm for the Constitution and laws of our once happy country..."

Recognizing the importance of maintaining good relations with the Mormons, Lincoln decided on a policy of benign neglect. Meeting with Mormon elder Thomas B. H. Stenhouse, he said, "Stenhouse, when I was a boy on the farm in Illinois there was a great deal of timber on the farms which we had to clear away. Occasionally we would come to a log which had fallen down. It was too hard to split, too wet to burn and too heavy to move, so we ploughed around it. That's what I intend to do with the Mormons. You go back and tell Brigham Young that if he will let me alone I will let him alone."

Such sentiments did not impress Connor, and at his initiative in November 1863, Capt. Charles H. Hempstead began editing Utah's first daily newspaper, the *Union Vedette*, at Fort Douglas. Previous newspapers in Salt Lake City had been weeklies. The Mormons had established the *Deseret News* in Salt Lake City in 1850, and several ephemeral sheets like the *Valley Tan* and the *Mountaineer* had circulated briefly during the late 1850s. In addition to news of the war and local affairs, the *Vedette* slung mud at the Mormons. In defense of his people, Stenhouse began publishing the *Salt Lake Daily Telegraph* as Utah's second daily. Given the small subscriber base for an anti-Mormon newspaper in Salt Lake City, the *Vedette* died in 1867.

Connor also found other means of infuriating Salt Lakers. During the Civil War, the federal government printed legal tender paper currency, nicknamed greenbacks. Since the notes did not circulate at par with gold and silver, prices in greenbacks tended to be higher than coins. Believing that the premium for gold and silver had resulted from a conspiracy by the LDS Church, on July 9, 1864, Connor ordered Hempstead to establish a provost guard on South Temple across from the Temple Square gates to arrest those who refused to accept greenbacks.

Understanding the provocation created by the provost guard and recognizing Lincoln's benign policy, Connor's superior, General Irvin McDowell at the Presidio of San Francisco, ordered the guard removed. Unlike Connor, McDowell undoubtedly realized that most people throughout the United States found the greenbacks unsatisfactory because they circulated at a discount with gold and silver.

In spite of the strained relationship between the Mormons and Connor's California volunteers, Salt Lake City prospered economically as it suffered morally because of the army. Estimates place the value of contracts let for supplying Fort Douglas during the Civil War at as much as $150,000 annually. Mormon merchants like Salt Lakers William H. Hooper, Horace Eldredge and William Jennings got most of the business. On the flip side, the quality of Salt Lake City's life declined as liquor flowed freely on Whiskey Street and prostitutes offered their bodies to willing soldiers and depraved camp followers.

In addition to contributing to the wealth of Salt Lake City merchants, Connor also helped to open a new chapter in economic development by fathering commercial mining. As early as 1848, Thomas and Sanford Bingham had discovered outcroppings of argentiferous galena (silver combined with lead-sulphide) in the Oquirrh mountain canyon located southwest of Salt Lake City. Unable to exploit these discoveries because of lack of transportation, milling and smelting facilities, the Binghams ignored the minerals.

By the 1860s, however, mining rushes in Nevada and Colorado had changed attitudes. In September 1863 a party of

Mormon ranchers including George and Alex Ogilvie, John Egbert and Henry Beckstead uncovered silver ore while dragging logs. The Ogilvies took the ore to Connor, who had it assayed. Since Utah had no mining laws, Connor, who had mined in California before volunteering for service in the Civil War, followed Golden State customs. Assembling at LDS Bishop Archibald Gardner's Jordan Ward meeting house, Connor helped the prospectors organize the West Mountain Quartz Mining District that covered the Oquirrh Mountains.

A silver rush around Salt Lake City decisively altered the territory's economy. Miners hurried to Bingham Canyon and to Wasatch canyons like Big and Little Cottonwood and American Fork. They also crossed to the eastern slope of the Wasatch to stake claims at Park City, and they moved south of Provo to found Eureka in the Tintic District. In 1870 Utah produced 23 percent of the nation's lead in addition to substantial portions of its gold and silver.

Troops from Fort Douglas firing artillery
C. W. Carter photo
LDS Church Archives

Convinced that he could defeat the Mormons by flooding the territory with gentile miners, Connor inaugurated a liberal leave policy for soldiers who agreed to prospect for minerals. The *Vedette* helped advertise such prospects by carrying stories of mining riches. Even Connor's wife Johanna and eight other women filed a claim they named the Women's Lode.

Nevertheless, miners could not effectively exploit these discoveries until the completion of the transcontinental railroad reduced the cost of transporting the ore. In the absence of railroads with no alternative water transportation, Utahns found wagon trains an extremely expensive way to get their goods to or through Salt Lake City. As a result, prices and wages in Utah's capital were higher than in the Midwest or on the West Coast, and the shipping of ore by wagon train seemed prohibitively expensive.

Contrary to popular belief, Salt Lake City had never been economically or socially isolated from the remainder of the nation. Beginning with the Gold Rush of 1849, the city had served as a pivot on the east-west route between the Missouri River and Northern California and the north-south trail between Southern California and Montana. Moreover, Euroamerican culture including books, music, plays, clothing and architectural styles all filtered into Salt Lake City.

Nevertheless, in spite of its benefits, the railroad posed something of a challenge to Utahns. They understood that larger and more efficient Midwestern businesses would inevitably

A group of American Indians posed in front of the ZCMI store in downtown Salt Lake City, 1869. *LDS Church Archives*

compete in Utah markets, and both prices and wages would certainly drop. Footloose miners and businessmen who mined the miners, many of whom had little respect for the unique aspects of Utah's culture, would clearly join the rush for riches.

Nevertheless, Latter-day Saint leaders recognized the potential long-term benefit of the railroad. Mormons gathering from Europe and the eastern United States would find it much less expensive to travel to Utah. In the long run the community would also benefit from cheaper goods.

Anxious to mitigate the immediate impact of the rapid changes thrust upon them by the new technology, Brigham Young and the church leadership inaugurated a number of economic and religious expedients. Beginning as early as 1865, the church leaders urged members to boycott merchants who attacked the Mormon people. Then, as the railroad neared the territory in 1868, the church leadership organized a full-scale boycott of gentile merchants.

William S. Godbe, spiritualist and leader, opposed the cooperative program of the Church of Jesus Christ of Latter-day Saints *Utah History Information Center, USHS*

Since 19th-century Mormons recognized no separation between the secular and religious, church leaders gave temporal as well as ecclesiastical direction to members. In 1868 Brigham Young reorganized the Salt Lake City School of the Prophets, an adult educational institution that had previously functioned in Kirtland, Ohio.

In the school, church leaders and prominent men from throughout the city met at the Salt Lake Tabernacle to discuss economic and religious matters. Attendees at the school agreed to trade with the church's newly organized Zion's Cooperative Mercantile Institution (ZCMI) instead of with other merchants. They agreed also to reduce the wages of working men, to tend to other businesses rather than rushing to the hills to prospect for minerals and to promote frugality in order to assist worthy members to immigrate to Utah.

The Salt Lake City School of the Prophets functioned as the central organization for a series of similar schools in communities throughout the territory. The central school in Salt Lake City continued to operate until August 1872, while schools in some of the other communities functioned as late as 1874.

Mormon women also organized to meet these new challenges. In 1867 Young called Eliza R. Snow to reorganize the Relief Society, a women's benevolent and educational institution that had functioned in Nauvoo in the 1840s and in Salt Lake City wards during the 1850s. From Salt Lake City, membership too spread throughout the various communities. The women ministered to the temporal needs of people; urged members to live moral lives; advised people to avoid vices such as tea, coffee and strong drinks; and promoted modesty and frugality in dress. Young women organized Retrenchment Societies for the same purposes.

The church leadership envisioned ZCMI as a cooperative enterprise to mitigate the impact of economic changes associated with the railroad. To establish ZCMI, Brigham Young and the other church leaders called upon Salt Lake City's Mormon retailers to pool their goods in exchange for stock in the new company. In addition, ZCMI opened factories to manufacture clothing and other goods, and it became the territory's largest importer.

Not everyone agreed with these cooperative measures. A group of people associated with Salt Lake City merchant William S. Godbe and author, publisher and designer Elias L.T. Harrison, generally called the Godbeites, favored instead a free market approach. In 1867 the Godbeites began publishing the *Utah Magazine* that focused at first on literary and social matters. In 1869, however, the magazine openly opposed Brigham Young's policy of reducing wages and discouraging prospecting. Opposition to Young's policy led to the excommunication of

Godbe and Harrison in a meeting held at the Council House in October 1869.

Five months before the Godbeite trial, the transcontinental railroad had come. The Latter-day Saints wanted the line to pass through Salt Lake City and to run south of Great Salt Lake. After preliminary surveys, the railroad engineers found the route down Weber Canyon and around the northern end of Great Salt Lake superior. On May 10, 1869, in a celebration at Promontory Summit in Box Elder County, dignitaries from throughout the nation met to drive the golden spike and join the Union Pacific and Central Pacific railroads.

Almost immediately, the Mormons broke ground to construct the Utah Central Railroad to connect Salt Lake City with the transcontinental railroad at Ogden. Crews completed the Utah Central to Salt Lake City on January 10, 1870 after a year of construction. During the 1870s, the church leadership built the Utah and Northern Railroad north from Ogden into Cache Valley and the Utah Southern south from Salt Lake City into Juab County. In 1884 the Union Pacific completed the Utah and Northern to Garrison, Montana, where it connected with

the Northern Pacific. The Union Pacific also constructed the railroad south from Juab County to the mines at Frisco in Beaver County in 1881 and to Los Angeles in 1905.

The coming of the railroad in 1869, the completion of the Utah Central to Salt Lake City in 1870 and the simultaneous opening of commercial mining ushered in an era of change for Salt Lake City. From a plowed field in July 1847, Salt Lake City had become a bustling regional center of 12,900 people by 1870. Visitors like the renowned British adventurer Sir Richard Burton commented favorably during the 1860s on the beauty of the city, its well-tended yards, lovely homes and friendly hospitality.

Conflicts such as those with the Godbeites, with Connor and with federal officials would persist, but in the long run these proved much less important than the salutary changes taking place in the city. By 1870 Salt Lake City was still about 90 percent Mormon, but it boasted a growing population of Protestants, Catholics, Jews and former Latter-day Saints who had found a home they liked but who accounted themselves, nevertheless, more comfortable outside the LDS Church.

The completion of the transcontinental railroad in 1869 nourished Salt Lake City's economic, cultural and social life. By contrast with some towns on the overland wagon trail like Forts Laramie and Bridger that shrank into obscurity, growth remade the Mormon capital from a wagon town of 12,900 in 1870 to a mining, commercial, financial and manufacturing center of 53,531 in 1900.

The Americanization of a Latter-day Saint Commonwealth

CHAPTER TWO

At the same time, change facilitated by the railroad contributed to the city's ethnic and religious diversity.

By the turn of the 20th century, Salt Lake City had become the hub of a thriving region that covered the eastern Great Basin, Upper Snake River plain, Western Rockies and Northern Colorado Plateau. In 1900 Salt Lake City was larger than any city in the 13 far-western states and territories except Denver (133,859) and the Pacific Coast ports of San Francisco (342,782), Los Angeles (102,479), Portland (90,426), Seattle (80,671) and Oakland (66,960). Like these and other regional centers, Salt Lake City tapped into the surrounding country to draw in and spew out the fruits of enterprise.

Expanding railroad connections enlarged Salt Lake City's economic and cultural domain between 1871 and 1909. In August 1871 workers began laying rails northward from the Central Pacific line at Brigham City through Box Elder County, into Cache Valley and on to Franklin in southeastern Idaho. In 1884 Union Pacific crews completed the line from Franklin to a Northern Pacific connection at Garrison, Montana. By 1879 the Utah Southern had ribboned the ground from the Utah Central terminal at Salt Lake City to Chicken Creek in southern Juab Valley.

The Union Pacific continued to construct the road to southern Utah. The U.P. reached the mines at Frisco in southwestern Utah's Millard County in 1880. In 1883 the Denver and Rio Grande Western linked Salt Lake City to eastern Utah's coalfields and to Denver. The Salt Lake and Los Angeles connected the Union Pacific to Southern California in 1905 and the Western Pacific provided an additional connection from Salt Lake City to San Francisco in 1909. As mining boomed, branch lines snaked up the nearby Wasatch and Oquirrh canyons.

As these connections multiplied, Salt Lake City became the center of a string of mining, milling and smelting districts

that spread through the canyons of the Wasatch and Oquirrh Mountains and through central and western Salt Lake County. Mining companies built most of the mills and some of the smelters in the canyons. Smelting companies, however, built the largest facilities adjacent to Salt Lake City on the south and west. In 1870 the Woodhull Brothers constructed a silver-lead smelter on Big Cottonwood Creek in Murray, a town just south of Salt Lake City. A handful of poorly designed smelters followed in the Woodhulls' wake.

By 1884, however, a number of efficient reverberatory furnaces had replaced the early jerrybuilt operations. A European invention that used a sloping roof to deflect heated gasses onto the ore mass, reverberatory furnaces operated at the Germania, Mountain Chief/Mingo and Hanauer smelters, all located at Murray. Other smelters opened in Midvale and Sandy, towns just south of Murray. By the early 20th century Salt Lake Valley had become one of the nation's most productive smelter districts.

The exploitation of the mineral lodes near Salt Lake City benefited not only from the introduction of smelting technology but also from other late 19th-century inventions. Alfred Nobel's fabrication of dynamite in 1866 preceded Charles Burleigh's development in 1870 of the mechanized drill. These new technologies together with the introduction of rapidly moving elevator cages facilitated the removal of large bodies of ore at previously unreachable depths and with previously unattainable rapidity.

Utah mines yielded mainly lead, silver, gold and copper. The richest sprang up in Big and Little Cottonwood canyons, American Fork Canyon and Park City in the Wasatch Mountains southeast of Salt Lake City, and at Bingham Canyon, Mercur, Ophir and Tintic in the Oquirrhs to the west. The mines attracted foreign investment until 1898 when British stockholders owned a significant stake in 25 Utah companies.

Although mining boomed, promotional costs inflated the price of the stock in some of these mines far beyond the value of the ore buried in them. Investors who held shares in the Emma Mine at Alta in Little Cottonwood Canyon, for instance, could have just as profitably pasted them up as wallpaper. The subsequent collapse of the Emma's paper profits tarnished the

The Kearns family: (Back row) Thomas Kearns, Helen Kearns and Edmund Kearns (seated front) Jennie Judge Kearns and Thomas F. Kearns
Utah *History Information Center, USHS*

reputations of Yale geologist Benjamin Silliman, Nevada Senator William M. Stewart, U. S. Ambassador Robert C. Shenck and a handful of British peers.

Although the Emma became an international scandal, other mines prospered and considerable wealth poured into the pockets of investors. The lure of mineral wealth drew some of America's millionaires to Utah's mines. Purchase of the Ontario lode at Park City added to the fortunes of Californians George Hurst and James Ben Ali Haggin.

The Kearns Mansion at 603 East South Temple Street is currently the Utah Governor's Mansion. *Utah History Information Center, USHS*

While Hurst and Haggin lugged their profits off to California, a number of investors and managers contributed to the wealth and cultural diversity of Salt Lake City. Mining wealth brought a number of new entrepreneurs to Utah's capital city. These included Thomas Kearns, a Canadian-born Catholic; David Keith, a Nova Scotia-born Presbyterian; Samuel Newhouse, New York-born son of Russian-Jewish immigrants; and George H. Dern, a Nebraska-born Congregationalist.

Born to Irish immigrants, Kearns arrived in Park City in June 1883. While working eight-hour shifts at the Ontario mine, he studied geology in his off hours. He began taking independent contracts, and he and David Keith saved enough money to purchase the Silver King, which they reorganized in 1892 with Kearns as manager and vice president.

Between 1895 and 1902 Kearns, Keith, and their associates, including Salt Lake City businessman and mayor John S. Bransford; Salt Lake City businessman Frank Westcott; and Salt Lake City banker William S. McCornick purchased five

additional Park City mines, which they reorganized as the Silver King Coalition Mining Company in 1907.

Kearns, Keith and Newhouse all built mansions on Salt Lake City's South Temple Street. After Kearns' death, the family donated his magnificent Renaissance Revival mansion to the state of Utah. Renovated and restored, it stands today at 603 East South Temple as the governor's residence.

Kearns served as a United States senator from 1901 to 1905, and in 1901 he purchased Utah's largest daily newspaper, the *Salt Lake Tribune*. Kearns and his wife Jennie Judge Kearns, devout Catholics, contributed lavishly to various philanthropies in Salt Lake City including Kearns St. Ann's Orphanage and the Cathedral of the Madeleine. Kearns served as chair of the construction committee for the cathedral.

Active in Salt Lake City's Masonic order, George H. Dern earned his fortune as a manager, inventor and investor in mines at Tintic and Merkur. He invested with Mormon mining magnate Jesse Knight in the Tintic Milling Company, and the two shared a patent for a process used in milling low-grade ores. After settling in Salt Lake City, Dern served in the state legislature and as governor of Utah (1925-1933). In 1933 President Franklin Roosevelt appointed Dern as secretary of war, a position he held until his death in 1936.

Mormon businessmen also benefited from Utah's mineral wealth. William Jennings, English immigrant and Utah's first millionaire, was born in Yardley near Birmingham. After coming to the United States, he married Mormon immigrant Jane Walker. Converted to the LDS Church, Jennings married Priscilla Paul as a plural wife.

After opening a meat market, he diversified into tanning, leatherwork, dry goods and general merchandizing. In 1864 Jennings opened the Eagle Emporium on Main Street, which became the first affiliate of ZCMI. He invested in the Deseret National Bank and the Utah Central and Utah Southern railroads, a number of mines and the Germania Smelter. Jennings served as Salt Lake City mayor from 1882 to 1884, and he purchased and remodeled the Second Empire style Devereaux House which stands restored on West South Temple, a block east of the Union Pacific Depot.

In addition, Salt Lake City residents George Q. Cannon and John Taylor, members of the Quorum of the Twelve and, from 1880 to 1887 president and first counselor in the LDS Church's First Presidency, invested in the mines. Both owned stock in the Bullion, Beck and Champion mining company in Tintic, and Cannon had a number of other mining interests in Utah and Nevada, including iron mines near Cedar City.

A number of lapsed Mormon Salt Lake businessmen also engaged in mining. These included William S. Godbe and the Walker brothers: Samuel Sharpe, Joseph R. David Frederick and Matthew Henry. Born in England, the Walker brothers converted to Mormonism and moved to Utah prior to the Utah War, where they engaged in merchandising. They left the LDS Church in a dispute with Brigham Young over business practices. In 1871 Joseph opened a stamp and amalgamation mill in the Ophir district. He also invested in the Germania Smelter and in mines in Bingham, Park City, and American Fork Canyon and in Montana, Idaho and Nevada.

Salt Lake City also benefited from the products of Utah's farms and ranches. Until the 1890s, Utah's fields and orchards managed to produce only slightly more than enough vegetables, grains and fruit to fill the stomachs of people in the territory. That changed in 1891 as the Utah Sugar Company opened its first plant at Lehi. Utah farmers rapidly replanted some of their best fields in sugar beets.

Utah's ranchers contributed a substantial volume of wool, beef and hides to national commerce in the 1880s. Mormon farmers and Gentile ranchers learned that they could graze sheep and cattle on the public lands in the mountains and high plateaus in the summer and pasture them in the desert west of the Wasatch Oasis in the winter. Between 1880 and 1900 the number of cattle raised in Utah grew from 91,448 to 343,690, while the number of sheep increased from 233,121 to a whopping 3,818,423. Many of these animals or their products left Utah by train for national markets, enriching Salt Lake City merchants and investors in the process.

Salt Lake City businesses engaged in local and national commerce as well. ZCMI, the parent store for a string of Mormon cooperatives throughout the territory, conducted nearly all Utah's wholesale trade and the bulk of the retail trade from its Salt Lake City headquarters. Since the LDS Church had asked its members to boycott all non-Mormon businesses, the various gentile-owned companies complained that they could not compete. Records of the Walker Brothers store

showed, however, that they prospered after ZCMI opened, apparently by capturing the gentile trade. Some other gentile businesses did not do so well.

Jewish businessmen survived in various ways. German-Jewish immigrants, Samuel H., Frederick S. and Theodore Auerbach opened the People's Store in Salt Lake City in 1864. They survived the boycott by opening stores in other towns. Jewish immigrant Nicholas S. Ransohoff merged his business with ZCMI.

Adding to the wealth generated by mining and commerce, various companies began manufacturing in Salt Lake City as well. In 1870 ZCMI opened a factory to make boots and shoes. By 1888 the company had expanded these operations as 180 employees produced more than 160,000 pairs annually. In 1888 ZCMI opened a plant to manufacture clothing. By 1900 the company had a thriving business that supplied the western market with overalls, shirts, coats, vests and men's underwear.

Consolidated Wagon and Machine Company, organized in 1883, manufactured wagons and various types of machinery for the Utah market. Jewish immigrants Nathan Rosenblatt and his sons Simon, Morris and Joseph opened an iron foundry and machinery business in Salt Lake City which eventually expanded into EIMCO, an internationally successful heavy machinery company.

As immigrants poured into Salt Lake City, they brought not only their economic skills but also their deepest religious beliefs. Most were Mormons, largely from the British Isles and Scandinavia. By 1892 the city supported 46 churches including 25 Latter-day Saint, four Methodist, three each for the Episcopalians and Lutherans, two each for the Baptists, Catholics, Congregationalists and Presbyterians, and one each for Christian Scientists, African Methodist Episcopal and Jews.

In addition to the churches throughout the city, the LDS Church owned the principal buildings in the center of Salt Lake City. The tithing yard occupied the space now housing the Joseph Smith Memorial Building on the corner of Main Street and South Temple. Brigham Young's homes and office occupied the north side of South Temple between the tithing yard and State Street. Across the street stood the Gardo House, an attractive Second Empire building that was completed after Brigham Young's death and the much smaller Historian's Office. In 1893 after 40 years of struggle, the Latter-day Saints dedicated the beautiful Fortress Gothic Salt Lake Temple.

Samuel H. Auerbach, along with Frederick S. and Theodore Auerbach, founded Auerbach's Store in 1864.
Utah History Information Center, USHS

Protestants who lived in Salt Lake City organized the Young Men's Literary Institute in December 1864. After meeting in a rented hall, members of the institute got help from the Rev. Norman McLeod, a Congregationalist minister and chaplain at Fort Douglas, to construct Independence Hall, an adobe structure seating 200 people and located on Third South near Main Street. McLeod held services there while he preached in Salt Lake City. Throughout his tenure, he carried on a predictable set of tirades against the Latter-day Saints, lecturing on such subjects as polygamy, the Mountain Meadows Massacre and whether the "Profit [sic] is celestially inspired or only a clever humbug.

From their mother house in Notre Dame, Indiana, these Sisters of the Holy Cross came to Salt Lake City to educate children and care for the sick. *LDS Church Archives*

Catholics established a presence in Salt Lake City in June 1866 when Fr. Edward Kelly from Marysville, California, celebrated the first mass in the city. Kelly gave sermons on such subjects as transubstantiation and divine revelation.

Other priests followed, but the 19th century's most enduring Catholic influence came from the Rev. Lawrence Scanlan who arrived in Salt Lake City in August 1873. Under Scanlan's direction, the Sisters of the Holy Cross sent a delegation from their motherhouse at Notre Dame, Indiana, to launch Catholic education and medical service. The sisters opened academies for girls and young boys in Salt Lake City in 1875. In 1886, with Scanlan's support, priests started All Hallows' College in Salt

Lake City. Marist Fathers assumed supervision of All Hallows' in 1889. Consecrated a bishop in June 1887, Scanlan carried the responsibility for Catholic parishes in Utah and eastern Nevada. He also promoted the construction and dedication in 1909 of the Cathedral of the Madeleine on East South Temple Street in Salt Lake City.

In 1866 the Episcopal church called Daniel S. Tuttle to the episcopate and assigned him as Missionary Bishop for Montana, Idaho and Utah. Tuttle's introduction to Utah came from Warren Hussey, an Episcopalian and a banker, who had developed a good relationship with the Mormons. Calling the Mormons "the worst lied about... of any people living," Hussey helped shape Tuttle's friendly attitude. Unlike a number of other Protestant representatives, Tuttle, like Scanlan, maintained a good relationship with the Mormons while disagreeing with their doctrines and practices.

After arriving in Salt Lake City in June 1867, Tuttle spent some time in Montana and Idaho before making his home in Salt Lake City in 1869. The Episcopal Church held services in Independence Hall until the completion of the basement of St. Mark's Cathedral in May 1871. Tuttle supervised the opening of St. Mark's Day School for Boys and Girls, St. Mark's School for Girls, and Rowland Hall, a boarding school and day school for girls. Non-Mormons constituted the majority of the student

The Lion House, an office building (center), and the Beehive House made up Brigham Young's 19th-century home and the church administrative complex on South Temple Street. *C. R. Savage photo, LDS Church Archives*

body of these schools, but some Mormons attended, though most went to the district schools.

While liturgical churches like the Catholics and Episcopalians disagreed amicably with the Mormons, Evangelicals like the Methodists, Congregationalists, Presbyterians and Baptists saw Utah as a field to convert the Mormons to "Americanism" and "Christianity." Since the Latter-day Saints carried on an active proselyting campaign themselves, they could understand the efforts of the Evangelicals to convert them to Protestantism. They chafed, however, at the bigotry of the Protestants who boasted that they would remake the Latter-day Saints into Christians and Americans, since the Mormons already believed in Christ and His atonement, and they counted themselves as loyal citizens.

Unlike the Catholics and Episcopalians, the Evangelicals tried to bring about these conversions by opening denominational schools where they offered free education to Mormon children. In general, these schools received heavy subsidies from Protestant missionary societies like the Methodist Woman's Home Missionary Society and the Congregationalist New West Education Commission.

In 1875 the Presbyterians established a high school called the Salt Lake Collegiate Institute. In 1895 they renamed the institute "Sheldon Jackson College," where a junior college curriculum was offered. In 1902 it was renamed Westminster

College. Operating on Thirteenth East as a liberal arts college, it remains one of the few vestiges of the mission schools.

Perhaps the most persistent controversy developed with the Methodists. For some unknown reason, in 1870 the Rev. John Philip Newman, pastor of the Metropolitan Methodist Episcopal Church of Washington, D. C. and chaplain of the United States Senate, labored under the impression that Brigham Young had challenged him to debate the question: "Does the Bible sanction Polygamy?" Newman, who had already carried on a running battle with Apostle Orson Pratt in the pages of the *New York Herald*, hurried to Salt Lake City where he wrote to Young accepting the nonexistent challenge. Taken aback by Newman's letter, the elderly Young answered that he was unable to appear but that John Taylor or Orson Pratt might debate him.

Disappointed that he could not beard the Lion of the Lord in his own lair, Newman reluctantly agreed to debate Pratt. The LDS Church offered the use of the Salt Lake Tabernacle, and the debate ran three evenings from August 12 through 14, 1870. As is usual in such debates, partisans of both antagonists thought their champion had won.

Enthused with the prospect of converting the Mormons, the Methodists continued to send missionaries to Utah. The Methodists established a high school and grammar schools in Salt Lake City and throughout the territory. The Rev. Thomas

Students gathered in front of St. Marks School, established by Episcopal Bishop Daniel Tuttle.
Utah History Information Center, USHS

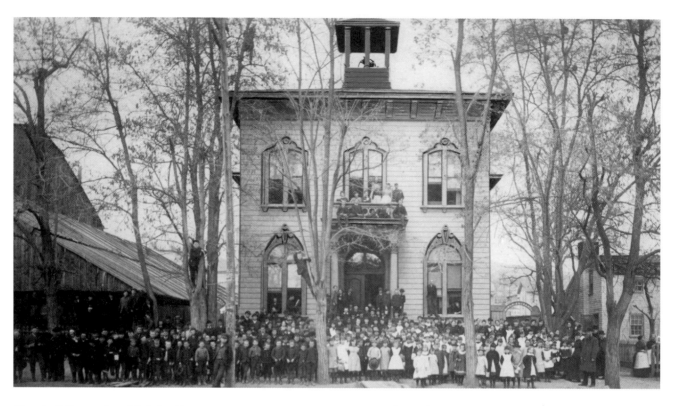

Corwin Iliff arrived in Salt Lake City in 1882 to serve as pastor and later superintendent of missions for the Rocky Mountain Conference of the Methodist Episcopal Church.

Following their excommunication from the Mormon fold, the Godbeites founded the short-lived Church of Zion; but they made a more lasting contribution in 1870-71 by constructing the Liberal Institute on the east side of Second East between First and Second South. They also succeeded in attracting Amasa Lyman, a former member of the LDS Church's Quorum of the Twelve, into their ranks.

Lyman, whom the Latter-day Saints excommunicated for denying the necessity of Christ's atonement, reveled in the Godbeite emphasis on spiritualism and seances. Designed to seat 1,000, the Liberal Institute played host to twice that number on occasion. National suffragists like Susan B. Anthony and Elizabeth Cady Stanton spoke there on visits to Salt Lake City. At various times Catholics, Methodists, Presbyterians, Lutherans and Re-organized Latter Day Saints held services at the Liberal Institute.

Martha J. Perkins Howell, Lucinda Flake Stevens and Belle Oglesby, representative women of Salt Lake City's African American community *From the Peoples of Utah Collection, Utah History Information Center, USHS*

By the mid-1860s Jewish immigrants had begun holding services in Salt Lake City. In 1866 Brigham Young gave them permission to celebrate High Holy Days at the Seventies Hall on Temple Square. Jewish congregations held services in homes and halls until 1883 when they dedicated Temple B'nai Israel at Third South and First West. At first following the Orthodox tradition, B'nai Israel soon adopted the Reform ritual. After selling the first temple, the congregation constructed a new synagogue on Fourth East between Second and Third South that replicated in miniature the Great Synagogue in Berlin. Orthodox and Conservative Jews constructed a building for Congregation Montefiore with twin Moorish towers flanking the central structure.

Salt Lake City's African-American population dated from the first pioneers of 1847. Elijah and Mary Ann Abel managed the Farnham Hotel in Salt Lake City. Elijah Abel also worked as a carpenter on the Salt Lake Temple. Detective Paul Cephas Howell served on the Salt Lake City police force for more than 20 years during the late 19th century. The railroad brought additional blacks to Salt Lake City where many worked as porters and waiters.

Asians added to Salt Lake City's ethnic mix. Only a few Japanese settled in Utah during the 19th century. Territorial and Salt Lake City officials, however, hosted the 50 members of a mission headed by Ambassador Extraordinary Iwakura Tomomi from February 3 through 22, 1872.

Utah's earliest Chinese came on Central Pacific construction crews. By 1890 271 Chinese lived in Salt Lake City, principally in the Plum Alley district between Main and State streets and First and Second south. During the 1890s the Chinese celebrated the lunar New Year on Plum Alley with a huge canvas dragon measuring at least 200 feet long fronted by a six-foot-high fire-spitting head. Although a Buddhist church was apparently not constructed in Salt Lake City until 1912, and then by Japanese, the Plum Alley Chinese maintained the reverence for family central to the beliefs of Buddhism, Confucianism and Taoism; and many returned the bones of their dead ancestors to China for burial.

A family enjoys an outing at Liberty Park.
Utah History Information Center, USHS

In addition to the churches, Salt Lake City hosted a number of benevolent and charitable societies. The Masons had eight lodges in Salt Lake City by 1892, and a broad range of other societies boasted lodges as well. Christian societies such as the YMCA, Christian Endeavor, the LDS Women's Relief Society, and the LDS Young Men's and Young Women's Mutual Improvement Associations all had organizations.

If the churches, synagogues and temples offered spiritual comfort to Salt Lake City's population, and the societies, associations and lodges offered opportunities for service, education and rituals, the city also hosted a number of athletic and cultural organizations. These included by 1892 the Salt Lake Fencing Club, the Harmony Dancing Club and the Salt Lake Rowing Club. The city had numerous literary and women's clubs such as the Ladies Literary Club and the Reapers, and it sported a number of libraries. Visitors could attend a play at the Salt Lake Theatre or the Walker Opera House, they could listen to a performance of the Mormon Tabernacle Choir, or they could visit the Deseret Museum to see a potpourri including paintings, Kit Carson's boat, Indian artifacts, and stuffed animals and birds. Those so inclined could play at one of several bowling alleys, shoot billiards at the Clift House or Trobridges, or watch and bet on trotter races at Faust's track.

The city also boasted a number of parks and other resorts. Some escaped to the nearby canyons or to Saltair on Great Salt Lake where they could dance and bathe. The city opened Liberty Park by purchasing farm property west of Seventh East between Ninth and Thirteenth South. Other parks included Arsenal Block (the current site of the State Capitol Building), Calder's Park (currently Nibley Park Golf Course west of Seventh East and south of Twenty-seventh South), the Salt Lake Driving Park (Fifth East and Twelfth South), Smoot's Gardens (on Eleventh East and South Boulevard) and Washington Square (the current site of the City and County Building).

During the 1870s and 80s intense rivalry brought many of Salt Lake City's residents to Washington Square to watch baseball. From 1877 through 1879 rivalry blossomed between

Participants activate a large dragon for a celebration in the Chinese community of *Utah History Information Center, USHS*

the gentile-dominated Deseret Club and the Red Stockings, a Mormon club. Interest became so intense that fully a fourth of Salt Lake City's population crowded onto Washington Square to watch the games. During the 1880s the Deserets became a professional team, hiring players from outside Salt Lake City. With professionalization, the interest of Salt Lakers in the Deserets waned and the city refused to allow them to play on Washington Square.

Rivalry between the Deserets and Red Stockings represented one facet of the conflict between Mormons and gentiles in Salt Lake City, Utah and the nation. Issues between the two communities included economic exclusiveness, ecclesiastically aligned politics and conflicting religious doctrines.

The division between the Mormon and non-Mormon communities had resulted from a number of conditions. Evangelical Protestants had labeled the Latter-day Saints as non-Christian, un-American and deluded fanatics since shortly after the founding of the Church in 1830. State-supported violence, approved by some Evangelicals, had led to the Mormons' expulsion from Missouri, and state-tolerated violence had led to the murder of their two most important leaders and their eventual exodus from Illinois.

Twice burned, the Mormons declined to trust outside leaders. Although the federal government sent governors, judges, and U.S. attorneys and marshals to the territory, real power rested with the LDS Church leadership with headquarters in Salt Lake City. Until 1890, a succession of prominent Mormons served as Salt Lake City's mayor, aldermen and councilors, while non-Mormons with the backing of the federal government tried to wrest power from the Latter-day Saints.

Many gentiles in Salt Lake City hoped that the federal officials could control Mormon power. By 1873 Protestants,

Catholics and Jews made up about a quarter of the city's population. Most had come with the expectation of making a living in the Mormon capital. A large percentage ran businesses or belonged to the learned professions. A study in 1874 showed that gentiles contributed 42 percent of the taxes and license fees the Salt Lake City government collected. Nevertheless, the city government operated like a private business and refused to allow the non-Mormons to review the books.

In addition to political domination, the Mormon practice of polygamy generated abundant tension with other Americans. Mormons considered polygamy part of the restoration of the fullness of the gospel and of Christ's new and everlasting covenant. The Saints expected plural marriages to reduce marital infidelity and to open the pathway for righteous spirits to leave God's presence and occupy bodies on earth.

During the 1880s, 20 to 30 percent of Latter-day Saint families were polygamous, though the percentage may have been somewhat lower in Salt Lake City. Thus, although 70 to 80 percent of the Mormon households were monogamous, most of the general authorities, stake leaders and bishoprics lived what many called "the Principal."

Since most Americans considered polygamy a deviant and immoral practice, anti-Mormons had little difficulty in convincing the federal officials to take a strong stand against these marriages. After his inauguration as U.S. president in 1869, Ulysses S. Grant sought a jurist to enforce laws against polygamy. James B. McKean of New York seemed to fill the bill, and Grant appointed him as chief justice of the Utah Territorial Supreme Court. The territorial governor assigned McKean to the third judicial district headquartered in Salt Lake City.

McKean arrived in the Mormon capital in the fall of 1870, and he immediately launched an attack on the city administration and the Latter-day Saints. Ignoring the territorial law on empaneling juries, McKean ordered the U.S. Marshal to recruit men off the street for jury service. After the marshal had packed the grand jury with Anti-Mormons, McKean secured indictments under the territorial law for lewd and lascivious cohabitation and adultery against LDS leaders Brigham Young, George Q. Cannon and Daniel H. Wells, who also served as Salt Lake City mayor, and Henry W. Lawrence, a prominent Godbeite leader.

In a dramatic announcement from the bench as he opened the trial against Young, McKean said that although the "case at

Logging in Little Cottonwood Canyon in the 1870s
Nelson Wadsworth

The Salt Lake Red Stockings baseball team
Utah History Information Center, USHS

bar is called, 'The People versus Brigham Young,' its other and real title is, 'Federal Authority versus Polygamic Theocracy.'" By this bit of hyperbole, McKean lost the support of many moderate gentiles. Patrick Edward Connor, for instance, had since resigned his general's commission and had remained in Utah to engage in mining and other business activities. Having mellowed since the heady days of the Civil War, he thought the charges ill advised. The Walker Brothers deplored McKean's actions. Even U. S. Attorney George C. Bates could not understand why McKean had secured the indictments under territorial laws clearly not written to prosecute polygamists rather than the federal 1862 Morrill Anti-bigamy Act.

McKean broadened his crusade against the Mormon leaders. On the questionable testimony of confessed murderer William H. "Bill" Hickman, McKean also secured indictments against Young, Wells and Hosea Stout for the murder of Richard Yates during the Utah War.

Not content with such actions, McKean trumped himself in 1875 when he agreed to preside over the divorce suit of Ann Eliza Webb Dee Young, Brigham Young's 27th wife. Young replied to Ann Eliza's petition by arguing that her divorce from James Dee had not become final, so she was not free to marry. Had she been free to marry, he could not have since he was legally married to Mary Ann Angell. In addition, he said, the sealing to Ann Eliza was a "plural or celestial marriage" performed under the rites of the LDS Church rather than a marriage recognized under Utah law.

Ignoring Young's arguments, McKean ordered the 74-year-old man to pay $500 per month alimony pending the outcome of the litigation. Young appealed McKean's order to the territorial supreme court, but the judge nevertheless fined him $25 and ordered him to spend a day in prison for contempt of court. Most in the Mormon community as well as a number of prominent non-Mormons thought that McKean had exercised poor judgment. Still, Young spent a night in the territorial penitentiary at Sugar House.

Young's imprisonment proved anticlimactic because the U.S. Attorney General ordered the case dismissed on the ground that Brigham could never legally have married Ann Eliza. To have recognized such a marriage would have tacitly acknowledged the legality of plural marriage, which the Morrill Anti-bigamy Act had declared a felony.

Not satisfied with attacks on the Mormon leadership, McKean assaulted the Salt Lake City administration as well. In an attempt to control the liquor traffic and to provide revenue, the city council had set up license fees and bonding requirements for dealers. McKean struck down the fees as excessive. Paul

Ann Eliza Webb Young, plural wife of Brigham Young who sued the aged church president for divorce
LDS Church Archives

A crowd gathered outside Faust's and Houtz Livery Stable awaiting the verdict in the case of Young v. Young. The stable was located on the south side of Second South between Main and State streets and was the site of Judge James B. McKean's United States District Court.
C. W. Carter photograph, LDS Church Archives

Englebrecht, a wholesale and sometime retail distributor, refused to secure performance bonds, and Jeter Clinton, Salt Lake City alderman and justice of the peace, ordered City Marshal John D. T. McAllister to destroy Englebrecht's stock of booze. McAllister complied, and Englebrecht retaliated by suing Clinton for three times the value of the liquor under a territorial statute. In a trial before McKean's court, an unsympathetic jury ordered Clinton to pay $59,000 in damages.

Clinton appealed to the U.S. Supreme Court, pointing out that McKean had failed to follow territorial law in empaneling the jury. In April 1872 the Supreme Court unanimously agreed with Clinton. This ruling overturned Englebrecht's award and threw out the indictments returned by McKean's stacked juries including those for adultery and murder against Young and Wells.

A collection of polygamous prisoners surround George Q. Cannon at the Utah Territorial Penitentiary in 1888. *Utah History Information Center, USHS*

McKean also attacked Salt Lake City's zoning and regulatory policies. In an apparent attempt to maintain the city's residential character, Salt Lake City's administration required all grocers and meat markets to locate in the center of town. To regulate potential gambling, the city established license fees for billiard establishments at several times higher than levies in other American cities. McKean struck down the zoning regulations and license fees as unreasonable.

To nullify Utah's victory in the Englebrecht decision, in 1874 Congress passed the Poland Act, which changed the method of empaneling juries by allowing the federally appointed clerk of the territorial supreme court to select half the panel. With more sympathetic juries, the territorial marshal arrested Brigham Young's secretary George Reynolds under the Morrill Anti-bigamy Act for practicing polygamy. Reynolds's trial took place in Judge Philip Emerson's court in Salt Lake City on March 31 and April 1, 1875. The jury found Reynolds guilty, but the Utah territorial supreme court overturned the verdict on a technicality.

Convicted again on December 21, Reynolds appealed to the U.S. Supreme Court. On January 6, 1979, the court upheld Reynolds's conviction in an interpretation of

Judge Charles S. Zane, whose rulings led to the conviction of hundreds of Latter-day Saint men for unlawful cohabitation *Utah History Information Center, USHS*

the First Amendment's Free Exercise of Religion clause that has since provided the basis of American law on the subject. Writing for the court, Chief Justice Morrison R. Waite said that Americans could believe anything that they wished, but they could not engage in acts that the general sense of the community considered immoral or illegal. Polygamy fell under that category.

In practice, however, the courts convicted few people under the Morrill Act, because the government had to demonstrate that a plural marriage had actually taken place. This proved extremely difficult because Utah had no civil registration until 1887 and Latter-day Saint temple records were generally unavailable.

Congress remedied this deficiency in 1882 with the passage of the Edmunds Act, which defined the misdemeanor of unlawful cohabitation. To prove unlawful cohabitation, the prosecution simply had to show that the couple lived together. To enforce the Edmunds Law, in 1884 President Chester A. Arthur selected Illinois jurist Charles S. Zane. Zane took the oath of office on September 1, 1884, and on November 3, a jury in his Salt Lake City court convicted Rudger Clawson, a 27-year-old church leader, of unlawful cohabitation. Like Reynolds, Clawson appealed his conviction to the U.S. Supreme Court. Also like Reynolds, the court sustained his conviction.

Reynolds and Clawson were two of more than 1,000 men convicted of practicing plural marriage, a large number of them in Salt Lake City's third district court. Judges also sentenced a number of women, usually plural wives and generally for contempt of court for refusing to testify against their husbands. The courts required such testimony because unlike first or monogamous wives, who could not testify against their husbands, plural wives were not legally married.

Although Zane usually sentenced unrepentant polygamists to the full extent of the law, he gained some admiration from Salt Lake City residents for what they perceived as his lack of anti-Mormon prejudice. He offered leniency to the few who agreed to obey the law. He also sustained the Salt Lake City council and local school districts in their attempts to regulate local affairs and to raise taxes to build new schoolhouses.

Nevertheless, he came down with the full wrath of the law on city officials who tried to use the law for political advantage. For example, in a bizarre case, Brigham Y. Hampton, a member of the Salt Lake City police department, had hired prostitutes (he called them detectives) to try to compromise local federal officials. Following Hampton's conviction, Zane sentenced him to a year in the Salt Lake County jail.

Such conflicts notwithstanding, Utahns granted women the right to vote in 1870. In a meeting in Salt Lake City on January 6, 1870, to protest new anti-polygamy legislation, Bathsheba W. Smith, wife of George A. Smith, first counselor to Brigham Young, and a prominent LDS Relief Society leader and women's rights advocate, secured the adoption of a resolution demanding "the right of franchise." George Q. Cannon, a counselor to Brigham Young and editor of the *Deseret News*, editorialized in favor of women's suffrage as a progressive measure that would lead to improvement of society. After the legislature passed a bill granting women the vote and Acting Gov. Samuel A. Mann signed it,

Members of a midwife class taught by Ellis Reynolds Shipp pose for a photograph in about 1896.
LDS Church Archives

The Utah Territorial Penitentiary, 1887, was located in what is now Sugar House Park in southeastern Salt Lake City.
LDS Church Archives

Seraph Young, the first woman to vote in an election in Salt Lake City after the passage of the Utah Territorial statute giving women the vote in 1870
Utah History Information Center, USHS

the Salt Lake City women sent a delegation to his office to thank him.

Two days after Mann signed the act, Seraph Young, a niece of Brigham Young, voted in the Salt Lake City municipal election and women began to take a part in public affairs. Georgia Snow, a niece of former federal judge Zerubbabel Snow, was the first Utah woman admitted to the bar. Other women were sworn in as lawyers, and 19th-century Utah women also served on school boards and on coroner's juries.

Unfortunately, this first progressive effort lasted only 17 years. Since neither the Morrill nor the Edmunds Act proved capable of eradicating polygamy in Utah, Congress passed additional measures. The Edmunds-Tucker Act, passed in 1887, repealed Utah's woman suffrage act, disbanded the territorial militia, turned management of the public schools over to a federal appointee and

provided for the confiscation of all of the LDS Church's secular property.

After some legal wrangling, the court appointed U.S. Marshal Frank H. Dyer as receiver of the church's property. He took possession of the Tithing Office, the Gardo House, the Church Historian's Office, the Church President's Office and numerous other pieces of property.

The LDS Church appealed the confiscation to the U.S. Supreme Court, which ruled the seizures legal in May 1890. Moreover, the decision left open the possibility that the receiver might also commandeer the Church's religious properties since they were being used for an illegal purpose — the practice of polygamy.

Concerned about the possibility that the government might confiscate the church's meeting houses and especially its temples, church President Wilford Woodruff prayed for guidance and sought a way out of the dilemma. In August 1890, he and his first counselor, George Q. Cannon, visited members throughout the Western states urging the members to divide into the two national political parties. In September the two traveled to San Francisco to consult with business and political leaders.

Wilford Woodruff and Emma Smith Woodruff in the 1890s
LDS Church Archives

After returning to Salt lake City late on September 21, Woodruff spent the next two days in normal business, in prayer, and in dictating the document that was to end the practice of plural marriage in the LDS Church. On September 24 he consulted with his counselors, Cannon and Joseph F. Smith and with apostles Franklin D. Richards, Moses Thatcher and Marriner W. Merrill. The same day, he issued the Manifesto that declared his intention to obey the law on plural marriage and to encourage all church members to do the same.

In the two weeks between the publication of the Manifesto and the church's Semi-annual General Conference, Woodruff met with other church leaders. He told them that the Manifesto meant ceasing to enter new plural marriages and ceasing to live with their plural families. At a session of the general conference, on October 6, members of the church approved the Manifesto with upraised hands.

Already, however, Utah's Mormon, Catholic, Protestant and Jewish communities had begun to come together. In some fields Salt Lakers accomplished the combination of the communities easily, in others it moved with exceeding slowness.

Interior of the George M. Scott and Company Store, 168 South Main Street, probably in the 1890s
Utah History Information Center, USHS

The economic rivalry began to melt away in 1882 when Brigham Young's successor as LDS Church president, John Taylor, lifted the boycott on gentile businesses. It further receded in 1887 when Territorial Governor Caleb W. West urged Mormon, Catholic, Protestant and Jewish businessmen to put aside their differences and organize a chamber of commerce, then called the Commercial Club. West rightly believed that the religious rivalry had poisoned Salt Lake City's business climate. Electing Salt Lake City businessman and banker William S. McCornick as the club's first president, members adopted the rule that politics and religion must remain outside the door.

After the passage of the Edmunds-Tucker Act and the disenfranchisement of Mormon women, the relative parity of adult gentile and nonpolygamous Mormon males in Salt Lake City led the Mormon People's Party leaders to propose a change in political policy. Instead of offering Salt Lakers a straight Mormon ticket, in February 1888 they proposed a slate including McCornick as one of the five alderman slots and John E.

Dooley, M. B. Sowles and Bolivar Roberts as three of the nine counselors. Mormon businessman Francis Armstrong led the ticket as mayoral candidate. Then, instead of running the ticket under the People's Party label, they called themselves the Citizen's Ticket. The Citizen's Ticket won by more than a two-to-one majority.

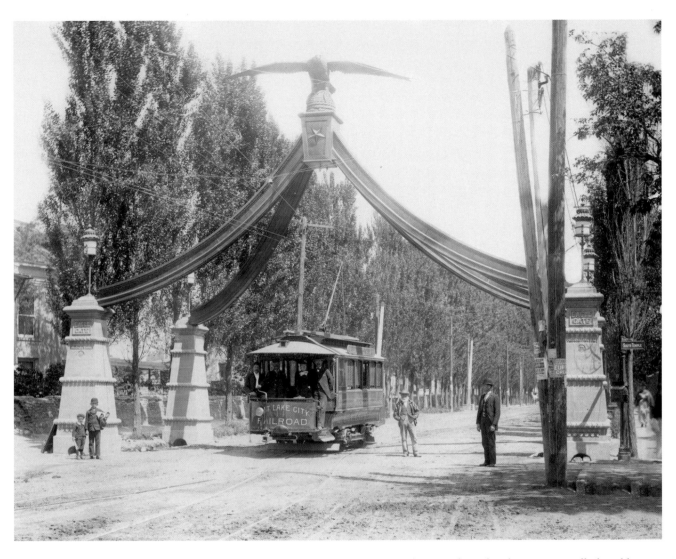

An electric streetcar passes under Eagle Gate on State Street in about 1893.
C. R. Savage photo, LDS Church Archives

Nevertheless, the anti-Mormon Liberal Party gained in strength. In the August 1889 elections for the legislature, Liberal candidates captured one Salt Lake City seat in the territorial council and three in the house. Buoyed by these victories, Liberal prospects seemed even more promising in November 1889 when Territorial District Court Judge Thomas J. Anderson ruled that Mormons could no longer become American citizens because he considered them disloyal.

In the hotly contested February 1890 city election, Liberal Party candidate George M. Scott, a businessman, defeated People's Party candidate and Mormon businessman Spencer Clawson. Born in New York in 1835, Scott migrated to California in 1852 and moved to Salt Lake City in 1871. There, he achieved considerable success in the hardware business, especially in selling mining machinery. The Liberal Party won all the alderman seats and all but three seats on the council. Election officials, however, gave victory certificates for those seats to the Liberal Party members. Appeals to Judge Zane and to the Territorial Supreme Court eventually returned the three seats to the People's Party, but not before 18 months of a two-year term had already expired.

When Scott's administration began to govern Salt Lake City in on February 18, 1890, they inherited a city deficient in improvements. Salt Lake City had no paved streets, and like Stockton, California, and Kansas City they were rated among the dirtiest in the West.

Most people moved by horse and buggy or the street railway system that had opened in 1872. In 1889, two years after the successful inauguration of an electric street railway

In this stereoscopic photo, a crowd gathers around the Salt Lake City fire department's first steam fire engine.
LDS Church Archives

system in Richmond, Virginia, the company then named the Salt Lake Rapid Transit Company converted the Salt Lake City line to electricity.

During the 1870s and 1880s companies began offering lighting options other than candles and lanterns. In 1872 the Salt Lake City Gas Company piped in gas manufactured from coal. In 1880 entrepreneurs turned on electric lights on Main Street. They then strung the lines into other parts of the city.

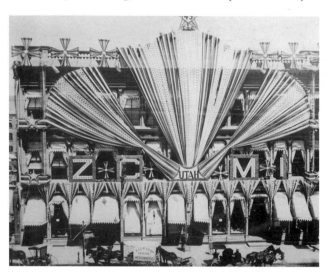

ZCMI decked out in celebration of the admission of Utah into the Union
Utah History Information Center, USHS

Like most American cities, Salt Lake moved slowly in the 19th century to provide a public water system. Largely because of the leadership of Mayor Feramorz Little, by 1884 the city had constructed enclosed water mains with a settling system. This system fed into hydrants rather than to user's homes. By 1890 the city had only five miles of sewer pipe along 275 miles of streets.

Petitions for street, water and sewer improvements poured into Scott's office. Responding to what they perceived as a public groundswell, the city council approved a massive urban improvement program. The city inaugurated a board of health and floated bonds to improve the streets and the water and sewer systems. In March 1891 the city administration entered into an agreement with Salt Lake County to construct a city and county building on Washington Square, which was completed in 1894.

Shortly after Scott's inauguration, Salt Lake City's political landscape began to change even more dramatically. Leaders of the LDS church recognized that conditions made compromise necessary, and that Utah's progress and eventual statehood required that they divide into separate political parties. On June 10, 1891, the LDS First Presidency and leaders of the People's Party met in the Gardo House, which the church had rented from the federal government. They agreed to disband the People's Party, and the church leadership encouraged Latter-day Saints to divide "about evenly between the [Republican and Democratic] parties." Mormons and gentiles cooperated in organizing the two national parties. At first a number of anti-Mormons declined to abandon the Liberal Party. Eventually, however, Liberal Party numbers became so few that a small remnant disbanded the party in December 1893.

In the meantime, a backlash against the massive expenditures of the Scott administration led Robert N. Baskin and a number of Salt Lakers to bolt the Liberal Party to organize a citizen's reform ticket for the February 1893 elections. In the changing political climate, a number of Mormons supported Baskin, who had been anti-Mormon during the 1870s. Baskin won, and he cancelled a number of contracts for urban improvements sponsored by the Scott administration.

In 1895, James J. Glendinning, a local businessman, won the mayoral election on the Republican Party ticket. He defeated former Mayor Francis Armstrong, a Democrat, and Elijah Sells, a Populist. Eight Republicans and seven Democrats won election to the city council.

In 1894 Salt Lake City and Salt Lake County dedicated the stunning Richardson Romanesque City and County Building downtown on Washington Square. The building became the stage on which Utah culminated its struggle for statehood. After Congress approved the Utah Statehood Enabling Act in July 1894, the people elected members to a constitutional convention that met in the City and County Building during March, April and May 1895. In November 1895 the people of Utah approved the constitution and a slate of state officers. Elected the first governor of the state of Utah, Heber M. Wells, son of former Salt Lake City Mayor Daniel H. Wells, was inaugurated in the Salt Lake Tabernacle on January 6, 1896.

Between 1870 and 1896, Salt Lake City had undergone sweeping changes. The Mormon, Protestant, Catholic and Jewish leaders had pulled together to make Salt Lake City the economic and cultural center of the Intermountain West. After weathering the ethnic and religious conflicts that had characterized Utah's communities during the 1870s and 1880s, Salt Lake City emerged politically and economically unified during the early 1890s. Religious division persisted as it did in other American cities, but for a time issues of public policy rather than religious persuasion divided Salt Lake citizens. Salt Lake City was to weather further struggles before it became fully integrated into the family of American cities, but for the time being people of various persuasions lived together in relative harmony.

The Gardo House or Amelia's Palace, shown here in about 1879, was constructed by Brigham Young for his wife Amelia Folsom Young. It was located on the south side of South Temple Street on the site of the present ZCMI Center.
LDS Church Archives

During the 1890s Salt Lakers enjoyed amenities similar to those of other large American cities. In a competition for customers, two streetcar companies had rushed to lay tracks from the central city into the Avenues subdivisions on the hill north of South Temple and east of State Street, into the Capitol Hill district west of the site for the State Capitol, onto the east bench near the

The Progressive City

CHAPTER THREE

new University of Utah campus, and into the farming country south of Liberty Park and in Sugar House. Freed by streetcar mobility, residents could ride to work, to shop or to school. Streetlights brightened the night and electricity illuminated newspapers and books, plays, musicals and vaudeville. People at home or at businesses could ring up one another on two systems — the Bell or the Independent.

Nevertheless, like the residents of many other American cities, Salt Lakers also wallowed in dirt, drank polluted water and breathed foul air. In 1880 observers rated Salt Lake City's 275 miles of dirt streets with Stockton, California, and Kansas City, Missouri, as among the filthiest in the West. During the 1890s some sewage seeped into wells and ditches, while some channeled into the rudimentary five-mile system, fed into the

The Cathedral of the Madeleine on east South Temple served as the center of Catholic life for Utah. *LDS Church Archives*

Jordan River, and washed into the wetlands south and east of Great Salt Lake. Fumes from factories, shops, railroads, homes and smelters fouled air and lungs as it soiled carpets, drapes and clothes. Diseases such as tuberculosis, diphtheria and smallpox spread through the city in periodic epidemics.

Amazingly, by 1930, like most American cities, Salt Lake City had eliminated or mitigated most of these health hazards and annoyances. Persistent lobbying by civic improvement leagues and the city's women's and men's clubs, the efforts of the city engineer and the cooperation of the city government led to the elimination or minimization of such dangers and inconveniences. During the mid-teens the city buried an adequate water and sewer system under paved streets, parklike boulevards

festooned a number of streets and vaccination had become more frequent. During the 1920s, when smoke abatement had taken its toll on air polluters, the city adopted a zoning system in an attempt to prevent the encroachment of industry into residential areas, and the administration had begun to provide rudimentary, if irregular, garbage collection.

By the 1920s new buildings had changed the cityscape. Mining magnates and wealthy business people had constructed a string of elaborate and beautiful mansions along South Temple, a street locals fondly called "Brigham Street." Apartment houses flourished near the downtown area. Middle- and upper-class homes sprang up in an arc of subdivisions ringing the central business district on the north, east and south. At the same time new immigrants crowded into apartments and houses in the downtown area and on the city's west side.

As residents built homes, buildings in the downtown area soared ever higher to dwarf the older one- or two-story structures like the Lion and Beehive houses and the tabernacle. On the south end of downtown at State Street between Fourth and Fifth South, Salt Lake City and County cooperated in building the City and County Building, a beautiful example of Richardson Romanesque architecture. The building was designed by Henry Monheim, George W. Bird and Willis T. Proudfoot and completed in 1894.

A block west and a half block north of the City and County Building on Exchange Place at Main Street stood the twin Boston and Newhouse buildings, designed by Chicago architect Henry Ives Cobb and completed in 1909. In the center of the downtown area at Temple Square, in 1894 the LDS church dedicated the Salt Lake Temple, an eclectic Fortress Gothic and Norman structure.

On the corner of South Temple and Main streets, the Hotel Utah (now the Joseph Smith Memorial Building) a Second Renaissance Revival building replaced the low-lying Tithing House and Yard. Designed by Los Angeles architects Parkinson and Bergstrom, it was completed in 1911.

Just east of the hotel, the LDS Church Office Building, designed by Joseph Don Carlos Young, the architect who supervised the final stages of Salt Lake Temple construction, was completed in 1917.

To the east and across the street at the corner of South Temple and State Street stood the Alta Club, a Second Renaissance Revival structure, designed by Salt Lake City architect Frederick Albert Hale and finished in 1897.

On Arsenal Hill overlooking the city, the State Capitol dominated the city. A Beaux-Arts Classical structure reminiscent of the national capitol in Washington, D. C., the state capitol was designed by Richard K. A. Kletting, a German immigrant and one of Utah's most distinguished early 20th century architects, and completed in 1916.

West of the city's downtown arose the Union Pacific Depot at the base of South Temple and the Rio Grande Depot at the end of Third South. The Rio Grande Depot, a fine example of Beaux-Arts Classicism, was designed by Chicago architect Henry Schlachs and completed in 1910. The Union Pacific Depot, matching the French Second Empire style of the nearby Devereaux House was designed by D. J. Patterson and completed in 1909.

Businesses, churches and local governments began to construct additions to the city's architecture and to some public utilities during the 19th century's worst depression. The depression began in Europe in 1890 as a recession that followed upon the breakup of the Baring Brothers' London financial empire. The recession washed from Europe to the United States and across the continent to Utah during 1891. By 1893 the nation and the Beehive State had fallen into full-scale depression. In 1894 fully 48 percent of Salt Lake City's work force pounded the streets looking for jobs while private and religious agencies offered temporary assistance. The LDS Church cooperated with local and national capitalists to offer jobs at companies in the newly inaugurated electric, sugar and salt industries. Depressed conditions retarded the rate of growth of Salt Lake City's population from the 116 percent it had experienced during the 1880s to just 19 percent during the 1890s.

By 1896, however, Utah and Salt Lake City had begun to emerge from this economic mire and citizens became more

Emma Lunt was chosen as Miss Utah for the 1897 semicentennial of the entry of the Mormon Pioneers into the Salt Lake Valley. Her attendants were Lou Groesbeck and Allie Miller. Pages were Allen Spencer and Curtis Y. Cannon. The driver is unidentified. C. R. Savage photo, LDS Church Archives

A crowd gathered for the 1897 semicentennial of the entry of the Mormon Pioneers into the Salt Lake Valley. At left is the papier maché "Hall of Relics" that housed artifacts contributed by various citizens. In the background is the Salt Lake Temple of the Church of Jesus Christ of Latter-day Saints. *LDS Church Archives*

concerned about how to govern themselves. Although Salt Lakers had abandoned the religious partisanship of the 19th century, during the early 1890s they traded religious parties for the political partisanship of mainstream America. While partisanship had only a slight effect on private enterprise in the city, it clearly retarded the improvement of the city's public amenities.

Partisanship led Republican James Glendinning, a former Liberal Party member who was elected mayor in 1896, to abolish the job of the city's Inspector of Provisions. Without the inspector, and in the absence of federal and state pure food laws, citizens stood in mortal peril from unscrupulous businesses that sold adulterated food and drinks. Some businesses, for instance, actually delivered milk laced with formaldehyde (embalming fluid) that they used to prevent spoilage.

Glendinning's ill-conceived partisanship led citizens of various parties to join together in offering a fusion ticket for the 1897 elections. Nominating businessman John Clark, a nominal Democrat and member of the Salt Lake LDS Stake high council, and hoping to banish partisanship from city elections, the fusionists called themselves the "Citizen's Reform Ticket." After Clark's two-year term, the Republicans and the Democrats captured the mayoral office in succession until religious bigotry captured the city again in 1905.

Bigotry reared its ugly head in 1903, after the Republican-dominated legislature elected Reed Smoot as a U.S. senator from Utah. A popular politician, Smoot also served as a member of the Quorum of Twelve Apostles, the second-highest governing body of the LDS Church. Immediately after Smoot's election, a coalition of Protestant ministers and non-Mormon businessmen fired off a protest to the U.S. Senate. They

charged that Smoot had made covenants as an apostle that were incompatible with the oath of a U.S. Senator. They alleged also that he and his colleagues promoted the practice of polygamy, which was illegal under Utah law and repugnant to traditional Christians.

Smoot denied the charges, and the senate seated him. Because of the protests, however, the senators turned the petitions against Smoot over to the Committee on Privileges and Elections, chaired by Sen. Julius C. Burrows of Michigan. The committee conducted extensive hearings into Smoot's life and into the teachings and practices of the LDS Church Between 1904 and 1907. After the hearings ended, the Senate voted to allow him to retain his seat.

Nevertheless, revelations of continued church involvement in politics and business and the continued practice of polygamy led to a number of changes in the LDS Church. Church President Joseph F. Smith issued a Second Manifesto in the Salt Lake Tabernacle at the April 1904 General Conference. In it he instructed members to stop entering into new plural marriages. Subsequently two of Smoot's colleagues among the Twelve were expelled from the quorum, and church courts excommunicated numerous members for refusing to stop entering polygamy.

Still, a group of anti-Mormons fine-tuned religious partisanship by organizing a new political party. Calling themselves the American Party, the anti-Mormons failed in elections throughout Utah except in Salt Lake City where they controlled the city government from 1905 through 1911. To its credit, the American Party began to build a number of needed urban improvements in Salt Lake City.

Nevertheless, in spite of their claims of high moral standards and official integrity, scandals plagued the American Party administration. Allegations of official collusion in the theft of $10,000 from two Scottish tourists in a rigged poker game led to the resignation in August 1907 of Chief of Police George A. Sheets and Chief of Detectives George Raleigh. Sometime afterward, Mayor Ezra Thompson also resigned, citing ill health. The city council appointed John S. Bransford, a businessman associated with Thomas Kearns, as mayor. Bransford ran successfully for election in 1909.

In the meantime, the Bransford administration itself weathered a scandal, this time over prostitution. In Salt Lake City, as in most American cities, prostitution flourished during the 19th century. During the 1890s Salt Lake City police operated an informal system of regulation by raiding parlor houses and small apartments called "cribs" each month. After hauling the prostitutes to the police station, they fined those who ran the operations $50 and charged the hookers $8.50 each. They also brought in doctors to give physical examinations to the prostitutes. After assuming power in 1905 the American Party refined this system by requiring each madam to turn in a list of her women and to pay a $10 "fine" for each.

At the turn of the century Salt Lake City's red-light district was located around Commercial Street, currently named Regent Street. Well known for its parlor houses, Commercial Street offered both booze and women. After the Johns rang the houses' doorbells, uniformed maids and butlers greeted them, and the customers proceeded into salons where they could enjoy a drink and listen to a "Professor" entertain them on the piano while they waited for their turn at hired sex.

In a dubious effort to reform this system, the American Party opted for open prostitution. In 1908 with the support of the city council, Bransford and Councilman Martin E. Mulvey approached Dora B. Topham, who, under the business name of Belle London, ran a number of brothels in Ogden's Electric Alley, a half street lying north of the city's notorious 25th Street. Topham agreed to build and operate a "stockade" with half a dozen parlor houses for the upscale trade and numerous cribs for independent prostitutes. Lying between 5th and 6th West and 1st and 2nd South, the property seemed ideal, since railroad tracks nearly surrounded it. As an added advantage in an age intolerant of southern and eastern European immigrants, the stockade lay in the middle of a district increasingly peopled by Italians and Greeks that locals derisively called "Greek Town." Topham's cribs rented for $1 to $4 per day and the parlor houses brought her $175 per month.

To the irritation of Belle London and the American Party, the erection of the stockade coincided with the nationwide reform movement called "Progressivism." Some Progressives, concerned about personal morality, launched what historian David J. Pivar called a "Purity Crusade." These reformers sought to eliminate prostitution. In a contrary movement, reformers in a number of American cities, like their European counterparts, lobbied for a regulated flesh trade. Convinced by the purity crusaders, Congress entered the fray in 1910 by passing the Mann Act, which outlawed the interstate transportation of prostitutes.

Attempting to solve the problem of prostitution was only one aspect of the Progressive movement. Along with sexual purity, many progressives sought to prohibit the sale of alcoholic beverages, to break up large monopolies like Standard Oil, and to regulate railroads and other public utilities. Some sought

The Second South stockade regulated the vice district under construction. *Shipler photo, Utah History Information Center, USHS*

pure food and drug laws. Many also agitated for urban amenities like street paving, water and sewer systems, parks and playgrounds. Progressives also generally favored efficient, economical and nonpartisan urban government.

In Salt Lake City monopolies controlled some of the city's utilities. Edward H. Harriman, owner of Union Pacific Railroad, bought and consolidated both of the streetcar companies. Mountain States Telephone put the competing Independent system out of business. Utah Power and Light controlled the city's electric service.

Men and women cooperated together in Progressive reform. After its organization in 1890, the General Federation of

and Daniel H. Burnham, a noted Chicago architect who designed the White City, the City Beautiful movement captured the imagination of many who deplored the ugliness of the places they loved.

As early as 1900 the Salt Lake City administration responded to similar sentiment by undertaking programs of urban beautification and improvement projects. In 1900 the city planted trees in Liberty and Pioneer parks and on Washington Square. At Liberty Park, city crews improved the walks and drives, placed large iron gates on the north entrance and built a playground for children.

Womens Clubs urged women to extend their attention to matters beyond the walls of their homes. Following this trend, women from Salt Lake City, Ogden and Provo organized the Utah Federation of Women's Clubs in April 1893. In 1912 representatives of Salt Lake City women's clubs organized the Salt Lake Council of Women to correlate activities of the various clubs. These organizations supported civic housekeeping by working to improve conditions in the city. Civic-minded men, generally members of the Chamber of Commerce or of one of the service clubs, promoted similar urban reform.

In addition, men and women joined together to organize special interest associations through which they lobbied for urban reform and civic improvements. In March 1906 a group of Salt Lakers organized the Civic Improvement League (CIL). Made up of women and men, Mormons, Protestants, Catholics and Jews, CIL leadership included Susa Young Gates, a Republican and daughter of Brigham and Lucy Bigelow Young; former Congressman William H. King, an attorney, a Mormon, and a Democrat; Orlando W. Powers, a Protestant Democrat and former federal judge; Episcopal Bishop Franklin S. Spalding; Frank B. Stephens, former city attorney and first president of CIL; W. Mont Ferry, a prominent Congregationalist and businessman; Ida Maas Bamberger, wife of Jewish businessman Simon Bamberger; and Republican businessman and Salt Lake LDS Stake President Nephi L. Morris. Captivated by a similar vision, women and men in various neighborhoods throughout the city organized improvement or betterment leagues to lobby for civic improvements such as street paving, water systems, sewers and parks.

Salt Lakers found a model for urban improvement in the "City Beautiful" movement, which furnished the inspiration for the construction of the "White City" for the World's Colombian Exposition held in Chicago in 1893. Under the leadership of Frederick Law Olmsted, who designed New York's Central Park,

Improvement league members also agitated for other urban improvements. High on their list was the expansion of the city's sewer and water systems, which the city built over the next decade. With the approval of the CIL, the American Party paved streets with macadam, a compacted conglomerate of gravel bound with asphalt. Unfortunately, in this early effort the city did not test the batches of macadam for durability, and the streets soon broke up under the pounding of weather and traffic.

In addition to the improvement of streets and utilities, the inauguration of nonpartisan government became the CIL's principal accomplishment. In May 1908 the CIL called for the consolidation of the Salt Lake City and County governments and for the reduction of the city council to five members. In September the league urged the reorganization of city government into a commission system.

George Sutherland, Utah's junior senator, also lobbied for a change to the commission system. Later, as a U.S. Supreme Court justice, Sutherland wrote the majority opinion in the Euclid case, which confirmed the right of cities to zone in order to separate business, industrial and residential districts.

In a commission system, a board of commissioners — usually five — sit together to develop policy and pass ordinances for city government. The chair of the commission, usually designated as mayor, has no more authority than the other members. Each commissioner also manages a group of city departments. For instance, the public safety commissioner might manage the police and fire departments, and the public utilities commissioner might supervise the water and sewer systems.

During the first decade of the 20th century, Galveston, Texas; Des Moines, Iowa; and Washington, D. C. had adopted this system. Each of these cities had realized considerable savings with the apparent benefit of increased efficiency.

Responding favorably to agitation of the CIL and other Progressive reform organizations, the state legislature passed laws authorizing cities to adopt the city commission system. In 1909 the legislature passed a commission bill but Utah's conservative Republican governor, William Spry, vetoed it. Undiscouraged by this setback, the CIL organized an ill-starred Citizen's ticket movement in 1909. When that failed, they lobbied with the legislature for the passage of a commission government bill in 1911. This time Spry signed the bill.

By 1911 public sentiment in Salt Lake City against the stockade and religious partisanship had reached a fever pitch. The CIL and the West Side Citizens League took strong stands against prostitution, and the Salt Lake Ministerial Association spoke out frequently against the stockade. Significantly, despite the support by Bransford and the city government, the American Party organization came out in opposition.

Local newspapers were divided on the issue. The *Salt Lake Tribune* and the *Salt Lake Telegram*, both Bransford enthusiasts, supported the stockade. *The Deseret News*, owned by the LDS Church; the *Salt Lake Herald*, a Democratic Party newspaper; and the *Intermountain Republican* opposed it.

In a slap at the Bransford administration, the Salt Lake County sheriff raided the stockade on several occasions. Deputies arrested Belle London and some of the prostitutes, but the raids accomplished little since the courts ordinarily dismissed the charges or convicted only a few of the women.

In September 1911 as the first election campaign for the new commission government heated up, Belle London announced that she would close the stockade. Supporting her decision, Mayor Bransford said that the stockade could not remain open in the face of such heavy public opposition.

In an attempt to save the prostitutes from a life of sin, women's organizations established a rescue station to find them jobs as maids and domestic servants. Fewer than a dozen women accepted the offer. Most of the former stockade tenants remained near West Second South or returned to the area around Commercial Street. Prostitutes continued to offer their services on Commercial Street until the late 1930s and on West Second South until the late 1970s.

As women's groups tried to lure Salt Lake City's hookers into respectable jobs, the election campaign under the newly approved commission system heated up. Despite the presumably nonpartisan character of the commission, various political groups jockeyed for advantage. Leading the list was a "businessman's ticket" headed by Salt Lake City jeweler Samuel C. Park and consisting of two Republicans, two Democrats and a Socialist. The American Party ran a slate headed by Mayor Bransford. The Republican Party nominated a "Good Government Ticket" headed by Elmer O. Leatherwood, an attorney. Other candidates included Socialist Welcome F. Ramsay and former Mayor Robert Baskin. A primary election on October 25 eliminated all except the businessman's and American Party candidates. In the general election, the businessman's ticket won handily. Handed this defeat in the only jurisdiction in which it had enjoyed any success, the American Party disbanded.

Salt Lake City inaugurated the commission system just as the City Beautiful movement came under attack by a group of competing reformers. Nationally prominent housing reform advocates like Benjamin C. Marsh, architects like Cass Gilbert, and landscape architects like Robert A. Pope promoted the "City Practical" in an attempt to offer function and beauty to all residents of the city. They criticized the City Beautiful as elitist because many of its proponents concentrated on beautifying middle- and upper-class city neighborhoods while neglecting the lower-and working-class areas. Responding to this challenge, a number of City Beautiful partisans such as George E. Kessler of St. Louis and White City designer Daniel Burnham tried to compromise between the two movements in order to achieve both aesthetic and practical objectives.

Salt Lake City chose at first to follow the City Beautiful model. Following the lead of Hartford, Connecticut, and other cities, the city commission organized the Civic Planning and Art Commission in November 1913. Mayor Park served as chair of the commission, which included prominent citizens, representatives of women's organizations, members of the Chamber of Commerce, business people, artists and architects.

Martha Hughes Cannon, the author of public welfare legislation, was reportedly the first woman to serve as a state senator in the United States. She and her baby are shown here in 1897. *LDS Church Archives*

Until 1918 when the City Commission reorganized the art and planning commission, J. Leo Fairbanks, the commission's executive secretary, exerted the decisive influence over its activities. A partisan of the City Beautiful movement, Fairbanks was a distinguished artist who later joined the Oregon State University faculty. He considered the commission as conducive to "a healthful, efficient and beautiful city." The commission would, he said, " work out a general plan... seek to have all material changes conform to that plan... minimize ugliness, and give a just cause for city pride."

In concert with the Civic Improvement League and the planning commission, the city engineers, and especially Sylvester Q. Cannon, an engineering graduate from Massachusetts Institute of Technology, played a decisive role in the development of urban improvements. Cannon, an advocate of the combined City Beautiful and City Practical movements, served from April 1913 through August 1925. In 1914 city residents approved a municipal improvement bond and virtually every week during 1914 one of the neighborhood improvements leagues, groups of neighbors, or individuals appeared before the city commission to lobby for new street paving, curbs, gutters, and sewer and water pipes. The commission disappointed very few. In addition, the city rebuilt a number of streets into beautifully landscaped boulevards.

In large part because of the construction that accelerated in 1914, a survey of U.S. and Canadian cities with more than 100,000 residents in 1916 ranked Salt Lake City among the first echelon in certain urban utilities. With 2.7 miles of water pipe per 1,000 residents, Salt Lake City ranked fourth among large American and Canadian cities, and far above the average of 1.72 miles per 1,000. With 2.56 miles of sewer pipe per 1,000 residents, it ranked third. The average city had only 1.4 miles per 1,000. Salt Lake City ranked fourth in street mileage at 4.5 miles per 1,000 residents, compared with an average of 2.17 miles per 1,000. Clearly, Salt Lake City had changed dramatically since 1890 when it had only a small protected water system, virtually no paved roads and only five miles of sewers.

Unfortunately the city did not rank in the first echelon in parks and playgrounds. Under pressure from the CIL, the American Party administration established a parks board in January 1908. In December 1909, like citizens in 90 other cities nationwide, a group of women and men met at the home of Corinne T. and Clarence E. Allen to organize a Parks and Playgrounds Association. The association consisted of men and women, Mormons, Catholics, Protestants and Jews including Kate Williams, John E. Dooley, Russell L. Tracy and Willard Young.

In part because of lobbying by this organization and the CIL, the city established its first playground for children in 1910, and in succeeding years installed playground improvements in Liberty and Pioneer parks. With the cooperation of various voluntary associations such as the Free Playground Society, various women's clubs and the Chamber of Commerce, the city opened new playgrounds in 1914 and afterward.

The city still lagged behind other American and Canadian cities in the development of public parks. With only 0.47 percent of its area in parks, Salt Lake City ranked far below the average

of 4.87 percent. The city also had only 15 acres of playgrounds. In part the undeveloped and readily accessible land in the foothills and canyons east of the city made up for part of the absence of parks and playgrounds.

Recognizing the shortage of parks and playgrounds, voluntary associations lobbied for the opening of facilities. In 1914 the Chamber of Commerce Field Sports Committee under A. J. Armstrong endorsed a plan for a municipal golf course. In spite of the support of Utah's former governor and current Salt Lake City Commissioner Heber M. Wells, opposition arose from members of the Salt Lake Country Club who feared that a municipal course might cut into their membership. Ignoring this opposition, in 1922 Charles W. Nibley, presiding bishop of the LDS Church and a Scottish immigrant, donated land for a

nine-hole course formerly occupied by the privately owned Wandamere and Calder's Parks. The land stretched south and west from Twenty-seventh South and Seventh East. Nibley said he hoped people might "find healthful enjoyment and rare pleasure... playing that splendid outdoor Scotch game."

While men's groups promoted a municipal golf course, in February 1921 the Salt Lake Council of Women planned for the development of new parks. Chairing a committee established by the council, Kate May Erskine Hurd began collecting petitions calling on the commission to establish a park on the city's east bench. Unsuccessful at first, in May 1923 the women succeeded in convincing the city commission to lease land west of the city cemetery from the Auerbach estate. In 1928, largely through Hurd's efforts, the city agreed to purchase the land for $15,000.

(Far left top)
"Old Folks" gathered for a picnic at Liberty Park.
LDS Church Archives

(Above)
Couples dancing in the ballroom at Saltair; better known as a resort for swimming at Great Salt Lake. Saltair also hosted dancing and an amusement park.
Albert Wilkes photo, c. 1900-1910, Nelson Wadsworth

A group of young adults held an egg race at Pioneer Park in 1911.
Shipler photo, Utah History Information Center, USHS

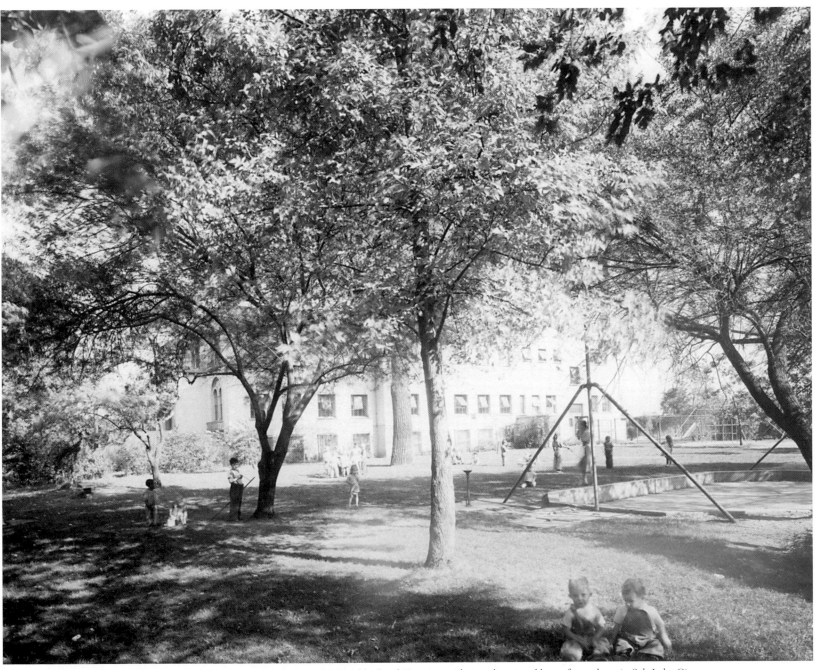

Children enjoyed themselves at the playground at Neighborhood House, a settlement house and home for orphans in Salt Lake City.
Utah History Information Center, USHS

Germany and was adopted first in the United States in 1916 by New York City and Berkeley, California. Zoning found its greatest support among partisans of the City Practical, but along with advocates of a combined movement, Cannon conceived of zoning as a means of controlling abusive development and promoting both practicality and beauty.

Cannon hoped that the adoption of zoning would prevent problems like the one the city faced in City Creek Canyon. The city had designated the canyon as a nature park. Nevertheless, a previous administration had leased part of the canyon as a gravel pit. In the absence of zoning, in an effort to protect the nature park, Cannon convinced the city administration to cancel the lease and close the pit.

Cannon had other interests that reinforced his support of zoning as a means of regulating growth. While he served as city engineer, he was also president of the LDS Pioneer Stake. This calling made him ecclesiastical leader of the Mormons in the southwest quarter of the city. Although this area included Pioneer Park, in which the neighbors took considerable pride, since both the Union Pacific and Denver and Rio Grande railroad tracks passed through the area, it became a prime target for manufacturing and commercial businesses.

Significantly, this was also the area into which most of the southern and eastern European immigrants had begun to move. In practice, Cannon tried to make their neighborhoods more pleasant at the same time he controlled industrial and commercial development for members of his stake.

They named it Lindsey Park in memory of Mark Lindsey, whose family had previously owned the property.

Clearly the planning and development inaugurated by Brigham Young and the city's first leaders had played a decisive role in the city's urban development. In part because of the large residential lots and wide streets, at 1 percent, Salt Lake City had the smallest industrial and business districts of any city in the 1916 survey. The city also had slightly smaller than average residential and farming districts (49 percent and 18 percent), probably owing to the wide streets and the early policy of placing farms outside the city. Salt Lake also had a much larger area of undeveloped land (31 percent) than the average (20 percent).

In spite of the comparatively small business and industrial districts and the large areas of undeveloped land, Salt Lakers wrestled with the encroachment of manufacturing and commerce into residential areas. Optimistic to a fault, Fairbanks thought the city could use publicity and moral persuasion to thwart incompatible uses. Unrealistically, he expected to confine coercive planning to city-owned property.

When persuasion proved unsuccessful, City Engineer Cannon began to lobby for zoning as a means of prohibiting the use of private property in ways that destroyed or downgraded the property and amenities of others. Zoning had originated in

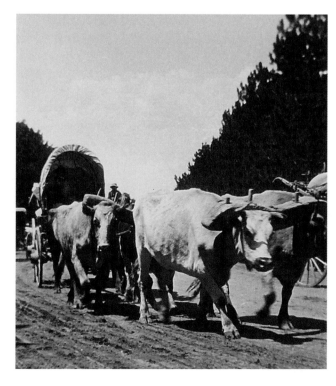

In an attempt to preserve the area for family residences, Cannon worked with the city commission to pass two stopgap zoning ordinances in 1917 and 1923 that covered the southwest section of the city. In promoting these ordinances, Cannon had the support of Mayors W. Mont Ferry (1916-1920) and C. Clarence Neslen (1920-1928) and the members of the city commission.

Cannon was educated as an engineer, not as a city planner, and although he studied urban planning, he and others believed that the city needed an expert to advise them on the subject. Responding to this need, in December 1917 and May 1918 the city brought in George E. Kessler, a St. Louis landscape architect, as a consultant. Kessler, who favored the merged City Practical and City Beautiful concepts, had studied and worked in Europe before returning to the United States to design parks and boulevards for New York City, Kansas City, Denver and Dallas.

Apparently relying on Kessler's advice and Cannon's skill, the city reorganized the planning commission in 1918. Cannon lobbied for the passage of a general zoning ordinance but was unsuccessful because the state legislature declined to approve a law authorizing such ordinances until 1925, just shortly before he resigned as city engineer. In 1927 the city passed a general ordinance, at the same time reorganizing the planning commission and establishing a zoning commission.

A family gathered on their front porch for the July 24 celebration in 1914.
Revel and LaRue Phillips

In addition to the problems of constructing urban amenities and keeping intrusive industry from residential areas, Salt Lake City faced a perennial problem with smoke pollution. In 1890 the city council adopted an ordinance to regulate the burning of soft coal. Unfortunately, city officials seldom enforced it. By the first decade of the 20th century, farmers in central Salt Lake County noted that smelter smoke had damaged their crops, and they secured an injunction to stop the damage. As early as 1908 Mayor Bransford, whose fortune came in large part from Park City mines, said that the reduction of smoke pollution constituted one of the city's most pressing needs.

In spite of pressure from smelting interests who argued that regulating smoke pollution would hurt Utah's economy,

In this view of Salt Lake City from Prospect Hill, smoke pollution is plainly evident.
C.R. Savage Photo, LDS Church Archives

representatives of the Salt Lake Council of Women and the Salt Lake Chamber of Commerce pressured businesses to reduce pollution and lobbied with the city commission to enforce anti-pollution regulations. In February 1914 the commission passed an ordinance requiring business to use the best available furnace technology and to train employees on how to run the furnaces. The city appointed George W. Snow, a graduate of the University of Utah and Lafayette College, as head of the Mechanical Inspection Department. Snow initiated an enforcement campaign to get business to rebuild their furnaces, and he met with various clubs and civic groups to explain the program and solicit their support.

Although Snow's efforts helped, Salt Lakers continued to suffer from unacceptable levels of air pollution. Responding to this problem, the state, the city and the United States Bureau of Mines set up a cooperative program to investigate and offer solutions. Osborne Monnett, a fuel engineer for the Bureau of Mines, conducted extensive research and completed reports in 1919 and 1920. Two thousand members of the Salt Lake Council of Women made a house-to-house survey to determine the types of furnaces and fuels used by the citizens. In an overly optimistic assessment, Monnett thought that $15,000 per year for two years would "largely" rid the city of the smoke problem.

Nevertheless, various groups in Salt Lake City tried to implement the plan. The Salt Lake Council of Women, the Chamber of Commerce, the Rotary Club, the Boy Scouts, the realtors' association and even school children supported the plan. In November 1921, under the leadership of Emily L. Traub Merrill, whose husband, Joseph F. Merrill, headed the University of Utah's College of Mines, the Salt Lake Council of Women questioned each candidate for the city commission on their views about eliminating smoke pollution.

During the years between 1922 and 1929 the city achieved some success in reducing smoke, then it ran into a political and technological brick wall. Virtually all manufacturing, commercial and railroad operations had redesigned or installed new furnaces, and by the winter of 1925-26, 75 percent of the smoke came from residential sources. Most of the remainder came from railroad engines. Between 1926 and 1929, while facing considerable resistance, the city continued to try to regulate residential furnaces.

Several technological changes eventually helped to control air pollution until the years following

Utah-born Maude Adams made it big on Broadway and earned an international reputation as an accomplished actress. *Utah History Information Center, USHS*

World War II when the flood of automobiles and the introduction of more heavy industry undid many of the previous successes. The shift of railroads from coal-powered steam engines to diesel electric power helped solve one aspect of the problem. During World War II many residences that continued to burn coal dropped the use of lump coal and began feeding their furnaces with stokers filled with oiled slack. These burned much more evenly and efficiently. By the late 1920s natural gas had begun to break into the coal market and during and after World War II most new construction and many existing homes installed gas instead of coal furnaces.

As Salt Lakers worked to reduce smoke pollution, they participated in another, much more controversial, aspect of the American Progressive Movement — prohibiting the manufacture and sale of alcoholic beverages. In 1911 the state legislature approved a local option law that allowed cities to vote on Prohibition. In the ensuing election, a number of mining camps and some of the larger cities including Salt Lake City voted to remain wet.

In 1917, however, the state legislature approved a statewide measure. This time Salt Lake City could not opt out and state and county officials raided the clandestine speakeasies, breweries and stills of Salt Lake City. Between January 1920 and April 1933 federal officials participated in the raids under nationwide Prohibition.

As the city government began to supply amenities such as improved streets, sewers and water systems, the city's culture underwent significant changes. In the late 19th century, the legitimate theatre enjoyed considerable patronage. People flocked to the Salt Lake Theatre to see performances by touring actors and actresses and the resident company. The great performers of the late 19th and early 20th century played there. Maude Adams; Ethel, John and Lionel Barrymore; Sarah Bernhardt; Billie Burke; William F. "Buffalo Bill" Cody; Eddie Foy; Al Jolson; and Lillian Russell all performed at the Salt Lake Theatre.

Increasingly, however, during the early 20th century, forms of entertainment with a greater mass appeal such as vaudeville and motion pictures began to cut into the theatre's patronage. The theatre management tried to meet the competition of such media by contracting with national theatre chains, but that proved unsatisfactory because they had to take good and bad, vulgar and virtuous, excellent and inferior.

In practice, the theatre succeeded only because of generous financing by the LDS Church. Unfortunately, during the 1920s, because of an agricultural depression and religious, business and educational obligations, the church ran into deep financial difficulty. Under these circumstances, the church leadership became increasingly dissatisfied with its subvention of the seedy entertainment the theatre had to offer in order to keep its head above water. Financially strapped and unable to afford renovations necessary to meet fire codes, the church leadership decided to sell the theatre property to the Mountain States Telephone Company.

The telephone company razed the theatre. For a time a service station shaped like a huge airplane occupied the site. A decade after demolishing the theatre, the company built a lovely Art Deco office building. Unfamiliar with the financial and artistic challenges that impelled the church to sell the property, someone scrawled in heavy black crayon on the boards surrounding the demolition site: "BUILT BY A PROPHET AND TORN DOWN FOR PROFIT."

As the people of Salt Lake City adapted to new forms of entertainment, the ethnic character of the city underwent a perceptible change. Although by far the largest numbers of foreign born continued to come to Salt Lake City from north-western Europe and Canada, between 1890 and 1910 newcomers whom historians have called the New Immigrants — southern and eastern Europeans, Japanese and African-Americans — poured into the city looking for jobs.

Each group contributed to the city's diversity. The largest percentage growth took place in the population of Greeks, whose numbers grew from virtually none in 1890 to 621 in 1910. The African American population grew from 218 in 1890 to 737 in 1910. The number of Italians grew from 100 in 1890 to 379 in 1910. The Japanese population grew from none in 1890 to 345 in 1910.

Salt Lake's earliest non-Caucasian immigrants lived south and east of the business district. The Chinese, who had begun to come with the railroad, centered their community around Plum Alley which ran between Main and State streets between First and Second South. African Americans, who had begun to arrive with the first pioneer company, tended to live between Third and Sixth South and Main Street and Third East. African American members of the 24th Infantry, which arrived at Fort Douglas in October 1896, and horsemen of the 9th Cavalry, which came in 1899, lived at Fort Douglas.

In contrast with these older immigrants, as the new Asian and southern and eastern European immigrants moved into the city after 1890, they settled in a ghetto whose imaginary boundary ran south and west from the intersection of West Temple and First South. The Japanese settled along First South between West Temple and Third West. Syrians congregated near Third South and Fifth West. Italians located near the railroad

Edward "Daigoro" Hashimoto, Japanese immigrant, merchant, and labor agent shown here in his office on West South Temple in Salt Lake City
Utah History Information Center, USHS

tracks. Greeks moved into Second South between Fourth and Sixth West.

As the oldest minority group in Salt Lake City, African Americans had long worked in service industries. Nevertheless, a number opened businesses. For instance, Frances H. Grice owned a restaurant at 153 South Main; and John Burns, Allen Smith, Andrew Campbell and A. D. McAlfred owned a mining company.

During the 1890s black Protestants launched religious services to meet the needs of Salt Lakers. In 1890 the Rev. T. Saunders organized the African Methodist Episcopal Church. The members held services in homes and rented facilities until 1902 when they dedicated the Trinity African Methodist Episcopal Church at 239 East 600 South, a street Salt Lake City recently renamed "Martin Luther King, Jr. Boulevard" in honor of the slain civil rights leader.

In 1892 Black Baptist women began meeting to pray in the home of Sister Emma Jackson at 176 East 700 South. Members held baptismal services at the First Baptist Church, and they continued to meet in homes until 1898. In June 1898 the Rev. A. E. Reynolds began holding services for the church, then known as Calvary Missionary Baptist Church, in a building at the rear of the First Baptist Church, 315 West Second South. The church met in several buildings until 1911 when they purchased the Immanuel Baptist Church at 679 East 300 South. In 1921 the church moved to a chapel on 700 East and 300 South. In 1922 the African American Baptists opened a second congregation, the Pilgrim Baptist Church.

Salt Lake City African Americans promoted a number of cultural activities for their community. Members organized the Alexander Dumas Literary Society to encourage reading and

Two African American waiters prepare to serve aboard a Union Pacific train.
Utah History Information Center, USHS

discussion of the African American experience. Black men organized lodges of the Odd Fellows and Elks, and women organized the Ladies Civic and Study Club of Salt Lake City, the Camelia Arts and Crafts Club and the Nimble Thimble Club. Many blacks and whites visited nightclubs such as the Dixie Land, the Jazz Bo, the Porters and Waiters Club, and the Hi Marine to dance and listen to music. Julius F. Taylor edited the *Broad Ax* from 1895 until he moved to Chicago in 1899. From 1897 through 1907 William W. Taylor edited the *Plain Dealer*. Rev. Manasseh H. Wilkinson of the Calvary Baptist Church edited the *Tri-City Oracle* for a short time.

Blacks suffered from discrimination perhaps more intensely than other racial groups. The Utah legislature passed an Anti-Miscegenation Law which remained on the books from 1898 to 1963. Although the law prohibited the mixing of all races, the legislators seem to have aimed it most particularly at African Americans. To counter such tendencies, in 1919 Salt Lake City residents organized a chapter of the National Association for the Advancement of Colored People to try to secure equitable treatment and civil rights for African Americans.

Buying into the ideas of white racists, some African Americans distinguished themselves by degrees of blackness. Lighter blacks organized Blue Vein societies to differentiate themselves from their darker skinned brothers and sisters.

Like the African Americans, economic opportunity beckoned many Japanese to Salt Lake City. Edward "Daigoro" Hashimoto, who opened a labor agency by 1902, recruited many of them. From his office at 163 West South Temple, Hashimoto furnished miners for companies in Carbon and Salt Lake Counties, section crews for the railroad and labor for farmers. Called the city's Mikado by white Salt Lakers, Hashimoto also ran a store through which he sold imported foods and clothing, and he helped the new residents find their way through the maze of forms and legal tangles.

Expanding his operations, Hashimoto recruited labor from other ethnic groups. Following a Greek-led strike at Bingham, the Utah Copper Company began to bring in Mexican strikebreakers. Hashimoto signed on as labor agent for the Mexicans, and Mexican President Venustiano Carranza made him honorary Mexican consul in Utah.

Hashimoto continued to live in Salt Lake City where he married and raised a family. In 1908 he married Lois Hide Niija, a graduate of Kobe College and the University of California. He built a home near the University of Utah campus at 315 South 12th East. His son, Edward I. Hashimoto, became a professor of anatomy at the University of Utah medical school.

The Salt Lake City Union Stock Yards, the center of the city's livestock sales in the early 20th century
C.R. Savage photo, LDS Church Archives

The mailing department of the Salt Lake City Post Office in about 1900
LDS Church Archives

Like the African Americans, Salt Lake City's Japanese opened various businesses and other institutions to provide goods and services to the community. In 1907 Japanese began publishing the short-lived *Rocky Mountain Times*, a tri-weekly publication. In 1914 the Terazawa family began printing the *Utah Nippo*. Japanese entrepreneurs opened the first noodle house on West Temple in 1907. During the teens the Japanese fielded a baseball team, the Salt Lake Nippon. In 1919 the Japanese opened a school to teach their language and culture.

Salt Lake City's Japanese community also organized to meet the spiritual needs of the immigrants. In 1912, only 13 years after the founding of the first Buddhist Church in the United States in San Francisco, Salt Lake City Buddhists organized the Intermountain Buddhist Church under the ministry of the Rev. Kenryo Kuwahara. Meeting first in a rented hall on West

Greek men to seek opportunity in the United States. Labor agents like the unscrupulous Leonidas G. Skliris of Salt Lake City offered them the chance to work in return for an upfront fee and a percentage of their wages. Called the "Czar of the Greeks," Skliris served as labor agent for the Utah Copper Company and the Western Pacific and Denver & Rio Grande Western railroads. He also operated the Pan Helenic Grocery Store and reportedly got the companies to fire workers who refused to patronize his store.

Like other immigrants, Greeks also brought their cultural habits with them. Since most of the earliest Greek immigrants were young single men, they found what historian Helen Papanikolas called "comfort, protection, and reassurance" in the coffeehouses. There the men sipped Turkish coffee, read Greek newspapers, smoked, played cards and talked.

A fleet of delivery trucks, reportedly the first in Utah, is shown lined up in front of the ZCMI building in 1922. (The oval appearance resulted from photographic distortion.) *LDS Church Archives*

South Temple, they dedicated a building at 247 West 100 South in 1924. Japanese Christians built their church directly across the street under the leadership of the Rev. H. Toyatome.

Like the African Americans, the Japanese suffered from legal and informal discrimination. In 1922 the federal Cable Act deprived American-born Japanese women of citizenship if they married immigrant Japanese men. The provision remained in force until 1931. In an additional example of discrimination, the 1924 Immigration Act prohibited the immigration of all Asians. Moreover, since many of the local schools excluded Japanese-American children from extracurricular activities, the Salt Lake Buddhist Church established a Young Buddhist Association in 1923.

Like most of the other ethnic groups, the Greeks came to Salt Lake City looking for jobs. Much of the Greek immigration to the United States and to Salt Lake City resulted from agricultural poverty. Crop failure and lack of work led young

Over time, however, life changed for the Greek men. Some married American women, and others had their families select wives from the homeland who were sent to Salt Lake City for marriages. Greeks dedicated their first church in Salt Lake City in 1905. Located on 400 West between 300 and 400 South, it served also the Serbian and Russian Orthodox. In 1924 they held the first service in the gorgeous Holy Trinity Greek Orthodox Church at 279 West Third South. Designed by Hyrum C. Pope, Harold W. Burton and N. A. Dokas, the church is a fine example of Byzantine architecture.

A decisive event in Utah Greek history occurred in 1912 when miners affiliated with the Western Federation of Miners struck at the Utah Copper Company mine at Bingham. Greeks who went out on strike called for higher wages and an end to servitude under Skliris. They occupied the high ground above the mines and engaged in a number of violent clashes with law enforcement officials and strikebreakers. After settling the dispute, the strikers got only part of their demands. The company agreed to pay somewhat higher wages and to fire Skliris, but it declined to recognize the union as the workers' bargaining agent.

Like the other immigrants, most Italians moved to the United States in search of work. Most 19th-century Italian immigrants had come from northern Italy. By contrast, most of the 20th century's newer immigrants came from southern Italy and Sicily. The earliest Italian immigrants generally moved to Carbon County to work in the coal mines. By the 1890s, however, some had begun to settle in Salt Lake City. Most of these worked for the railroads. Like members of other immigrant communities, they opened grocery stores, saloons, services and fraternal organizations.

As more and more immigrants came to Salt Lake City during the early 20th century, the United States witnessed the birth of a radical labor organization, the Industrial Workers of the World (IWW), which tried to organize workers into one big union. One of the leaders of the organization, William D. Haywood of the Western Federation of Miners, was born in Utah. The IWW conducted a free-speech crusade throughout the United States, including on the streets of Salt Lake City. Streetside speakers drew the wrath of the police, who threw many of them into jail.

One of Utah's most controversial murder cases had its roots in the controversy over the IWW. On January 10, 1914, during a robbery attempt someone shot Salt Lake City grocer John G. Morrison and his son, Arling. In the melee, Arling shot one of the robbers. Later in the evening, Joe Hill, a Swedish emigrant and itinerant IWW poet and songwriter, appeared at the home of Dr. Frank M. McHugh with a gunshot wound. On January 12 Salt Lake City police arrested him. Following Hill's conviction on circumstantial evidence, concerned citizens, the Swedish Consul and even President Woodrow Wilson sent letters and telegrams to Utah Gov. William Spry urging him to commute Hill's sentence from death by firing squad to life imprisonment. Spry declined the requests, and a firing squad executed Hill on the grounds of the old state prison in Sugar House, now the site of Salt

Lake City's Sugar House Park. After his cremation, supporters took Hill's ashes to every state except Utah.

Hill's death did not end the affair. Utah courts disbarred Hill's attorney, O. N. Hilton, and the University of Utah fired Virginia Snow Stephen, a daughter of former LDS Church President Lorenzo Snow, both opponents of the death penalty, for their denunciation of Utah's governor and judges.

Moreover, the events surrounding the murders and Hill's execution have taken on a life of their own in American labor and radical history. Gibbs Smith, Wallace Stegner and Barrie Stavis have memorialized Hill in a biography, a novel and a play. Nevertheless, labor historian Vernon Jensen in an interview with Dr. McHugh learned that Hill had confessed to the murders. McHugh, a Socialist who opposed capital punishment, declined to volunteer the information until much later. Nevertheless, given the extremely negative publicity about the IWW, it seems unlikely that Hill could have had a fair trial in Salt Lake City.

In spite of such setbacks, by the fall of 1929 Salt Lake City seemed to stand on the brink of even greater prosperity. Although agriculture languished during the 1920s, urban occupations like construction and retail sales boomed. Largely because of the activities of Progressives, Salt Lakers enjoyed urban amenities on par with other large American cities. Citizens took just pride in their wide-paved streets, cleaner air, modern water and sewer systems, and new parks and playgrounds. Unfortunately, the promise of a better life crashed with the stock market in October 1929.

The Open Heart Coffee House in Salt Lake City's "Greek Town," probably in the 1920s; owner Emmanuel Katsanevas is shown standing in the left center.
Utah History Information Center, USHS

During the 1920s many Americans thought that God had blessed them with unending prosperity. Stock prices rose to unprecedented heights, trade flourished, manufacturers prospered and construction boomed. People listened to programs on their newly invented radio sets, and talking pictures pushed the old silent movies from theaters.

Depression and War

CHAPTER FOUR

Pandora's box of economic depression, and the decline in business activity that followed unleashed the furies of unemployment, poverty and despair. Nationally, the unemployment rate rose from 4 percent in 1929 to 25 percent during the winter of 1932-33. This seemed almost like Paradise to Utahns whose unemployment rate stood at more than 35 percent. Per capita income in Utah dropped from $537 to $276 between 1929 and 1933. The latter figure was less than 80 percent of the national average. By 1934 more than 206 Utahns per 1,000 received public relief — the fourth highest among the states.

If anything, Salt Lakers suffered more than other Utahns. Few of them had farms on which they could grow their own food. Samples from the various quarters of the city indicated the depth of hopelessness. By the fall of 1930 more than 6,000 Salt Lakers had no jobs. In November 1932 the Southgate Ward on Salt Lake City's rather affluent southeast side reported that more than 63 percent of the heads of households were out of work. In the Pioneer Stake, which covered the city's working class southwest quadrant, more than half of the men and women could find no employment.

On February 23, 1933, hundreds of people stormed the Salt Lake City and County building to try to stop a sheriff's sale of the homes and farms of those who could not pay their taxes or on whose mortgages the banks had foreclosed. The county administration ordered tear gas and fire hoses to drive them away. Families expelled from their homes camped out on vacant lots throughout the city.

In July 1933 more than 24,000 residents of Salt Lake County could not find work. The streets filled with the unemployed, many of whom set up carts and stands to hawk everything from shoelaces to apples. Soup kitchens sprang up throughout the city, and various councils and leagues organized unemployment bureaus.

Both public and private agencies offered assistance. In August 1931 Salt Lake City Mayor John F. Bowman appointed an advisory committee on unemployment with LDS Church Presiding Bishop Sylvester Q. Cannon as chair. Committee members tried desperately to find jobs for the unemployed. City construction projects required a minimum wage of $3.50 per day and mandated that where possible contractors

Most people thought the nation could solve what seemed like its few economic problems. Most businesses refused to bargain with their employees and unions floundered, but the nation enjoyed low unemployment and prevailing wages allowed many to buy cars, washing machines and vacuum cleaners. Agricultural prices declined but many thought that was a temporary downturn.

Although Utahns also seemed generally optimistic during the 20s, their economy suffered slightly more than the national average. Construction, transportation and trade all seemed solid. Manufacturing employment had grown rapidly between 1890 and World War I, but, after peaking during the war, between 1920 and 1929 total wages and number of employees remained steady. The value of Utah's mineral products had declined during the Depression of 1919-21, but in 1929 Utah's mines produced more than $115 million in minerals — a greater value than any previous year.

Still the prosperity passed some by. During the 1930s the state experienced a net out-migration when fewer people moved into the state than moved out. The value of Utah's farms actually declined by eight percent during the 1920s. For the first time in Utah's history, more than 100 businesses failed in 1922, and business failures never declined below 115 any year during the remainder of the decade.

Salt Lake City suffered with the rest of the state. In 1925 3,000 Salt Lakers were unemployed. Since neither the state nor the nation had established employment services, the city set up an employment bureau to help them find work.

During the early 1930s, even these problems seemed minor. The stock market crash of October 1929 cracked open a must use local labor and materials and that they rotate work to give the largest number of people some work.

The Salt Lake Chamber of Commerce helped out. In 1930 Gus P. Backman resigned as a manager at ZCMI to become executive secretary of the chamber. In 1931 under Backman's leadership, the chamber sponsored benefit performances in six Salt Lake City theaters to collect funds for the needy.

Women worked to relieve suffering as well. Often families had to rely on the income of women who found the only jobs available in pink-collar employment as secretaries, teachers and nurses. Many minority women worked in manufacturing, and a large number of African-American women got jobs in domestic service. Organizations of religious women helped families, and the Salt Lake Council of Women frequently showed up at commission meetings to lobby on various issues. The women's division of the city's make-work committee hired 20 women to sew quilts and repair clothing.

Various private charities pitched in to help. Neighborhood House at 727 West First South raised money for various worthy causes, provided day care and kindergarten services, ran a library, and offered help and comfort to shut-ins. In 1935 Neighborhood House opened a dental clinic that offered service with rates scaled by income. And citizens helped one another. A number of people who had jobs donated wages or approved wage deductions to try to help those without work.

Since a majority of Salt Lakers were LDS, Mormon leaders had particularly strong reasons to help relieve suffering. In February 1930 Bishop Cannon met with the presidents of the six stakes in Salt Lake County and with representatives of the Church's Deseret Employment Bureau. The leaders agreed to cooperate with ward bishops and Relief Society presidents to seek jobs and relief for members. The stake presidents assumed direction of the Deseret Employment Bureau and the Relief Society's employment service helped in finding jobs. Committee members agreed to seek employment for church members and to help needy Mormons get assistance from the county government.

City, county and private agencies cooperated closely on relief efforts. Early in the Depression, Salt Lake County public relief agencies used the LDS Relief Society's Social Service Exchange as a clearinghouse for employment assistance. Salt Lake City officials estimated that if they had not accepted the voluntary aid of the Relief Society they would have had to hire five or six additional employees.

To coordinate the welfare effort, the Council of Social Agencies consisting of the Community Chest, the LDS Relief Society Social Service Department and the Salt Lake County Charity Department worked to fill welfare orders. Virtually all private relief agencies including the Relief Society worked with the Community Chest to offer help to the unemployed. In 1930 Community Chest agencies spent $150,000 in Salt Lake City. The Utah Coal Producers Association donated thousands of tons of coal during the winter. In the October 1931 general conference, Cannon urged ward bishops to see that all who lived within their ward areas, whether LDS or not, received assistance as needed.

Many in Salt Lake City sought to cooperate with nearby farmers or sought land to farm themselves. The farmers welcomed this help because depressed conditions drove their cost of production below the market price of their commodities. Families, groups and religious organizations made sharecropping arrangements with the farmers, agreeing to harvest the crops in return for a part of the food. In the Pioneer Stake, members occupied vacant lots on which they planted various crops which they irrigated from city fire hydrants.

In addition, church organizations helped manage food and other supplies. In 1932 the Liberty Stake in central Salt Lake City under President Bryant S. Hinckley set up a bishop's storehouse to warehouse and distribute food and fuel for the sharecroppers. The Pioneer Stake stored sharecropped commodities in warehouses. Stake leaders set up a coal yard near the railroad tracks to give fuel to the needy and to sell to those who had money. As the Depression deepened, the federal government began to supply assistance. In July 1932 a reluctant President Herbert Hoover signed the Emergency Relief and Reconstruction Act which set up the Reconstruction Finance Corporation. The RFC lent funds to states for welfare and work relief. State, private and religious organizations used these funds in Salt Lake City and elsewhere to supplement local taxes and charitable contributions for the needy.

The inauguration in March 1933 swapped Franklin Roosevelt's commitment for Hoover's reluctance to use federal resources to help in restoring the nation's economy. During 1933 and 1934 the Federal Emergency Relief Administration

Amy Brown Lyman, First Counselor (1928-1939) and President (1940-1945) of the Relief Society of the Church of Jesus Christ of Latter-day Saints and a leader in the adoption of social welfare in Utah and in the LDS Church
Utah History Information Center, USHS

(FERA), the Civil Works Administration (CWA), and the Public Works Administration (PWA) provided direct relief payments, and, most importantly, these agencies hired people on public works jobs throughout the nation.

Until the mid-1930s local governments cooperated closely with private organizations in administering relief and works projects. Increasingly, however, federal rules separated government agencies from private and volunteer groups. In June 1933 FERA rules required that the staffs of public agencies distribute relief funds. This proved extremely disruptive since nearly 40 percent of all Mormons on relief resided in Salt Lake

This system of cooperation worked well until newly appointed public welfare officials wanted a neat system that adhered to the guidlines of federal regulations. In November and December 1934 the county dissolved District 7 and moved the Relief Society social workers into county offices. In part because of such rules, in part because of the anti-government antagonism of some LDS general authorities, and in part because some of the church leaders believed the church could "care for its own," the LDS Church established its own relief programs under the Church Welfare Plan in 1936.

After the Roosevelt administration took over, Salt Lake

The University of Utah's Field House of Natural History, a Works Progress Administration Project
Utah History Information Center, USHS

County. The LDS Relief Society had the largest cadre of trained social workers in Salt Lake County at the time, and in order to meet the spirit of the regulation, the county redesignated the Relief Society Social Services Department as District 7 of the Salt Lake County Department of Public Welfare. Then the social workers from each of the local stakes moved into the Relief Society offices while the county paid them for their services.

City secured a great deal of federal money. In 1933 Mayor Louis Marcus, a businessman who had replaced Bowman in 1932, traveled to Washington to meet with Interior Secretary and PWA director Harold Ickes. He returned to Salt Lake City with a $2.5 million federal grant.

In spite of Roosevelt's early commitment of federal funds for the dole, he detested handouts as much as Hoover did. In

(Far right)
A photograph of the University of Utah campus, taken sometime between 1915 and 1920, includes Fort Douglas in the background.
Albert Wilkes Photo, LDS Church Archives

The University of Utah's Carlson Hall was constructed as a dormitory by the WPA and it now houses departments in the College of Humanities.
Utah History Information Center, USHS

1935 he sought to end federally sponsored direct relief. In its place, the administration substituted the Social Security program, which it financed through direct taxes on the people who received help — employers and workers. To provide jobs instead of handouts, the federal government expanded the construction projects sponsored by the CCC, the PWA and the now-defunct FERA by establishing the Works Progress Administration (WPA, later renamed the Works Projects Administration) and the National Youth Administration (NYA) to offer employment on various projects.

Deer Creek Reservoir, Highway 189 and Deer Creek Dam were constructed by the Bureau of Reclamation as part of the Deer Creek project during the 1930s. Mount Timpanogos rises in the background.
Utah History Information Center, USHS

Federal expenditures from these programs proved extremely helpful to Salt Lake City. Between 1935 and 1942 the WPA employed 3,000 people full time and an equal number of part-time workers in Salt Lake City. WPA workers built a field house, museum of natural history and Carlson Hall on the University of Utah campus; the Salt Lake School District administration building; the officer's club at Fort Douglas; and three runways, an administration building, and a drainage system at the Salt Lake City Airport. The federal government provided funds and commodities for a school lunch program in city schools, set up a nursery school for children of unemployed parents and established classes for the blind. By the end of the Depression, Salt Lake City had 16 parks and three golf courses, in part because of federal construction projects.

Perhaps the most important long-lasting project completed during the Depression increased Salt Lake City's supply of water. In a report issued in 1931, the U.S. Bureau of Reclamation (BOR) made recommendations on the use of water in the Colorado River and the Provo River-Utah Lake drainage systems. Concurrently, Mayor Bowman and the city commission appointed an advisory board to recommend ways of supplying water for 400,000 people. As part of the study, Salt Lake City Engineer W. D. Beers said that the city could get its water most economically from a proposed BOR dam on the Provo River at Deer Creek.

Franklin Roosevelt approved the dam as a PWA project in 1935, and Salt Lake City took steps to buy BOR water. A number of Salt Lake City and Utah County citizens helped to promote the project. Those from Salt Lake City included William R. Wallace, C. C. Parsons, John D. Rice, Fisher S. Harris, Mayor Louis Marcus and Commissioner George D. Keyser. In a 1935 referendum, Salt Lakers voted by a slim plurality to form the Metropolitan Water District, and in November 1938 they agreed to purchase water from the Provo River Project.

Principal opposition came from conservatives like A.C. Rees and William Langton. Langton chaired a "Property Owners Investigating Committee," and Rees succeeded in getting Mayor Marcus to appoint several people to the district board who opposed the project.

Nevertheless, after these votes and the advice of outside consultants, Salt Lake City purchased 46,000 acre feet of water in Deer Creek Reservoir. Salt Lakers also induced the BOR to construct an aqueduct to transport water from Deer Creek to the city. The aqueduct, which cost $5.55 million, actually exceeded the cost of the $2.65 million Deer Creek Dam and canal system.

The project continued from 1938 to late 1950. Construction of the dam continued from May 1938 to November 1941, but completion of the aqueduct had to await the end of World War II. Because of material and labor shortages during the war and the impact of postwar inflation, workers could not complete the aqueduct until October 1950.

In addition to the construction projects, the federal government also financed programs in the arts and humanities. After all, as one observer put it, artists had to eat too. In Salt Lake City a group of artists painted the murals for the rotunda of the State Capitol Building. The project was planned under the Public Works of Art Program of the FERA by noted Utah artist Lee Greene Richards, and artists who worked on it included Richards, Gordon Cope, Henry Rasmusen, Ranch Kimball and Waldo Midgley. In 1934 the artists executed the murals on

The WPA Orchestra, led by Reginald Beales in 1940, was the predecessor of the Utah Symphony.
Utah History Information Center, USHS

canvas at the state fairgrounds, then transported them to the capitol building for installation.

After the termination of FERA, the WPA's Federal Arts Project promoted various programs in Salt Lake City. Among the most important, WPA funds supplemented by a land grant and $1,000 from the city commission established the Salt Lake Art Center. Housed in a building called the "Art Barn" on the corner of South Temple and University streets near the University of Utah campus, the center offered schooling and display space.

The WPA also sponsored music projects. Most important among its offerings was the 1936 Utah Music Project. The orchestra sponsored by this project, later christened the Utah Symphony, became one of the nation's premier musical organizations after World War II.

The WPA writers project helped preserve the state's heritage. Dale Morgan published *Utah: A Guide to the State*, and historians inventoried records in county archives. Juanita Brooks and other historians made copies of old diaries collected from Utah pioneers, which they deposited in libraries and archives.

Significantly, in spite of the Depression, Salt Lakers found time for recreation. In part because of prize-giveaway nights, attendance at movies actually increased during the 1930s. Movie tickets for adults cost only 25 or 35 cents, and children could get in for 10 or 20 cents.

Salt Lakers also built a new zoo to replace the older facility that they had outgrown. By the 1930s the older zoo, which had opened at Liberty Park in 1911 with some ducks and a deer, hosted a larger number of animals including Princess Alice, an enormous elephant. To replace the inadequate facilities, Mr. and Mrs. James A. Hogle donated property for a new zoo at the mouth of Emigration Canyon. Only with considerable difficulty did the Salt Lake Zoological Society move Alice and her animal friends to the new Hogle Zoo.

To offer a replacement attraction at Liberty Park, in 1938 Russell Lord Tracy donated his collection of exotic birds. Tracy later added attractive landscaping and additional birds as well as deer, monkeys, seals and some Barbary sheep.

Like other Americans, Salt Lakers also enjoyed dancing and listening to the music of the era's big bands. At Saltair, Coconut Grove, the Hotel Utah's Starlight Gardens and Pinecrest in Emigration Canyon, local orchestras together with nationally famous bands like Xavier Cugat, Eddy Duchin, Glen Miller, Gene Krupa and Les Brown entertained the public.

In addition to attending movies and dancing, larger numbers of Salt Lakers began to enjoy skiing. Western Europeans had brought skiing to the United States. Ski-jumping and Nordic — or cross-country — skiing had blossomed in Norway from the mid-19th to the early 20th centuries. Alpine or downhill skiing had matured in Austria during the late 19th and early 20th centuries. The main differences in the two styles consisted originally in longer and narrower Nordic skis with bindings made of leather or hemp that left the heel free to move. By contrast, Alpine skis were wider and shorter and had metal (beartrap) bindings that clamped the entire foot tightly to the ski. More suited to shallower slopes or ski jumping, the Nordic equipment required the skier to employ wide Telemark or Christie turns when going downhill. Alpine techniques allowed the descent of steeper slopes through a series of short, controlled snowplow, stem-Christie, or parallel S-turns.

Norwegians brought skiing to the United States as early as the 1850s. Various skiing enthusiasts practiced the sport in the California mining camps and in the Great Lakes states. Skiing first came to Utah when the legendary John "Snowshoe" Thompson carried mail by ski in the late 1850s from Genoa, Utah Territory (near present-day Carson City, Nevada) to Placerville, California. By the early 20th century, miners at Alta

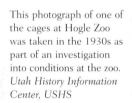

Juanita Brooks, noted Utah writer and historian, helped copy and preserve historical documents during the 1930s. *Utah History Information Center, USHS*

This photograph of one of the cages at Hogle Zoo was taken in the 1930s as part of an investigation into conditions at the zoo. *Utah History Information Center, USHS*

A crowd gathered at the Coconut Grove dance hall for Utah Governor Henry H. Blood's birthday party on October 6, 1937. *Salt Lake Tribune photo, Utah History Information Center, USHS*

teachers, physicians and business people, many of them from Salt Lake City, organized the Wasatch Mountain Club.

During the late teens Wasatch Mountain Club members engaged in long skiing expeditions. Usually leaving from Salt Lake City, they traveled by train to Park City. From Park City they skied across Catherine Pass in the Wasatch Mountains to Brighton. Most skied down Big Cottonwood Canyon and back to Salt Lake City. Some crossed from Brighton to Alta and skied down Little Cottonwood Canyon.

had begun skiing down Emma Hill or Rustler Mountain on home-fashioned boards they called "flipflops."

Most people in Salt Lake City knew little about skiing until the teens. In 1912 Brigham Young University coach Charles T. Stoney, his two sons, artists, scholars, photographers, writers,

Stoney and other enthusiasts generally used makeshift equipment. They made their own skis and scrounged bamboo poles from carpet stores. They used these poles as pivots in turns and as drags to slow their descent. Bindings usually consisted of a leather toe strap and a heel strap cut from an old innertube. Less adventurous skiers learned to ski at places like the first and ninth holes at the Bonneville Golf Course. Since there were no lifts, skiers climbed to the top of hills by herring boning (alternately advancing one ski after another at an angle with the line of ascent) or by tying gunny sacks or rope around the middle of their skis to stop them from slipping backward.

Ecker Hill ski jump in 1937 *Shipler photo, Utah History Information Center, USHS*

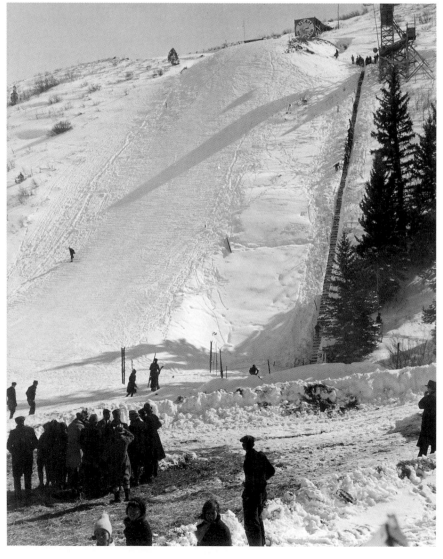

Only a few hardy souls skied during the teens and 20s, and by 1932 only about 3,000 Utahns had taken up the sport. Then, during the 1930s packs of skiers began to head for the slopes. Resorts improved their facilities and by 1940, 190,000 Utahns found their way into the winter sports areas each year. Most came from the Wasatch Front cities, and the bulk of these from Salt Lake City.

In Europe, in the United States, and in Salt Lake City, the earliest competition consisted in jumping for distance. In 1914 Martinius "Mark" A. Strand organized Utah's first ski-jumping competition at Dry Creek Canyon on what is now the University of Utah campus. Strand repeated the event in 1915, and he and a group of associates organized the

Norwegian Young Folks Society, which sponsored the jumping competition beginning in 1916. Later renamed the Norwegian-American Athletic Club, the members again renamed their association the Utah Ski Club in 1928.

In 1927 Mark Strand, Peter Ecker and Axel Andresen convinced Frank, James and Lawrence Rasmussen to build a ski-jumping facility at their ranch by Parley's Summit near what is now Interstate 80. The first jumping tournament was held at the Rasmussen Ranch on February 22, 1929, on a hill later named "Ecker Hill" in honor of Peter Ecker.

During the 1930s skiers became even more serious about jumping competition. In 1929 the Ogden Chamber of Commerce appointed Gus Becker, an Ogden Brewer, as chair of the Ogden Winter Sports Committee. Anxious to promote a sport that he loved, Becker supplied funds to construct a jumping hill east of present Pineview Reservoir in Ogden Valley at a site named "Becker Hill" in his honor.

Jumping competition began at Becker Hill on February 16, 1930, as part of a winter festival promoted by Becker, Mark Strand, Pete Ecker and others. The festival was extremely important since it began interstate cooperation among Ogden; Ashton, Idaho; and Lake Tahoe-Truckee, California. The Ogden Chamber of Commerce offered a $2,000 prize to anyone who could beat Henry Hall's record of 229 feet. First-rate jumpers like Halvor Bjorngaard, Alf Engen, Anders Haugen, Lars Haugen, Halvor Hvalstad, Sverre Engen and Sigurd Ulland competed. In order: Ulland, Alf Engen, Anders Haugen, Lars Haugen, and Sverre Engen had the longest jumps, but none bested Hall's record. Alf Engen, however, broke Hall's record in 1931.

Utah's premier skier was undoubtedly Alf Engen. Born in Mjondalen, Norway, Engen and his brother Sverre came to the United States in 1919. Their younger brother Corey later joined them. Although the Engens first lived in Chicago, they began participating in professional ski-jumping competition in Utah in 1930. They settled in Utah in 1948. In 1937 the National Ski Association named a new jump at the Spruces in Big Cottonwood Canyon in Alf Engen's honor.

Though exhilarating to the jumpers and exciting for the spectators, ski-jumping was an extremely dangerous sport.

A sequence photograph of Alf Engen running a slalom gate at Alta
Utah History Information Center, USHS

Jumpers often sprained ankles or cut themselves in spills. In February 1934 Calmar Andreasen, Utah amateur champion, died after losing control during a jump at Ecker Hill. After the 1934 season so many jumpers had sustained injuries that ski-jumping professionals like the Engens decided to disband their organization.

After the professionals disbanded, the National Ski Association agreed that if they refrained from competing for a year, they could apply for amateur status. Alf did so, and Mark Strand, by then vice president of the National Ski Association, announced that they had chosen Engen to represent the United States at the 1936 Olympics. In a disappointing ruling, however, Avery Brundage, head of the United States Olympic

Ski tow at Alta
Utah History Information Center, USHS

Committee, vetoed Engen's participation because his picture had appeared on a Wheaties Box in 1935. Engen had earned no money for the picture, but Brundage wanted to avoid even the taint of impropriety.

In 1937 the National Ski-Jumping Championship took place at Ecker Hill, and in 1939, Ecker Hill was the site for the combined national Jumping and Cross-Country Combined Championship. After cross-country skiing of 11.2 miles (18 kilometers) and jumping, Engen won the combined championship.

Among other championships, Engen won the 1940 national ski-jumping championship and the national four-event combined championship. He took first place in the downhill, slalom and jumping, and third in cross-country. To cap his career, in 1940, Engen received the American Ski Trophy awarded by the National Ski Association to recognize individuals who did the most to further skiing in America. He was inducted into the National Ski Hall of Fame in 1959, and his brothers Sverre and Corey were inducted in 1971 and 1973.

As the ski-jumping competition continued, recreational skiing became more popular. Several sites attracted the earliest patronage. Rasmussen Ranch, the site of Ecker Hill, hosted the largest number of brown-bag skiers from 1928 to the mid-1950s. For 50 cents skiers could take the Denver and Rio Grande Western Railroad to the ranch, and since there were no lifts or tows at first, they could ski all day for free. From Rasmussen's Ranch the hardier souls could continue by train to Park City or Snow Park (later renamed Deer Valley). During the 1930s, Community Camp in Big Cottonwood Canyon drew Salt Lake skiers as well.

Beginning in 1932 the Salt Lake Junior Chamber of Commerce sponsored skiing trips to Snow Park aboard a special train they called the Snow or Ski Train. To make the occasion more festive, the Chamber hired a band to play on the train.

Perhaps the largest impediment to widespread recreational Alpine skiing was the absence of easy ways to get to the top of the hill. Between 1905 and the late 1920s, Austrian, Swiss and French ski areas installed tows, lifts and a tram. As early as 1913, Truckee, California, had installed a toboggan tow, and in 1932 and 1934, ski areas near Shawbridge, Canada, and Woodstock, Vermont, installed rope tows.

The first lifts in the United States (1936 and 1938) owe their existence to cooperation between private developers and the U.S. Forest Service. Forest Service employees Felix C. Koziol, Alf Engen and James E. Gurr played the most crucial role in these developments. Engen worked for the Forest Service to conduct ski schools and to locate and develop ski areas on National Forests in Idaho, Wyoming, and Utah. Engen and Koziol, himself an avid skier and friend of Union Pacific Railroad magnate Averell Harriman who financed the Sun Valley resort, worked on the development of Sun Valley much of which operated under a special use permit on National Forest land. Sun Valley opened the nation's first lift in 1936.

At Alta George H. Watson and other businessmen consolidated mining claims that they transferred to the Forest Service. Watson and his associates then secured a special use permit through the cooperation of Gurr, who was then Wasatch National Forest Supervisor, for the construction of Utah's first lift at Alta in 1938.

The operators had considerable difficulty in maintaining the Alta lift until Fred H. Speyer, an Austrian engineer, emigrated to Utah. By the spring of 1939, Speyer had solved most problems and Alta's lift operated reliably. Lift rides cost 15 cents. During the 1950s Koziol, by then Wasatch National Forest supervisor, and his staff pioneered avalanche studies and methods of triggering controlled avalanches at Alta.

Felix C. Koziol (left) of the USDA Forest Service and Mayor George H. Watson of Alta were both instrumental in the growth of skiing in Utah.
Utah History Information Center, USHS

Chairlift at Brighton, 1947
Utah History Information Center, USHS

Utah Outdoor Skiing Camp at Engen Hill, Alta
Utah History Information Center, USHS

Skiers in line to get on the lift at its opening at Snow Basin in 1946
Utah History Information Center, USHS

Brighton developed as a ski resort in a much different way. After their emigration to Utah as Mormon converts from Scotland, William S. and Catherine Brighton had pre-empted 80 acres at Brighton. They built two hotels (the second replacing the first) at the site which James H. Moyle purchased after the Brightons' deaths. The resort hosted various cross-country and recreational skiers before 1939 when K. Smith and a number of Salt Lake businessmen constructed a T-bar tow at Brighton. An additional tow was added in 1941. In 1943 Zane Doyle purchased the ski area and in 1947 he added the Millicent chairlift.

In a way similar to Alta, Snowbasin near Ogden was developed on National Forest land that private interests had previously owned. Before 1934 the Ostler Land and Livestock Company had owned most land in Wheeler Basin, on the northeast slope of Mount Ogden. Severe overgrazing and destructive flooding led to condemnation of the land, its purchase by the federal government and its inclusion in the Cache National Forest.

As with many of the ski resorts in Utah, Alf Engen and Felix Koziol, working for the Forest Service, examined the area and found that the Wheeler Basin offered excellent possibilities as a ski area. In 1940 the Forest Service built a road into the basin which, at the suggestion of the Ogden Chamber of Commerce, had been renamed Snowbasin. In the winter of 1940-41 Snowbasin was the site of the Intermountain Downhill and Slalom Championships. The following summer, Civilian Conservation Corps recruits under Engen's supervision cleared Wildcat run, named for a litter of wildcats they found on the site. They also cleared Chicken Springs run. Snowbasin opened its first chair lift in 1946 under the supervision of Corey Engen.

Some other tow facilities were constructed prior to the end of World War II. These included a tow at Rasmussen's Ranch at Parley's Summit, one at Sundance — then called Timphaven — on the Alpine Loop above Provo Canyon and one at Beaver Mountain in Logan Canyon. Park City and Deer Valley, then called Snow Park, had some jumping facilities and were the sites of winter activities. Neither was adequately developed before 1945. Other Wasatch Oasis ski facilities such as Solitude,

Snowbird, Powder Mountain, Nordic Valley and the Canyons were not developed until after the war.

Without cooperation between private entrepreneurs and the Forest Service it seemed unlikely that Utah's ski areas would have developed as rapidly as they did. Sites at Park City and Deer Valley were undoubtedly as good as Alta and Snowbasin,

unemployment rate declined to 6 percent in 1936, and it remained below 9 percent for the remainder of the decade. The unemployment rate topped 10 percent in 1940 but declined rapidly thereafter as America geared up to challenge the potential threat of German Nazis, Italian fascists and Japanese Imperialists.

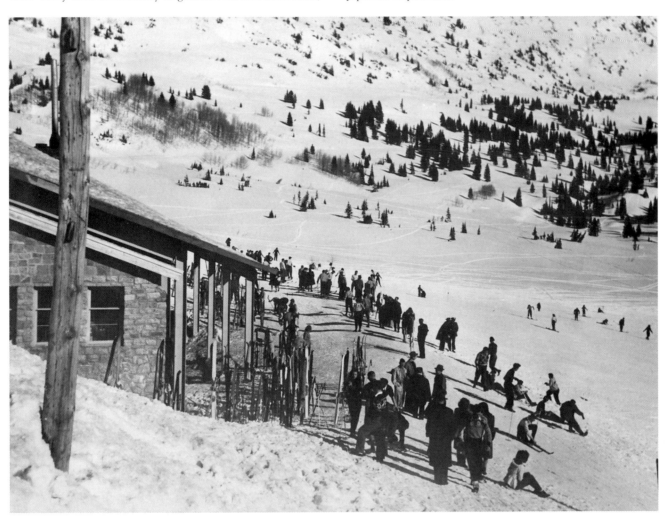

Snow Pine Lodge at Alta, built by Civilian Conservation Corp labor on the Wasatch National Forest
Wasatch National Forest photo, Utah History Information Center, USHS

but they did not develop as soon. National Forest land served as the sites for Alta, Snowbasin and part of Brighton. Civilian Conservation Corps (CCC) and WPA workers helped to build roads, bridges, campsites and outhouses in the mountains above Salt Lake City. At Snowbasin, particularly, CCC workers (under Engen's supervision) helped build roads and clear some of the runs. The WPA, under the supervision of Vern R. Thorpe, built skiing facilities at Park City and at Community Camp in Big Cottonwood Canyon.

In addition to the cooperation in developing ski areas, Salt Lakers along with other Utahns owed a considerable debt to the federal government for bringing an end to the Depression. Largely because of WPA, PWA and CCC projects, Utah's

As America began to prepare for war in 1941, the unemployment rate declined to just over 4 percent and Salt Lakers began to fear Adolph Hitler, Benito Mussolini and Hideki Tojo more than the loss of jobs. As preparations for war increased, the Wasatch Front region began to play an increasingly important strategic role. By the early 1930s the federal government recognized the potential threat to the West Coast from Japan which had begun its wars of conquest on the Asian mainland. To secure the nation's war materiel, the War and Navy departments sought sites for military installations at some distance from the western border. Since they needed portability as well as security for the war materiel, they also looked for adequate railroads and highways.

U.S. Army Mountain Troops in training at Alta during World War II
Utah History Information Center, USHS

The Salt Lake area seemed ideal for military installations. Transcontinental railroads served the area from all directions and because of the arcing of the U.S. West Coast, Salt Lake City stood within 175 miles of being equidistant from the major West Coast ports of Los Angeles, San Francisco and Seattle. In the 1930s WPA projects enlarged the Ogden Arsenal, about 25 miles north of Salt Lake City, and in 1938 the WPA began construction at Hill Air Force Base just east of the Arsenal site. Additional construction at the Ogden Arsenal and Hill Air Force Base made them major employers. By the end of the war, Hill Air Force Base had become the largest employer in the state of Utah.

After the bombing of Pearl Harbor on December 7, 1941, and America's subsequent entry into the war, the federal government became even more concerned about the possible damage a West Coast attack could cause. In all, the federal government financed construction of two dozen military depots, garrisons, manufacturing plants and a hospital in Utah, mostly in the region surrounding Salt Lake City.

Recognizing the potential threat of a West Coast invasion to the Presidio of San Francisco, in January 1942 War Department planners began upgrading the facilities at Fort Douglas. Considering the Ninth Service Command headquarters at the Presidio potentially vulnerable to attack, the army moved its personnel to Fort Douglas. As a result, the Salt Lake City facility became the command post for military activities in Washington, Oregon, Nevada, Utah, Idaho, Arizona and Montana.

Salt Lake City hosted numerous other manufacturing facilities operated by private companies but constructed or improved with federal appropriations. These included the Eitel McCullough radio tube plant; the Kalunite Alumina plant, which concentrated low-grade aluminum ore; the Remington small-arms ammunition plant, which opened in 1941 and employed 10,000 people until its closing in late 1943; the Union Carbide tungsten plant; and the Utah Oil Refining Company plant which produced 100 octane aviation gasoline. Just south of Salt Lake City the government constructed the Kearns Army Air Base, which housed airmen for training. In adjoining counties, the government constructed such installations and businesses as Clearfield Naval Supply Depot, Ogden General Depot, Tooele Ordnance Depot, Dugway Proving Grounds, Wendover Air Force Base, Geneva Steel Plant and the Gladden McDean refractories plant.

The construction of these facilities created problems for Salt Lake City that city fathers had never anticipated during the dark days of the Depression. Persistent housing shortages plagued the city and unemployment rates below 2 percent spawned inflation and left many employers including the city

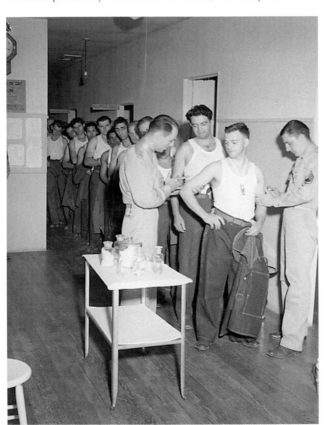

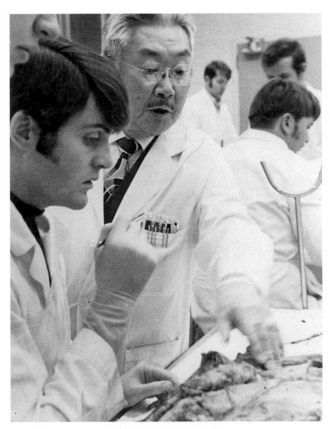

(Far left)
Soldiers line up to get their shots at Fort Douglas in January 1942. *Salt Lake Tribune photo, Utah History Information Center, USHS*

Dr. Edward I. Hashimoto, University of Utah professor of anatomy *Utah History Information Center, USHS*

Sharon Becker, a technician on the F-4 aircraft production line at Hill Air Force Base grabs a crimper to use while wrapping wires inside a cockpit. *Utah History Information Center, USHS*

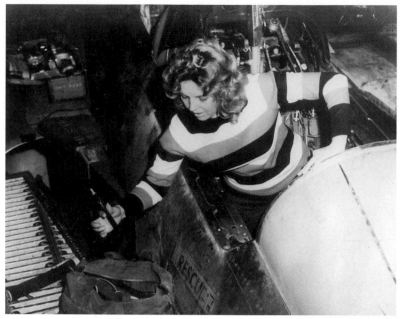

In February 1942 the city began searching for sites for housing projects. Officials located a place on the city's west side for a federal project that they named Glendale Gardens. Contractors built Glendale Gardens' cheap multi-story family units very quickly. At about the same time, private contractors constructed Ambassador Gardens containing 38 apartments, and Douglas Arms Corporation constructed a project with 36 units. The entities, both private, constructed additional housing between 1942 and 1944.

In some cases, private owners who recognized that they would have little trouble renting their units discriminated against families. As a result, some families had to live in substandard housing while seeking better accommodations. Some landlords refused to rent to non-Caucasian families.

Perhaps the Japanese Americans suffered most. Anti-Japanese signs appeared in Salt Lake City businesses and the Chamber of Commerce and the Salt Lake Federation of Labor urged Japanese not to open new businesses in the city. Dr. Jun Kurumada, a Salt Lake City dentist and chairman of the Japanese-American Citizen's League, met with other league members and assured the FBI of their cooperation and loyalty. "America's fight is our fight," he and other JACL members proclaimed.

government scrounging for workers. Absent parents and high wages increased crime rates among juveniles, and anti-foreign prejudice wreaked havoc among loyal Americans born outside the United States.

In 1941 prior to the outbreak of the war, representatives of the real estate industry and federal agencies both downplayed the emergency. On August 21 Richard F. Harding, secretary of the Salt Lake Real Estate Board, said that hotels, apartments, tourist courts and rooms in homes would take care of the city's immediate housing problem. A WPA survey in the fall suggested that no housing emergency existed. In addition to the privately constructed projects, public entities constructed additional housing between 1942 and 1944.

After the bombing of Pearl Harbor, the magnitude of the housing shortage quickly became apparent. Thousands of workers flooded into Salt Lake City and other Wasatch Front cities. They all needed housing, and many resorted to expedients such as

Women effectively run an electric engine in 1944. *Utah History Information Center, USHS*

bunking together with other families, trucking in temporary housing and constructing emergency units. In January 1942 when personnel from the Ninth Army Corps Area moved from San Francisco to Salt Lake City, city and county officials spent the day placing 150 families in temporary housing. When the temporary units proved inadequate, the army moved in 60 trailers and parked them on vacant land near the University of Utah stadium.

Some Japanese-Americans diffused prejudice in rather creative ways. When Dr. Edward I. Hashimoto walked into his anatomy class at the University of Utah's medical school the day after the bombing of Pearl Harbor, the students greeted him with stony silence. Taking the matter in stride, he said, "What are you fellows staring at? I'm Irish. I was home in Dublin at the time!" Taken aback and delighted by Hashimoto's wit, the students relaxed. Thereafter, since Hashimoto could draw human figures with either hand, students called him the "Ambidextrous Irishman."

Under wartime conditions, Salt Lakers no longer had difficulty finding jobs. Women went to work in unprecedented numbers. No longer did they have to confine themselves to pink-collar jobs. In the crisis "Rosie the Riveter" became a symbol of women's contribution to the war effort. Many high school students found after-school work at jobs they could never have hoped for only a couple of years before.

Servicemen poured into the city in unprecedented numbers. The Army stationed many of them at Fort Douglas, Kearns or Hill Air Force Base, and they came into the city on leave to seek recreation and companionship.

Wartime conditions changed the way people lived. The government conducted drives for such things as grease, newspaper, rubber and tin cans. People had to surrender ration coupons for gasoline, tires and oil, all of which appeared on the market only in short supply if at all. Rationing limited the consumption of such foods as meat, sugar, coffee and butter. Most women could not find nylon hose at any price, and children found it impossible to buy bubble gum. Juvenile crime increased, as did certain types of violent crimes and crimes against property. The divorce rate increased as some families disintegrated under wartime pressures.

In spite of Depression and wartime conditions, city politics continued as usual. During the Depression and World War II, Salt Lake City suffered through some of the most serious public scandals in its history. In 1938 Mayor E. B. Erwin, who had defeated Louis Marcus for re-election in 1935, and Chief of Police Harry L. Finch were charged with taking payoffs from gamblers and brothels and were sentenced to a year in the county jail. Erwin's successor Ab Jenkins, who earned local fame as a race car driver, carried on a running conflict with the other members of the city commission, especially Oscar W. McConkie and Fred Tedesco over city finances and employee relations. Apparently fed up with such infighting, the voters elected Earl J. Glade to replace Jenkins in 1943.

Still, all was not negative in Salt Lake politics. In 1936 Salt Lakers elected attorney Reva Beck Bosone as a city judge. As a state legislator, she had sponsored laws setting minimum wages and maximum hours for children and creating a women's division in the state Industrial Commission. As a judge she started assessing stiff fines to drunk drivers while offering them the option of securing help through Alcoholics Anonymous. In 1948 the voters of Utah's second congressional district elected her to Congress where she served for two terms.

Salt Lake City's experience during the Depression and World War II resembled an exciting roller coaster ride. From the heights of economic prosperity in 1929, the city rode to its low point in 1932-33. Employment on PWA, WPA, CCC and other federal projects helped lift the economy from the downturn during the mid-1930s. World War II lifted it even more. At the same time, the people paid a price for this uphill ride in crime and family disintegration.

Nevertheless, Salt Lakers gained important cultural advantages from the Depression and war. During the 1930s the arts flourished and the city saw the origins of the Utah Symphony. Salt Lakers could now see exotic animals under more favorable conditions at Hogle Zoo. Most importantly, the nearby ski resorts began early development and fame because of championship competitions and the development of ski lifts and tows.

Salt Lake City Commission, June 2, 1949 (Left to right) Fred "Feets" Tedesco, L.C. Romney, Mayor Earl J. Glade, J.B. Matheson and D.H. Afleck *Shipler photo, Utah History Information Center, USHS*

A group of Japanese-American servicemen belonging to the World War II Nissei War Loan Committee met with Governor Herbert B. Maw (center of the front row) on July 14, 1944. *Utah History Information Center, USHS*

On September 2, 1945, as the Japanese surrendered to General Douglas MacArthur aboard the battleship *Missouri* in Tokyo Bay, Salt Lakers joined in celebrating VJ Day. Then, cheered by the end of the conflict, with other Americans they began to convert their war machine to an engine of prosperity. Soldiers boarded trains for home, and the War and Navy departments and their successor, the Defense

Salt Lake City and its Hinterland

CHAPTER FIVE

Department, began to transform or sell off many of the depots, garrisons and plants that the government contractors had built during the war.

Although fear of a return to pre-war depression plagued many minds, excessively high unemployment, low profits and hard times did not come again. Instead, a combination of federal subsidies, entrepreneurial initiative, widening markets, the Korean War and the Cold War fueled Salt Lake City's prosperity.

Construction, commerce, mining and manufacturing boomed. By 1950 Salt Lake City stood at the center of a complex of nearly 600 manufacturing plants. *Business Week* called the Salt Lake region "the nation's greatest concentration of nonferrous mining, milling, smelting, and refining."

Like a drunk on a pay-day binge, the Defense Department began selling off the war plants and garrisons that had fueled Utah's wartime prosperity. Salt Lake City received a boost as the government unloaded the $20 million Remington Arms Plant to a syndicate headed by Salt Lakers John M. Wallace and Leland S. Swaner for $1.7 million. Wallace and Swaner poured in additional funds to refurbish the plant and convert it to a site

for light industry and commerce. For a fraction of its wartime cost, the government sold the Geneva Steel Mill in Orem, 45 miles south of Salt Lake City, to United States Steel. Entrepreneurs converted the Clearfield Naval Supply Depot, 25 miles north of Salt Lake City, into a shipping and storage facility they renamed the Freeport Center.

Government subsidies and private initiative made Salt Lake City into the Intermountain West's major oil refining center. In another government fire sale, AMOCO (Standard of Indiana) paid $4.1 million for the $15.9 million Utah Oil Refining Plant that Amco had run on a contract with the government during the war. The company then spent $10 million enlarging and refurbishing the facility. Between 1948 and 1950 Chevron (Standard of California) laid pipelines from Pasco, Washington, and Rangely, Colorado, to a plant it built north of the city. In 1950 Phillips Petroleum Company constructed a refinery in North Salt Lake. Later Northwest Energy, a major oil pipeline company, established offices in Salt Lake City.

The state of Utah benefitted from some of the surplus sales and give-aways. The State Road Commission purchased the Eitel McCullough radio tube plant and converted it into a storage facility. As the army phased out most of its operations at Fort Douglas, the state added much of the land and many of the buildings to the University of Utah campus.

In view of the potential for future military conflicts, however, the Defense Department did not unload all of the installations. The Army and Air Force decreased employment and slowed down operations at these locations immediately after the war, but the outbreak of the Korean War in 1950 led again to the expansion of their activities. Then, as the Cold War became more intense, these installations played an even more vital role in America's military defense. About 30 miles north of Salt Lake City, the personnel at Hill Air Force Base repaired airplanes and provided housing for pilots and their families. Hill Air Force Base, with more than 11,000 employees, had become Utah's largest business by the mid-1950s. In addition, Utah General Depot in Ogden, Tooele Ordnance Depot in Tooele and Dugway Proving Grounds (southwest of Tooele) also continued to serve the nation's defense needs.

Construction in Salt lake City boomed. A few months after the war ended the Federal Housing Administration estimated that the city needed 6,000 more homes. Mayor Earl J. Glade

appointed a committee to coordinate plans for financing the homes, and the National Association of Home Builders announced plans to construct low-cost dwellings for returning veterans. By the early 1950s builders had met most of the housing deficit.

Unfortunately for downtown Salt Lake City, most of the new homes sprang up on the city's affluent hillsides, on the city's northwest side and in the suburbs. Since no one paid much attention to the houses in the central city, the area deteriorated under the corrosive force of what some observers called "dry rot." Absentee owners and speculators built walls and cut in doors to divide the homes into small rental units. Many of these owners then left these apartments to decay until a study in 1971 considered 60 percent of the downtown housing as "blighted."

This moldering of homes in Salt Lake City's downtown resulted in part from county property assessment policy, in part from Federal Housing Administration policy and in part from market forces. The Salt Lake County Assessor continued to undervalue the land underlaying these homes while they rated the buildings at something approaching the market value.

The FHA contributed to the deterioration by singling out areas its agents called "declining," and outlining them in red on maps. Then the agency refused to guarantee loans for the purchase of homes in the redlined districts. Since banks and savings and loans followed FHA guidelines, even those owners

The Templeton Building on the corner of Main Street and South Temple as it appeared in the 1950s
LDS Church Archives

who might have wanted to refurbish rundown central city property had difficulty getting loans at reasonable rates to make repairs.

In part because of these policies and in part to meet the demand for low cost housing, absentee owners ignored repairs and let the buildings deteriorate. Objecting to the rotting condition of homes in their neighborhood, members of the Central Community Council organized a lobbying group called People Against Redlining. The group tried to get the FHA and lending agencies to stop discriminating against their neighborhood. They also urged the city administration to enforce compliance with building and safety codes.

Sometimes such citizen-based efforts worked, but just as often they failed. By 1970 the abject poor, 60 percent of whom earned less than $5,000 per year and 16 percent of whom scraped by on less than $1,600 per year, clung to a precarious life in these downtown hovels.

Nevertheless, in a startling development, while family dwellings in the downtown area declined,

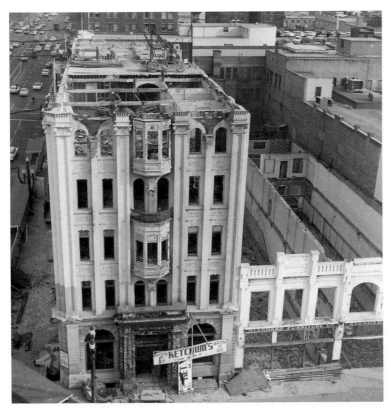

The Templeton Building is shown here during the demolition for the ZCMI Center.
Utah History Information Center, USHS

during the 1960s and 70s entrepreneurs, religious organizations and governments beautified the commercial district. Distinguished structures constructed during this period included the formal-looking University Club Building on east South Temple, the gigantic Kennecott Building on the west side of Main Street at South Temple, and the multi-functional Salt Palace on Second West between South Temple and Third South.

Entrepreneurs constructed two new downtown malls to draw shoppers to the central city. The LDS Church financed construction of the ZCMI Center. Completed in 1976, the mall faced the Kennecott Building from the east side of Main Street. In an effort to retain some of the flavor of Salt Lake City's 19th century downtown, ZCMI removed the Victorian cast iron facade from the former Building and reattached it to the Main Street surface of the new structure. Developers Sidney Foulger, Jack Okland and Richard Hemingway built the Key Bank Tower next to the Kennecott Building then wrapped the Crossroads Mall around the two buildings.

In practice, however, as people moved to outlying quarters of the city or to the suburbs, many Salt Lakers began shopping outside the downtown. New malls such as Cottonwood Mall at 4800 South and Highland Drive in Salt Lake; Fashion Place Mall at 6191 South State Street in Murray; and Valley Fair Mall at 3600 South and 2700 West in what later became West Valley City all took patronage from malls and stores in the downtown area.

In addition to the privately constructed buildings and malls, governments also added to the variety of the cityscape.

Salt Lake City and Salt Lake County collaborated in the construction of the Salt Palace as a convention center and site for professional basketball and hockey teams. They also built a nearby concert hall to house the Utah Symphony and to host nationally renowned musicians. East of the City and County Building, the city constructed a new library and Metropolitan Hall of Justice.

By the early 1970s, the LDS Church had begun to develop a large bureaucracy to manage affairs for what had become a world-wide organization. To house the bureaucracy, in 1973 the church completed construction of the towering church office building. Anchoring the northern end of the business district, the church office building faced North Temple. From there this massive New Formalist structure stretched from Main to State streets east and west and well into the block toward South Temple from north to south. The Church later added the Family History Library and the Museum of Church History and Art on West Temple across the street from Temple Square.

Controversy dogged what may have been the most important of the public projects, the Salt Palace. In characteristic fashion, Utah's former governor, J. Bracken Lee, who had ridden to election as Salt Lake City's mayor in 1959 on a wave of economy and anti-governmental activism and who had fired police chief W. Cleon Skousen shortly after assuming office, announced his intense opposition to the Salt Palace project. Moreover, although South Salt Lake and Murray favored the Salt Palace, their city administrations thought the county should build on Thirty-third South. By contrast, the Chamber of Commerce, the *Deseret News*, the *Salt Lake Tribune* and a number of city boosters campaigned passionately for its construction in downtown Salt Lake City. They found a champion in Commissioner Conrad Harrison, a former newspaper man, who had written a series of articles in the *Deseret News* in March 1961 supporting the project.

Several factors seem to have tipped the scales in favor of constructing the Salt Palace in downtown Salt Lake City. Many people had become embarrassed by the shabby appearance of the central district of Utah's capital city. They came to believe that a new sports complex, concert hall and convention center would lead the way to the revitalization of the downtown area. Moreover, the LDS Church took a proprietary interest in the area surrounding their world-wide headquarters. Touched by a sense of pride and civic virtue, the Church donated the land for the new center.

Even with the Church's donation, Lee persisted in his efforts to scuttle the project. Calling the center an intolerable burden on taxpayers, the mayor helped sponsor a petition drive for a referendum. The petition drive failed, in part because of the sense of pride shared by Salt Lakers, in part because they believed the project would revitalize the city's economy, and in part because they learned that the city and county had already invested $3 million in planning for the project.

Then, the complex hit another snag. The architect estimated the cost of constructing the complex at $12.6 million. When the county officials opened the bids, however, they learned to their horror that the lowest bid was $16.9 million. Moreover, the bids did not include an estimated $4.8 million for clearing and preparing the site. Since the bond they had floated could not cover the cost, they agreed to construct only the sports and exposition complex at a cost of $11.7 million. The county dedicated the Salt Palace in 1969.

Abravanel Hall
Photo by the author

In retrospect, it seems clear that the construction of the convention and sports complex helped to revitalize the downtown area. Professional hockey and basketball teams made the arena their home. National and local chains constructed hotels, restaurants and stores in the area. Entrepreneurs Essam and Adnan Khashoggi built the Triad Center to the west to house business offices and the broadcast facilities of KSL-TV and radio.

As these changes took place, Salt Lake City further entrenched its position as the center of Utah's arts and humanities. As a bicentennial project in 1976, Salt Lake City restored the historic Capitol Theater, which was originally built in 1912. It became the headquarters of the Utah Opera Company, Ballet West and the Ririe-Woodbury Dance Company. In addition to performances by these companies, the Capitol Theater served as the site for plays and musicals presented by national touring companies.

In 1979 the city added the music hall that the budgetary shortfall had deleted from the original Salt Palace construction. Symphony Hall, renamed Abravanel Hall in honor of Maurice Abravanel, rose on the corner of South Temple and West Temple, north of the Salt Palace. It has served since that time as the home of the Utah Symphony.

Other developments helped solidify Salt Lake City's place as a center for the arts and humanities. The Utah State Historical Society moved from cramped quarters in the State Capitol Building to the former Kearns Mansion at 603 East South Temple. In 1976 a coalition of humanists organized the Utah Endowment for the Humanities (later renamed the Utah Humanities Council) with Anne Levitt, a Cedar City civic leader, as founding chair. Headquartered in Salt Lake City and directed by Delmont Oswald, the UHC made grants for humanities projects from funds supplied by the National Endowment for the Humanities, private donations, and more recently, appropriations from the Utah State Legislature.

The Utah Arts Council grew from the earliest arts institute organized in the United States. In 1899 Representative Alice Merrill Horne, a member of the state legislature from Salt Lake City, sponsored an act to organize the Utah Arts Institute. The act established an annual art competition and exhibition, and it provided funds to purchase art for a state collection. In 1965 the arts council began to receive grants from the National Endowment for the Arts. It used money from the state and private donations to help support the collection and to provide funds for various arts organizations including the Utah Symphony and Ballet West.

Public works of art added to the city's distinction. As part of the observance of the centennial of the arrival of the Mormon pioneers in the Salt Lake Valley and the founding of Salt Lake City in 1847, the State of Utah planned the This is the Place Monument at the mouth of Emigration Canyon north of the Hogle Zoo. The state commissioned Mahonri M. Young, a grandson of Brigham Young who had earned international renown as a sculptor and painter while living in New York City, to design and sculpt the monument. The memorial constructed as a massive block topped by statues of Brigham Young, Heber C. Kimball and Wilford Woodruff, also holds panels commemorating the achievements of Native Americans, mountain men, Hispanic missionaries, explorers and others who contributed to the discovery and development of the state. Dedicated before an audience of 50,000 by LDS Church President George Albert Smith, the monument has served as a beacon for tourists, residents and art connoisseurs since 1947.

The year 1947 also witnessed the revitalization of the Utah Symphony, largely through the efforts of Maurice Abravanel.

Lighting ceremony at the This is The Place Monument, November 15, 1949
Utah History Information Center, USHS

Born in Salonika, Greece, to a Spanish Sephardic Jewish family, Abravanel grew up in Lausanne, Switzerland. Though he devoted his early life to music, his father wanted him to become a physician. Abravanel's love for music led him to drop out of medical school and move to Berlin in 1922 where he found an exciting music scene and where he became a close friend and student of Kurt Weill. Abravanel went on to conduct orchestras in Germany until 1933 when the selection of Adolph Hitler as Reichskanzeler and increasingly virulent anti-Semitism led him to move to Paris. Abravanel conducted orchestras there and in Australia before moving to New York City where he conducted the Metropolitan Opera Company orchestra and orchestras for Broadway musicals. Returning to Australia for a year in 1946, he was offered the conductorship of New York City's Radio City Music Hall orchestra for the next year.

Abravanel, however, dreamed of becoming a musical pioneer who could build and conduct an orchestra of his own. His chance came in 1947. As part of Utah's centennial celebration, the Utah Symphony board sought a conductor to replace Werner Janssen who had lasted only one year. Entranced by the city and the challenge, Abravanel turned down Radio City to take the Utah Symphony job. He refashioned the symphony from a well-respected local orchestra into an internationally renowned musical organization. The LDS Church donated the historic Salt Lake Tabernacle as a site for symphony performances (until the construction of Abravanel Hall), and the University of Utah furnished space for rehearsals.

Abravanel committed his life to Utah while he served as Utah's music teacher. Unlike Janssen, he and his wife settled in Salt Lake City. He took the symphony throughout the state, performing in elementary and high schools and in public gatherings. As a teacher, he introduced Utahns to such modern music as Stravinsky's *Firebird Suite* during his first season at the podium. At the same time, he conducted stunning performances of more familiar works such as Beethoven's *Eroica*.

He also helped Utahns to understand their own musical heritage. He introduced Utah audiences to Leroy Robertson's *Trilogy*, a three-movement symphony that had won the prestigious Reichhold Award as "the Western Hemisphere's best symphonic work." Robertson, who had grown up as a Mormon sheepherder, was at the time professor of music at Brigham Young University. Abravanel persuaded U of U president A.

Ray Olpin to bring Robertson to the University of Utah as chair of the music department.

Most importantly, Abravanel's tenure as music director and conductor helped demonstrate that the Mormon and non-Mormon communities could work together. In the second year of Abravanel's tenure, the symphony encountered serious financial difficulty. Then and in succeeding years Mormon and non-Mormon board members such as Glenn Walker Wallace, Calvin W. Rawlings, J. Allan Crockett, John M. Wallace, James L. White, Morris Rosenblatt, T. Bowring "By" Woodbury and Obert C. Tanner played significant roles in averting the symphony's financial crises. The symphony received a Ford Foundation Matching Grant which it used to double $1 million in contributions between 1966 and 1971.

Abravanel, played a crucial role in keeping the symphony afloat. He turned down an offer of twice his salary from the Houston Symphony. His perpetual good nature, optimism, and brilliance raised the symphony's stature and endeared him to Utahns.

Maurice Abravanel (right) with three noted Utah musicians: LeRoy Robertson (left), William Fowler (center), and Alexander Schreiner (seated at the piano) *Utah History Information Center, USHS*

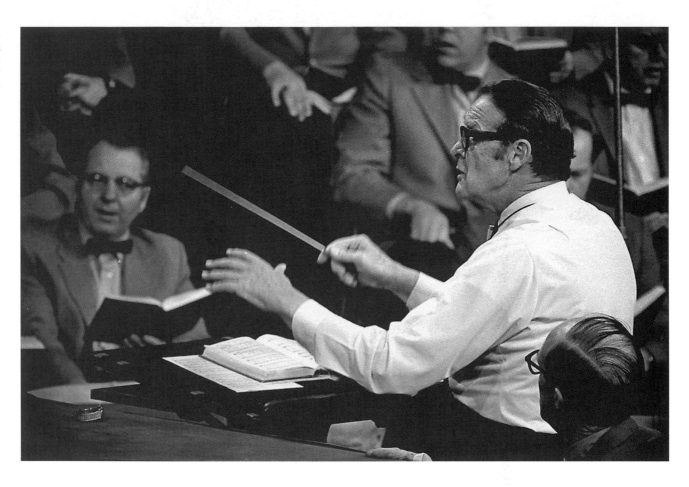

Conductor Richard P.
Condie rehearsing
with the Mormon
Tabernacle Choir
Nelson Wadsworth

Crawford Gates,
noted composer
*Utah History Information
Center, USHS*

Utah's music community also benefitted from the return to Salt Lake City of Utah native Willam Christensen. Born in Brigham City, Christensen performed in vaudeville before settling in San Francisco. He founded the world-renowned San Francisco Ballet in 1937. Then in 1951 he returned to Utah to accept a position at the University of Utah as professor of ballet. Christensen encountered opposition from the faculty in part because he had no degrees and in part because some thought ballet did not belong on a university campus. Utah's curmudgeonly governor, J. Bracken Lee, greeted him with a caustic outburst. "What?" Lee said, "A toe-dancer on the university faculty?" Rapidly silencing his critics, Christensen built not only a distinguished ballet program at the U, but he also made Ballet West — which he organized as the Utah Theater Ballet Company — into one of the nation's premier performing organizations.

Over the same period, the Salt Lake Tabernacle Choir achieved additional recognition. The choir continued weekly broadcasts of "Music and the Spoken Word" which had originated on CBS in 1929, and in 1955 it made the first of a series of major international tours. Under the leadership of J. Spencer Cornwall the choir joined with Eugene Ormandy's Philadelphia Symphony to cut recordings for Columbia Records. In 1959 the choir and symphony won the first of a number of Grammy awards for their performance of "Battle Hymn of the Republic."

In spite of the fact that they shared the Tabernacle together until the completion of Abravanel Hall, not until the bicentennial celebration in 1976 did the Tabernacle Choir and the Utah Symphony perform together. This collaboration came about largely because of the efforts of President Nathan Eldon Tanner, a counselor in the LDS First Presidency, Bicentennial Commission Chair Obert C. Tanner, Tabernacle Choir director Jerold Ottley and Abravanel. In a memorable performance, Abravanel and composer Crawford Gates, a California-born composer with ties to Utah, shared the podium to present a number of pieces, including the premiere of Gates's symphony *The New Morning*.

The maturing of Utah's cultural scene paralleled the efforts to solve Salt Lake City's increasingly severe transportation headache. As homes in the downtown area deteriorated and commercial buildings sprang up to change the city's skyline. Salt Lakers found themselves saddled with an archaic and dysfunctional transportation system. The system's deterioration had accelerated during the 1930s as the Utah Light and Traction Company found the trolley system unprofitable. The

Willam Christensen of Ballet West directs a rehearsal of the cast of the *The Nutcracker*.
Utah History Information Center, USHS

Service stations like this one owned by Lincoln Hanks fueled Salt Lake City's affair with the automobile.
LDS Church Archives

company then stopped running the trolleys, tore up the tracks and replaced them with busses. In 1944 an anti-trust suit against U L and T's parent company, the Utah Power and Light Company, forced U L and T to sell the bus system to Salt Lake City Lines, another privately owned company.

After the war ended and as cars again became available, America's love affair with the automobile proceeded from courtship to passion, and the public transit system fell into ruin. Enamored by the mobility private automobiles offered and flush with the cash to buy and drive them, Americans pressed local, state and national governments to construct new and better roads and highways. During the 1950s the Eisenhower administration had little trouble getting Congress to approve the Interstate Highway System with the promise that Americans could drive

their cars from coast to coast and Canada to Mexico without meeting a stop light.

Utah cooperated by furnishing matching funds, and, as highways stretched into rural areas near Salt Lake City, automobile suburbs replaced the older streetcar suburbs. In contrast with the city's decaying downtown, suburbanites reveled in their newly paved streets, single family homes, two car garages, superior schools, and shopping malls. Fathers and an increasing number of mothers drove from the suburbs to Salt Lake City for work, college or play. Many rushed home to join those who worked in the home and to drive station wagons and vans filled with children to homes, to schools, to sports and to churches. Under the weight of increasing numbers of automobiles, Salt Lake City's streets became rutted rivers flowing with streams of traffic. The cars created gridlock, anger and road rage as drivers sought convenient routes to their city destinations and to increasingly phantom parking places.

As the number of families with two or more cars increased, between 1945 and 1960 mass transit ridership declined in Salt Lake City and throughout the nation. Nationwide, ridership dropped by 61 percent. In Salt Lake City annual bus ridership plummeted by 64 percent from 33 million passengers in 1946 to 12 million in 1960. Faced with degenerating income, Salt Lake City Lines delayed repairs on the old busses and put off buying replacements. By the mid-1960s SLCL had decided to throw in the towel.

With no alternative except to turn the streets over to automobiles or to set up a public transportation system, the city worked out an interim arrangement that provided breathing

The last Utah Light & Traction Company streetcar to run in Salt Lake City, June 1, 1941
Utah History Information Center, USHS

time until they could buy the bus system. In 1968 the city signed an agreement with Union Street and Railway Company. Under the agreement, USRC acquired Salt Lake City Lines' franchise, busses and facilities. The city agreed to provide a $210,000 subsidy over a two-year period, and it reserved the right to purchase the line and operate the busses as a public transit system.

Salt Lake City was not alone in the deterioration of its public transportation system. In fact, by the late 1960s Salt Lakers along with residents and governments in other Wasatch Front cities faced problems similar to those in urban areas throughout the nation.

People in Utah as elsewhere came to believe that the only reasonable way to break automobile gridlock lay in the development of a publically subsidized transit system. After all, they observed, governments provided massive subsidies to automobiles, trucks and recreational vehicles through the construction of roads and highways. Why should government not also subsidize public transportation?

Responding to these needs, the state legislature approved a bill in 1969 allowing cities and counties to organize mass transit districts. The nearby cities of Salt Lake, Murray, Midvale, South Salt Lake and Sandy set up the Utah Transit Authority to operate a mass transit system. In 1970 Salt Lake, Davis and Weber counties joined, and then Utah County later entered the system. Using a grant from the U. S. Department of Transportation to pay part of the cost, Salt Lake City purchased USRC's busses. In 1972 the legislature approved a law allowing members of the transit district to levy a one-quarter of one percent sales tax to subsidize the system. Voters in Salt Lake City and the other cities and counties approved the tax which together with additional subsidies from the federal and state governments, allowed the system to offer reasonably priced rides.

As the transit system modernized, so did Salt Lake City's connections with the outside world. Since automobiles had rung the death knell of private interstate train passenger traffic in the Mountain West, the only major alternatives consisted of busses or airplanes. Bus companies like Greyhound continued to operate out of Salt Lake City, but the public became increasingly drawn to airplanes.

Understanding the public's preferences, Salt Lake City initiated improvements at its airport. After undertaking an extensive improvement and modernization program between the late 1950s and 1962, Salt Lake City Municipal Airport was redesignated Salt Lake City International Airport in 1968. On the heels of this designation, Mayor E. J. "Jake" Garn, who had been elected in 1971, began a project to renovate the airport that lasted years after his administration ended in 1976.

Unfortunately, Salt Lakers who wanted to fly had been hampered by the lack of competition. United Air Lines and Western Airlines dominated the Salt Lake City market, but they had established their major hubs in Denver. As a result, passengers could fly anywhere in the world from Salt Lake City if they changed planes in Denver. After the upgrade and the construction of a new terminal during the administrations of Garn and Ted Wilson, in the early 1980s Western Airlines moved its hub and headquarters from Denver to Salt Lake City.

Other changes took place in the city that helped its revitalization. During World War II, enrollment at the University of Utah had declined to 3,400 students. After the war, the student body boomed to nearly 10,000. Before 1945 most people thought that they needed only a high school education to make their way in the world. After the war, however, increasingly large numbers of employers demanded some college training, a college degree or even a graduate degree. The GI Bill of Rights offered a way for returning veterans to go to college at public expense, and those who had not served flocked to colleges as well. Enrollment at the University of Utah continued to increase until by the 1973-74 academic year it topped 21,000.

Faced with the flood of students, the university moved aggressively to construct new buildings and recruit new faculty. At first, the university held classes and housed students in many of the temporary buildings it inherited from Fort Douglas. Then between 1959 and 1969, under the administrations of A. Ray Olpin and James C. Fletcher, the university built 30 major buildings and a large number of auxiliary structures.

Nowhere was the change more evident than at the university's medical school. The University of Utah had upgraded its medical school from a two-year to a four-year institution shortly after the outbreak of World War II, and President LeRoy Cowles appointed Dr. A. Cyril Callister, a Salt Lake surgeon, as dean. Like deans and chairs of the university's other colleges and departments, Callister initiated an aggressive campaign to make the medical school into one of the nation's finest by scouring the United States for faculty and by promoting the construction of new facilities. During the 1960s, as part of the construction campaign, the university built a new medical center east of the campus and north of Fort Douglas.

(Above top)
The Utah Transit Authority demonstrates a device for loading and unloading handicapped passengers from UTA busses, January 1985.
Salt Lake Tribune photo, Utah History Information Center, USHS

(Above bottom)
Construction of a runway at Western Airlines (subsequently Delta Airlines) new terminal, Salt Lake International Airport, July 1984
Salt Lake Tribune photo, Utah History Information Center, USHS

(Left)
Salt Lake City Municipal Airport, September 19, 1962
Utah History Information Center, USHS

As education, the humanities, arts and transportation improved, Salt Lake City boosted its promotion of professional sports. Between 1915 and 1928, a minor league baseball team, the Salt Lake Bees of the Pacific Coast League, played at Community Park, which was later renamed Derks Field in honor of *Salt Lake Tribune* sports writer John C. Derks. The professional teams suspended play during World War II, but afterward, the Bees joined the Class C Pioneer League. As part of the Pioneer League, the Bees played teams from throughout the Mountain West from cities such as Boise, Twin Falls and Ogden. In 1958 the Bees returned to the Triple A Pacific Coast

With the increasingly easy access to Salt Lake City by air and automobile, the city stood ready to take advantage of America's increasing demand for winter sports. Colorado, Nevada, Wyoming, Idaho and California, had already begun the development of destination resorts like Sun Valley, Jackson, Aspen, Vail, Lake Tahoe and Squaw Valley.

To capitalize on the demand for winter sports, major new destination resorts sprang up at Park City and nearby Deer Valley on the east side of the Wasatch Mountains and at Snowbird, downhill from Alta in Little Cottonwood Canyon. Park City led the way. By the late 1950s United Park City Mines

The 1959 Salt Lake Bees baseball team
Utah History Information Center, USHS

League, and they capped their return in 1959 by winning the league championship.

With the completion of the Salt Palace, the city began to host basketball and hockey. The Salt Lake Golden Eagles hockey team debuted at the Salt Palace for the 1969-70 season. In May 1975, the Golden Eagles won the Western Hockey League championship.

In 1970 the Los Angeles Stars of the American Basketball Association changed their name to the Utah Stars and moved to the Salt Palace. The Stars won the ABA championship in 1971 by defeating Kentucky. Enamored of the new team, Salt Lake City renamed West Temple "Stars Avenue" until the team left in 1974.

Company had fallen on bad days. Revenues from their lead-zinc mining operations had declined dramatically, and the population of Park City had shrunk from more than 4,200 in 1930 to slightly over 1,100 in 1970. Many houses in Park City lay vacant.

A study conducted by Robert J. Wright and a second by M. Walker Wallace and Milton P. Matthews showed that, as a potential winter sports destination resort, Park City had conditions at least as favorable as such well-known sites as Aspen, Jackson Hole and Virginia City, Nevada. Moreover, unlike Aspen and Jackson, Park City stood within a half hour of a major city with a large population and an international airport. Although Reno, Nevada, the

Skiers scramble to get in line to ride the gondola to world-famous snow at Park City's opening in 1963.
Salt Lake Tribune photo, Utah History Information Center, USHS

Skiers aboard the original Prospector Lift at Park City
Utah History Information Center, USHS

largest city near Virginia City, billed itself as "The Biggest Little City in the World," neither its population nor the population of nearby Carson City could compete with that of the Wasatch Front. Under the circumstances, United Park City's board of directors thought they might make better use of their property by turning it into a recreation mecca. Moreover, since Park City had become a depressed area, the company qualified for an Area Redevelopment Administration grant.

After a considerable investment, and with the accompaniment of considerable fanfare, the company opened what it called Treasure Mountains resort on December 21, 1963. Salt Lake City businessmen John M. Wallace, president of United Park City Mines, and James E. Hogle, chair of the board's executive committee, stood with S. K. Droubay, the company's general manager to greet guests who traveled by gondola to the Summit House where a trio of yodelers and hot libations greeted them. On returning to the "Treasure Mountain Center," at the base, the guests could choose from hors d'oeuvres, non-alcoholic punch and hot spiced burgundy. Unfortunately, the expected crowds did not materialize immediately, and faced with increasing financial burdens, the resort was sold twice between 1969 and 1975.

Like Park City, Deer Valley developed on the site of previous skiing activity. After playing host to the Snow Train tours in the 1930s, Snow Park, the early name of Deer Valley, emerged as a resort in 1946 when Otto Carpenter and Robert Burns opened a T-bar tow. The two converted the T-bar into a chair lift, and they added a second lift in 1948. In the 1980s, Royal Street Development of New Orleans, then owner of the Park City ski area, had acquired an interest in Deer Valley. They poured in money to develop Deer Valley into an upscale resort with amenities such as Snow Park Lodge, glamorous in its rusticity.

Similar expectations of extensive patronage led to the development of Park West, later renamed Wolf Mountain, and more recently the Canyons. In 1968 Bob Autry and Don Redman opened the ski resort east of Snyderville, a town about four miles north of Park City. Like Park City, Park West experienced financial difficulty and the Ford Motor Credit Union acquired ownership for a short time in the mid-1970s before selling to Jack Roberts in the late 70s.

The expectations of catering to a world-class clientele that led to the development of Park City brought about the construction of Snowbird. During the early 1960s, G. Ted Johnson, who had worked as a handyman at Alta and ski instructor at Alf Engen's Alta Ski School, purchased a number of mining claims about a mile down Little Cottonwood canyon from Alta. With this base property, he applied to the Forest Service in 1966 for a special use permit to develop Peruvian Gulch and Gad Valley into a year-around resort. He acquired the permit in 1967 but lacked capital for development until 1969 when he sold an 80 percent interest in the project to Oklahoma oilman Richard D. Bass. Bass subsequently acquired Johnson's holdings, and in 1971 he opened a tram at Snowbird. A truly world-class resort, Snowbird offered vertical runs and powder snow that stoked envy in the hearts of skiers used to the terrain at Aspen and Sun Valley.

Solitude Resort just down Big Cottonwood Canyon from Brighton developed after 1950. Robert M. Barrett, fresh from a plunge in the Moab uranium boom, purchased a number of properties in the Honeycomb and Solitude Fork near Brighton. He secured a special use permit from the Forest Service and opened a base lodge and a mountain restaurant. In 1958 he started running a Pomalift and two chairlifts at Solitude.

Considered strong-willed and uncooperative by Forest Service personnel, Barrett quickly ran into conflicts. Complaints of watershed damage, unsafe lifts and failure to secure construction permits led the Forest Service to revoke Barrett's special use permit. Barrett's two daughters Judy Tschaggeny and Patty Barrett tried to run Solitude, but in 1968 they sold the family holdings to Paul Hunsaker. Hunsaker obtained a special use permit from the Forest Service and reopened the resort in 1969. In 1970 a cable-clamp failure threw several skiers from the lift to the ground, causing severe injury to a number of them. Poor design caused a number of other lift accidents until the operation closed in March 1974. In 1975 Richard Houlihan took over Solitude's operation. He renovated the lodge, replaced the chair lifts and made a number of other improvements.

Three other ski areas within a short distance of Salt Lake City developed by the mid-1970s. Powder Mountain and Nordic Valley in Ogden Valley offered services during the 1960s and 70s as local ski areas. Development began at Sundance about 15 miles northeast of Provo on the Alpine Loop during the 1940s. The Stewart family owned a ranch in the area and they ran sheep on 2,000 acres of the eastern slopes of Mt. Timpanogos. The beauty of Timpanogos's east side and easy access to the Provo-Orem area led Ray, Paul, Ava and Hilda Stewart to believe skiers would find the area attractive. Paul Stewart took the lead in the development, which the family named Timp Haven. The Stewarts successively installed a rope tow, a T-bar, a jumping hill and a 2,200-foot chair lift at the site. Timp Haven was an attraction for skiers mainly from Utah County.

In 1968, entranced by the Timp Haven area and believing in its potential, Robert Redford, the movie actor and director, put together a consortium to purchase and operate the ski area. Others in the company included Stan Collins, Hans Estin, Robert M. Gottschalk and Michael P. Frankfurt. They purchased the Stewart property, renamed the resort "Sundance," after the character Redford played in the film *Butch Cassidy and the Sundance Kid*, and made numerous improvements. They installed new lifts, extended the ski runs, constructed resort accommodations and added other amenities.

Other ski areas such as Beaver Mountain in Logan Canyon and Brian Head near Cedar Breaks National Monument east of Cedar City tended to cater to local clientele.

As ski areas sprang up in the mountains east of Salt Lake City, residents in the city tried to cope with racism. Increasingly large numbers of African Americans migrated to Salt Lake City during World War II seeking employment in the burgeoning defense industry. They often found it difficult to secure homes because of restrictive covenants prohibiting sale to African-Americans written into real estate contracts until they became illegal in 1948.

In addition, public accommodations often refused service to African Americans. Blacks could not swim in public swimming pools and many restaurants refused to serve them. Movie theaters made them sit in the balcony. The Normandy Skating Rink on Sixth South and Main opened their doors to African Americans only from midnight to 1 a.m. The Rancho Lanes bowling alley refused to allow blacks to bowl there.

By the late 1930s some Salt Lakers tried to follow the inspiration of the Nazis by creating ghettos for blacks. In 1939, Salt Lake realtor and Democratic speaker of the Utah House of Representatives Sheldon Brewster tried to get the Salt Lake City Commission to designate a portion of the city as an African

Rainbow Randevu, the successor to the Coconut Grove, was reportedly the earliest dance hall in Salt Lake City to admit African Americans on an equal basis with Caucasians.
Utah History Information Center, USHS

Salt Lake City attracted presidential candidates during the 1960 election. President David O. McKay of the
Church of Jesus Christ of Latter-day Saints is shown with John F. Kennedy (center) and
Utah Senator Frank E. Moss (right) in the Salt Lake Tabernacle.
LDS Church Archives

American ghetto. Although he gathered 1,000 signatures on a petition, the city commission refused to pass the ordinance. Undeterred by this rebuff, he tried to persuade blacks to sell their homes and to move to his ghetto. Insulted by this outrageous display of racism, African Americans and their supporters marched on the state capitol in protest.

African Americans who traveled to the city often encountered difficulty in securing hotel rooms. Salt Lake City hotels refused rooms to Metropolitan Opera contralto Marian Anderson in 1937, and Lionel Hampton and Ella Fitzgerald encountered similar discrimination. In 1938 Anderson rented a room at the Hotel Utah only by agreeing to ride in the freight elevator. The Hotel Newhouse made an exception to its discriminatory policy for Harry Belafonte.

After World War II, conditions began to change. In the late 1940s, Robert E. Freed integrated Salt Lake City's Rainbow Randevu ballroom and the swimming pool and ballroom at Lagoon resort north of Salt Lake City in Farmington. Adam (Mickey) Duncan and other officers of the American Civil Liberties Union met informally with restauranteurs and hotel owners urging them to integrate. Following Freed's lead and Duncan's lobbying, the better hotels and restaurants integrated their facilities and other businessmen dropped their discriminatory policies as well.

In practice, Utahns and Salt Lakers reduced the level of official discrimination at about the same rate as other Mountain Western states. In 1963 Utah repealed its anti-miscegenation law and in 1965 the state began to pass civil rights legislation requiring equal treatment of all people.

Most importantly, perhaps, the Mormon Church changed its policies. Prior to 1978, while African Americans could belong to the Church, participate in meetings, and hold church positions, they could not hold the priesthood or enter the temples. Hugh B. Brown, first counselor in the Church's First Presidency, had spoken out against discrimination, and Church President David O. McKay urged members not to discriminate against African Americans. In 1978 Church President Spencer W. Kimball announced a change in policy. Henceforth all worthy males regardless of race could receive the priesthood and all worthy persons could participate in temple ordinances and officiate in the Church's temples.

Patricia and Richard M. Nixon are shown with Elder Nathan Eldon Tanner, then an Assistant to the Quorum of Twelve Apostles and later First Counselor in the First Presidency of the Church of Jesus Christ of Latter-day Saints (left), and Utah Senator Wallace F. Bennett (right). *LDS Church Archives*

By the late 1970s Salt Lake City resembled other American cities in many ways and differed from them in others. Unlike many cities, Salt Lake City's downtown did not die after 5 p.m. when workers left the area. Because of the construction and development, downtown continued to attract many people well into the evening hours. Like many other cities, however, those who lived in the downtown area tended to be the dregs of society — the poorest of the poor.

Nevertheless, changes in and around the city continued to make Salt Lake a desirable place to live and to visit. The LDS Church took a particular interest in the downtown area, constructing buildings and beautifying Temple Square at various seasons of the year. The University of Utah had emerged as a significant university with a world-class medical school. The city's transit system had improved considerably since the decline of streetcar and bus traffic during the 1930s and 40s. The Utah Transit Authority provided bus service along the Wasatch Front with Salt Lake City at its center.

The available interstate and international transportation and well-educated labor force continued to attract businesses to Salt Lake City. Entrepreneurs had begun to develop world-class ski areas, and the cooperation of the city, the county, the state and private individuals promoted the arts and humanities. By the mid-1970s Salt Lake City stood on the verge of a quarter century of growth and prosperity.

Gus P. Backman, executive secretary of the Salt Lake Chamber of Commerce met regularly with President David O. McKay of the Church of Jesus Christ of Latter-day Saints and John F. Fitzpatrick, publisher of the *Salt Lake Tribune*, to discuss the city's affairs. *Utah History Information Center, USHS*

Between the mid-1970s and the early 21st century, Salt Lake City underwent a dramatic and fundamental face-lift, and during the 1990s, people in the city experienced a psychic transformation. New and restored buildings and houses graced the city streets. Apartment houses and condominiums sprang up in some neighborhoods, and a new trolley system flowed through the center of the city during the 1900s.

The Face of a Mature City

CHAPTER SIX

The Pearce-Browning-Auers home, an 1875 adobe home restored by Mike and Cindy Mitchell
Photo by the author

Committed to beauty and diversity, many families who chose to live in the city restored historic homes. In 1989, for example, Cindy and Mike Mitchell purchased the Pearce-Browning-Auers home on Center Street in Salt Lake City's Marmalade District. The adobe-stucco home, built in 1875 for a Salt Lake City basketmaker named Elijah Pearce, had belonged to a succession of families. The Auer family, who owned it from 1910 until the early 1980s, had remodeled it as a duplex. A subsequent owner had begun to restore it as a single-family dwelling when the Mitchells bought it.

The Mitchells spent two years planning the restoration and two years in reconstruction. With a considerable investment of money and sweat, they completely replaced the leaking roof, restored the exterior and reconstructed part of the interior including the beautiful hardwood floor. They renovated the remainder of the interior into a lovely two-story, single-family home. Professionals did about 80 percent of the restoration including rebuilding two original dining room windows. Although they had the exterior restuccoed to match the original owner's design, visitors can see the adobe walls in the basement. The Mitchells proudly attached a plaque showing that the house is listed on the National Register of Historic Places.

The Mitchells and their Marmalade district neighbors have restored a sense of community to what was previously a deteriorating neighborhood. For example, since the early 1990s, each year on the Sunday before Ash Wednesday, the residents of the Marmalade district sponsor a colorful parade and Mardi Gras celebration. Although the parade occurs on Sunday rather than Tuesday, participants march along Apricot, Center and Almond streets to a party at one of the nearby homes.

From 1960 to 1990, as the deterioration that the Mitchells and their neighbors deplored had taken place, many people chose to leave the city. A peak of 189,454 people lived in Salt Lake City in 1960. Then, as families moved to the growing communities of southern and western Salt Lake County, southern and central Davis County and northern Utah County, population declined. By 1990 the number of Salt Lake City residents had dropped to 159,936.

Observers have generally referred to the movement of people to surrounding areas as "suburbanization." In the late 19th and early 20th centuries, Salt Lakers, like residents of other cities, had followed the streetcar tracks into the countryside. The city fathers incorporated many of these areas into the city, especially those in the southeastern quarter. After 1960, as the automobile simplified outward mobility, an even wider dispersion of people occurred, and Salt Lake City either did not or could not annex most of these areas.

We should not, however, confuse suburbanization with a flight to the farm. Most of those who moved to the suburbs were city people as surely as those who remained in the urban core. In fact, suburban lots looked more like the homesites of 19th century Salt Lakers than like farmyards. The major differences between the 19th and 20th city, suburban and farm lots were conspicuous in such modern amenities as automobiles, sewer and water systems, electricity, television and dishwashers. Modern suburban homesites appeared less rural even than Salt Lake City's 19th century town lots, since they were generally smaller and most homeowners kept no cows, horses, chickens or pigs in their yards.

Moreover, as Salt Lake City's population shrank, the urban population of nearby counties and cities grew rapidly. Salt Lake County grew from 383,035 people in 1960 to 898,387 in 2000. Davis County surged from 64,760 in 1960 to 238,994 in 2000. Utah County expanded from 106,991 in 1960 to 368,536 in 2000. In bountiful northern Davis County, the population increased from 17,039 in 1960 to 41,301 in 2000. Murray, south of Salt Lake City grew from 16,806 in 1960 to 34,024 in 2000. Sandy, in southern Salt Lake County, sprouted from 3,322 in 1960 to 88,418 in 2000. In 1960 West Valley City, which adjoined Salt Lake City on the southwest, Taylorsville south of West Valley City, and Holladay, Southeast of Salt Lake City, were unincorporated parts of Salt Lake County. By 2000, they boasted populations of 108,896, 57,439 and 14,561, respectively. Moreover, West Valley City had surpassed Provo as Utah's second-largest city.

Although farmers still plowed and planted in Salt Lake, Davis and Utah counties, single-family homes together with some rambling apartments and condominiums rapidly chewed up the agricultural land. During the 1990s the unincorporated areas of the three counties actually lost population. Some of this is attributable to annexation of previously rural areas into nearby cities. Much of this development together with the loss in population came from a flight from the farm.

In general, then, the difference between Salt Lake City and the surrounding counties and cities was not that one was urban and the other was rural. Rather, it appeared most evident in the relative diversity of population. I use the term "relative" advisedly because a wide range of ethnics and classes lived in all areas. On the whole, however, Salt Lake City, tended to exhibit a greater degree of diversity in both ethnicity and class than the other cities, since a higher percentage of people of Western European ancestry tended to live outside the core city. In 2000, for instance, 89 percent of Utah's population was white. Salt Lake City, by contrast had a 79-percent white population.

Significantly, during the population decline, the number of Salt Lake City's housing units actually increased as older families and families with fewer children elected to live in the city in apartments and condominiums. The decision to move to collective housing was not unprecedented. Many of the poor had always lived in apartments, and some middle and upper class people had traditionally chosen apartments or condominiums as well.

Unlike the Mitchells and their neighbors, in the late 20th century, larger numbers of middle and upper-middle class Salt Lakers abandoned single-family houses which had been the ideal of 19th- and early 20th-century Americans. Some of these moved instead to upscale apartments and condominiums. Builders tended to concentrate these structures and their attendant work-out rooms, swimming pools and shopping centers on the northern and northeastern perimeter of the central city, on South Temple and on Thirteenth East.

As apartments, condominiums and shopping centers sprouted up in middle and upper-middle class neighborhoods some people stood their ground, and some, like the Mitchells, began to trickle back to the deteriorating neighborhoods. Many who loved city life opposed the eclipse of qualities such as single family homes, open spaces, gardens and private yards that had been the hallmark of 19th and early 20th century Salt Lake City life; and, as they experienced the loss of such amenities, they organized to exclude the apartments and condos. Since higher zone numbers represented more dense housing, partisans of single family homes crusaded for "down-zoning," and

battles between neighbors and developers intensified between 1975 and 1980.

No place did such disputes touch more raw nerves than in the Avenues. By the late 1960s many homes between A and Virginia streets and First and Sixth Avenue wore a patina of shabby decadence. Private owners and developers had constructed most of the homes between the 1880s and 1920s. As life in the Avenues became less attractive, families moved out and absentee landlords allowed the houses to deteriorate. Many owners punched in doors and added walls to cut up the homes into small apartments. There followed an almost inevitable decline in value, and when the time seemed ripe, many owners simply tore down the houses and erected apartment buildings, condominiums or shopping centers on the sites.

At the same time, confirmed urbanites began to recognize diamonds in the rough under the dingy exterior of the older Avenues' homes. Following a model well established in places such as the Georgetown quarter of the District of Columbia, well-educated couples and families began to restore the houses.

During the 1990s, as the population in other centers like Chicago, New York City, Indianapolis and Kansas City began to rebound, Salt Lake City's population grew as well. By 2000 it had reached 181,743, only 7,711 fewer than the peak 1960 population. Moreover, if the current rate of growth continues, the city will eclipse its previous high well before the 2010 census.

The motivation of those who chose to live in the city varied. Many chose city homes for the chance to live in a beautiful home, preserve a chunk of history and reside in a neighborhood of families who valued the arts, humanities and education. Many chose the easier access to cultural events, the absence of planned cookie-cutter development and the ethnic diversity that city living afforded. Some people with jobs in the city relished the idea of saving money by walking to work or by commuting on public transportation.

Some observers began to speak of "gentrification" — the transformation of a neighborhood from a deteriorating slum to a community of middle-class families. Anxious to preserve the historic character of the Avenues, critics of the destroy-the-old and build-the-new mentality gained control of the Greater Avenues Community Council, and they pressured the landmarks commission and the city commission to protect the historic character of their neighborhood. Through the community council they lobbied to revise the 1967 city master plan by downzoning the neighborhood to favor single family homes and to block out condominiums and shopping centers. They succeeded by getting the landmarks commission to designate the area as the Avenues Historic District, and in 1979, during the administration of Mayor Ted Wilson, the city commission revised the master plan to down-zone the area for single family homes.

Homeowners in other sections of the city replicated the success of Avenues residents until the landmarks commission had designated nine more historic districts by March 2001. These designations took place during the Wilson administration and the administrations of Mayors Palmer DePaulis, Deedee Corradini and Ross "Rocky" Anderson. Along South Temple, in the Central City, in the Capital Hill and Marmalade neighborhood, in Gilmer Park, in the University, Highland Park, and Warehouse districts, and even in the Fairpark district west of I-15 and north of North Temple, owners refurbished and restored family homes, mansions and commercial buildings.

Some found gems of art and history. While stripping buildup on the walls of an Avenues home, one owner uncovered the murals of a distinguished 19th-century artist. Others removed aluminum or asphalt siding to discover the grey sun-baked clay of adobe homes built in the mid-19th century. Owners engaged in the restoration of the Wilford Woodruff

farm home on Fifth East near Seventeenth South uncovered interior walls covered with plaster bonded with horsehair.

Significantly, middle class and professional families have moved into the city's west side. In 1995 Alan Barnett bought a home at 700 West and 200 North in the Fairpark district. A previous owner had cut the house into a triplex. Barnett did not know how old the house was, but after searching the attic, he found a circus poster, some old newspapers and a note left by a long-forgotten carpenter verifying construction in 1877. Barnett, a loan manager for the Utah Heritage Foundation, undertook a $60,000 project to restore the residence as a single family home.

The restoration of 19th- and early 20th-century homes led some businesses to recognize that many clients had lost their infatuation with the stark lines of the International and Bauhaus schools and that they had rekindled a love for Gilded Age styles such as Greek Revival, Victorian Gothic, Queen Anne and Second Empire. Recognizing the trend, many firms decided to preserve older homes rather than knocking them down to make way for new buildings. They purchased the homes, restored the exteriors and adapted the interiors as business space.

Many came to think of a restored home as a mark of taste and prestige for a law firm, insurance agency, accountant or other business. Signature Books' owner George Smith purchased a number of homes and buildings on the city's west side. The publishing company moved into an adobe home built in 1854. Smith restored a mom-and-pop grocery store with an apartment above that he rented to the Utah Humanities Council. Cooper-Roberts Architects restored and moved into an abandoned Latter-day Saints Chapel.

After his inauguration as governor in 1977, Scott M. Matheson and his wife Norma Warenski Matheson decided that they wanted to leave the modern home in which governors George D. Clyde and Calvin L. Rampton had lived and return the governor's residence to the Kearns mansion at 603 East South Temple. Occupied by the Utah State Historical since 1957, the mansion had remained in excellent condition, but the state had reconfigured the interior as office, storage and display space. Norma Matheson oversaw the 1978 restoration of the mansion.

The Historical Society vacated the building and moved to temporary quarters in the Crane Building, then to the Denver

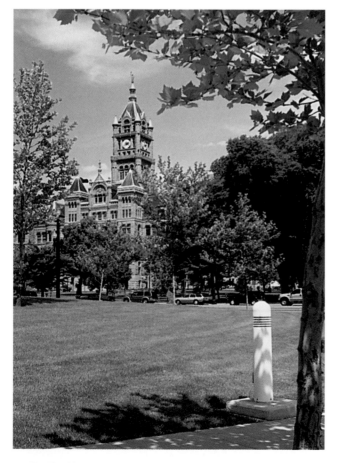

The Salt Lake City and County Building
Photo by the author

and Rio Grande Depot which the railroad company donated to the state. After acquiring the depot, the state renovated it as office, storage, library and display space.

Later the Union Pacific Railroad donated its depot to the state as a home for the Utah Arts Council. In the late 1990s, after the Arts Council found the space was unsuited for its needs, the state sold the building and the council occupied administrative offices with the Historical Society at the Rio Grande Depot. The Arts Council rented space in another building to store its collection, and it housed its folk arts collection at the restored Chase Home in Liberty Park as it had for a number of years previously.

As in the adaptive reuse of the Rio Grande Depot, some developers undertook the restoration of larger buildings and building complexes. The old trolley barns between Sixth and Seventh East and Fifth and Sixth South, for instance, had remained vacant for many years. Converted to the utility of adaptive reuse, developers Wallace A. Wright, Jr. and I. J. Wagner decided to renovate the rundown and seedy structures. Workers sandblasted layers of unsightly yellow paint to uncover the red brick often used in such early 20th-century industrial buildings. To complement the adaptive reuse, Wright scrounged wrought-iron light fixtures and memorabilia from old buildings scheduled for the wrecker's ball. The developers opened Trolley Square Mall in 1972 that included shops, theaters and restaurants. The mall became such an important tourist attraction that many visitors consider their visit to Salt Lake City a failure if they have not wandered through its maze-like corridors.

Similar adaptive reuse or restoration occurred in larger buildings in other sections of the city. Buildings near the Salt Palace became favored sites for such activities. Restored as a mall of shops and restaurants, Arrow Press Square on West Temple between First and Second South, was constructed around the site of a former printing establishment. As part of the Triad Center project on the city's west side, Essam Khashoggi and his family and associates restored the historic Devereaux House on West South Temple before abandoning the Triad project and leaving a large number of unpaid workmen and suppliers. Sculptor Stephen Goldsmith founded not-for-profit Artspace, Inc., and restored warehouses on the city's west

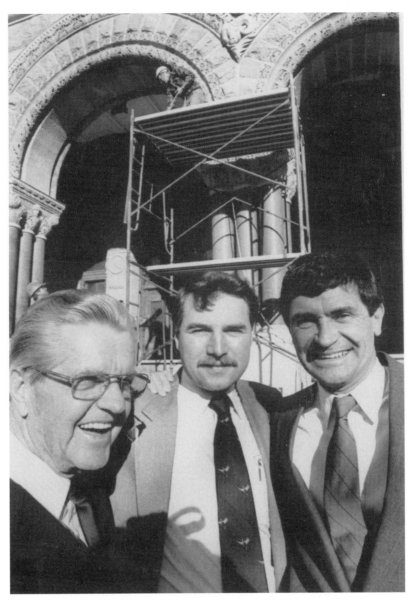

(Left to right) Commissioner Conrad B. Harrison, future Mayor Palmer DePaulis and Mayor Ted Wilson gather outside the Salt Lake City and County Building on March 9, 1989, as workers remove the scaffolding following the building's restoration. *Utah History Information Center, USHS*

side into commercial space and housing and workspaces for artists and their families.

Restoration took place in other sections of the city as well. After a large block of sandstone fell from the roof of the Cathedral of the Madeleine on South Temple Street, the Catholic Church undertook an extensive restoration of that historic structure. Salt Lake County decided to vacate the City and County Building in favor of a newer facility in the renovated Salt Lake County General Hospital on Twenty-first South and State. As sole occupant of the City and County Building, Salt Lake City undertook a $33 million restoration project under the leadership of Mayors Ted Wilson and Palmer DePaulis between 1985 and 1988 which brought the building up to seismic code and restored the beauty of the Richardson Romanesque structure.

In another example of adaptive reuse, in 1965 the Hansen Planetarium moved into the former Salt Lake City Library. Located at 15 South State Street, the Beaux Arts Classical library building was designed by Hines and LaFarge of New York City. Salt Lake City architect Albert Hale had supervised the building's 1905 construction.

The Delta Center shown here during the 1995 NBA playoffs
Photo by Craig W. Fuller

In some cases, however, restoration seemed impractical. Owner Larry H. Miller and other Utah Jazz officials found the Salt Palace far too small to seat the throngs of people who wanted to see games played by the major NBA franchise. Constructing an alternate venue, in October 1991 they dedicated the imposing glass and steel Delta Center on property north and west of the Salt Palace and south of the Triad Center. With a seating capacity of 20,400 people, the Delta Center has served as home for the NBA Utah Jazz and the WNBA Utah Starzz. The center also hosts such attractions as touring concerts of major artists, ice shows, rodeos and motor sports.

Similarly, the local governments state tore down Derks Field. Home of the Triple-A Pacific Coast League Salt Lake City Stingers (earlier called the Buzz) baseball team, the field had become unsafe and inadequate. Salt Lake Mayor Deedee Corradini wanted the new field built downtown, but she failed in the negotiations to do so. Rather, a cooperative agreement led to the erection of Franklin-Covey (earlier called Franklin-Quest) field, named for a planning and consulting firm that donated $1.4 million to the project. Franklin-Covey Field opened in April 1994.

The early 1990s witnessed a further transformation of Salt Lake City's large structures. Although the Utah Jazz vacated the Salt Palace in 1991, by 1993 Salt Lake County, Salt Lake City and the State of Utah had concluded that it lacked the space necessary for a convention and display center. The owners tore down the Salt Palace and spent $70 million to construct a much larger complex.

By the early 1990s, the state, county and city decided that they needed better judicial facilities than those supplied in the state capitol and in the Metropolitan Hall of Justice east of the City and County Building. To meet the need the Scott M. Matheson Courthouse was built. It anchors the southern end of the city's downtown directly west of the City and County Building. Completed in 1998 at a cost of $68 million, the limestone and green glass building rises five stories above State Street. The building houses the Utah State Supreme Court, the Utah Court of Appeals, district courts and court administration offices. Courtrooms in the building are the scene of most cases filed in Salt Lake County.

The Scott M. Matheson Courthouse on State Street west of the City and County Building
Photo by the author

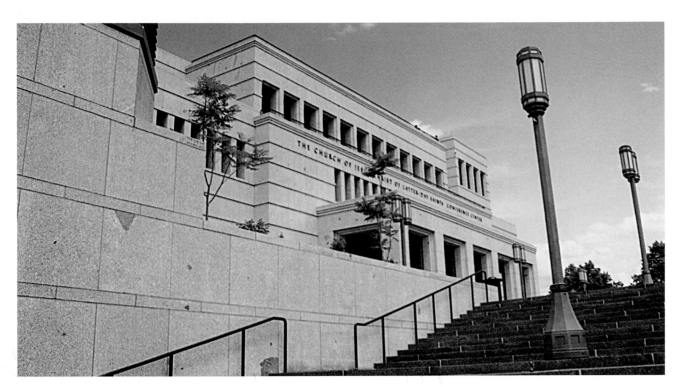

Salt Lake City then planned to fill the space east of the City and County Building with a new library complex. After tearing down the former jail and two court buildings in 2000, in March 2001 the city demolished the Metropolitan Hall of Justice. A new library complex is rising on the site formerly occupied by the structures. Salt Lake Mayor Rocky Anderson wanted to move the Hansen Planetarium to the library complex, but Salt Lake County Mayor Nancy Workman and the Boyer Company succeeded in providing a place for the planetarium in the Gateway District.

The Gateway project, begun in 1997 and opened in November 2001, is expected to revitalize the area near the railroad tracks on the city's west side. In addition to some working and middle-class residences, the Gateway District, as planned, will include a million square feet of offices and 700,000 square feet of retail space.

The Gateway development promised the rehabilitation of an area that had deteriorated in attractiveness and safety. In the late 19th and early 20th centuries, children and families had enjoyed the grass, trees and playground equipment at Pioneer Park, which lay near the district. At the turn of the century most people still traveled long distances by train, so the city's Rio Grande and Union Pacific depots offered many travelers the first sight of Salt Lake City. At the same time the area to the west and north of the park near the two depots, had provided homes for working people of the "new immigration" from southern and eastern Europe.

Then, as increased wealth allowed immigrant and second-generation families to move from the district, the homeless and poverty stricken remained. Moreover, people shied away from the depots. By the last quarter of the 20th century most people preferred airplanes, autos or even busses for long distance travel; and, as train traffic declined, the only passenger depot that remained consisted of a small AMTRAK station in the south end of the Rio Grande Depot. Even that was moved west of the tracks. The homeless — forgotten people, many suffering from mental illness, and most left in the wake of America's late 20th- and early 21st-century prosperity — began to dominate the area. In acts of charity, various organizations set up nearby centers to offer goods and services. The Rescue Mission of Salt Lake City men's homeless shelter on 400 West offered a place to sleep, the St. Vincent de Paul Center on 200 South offered comfort, the Salvation Army Thrift Store on 300 South offered low-cost clothing and furnishings.

With the deterioration of the city's west side, Pioneer Park became a notorious resort for the city's violent drug culture. Police ran periodic sweeps through the park, and the city has restricted access at times. The Utah State Historical Society, located a block west of Pioneer Park and a block south of the homeless shelter, had to monitor access to the building to prevent the harassment of patrons and the loss of valuable collections.

Many in Salt Lake City expect the Gateway District to reduce violence and drugs in the city's west side, but the plans make no provision for the relocation of the city's poorest citizens.

The Brigham Young monument was relocated on the south end of the park that stretches from South Temple to North Temple at Main Street.
Photo by the author

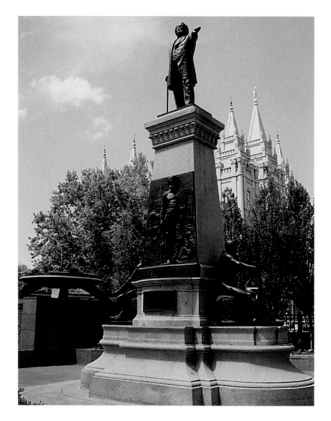

Under construction on a three-city block area running from North Temple to 200 South, the first phase of the Gateway project surrounds the Union Pacific Depot. By October 2000, the Boyer Company had obtained commitments from retail stores to occupy three-quarters of the $375 million complex. The company opened the first phase in November 2001, to precede holiday shopping and to welcome visitors to the 2002 Winter Olympics. Projected as a combination retail, office and residential space, the first phase of the Gateway will include a total of 503 condominiums and apartments. Utah Jazz owner Larry Miller manages a movie complex, and the Children's Museum of Utah and the Hansen Planetarium will both relocate to the center.

Other construction has changed the face of Salt Lake City's downtown. In 2000 the Church of Jesus Christ of Latter-day Saints dedicated a new conference center on the block north of Temple Square. The Tabernacle, which had served the church's faithful since the 1860s, had become clearly too small for even a small fraction of the 10 million members, so the First Presidency approved the construction of a new building to use for General Conference and other large church meetings. Although even this building serves only a small percentage of the church membership, it is much larger than the Tabernacle. In order to place the building on the block, the Church demolished the Deseret Gymnasium on North Main Street and

several small buildings and a parking lot on the corner of North Temple and Main Street.

Other changes took place in the city's downtown. Concerned about the impediment to traffic, the city moved the Brigham Young Monument, which had stood for most of the century at the intersection of South Temple and Main Street to a spot on north Main Street across from the west entrance to the Hotel Utah. The LDS Church remodeled the hotel into an office building that it renamed the Joseph Smith Memorial Building. The church owned the blocks on both sides of Main Street between North and South Temple, and in April 1999, the Salt Lake City Council and Mayor Corradini voted to sell the street to the church for $8.1 million for conversion into a park over an underground garage.

The church agreed to open the park to the public under certain restrictions with which the city agreed. Landscape architects designed the park as a quiet space for public rest, enjoyment and contemplation. The deed allowed the church to prohibit activities inconsistent with such peaceful uses such as demonstrations; skateboarding; sunbathing; smoking; or illegal, offensive, obscene, or lewd speech, dress, or conduct. Many people welcomed the quiet and beautiful open space in the middle of the city's busy downtown, and the church leadership believed that the restrictions on the park protected its property while allowing residents and visitors to enjoy serenity and solitude. In addition, these restrictions seemed particularly important since the public streets outside Temple Square had regularly drawn pickets and protesters, many of them extremely vocal, especially during General Conference weekend.

Nevertheless, the sale evoked almost instant controversy. Critics viewed the sale of the street as an LDS power play, and some resented the restrictions on speech and conduct. The American Civil Liberties Union, the Unitarian Church and several other groups entered a suit to rescind the sale, but at the time of this writing, the courts have ruled against them.

The controversy over the sale of the street for a park emphasizes the divergent responses of some visitors and non-Mormon residents to Salt Lake City. An in-depth study by Anne-Marie Waddell, a student at the University of Utah, revealed that most outsiders who came to Salt Lake City found Salt Lakers friendly and outgoing. Nevertheless, most newcomers had to adjust to the predominantly Mormon culture. Some found the liquor laws in Salt Lake City stricter than other places in which they had lived, though more lenient than in some midwestern and southern states. Some found it disconcerting that most stores closed on Sunday for lack of patronage, although Utah has no Sunday-closing laws. Nevertheless, most got along quite well with other the Salt Lakers and said that the Mormons they knew or worked with were generally friendly and tolerant.

As Salt Lakers experienced these developments, they anticipated the 2002 Olympic Winter Games. Salt Lakers had dreamed of hosting the Winter Olympics at least since the 1930s, but John W. "Jack" Gallivan, publisher of the *Salt Lake Tribune*; Maxwell Rich, former adjutant general of the Utah National Guard; and Governor Calvin Rampton rescued the idea from the wishing stage in the mid-1960s as they sought to host the 1972 Winter Olympics. Rampton appointed a planning committee and Salt Lake City put in a bid. The city lost the 1972 bid to Sapporo, Japan, and succeeding bids went to other cities as well.

After these losses, Utahns marshaled their forces to make a serious run for the 1998 Winter Olympics. In order to do so, the state constructed the Utah Winter Sports Park at Bear Hollow near Kimball Junction just off Interstate 80 north of Park City. To lead the bid effort, in 1989 the city hired attorney Tom Welch as president of the Salt Lake Organizing Committee (SLOC). Although some expressed vocal opposition to the Olympic bid, polls showed that a majority of Salt Lakers favored the games. Still, to SLOC's disappointment, after three rounds of voting, the International Olympic Committee (IOC) awarded the 1998 games to Nagano, Japan.

After losing to Nagano, whether accurate or not, SLOC officials believed that they had failed because of favors the Japanese did for IOC members. They believed that while they had handed out cowboy hats and salt-water taffy, the Japanese had contributed millions to get the games. Nagano Mayor Tasaku Tsukada denied the charges, but the SLOC officials, especially Tom Welch and his deputy Dave Johnson believed Salt Lake City had lost because they had not been aggressive enough.

After the loss to Nagano, SLOC officials decided to conduct an expensive and aggressive campaign to secure the 2002 games. Following this strategy, SLOC spent more than $1 million in providing scholarships, trips and presents to IOC members and their families. The campaign proved successful, and in June 1995, the IOC voted to award the 2002 Winter Olympic games to Salt Lake City.

In 1997 Welch resigned as SLOC president to pursue other professional activities, and Frank Joklik, a prominent businessman and SLOC board chair, succeeded him. Later Joklik resigned and Mitt Romney, a Massachusetts businessman and politician with links to Salt Lake City, replaced him.

In late 1998, however, the United States Justice Department threw ice water over Salt Lake City's winter game plans. Evidence of the payments and presents to IOC members and their families came to light, and the Justice Department

A view of the park sold by Salt Lake City to the Church of Jesus Christ of Latter-day Saints. The Salt Lake Temple stands on the right, the Joseph Smith Memorial Building in the center and the Relief Society Building on the left.
Photo by the author

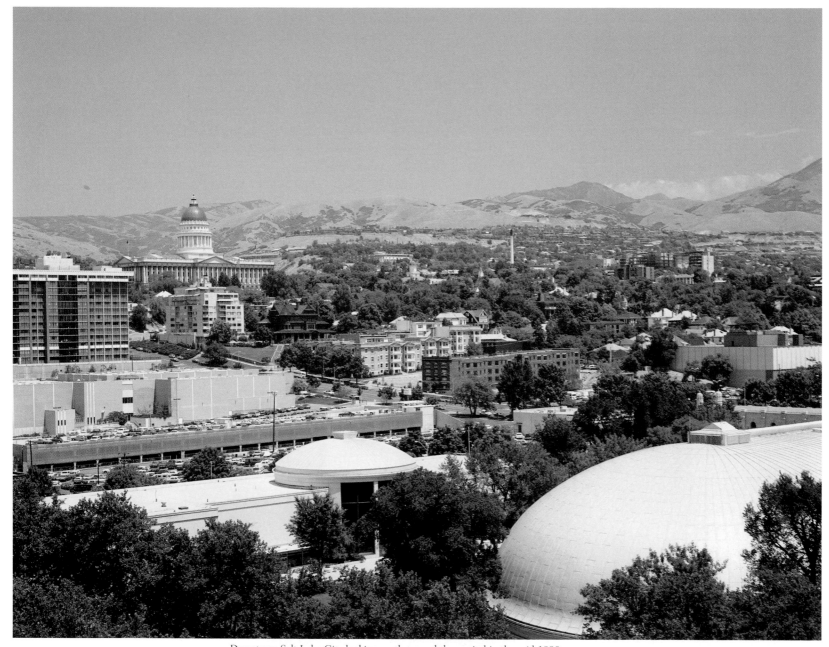

Downtown Salt Lake City looking north toward the capitol in the mid-1990s
Heritage Media collection

slapped Welch and Johnson with 15 indictments alleging offenses such as mail and wire fraud and conspiracy. On February 9, 2001, one year to the day before the Olympic games were scheduled to begin, Welch, Johnson and their attorneys sat through a preliminary hearing before U. S. Magistrate Ronald Boyce. Boyce refused to throw out any of the indictments, but on November 15, 2001, Judge David Sam dismissed the suit. Shortly thereafter the Justice Department appealed Sam's decision. The outcome is still uncertain.

Although these charges have cast a gloomy pall over the events, under Romney's leadership, Salt Lake City and the state of Utah have gone ahead with the preparations for the February 2002 games. The organizers found a large number of companies willing to host the games, the state legislature offered enthusiastic assistance, the federal government chipped in funds, most Utahns favor the games and patrons worldwide have oversubscribed the ticket sales. Both the Corradini and Anderson administrations have supported the efforts as well. As of March 2001 the federal government had spent $142 million (excluding highway funding) for the games, and it was expected Washington would spend nearly $400 million in support.

Most importantly, Utah has pushed ahead with the preparation of venues for the games. Although the IOC awarded the Olympic bid to Salt Lake City, the SLOC selected various sites at nearby cities and resorts in addition to those in Salt Lake City. The Delta Center, which during the games will be temporarily renamed the Salt Lake Ice Center, will host the figure skating and short-track speed skating. Organizers will have to remove several rows of seats to fit an Olympic-sized ice rink into the center. Long track speed skating will take place at the Oquirrh Park Oval in Kearns, a city about 6 miles south of Salt Lake City. About 25 of the men's and women's hockey games occur at the Peaks Ice Arena built in Provo, about 45 miles south of Salt Lake City. The remaining hockey games will follow at the E Center in West Valley City, home of the Utah Grizzlies Hockey Team. Teams will slide their curling stones in an arena on the campus of Weber State University in Ogden, 30 miles north of Salt Lake City. Competition between bobsled, luge and skeleton drivers will take place at the Utah Olympic Park north of Park City near the Canyons. Soldier Hollow near Wasatch Mountain State Park in Midway, Wasatch County, will host the biathlon, nordic combined and cross-country skiing. Freestyle mogul skiing, slalom and freestyle aerials will take place at Deer Valley. Participants in the alpine giant slalom and snowboarding's giant slalom and snowboarding half pipe events will compete at Park City. Snow Basin will serve as a venue for the combined downhill and Super-G alpine ski races.

The opening and closing ceremonies and the award of medals will take place in Salt Lake City. In order to accommodate the various Olympic administrative and media sites, the Salt Lake City administration has agreed to block off much of downtown around South Temple from West Temple to 400 West. The Salt Palace Convention Center will serve as the main media center. A lot owned by the LDS Church facing South Temple between 200 and 300 West will serve as the Medals Plaza.

The University of Utah will host the opening and closing ceremonies and house the athletes. The state of Utah has renovated Rice-Eccles Stadium on the University of Utah Campus for the ceremonies. To house the athletes, the state constructed a large housing complex on land formerly belonging to Fort Douglas. Since the fall semester, 1999, University of Utah students have lived in the apartments. The students will have to vacate their digs in fall 2001 to prepare for the games.

The games have necessitated new construction at some sites and the massive overhaul of others. The state of Utah built new facilities for the cross-country and biathlon competition at Soldier Hollow. Snow Basin owner Earl Holding, under a federal law sponsored by Utah Representative Jim Hansen and Senator Orrin Hatch, negotiated a trade with the Forest Service for land

(Left and following page top two photos) Demolition and construction of Interstate 15 near Salt Lake City. Power equipment has punched enormous holes to demolish the old freeway.
Paul Harbrech Collection, Utah History Information Center, USHS

(Far right)
A crane places a steel girder on an I-15 overpass.

(Right)
A backhoe and a crane tear apart Salt Lake City's Fourth South bridge.
(Both photos)
Paul Harbrech Collection,
Utah History Information
Center, USHS

abutting the resort. On the land, the resort has built new base facilities and other amenities, and it has redesigned its runs. In addition, the state of Utah constructed a new road from Trapper's Loop (State Highway 167) to Snowbasin to reduce the distance to the ski runs and to eliminate the need to negotiate the curves on State Highway 226.

The Winter Olympics and the needs of Utahns have necessitated a massive overhaul of Salt Lake County's transportation system. In anticipation of the games and at enormous inconvenience to the motoring public, the federal government and the state legislature financed a multi-million dollar rebuilding of Interstate 15 through Salt Lake Valley. Designed to meet the state's needs in Salt Lake County for 50 years, the project consisted of the reconstruction of 17 miles of freeway from 600 North in Salt Lake City to 10600 South in Sandy. Sections of the freeway reopened at various times during 2000 and 2001. The state announced completion of the project on July 15, 2001, and officially accepted the highway from the contractor on October 16.

In addition, with a massive infusion of federal funds, the state undertook an extensive addition to its public transportation system by installing a trolley in Salt Lake Valley. Following a lengthy period of construction, the Utah Transit Authority

(UTA) opened the trolley line, called TRAX, in December 1999. Trolley cars run between 10000 South at the Sandy Civic Center in southern Salt Lake County to the Union Pacific Depot in downtown Salt Lake City. The tracks run parallel to and east of I-15 to 700 South in Salt Lake City where they curve east to Main Street. The line then follows Main Street to South Temple, where it bends westward passing Temple Square, the future Olympic medals plaza, and the Delta Center to a terminus east of Union Depot. At this writing, UTA is constructing a TRAX line east along 400 South that is expected eventually to connect the University of Utah campus to the Salt Lake International Airport. The line from downtown Salt Lake City to the Rice-Eccles Stadium was completed in December 2001, slightly less than two months before the Olympic games begin. It is unclear just when UTA will construct the line to the airport, which itself has undergone a massive construction project.

Although polls have shown that the majority of Utahns favor the Olympics and are quite satisfied with the preparations for the games, controversy has dogged some of the decisions. SLOC has promised Utahns that they will not have to pay for any cost overruns, but some critics doubt their ability to live up to the promise. Some advocates for the poor and minorities have

(Far right)
A TRAX train, bound for Sandy in the south end of Salt Lake Valley, stops for passengers in downtown Salt Lake City.
Photo by the author

Mayor Deedee Corradini (holding the poster) and others celebrate the beginning of construction of the TRAX system.
Photo by Craig Fuller

complained that the SLOC seems heavily weighted in favor of the wealthy and the business community and that minorities and the poor have been underrepresented in the planning. Some critics led by the *Salt Lake Tribune* have complained about the number of Latter-day Saints involved in the preparation for and staging of the games.

As Salt Lake City prepares for the 2002 Olympic Winter Games, and as the restoration and demolition of old buildings and the construction of new ones have changed the city's landscape, the quarters of the city in which various classes live have remained relatively stable. Salt Lake City's middle and upper classes have tended to live on the city's hillsides, though in recent years, middle-class families have moved to the city's west side. Like spectators in an amphitheater, hillside people overlook the Gateway District with its poor and homeless and the working class districts in the central, western and northwestern sections of the city.

A quintessential neighborhood of single-family, working-class homes, for instance, Rose Park lies between Interstate 15 and the Jordan River in the northern part of Salt Lake City. Rose Park got its name because the developer chose varieties of roses for the names of the streets in the subdivision. Like many working class neighborhoods, Rose Park became more diverse as Salt Lake City's ethnic mix changed. In 1990 Rose Park was 15 percent Hispanic, and since that time the percentage of Hispanics has increased.

These Hispanics are part of a new migration that has changed the character of the United States. Unlike the "new immigration" of the late 19th and early 20th century, these recent immigrants generally came to Salt Lake City as families rather than as single men, and, instead of coming from southern and eastern Europe, most have emigrated from Southeast Asia, the Pacific Islands and Latin America.

The immigration to Salt Lake City from Southeast Asia radically changed the city's character. Prior to 1970, most Asian immigrants had come from China and Japan. The cease-fire in the contentious and unpopular Vietnam War brought more than 12,000 Vietnamese refugees to Utah. Refugees from the war-ravaged countries of Laos and Cambodia and from neighboring Thailand quickly joined them. A larger percentage of these

expatriates in proportion to the population settled in Utah than any other states except California and Washington state, as well as Washington, D.C. Many settled in Salt Lake City, especially in the central city and on the city's west side.

Like most new immigrants, the Southeast Asians generally took entry-level jobs and sought to retain their previous culture while adjusting to the mores of Utah's predominantly Euro-American culture. In some cases urbanites with managerial and technical skills found themselves flipping hamburgers in fast food restaurants. Others who had worked as farmers or fishermen had to remake themselves into urbanites. Although some were Latter-day Saints and others were Protestants or Catholics, most fishermen or farmers practiced Buddhism, and the Buddhists opened three temples in Salt Lake County.

Pacific Islanders, many converted by Latter-day Saints missionaries, poured into Utah. Utah's earliest Pacific Island immigrants had generally come from Hawaii, New Zealand and Tahiti. After 1970 an increasingly large number of Tongans, Samoans and Fijians found a new life in Salt Lake City. Many of these were Mormons, and the LDS Church organized several Tongan and Samoan wards. The Polynesians organized choirs that sang hymns in Polynesian languages and in English. They also performed traditional dances and served traditional food at home and at parties.

As members of Salt Lake City's oldest non-European immigrant minority, some African Americans moved into the city while many had longtime family

Drummer performs at the Obon Festival at the Buddhist Church, July 8, 1989. *Salt Lake Tribune photo, Utah History Information Center, USHS*

A Vietnamese couple take their marriage vows in March 1985. *Salt Lake Tribune photo, Utah History Information Center, USHS*

Utah Jazz forward Karl Malone, who helped sponsor the Special Olympics, is shown here with Marilyn Alexander at the Utah Special Olympics in about 1992. *Marilyn Alexander photo*

Dr. Ronald Coleman, professor of history at the University of Utah, accepts the congratulations of well-wishers after receiving the Governor's Award in the Humanities, October 2000.
Utah Humanities Council

The Rev. France Davis, chair of the Utah Humanities Council, presents Alan Roberts of Cooper-Roberts Architects a Friend of the Humanities Award, October 2000.
Utah Humanities Council

state. At the university he earned a reputation as an excellent teacher, served as an administrator and documented the experience of Utah's African Americans. In 2000 Coleman won the governor's award in the humanities.

As a community leader, none has surpassed the Rev. France A. Davis. A graduate of the University of California, Rev. Davis moved to Utah in 1972 to study as a teaching fellow at the University of Utah. He was invited in 1973 to serve as interim pastor at Calvary Missionary Baptist Church and has remained in the post to the present time. As a leader in Salt Lake City's religious community, Davis succeeded in getting the county to end the taxation of church properties. He helped organize the Utah Opportunities Industrialization Center that functioned from 1974 to 1996 to provide training for welfare recipients, to place them on upwardly mobile jobs and to develop low-cost housing. Davis also chaired a committee established by the NAACP to promote the adoption of a bill introduced by Sen. Terry Williams to designate Martin Luther King, Jr. Day as a state holiday. Later Davis led a successful effort to rename Salt Lake City's 600 South Street after the Rev. Dr. King. Davis also served as chair of the Utah Humanities Council and was one of the signers of the Alliance for Unity statement.

connections in the community. Even after the 1978 revelation announced by President Spencer W. Kimball of the Church of Jesus Christ, blacks continued to suffer discrimination in the state. Apparent racial profiling by the police tended to result in the more frequent arrest of African Americans and Hispanics, and the state legislature has declined to pass an effective hate crime bill such as that sponsored by Salt Lake state Sen. Pete Suazo, who died in an accident in the late summer of 2001.

Nevertheless, a number of Utah's most prominent citizens are African Americans. Undoubtedly the best known is Karl Malone, star forward for the Utah Jazz. Drafted by the Jazz after graduating from Louisiana Tech in 1985, Malone has regularly performed as the leading scorer on the Jazz team. He has set a number of NBA records, and he won Most Valuable Player honors in 1996-97 and 1997-98.

Well known also is University of Utah history professor Ronald Coleman. Coleman, who came to Utah to play football in the early 1960s, earned a Ph.D. and made his home in the

Although African Americans constituted Salt Lake City's oldest minority, Hispanics have become the city's largest. By 2000, 19 percent of Salt Lake City's residents considered themselves at least part Hispanic. Attracted to Utah's capital city in the late 19th century by the economic boom, immigrants from Mexico came to work as laborers in mining, sugar beet farming and the railroads. During World War II, Hispanics from New Mexico and Colorado moved in to take jobs in the burgeoning war industries.

The Hispanics belonged to a number of churches. Thirty to 40 percent of Hispanics belong to the Church of Jesus Christ of Latter-day Saints. For Mormon Hispanics, the LDS Church organized Spanish language branches and wards where they could worship and socialize. Through their LDS connections, Mormon Hispanics enjoyed some of the benefits of belonging to Utah's largest church, including access to a network that helped to find jobs.

Although the number of Utah Catholics is smaller than the number of Mormons, a larger percentage of Hispanics belong to the Catholic church. To serve the Catholics, Sisters of the

Order of Perpetual Adoration established a convent-chapel called Our Lady of Guadalupe in Salt Lake City at 528 West 400 South. Fr. James E. Collins served as pastor there from 1930 to 1957, and in 1961 Fr. Jerald H. Merrill succeeded him as parish priest. In 1965 Merrill helped organize a branch of the Guadalupana Society, and in 1966 the society opened the Guadalupe Center.

Beginning in the 1930s, many Hispanics founded associations to support their needs. These included the Centro Civico Mexicano, the Sociedad Proteccion Mutua de Trabajadores Unidos, the American G. I. Forum and the Spanish-Speaking Organization for Community, Integrity and Opportunity (SOCIO).

SOCIO was a collaborative effort of Hispanics from various backgrounds. Founders included Orlando Rivera, a professor of educational psychology at the University of Utah and bishop of the Lucero LDS Ward; Father Jerald Merrill of Our Lady of Guadalupe Parish; and others such as Robert "Archie" Archuleta, Jorge Arce-Larreta and Roberto Nieves. Working with Asian American and African American organizations, SOCIO promoted the organization of a Minority Advisory Board in the Utah State Department of Employment Security. SOCIO also promoted the education and training and set up a loan fund to start businesses.

During the 1970s and 80s large numbers of Hispanics accelerated the migration to Utah. By 1980 more than half of Utah's 60,000 Catholics bore Spanish surnames, and by 2000, 9 percent of Utah's population was Hispanic. Recognizing this condition, the Vatican called William K. Weigand, who had served as pastor of St. John the Baptist Parish in Cali, Colombia, and who spoke fluent Spanish, as bishop of the Salt Lake Diocese.

As numbers accelerated, changes took place in the Hispanic community, especially during the 1980s and 1990s. By 1990, 41 percent of the Hispanics held white-collar positions, and nearly 13 percent earned more than $50,000 per year. Whereas previously the bulk of the community had consisted of Mexicans and Hispanics from Colorado and New Mexico, by the 1980s, Peruvians, Chileans, Guatemalans and Cubans came to Salt Lake City to join the more established groups.

Although smaller than a number of other minorities, American Indians constitute Utah's oldest minority. In the 20th century, large numbers of Utes, Paiutes, Goshutes and Navajos have left their reservations to live in Utah's cities. The 1990 census showed that Salt Lake County had the second-largest number of Indians of any county in the state after San Juan County, which had a large Navajo population. The migration from the reservations to Salt Lake City and other Utah cities seemed reasonable to many because of the high unemployment rates and lack of well-paying jobs on the reservations. Many of the younger generation who have grown up in the city have forgotten the native languages, beliefs and ceremonies.

A number of organizations in Salt Lake City attempt to deal with Indian concerns. Established in 1953 and currently under the direction of Forrest S. Cuch, a Northern Ute, a graduate of Westminster College, and former head of the Social Studies Department of Wasatch Academy, the Utah Division of Indian Affairs has a number of committees and boards that address Native American interests.

In Salt Lake City the Indian Walk-In Center, established in 1977, helps to promote Native American cultural values and heritage, provides material assistance, offers counseling services and has a program for alcohol abuse rehabilitation. The center sponsors a monthly powwow for 400 to 500 participants and presents Christmas dinners and toys to about 600 needy people. The center hosts a number of fund-raising activities to help support its programs such as renting parking space for Salt Lake Buzz baseball games, selling Indian arts and crafts and holding auctions.

Salt Lake City is also the site of the Indian Training Education Center. Established in 1988, the center offers job training, counseling, education, GED preparation and other educational and job-related programs to Indians over age 14.

As Salt Lakers accustomed themselves to greater diversity, the city's business community changed in fundamental ways as well. During the late 1980s and early 1990s a significant development took place in Utah business when a number of regional and international businesses established their headquarters in Utah. Many of those have retained their independence and kept their headquarters in Salt Lake City. These include companies such as Evans and Sutherland, a company that produces computer software graphic applications; Huntsman Chemical Corporation, the largest privately held chemical company in the United States; Zions Bancorporation, a major interstate bank holding company; and Morris-Murdock, one of the nation's largest travel agencies.

Recently, however, a number of out-of-state firms have purchased Salt Lake City-based companies and located their headquarters elsewhere. In late 1999 many Utahns were stunned by the announcement that Meier & Frank, a Portland, Oregon-based department store chain, owned by the May Company and with outlets in the Pacific Northwest, had purchased ZCMI, a Salt Lake City-based corporation with 14 stores in Utah and Idaho. Established by Brigham Young in 1868, ZCMI billed itself as the nation's oldest department store. Most observers knew that ZCMI had lost money in recent years, but many believed that the company's management would institute cost-cutting measures to restore profitability. Instead, the company continued to amass significant debt, and its management negotiated the sale to Meier & Frank. For over a year, Meier & Frank operated the stores under the ZCMI name, but early in 2001 the company announced that it would change the outlets to its own name.

Utah's largest banking company sold to a West Coast interest as well. In March 2000 First Security Corporation announced that Wells Fargo, a San Francisco-based company with banks throughout the west, had purchased it. Organized in 1928 by Marriner and George Eccles and Jonathan Browning, First Security had acquired companies whose histories stretched back into Utah's mid-19th century. During the late 20th century under the leadership of Spencer Eccles the bank had flourished, though its stock had declined in value in recent years. By late 1999 the presidents of First Security and Zions Bancorporation had negotiated an agreement to merge the two corporations. In March 2000, however, Zions' shareholders refused to approve the deal, and Eccles worked out an agreement to sell First Security to Wells Fargo.

Other acquisitions have diminished the local ownership of Salt Lake City-based corporations. In 1971 June Morris, who had grown up in Manti and Salt Lake City, opened a small travel agency. Over time, she added services, clients and employees until by 1985 Morris was the 30th largest travel agency in the United States. In 1984 Morris started a charter flight company known as Morris Air, and in December 1992, Morris's company became a scheduled airline serving 28 cities in the Western United States. Morris Air offered low-cost service by pioneering such measures as ticketless travel, and the company became Utah's second largest airline after Delta. In January 1994, however, Morris sold out to Texas-based Southwest Airlines. A low-fares airline in the Morris mold, Southwest has expanded to include flights to most major American cities except those in the northern Great Plains. Several years after selling Morris Air, Morris merged her travel agency with Murdock Travel to create Morris-Murdock, the state's largest agency.

Although these changes have reduced the autonomy of some Utah businesses, they are evidence of the maturity of Salt Lake City's economy and society. During the early 20th century Utah's and Salt Lake City's economies operated as colonies of major corporations headquartered outside the state like Kennecott Copper, Utah-Idaho Sugar and Union Pacific. From the 1930s through the mid-1970s the dependence on federal expenditures during the depression and on defense installations during the Korean and Vietnam wars and the Cold War made Utah a colony of Washington. Since the mid-1970s, however, Utah's and Salt Lake City's economy have diversified so broadly that such outside acquisitions do not make the state completely an economic colony of those interests. The sale of such companies as ZCMI, First Security and Morris Air to other western companies, may actually benefit Salt Lake City. Each of these companies has considerable competition from other firms such as Dillards, J C Penney, Sears, Nordstrom, First Interstate Bank, Zions Bank, Key Bank, Delta Airlines and United Airlines.

The mix of local and national businesses in a city consisting of old, new and restored buildings and a wide range of ethnic groups underlines Salt Lake City's current vitality. From the restored houses throughout the city to adaptive reuse such as the railroad depots and trolley square, to new buildings such as the Delta Center and the Scott M. Matheson Courthouse, the city exhibits a vibrancy and beauty unexcelled in any of America's major cities. The new trolley system, construction at the airport, and the reconstruction of Interstate 15 when coupled with Salt Lake City's wide streets make travel to and in the city convenient and pleasant.

At the same time, Salt Lake City's population has become increasingly diverse. Though the city was founded by Mormons, only about half of the city's population are now Latter-day Saints. Catholics make up the second largest minority, but Protestants constitute a sizeable group as well. In addition, the influx of Asian and Near Eastern immigrants brought increasing numbers of Buddhists and Moslems to the city. The large numbers of Hispanics and other ethnic groups in the city highlight the increasing diversity.

Clearly, Salt Lake City is an urban place of grace and grandeur. As Brigham Young might have predicted in 1847, this is the "Right Place" for the Olympics and for other internationally significant events and activities.

Bishop Duane Hunt and Father James Collins dispense first communion to Hispanic Catholics at Guadalupe Church. *Utah History Information Center, USHS*

University of Utah intercollegiate champion, Cristl Hager, skis around a gate at Park City.
Manuscripts Division, J. Willard Marriott Library, University of Utah

PARTNERS IN SALT LAKE CITY

CONTENTS

Building a Greater Salt Lake City 126

Business & Finance 140

Community Commitment 150

Manufacturing & Distribution 164

Marketplace 188

Networks 210

Quality of Life 224

Technology 252

Building a Greater Salt Lake City

Salt Lake City construction and engineering firms shape
tomorrow's skyline, providing and improving working and
living space for area residents.

Bush & Gudgell, Inc 128

Thorup Brothers Construction 130

Granite Mill 132

Standard Builders Supply, Inc. 134

New Star General Contractors 136

Ralph L. Wadsworth Construction Co., Inc. 138

Bush & Gudgell, Inc.

ON September 1, 1948, Clarence C. Bush and George B. Gudgell entered into an agreement as co-partners of Bush & Gudgell Engineers to conduct a civil engineering business in Salt Lake City. Bush was a registered land surveyor and Gudgell, a registered professional engineer. Salt Lake City and surrounding area was then experiencing the need for additional housing. Realizing this, the partnership concentrated on subdividing land for many developers with whom Bush had become acquainted while working in the County Surveying Department. In a very short time Bush & Gudgell became the area's leading firm, designing more than 90 percent of the subdivisions in the Salt Lake Valley.

The partnership was dissolved on July 1, 1956, and a small business corporation, with six stockholders, was established in its stead. The firm was expanded to provide additional services in civil engineering, disciplines of road design, sanitary engineering, water treatment, storage and distribution, and planning.

The company has long been in the avant garde of technology. In the early 1960s the firm began using computers located in California to analyze water system networks. Preliminary designs were laid out with the components punched into a tape that was telephoned to the computer. The analysis was returned to Bush & Gudgell the following day to allow the firm to evaluate and make changes that would satisfy the demands of various areas. A few years later punch cards were used to assimilate the data read and analyzed on large computers located at the University of Utah. When desktop computers became readily available, Bush & Gudgell incorporated these into their work program.

When George B. Gudgell retired on June 30, 1977, the subchapter S was revoked and Bush & Gudgell, Inc. was established. John L. Probasco, P.E. and P.L.S., a Colorado A&M College graduate who joined the company as a junior engineer in June 1953, became president in 1984. The corporation's principals and officials are registered professional engineers and/or professional surveyors who have more than two centuries of combined experience and expertise in various technical fields. Robert Jones, P.L.S., chairman of the board, has been with the company for 52 years.

Emerging from an era in which engineers were largely concerned with parameters of cost, utility and the physical sciences, Bush & Gudgell has kept pace with changing societal values and the ever-increasing challenge to make creative contributions to the environmental relationship. The company has established and maintained meaningful interaction with professional societies, citizen groups, planners,

The 500,000-gallon reservoir at Bullfrog, Glen Canyon, was part of the water system improvements designed by Bush & Gudgell.

Bush & Gudgell prepared the master plan for this major marina on the Great Salt Lake.

ecologists, economists, sociologists and the business and political structures vital to the design and construction of both simple and sophisticated projects. This range of services includes economic and engineering feasibility studies and reports, site selection and land planning, preparation of conceptual and final design, contract drawings and specifications, and construction engineering and inspection to assure that actual construction carries out design intent.

Bush & Gudgell tailors each project team to include the personnel required to handle the complexities of a total project, engineering, technical, financial, legal and public relations. This begins with every effort being made to define the needs and purposes that the owner intends the project to serve. Combining this understanding with an understanding of other significant constraints facilitates the resolution of conflicts frequently encountered between the technical, financial, legal, interagency, environmental and social issues.

Bush & Gudgell has completed more than 50,000 projects, both locally and throughout the Rocky Mountain region, from Colorado to the Pacific Ocean. With such a history it is possible to list only a few of the firm's noteworthy projects. A major activity for Bush & Gudgell for more than four decades has been planning and engineering for the development of residential building sites. The company has planned more than 2,000 subdivisions, comprising 60,000 lots, including the only two master planned communities in the state, Stansbury Village near Salt Lake City and another community at St. George. Another major function is the planning and design of recreational sites including all utilities, road studies and landscaping. Bush & Gudgell has played a major role on many Lake Powell projects for more than 20 years, with the National Park Service overseeing and approving all engineering and design. Bush & Gudgell planned microwave tower stations across the western United States for MCI Telecommunications, a major longtime client. When MCI created its fiber optic network, the firm performed all site work necessary for repeater stations erected every 30 miles along railroad tracks in Utah, Arizona, Nevada and California.

Unlike some engineering firms that bring in business through low bids or expensive marketing presentations, Bush & Gudgell attracts and retains clients with the oldest and least expensive method of advertising — word of mouth. By providing only the highest quality service, the company has received a large portion of its work through client referrals. The firm has 40 to 50 full-time employees and conducts $2 million to $4 million in business each year. In addition to regular projects Bush & Gudgell also provides professional services to cities, counties and special service districts to help guide the governing officials important decisions related to capital improvements, control of developers and many other engineering-related items.

With members of the firm serving on various committees and boards such as the Professional Engineers, American Society of Civil Engineers, American Public Works Association, the Chamber of Commerce and Utah Council of Land Surveyors, it is not surprising that local work has always held a special interest for Bush & Gudgell. The firm hopes to lengthen its list of engineering contributions not only to Salt Lake City and the state of Utah, but also throughout the intermountain area.

The pumping facilities and water storage ponds for secondary irrigation facilities at Hyrum are examples of Bush & Gudgell's water development engineering.

Thorup Brothers Construction

THE three Thorup brothers — Kenneth F., Donald L. and Douglas O. — who co-founded and incorporated Thorup Brothers Construction in 1971 are third-generation pioneer stock whose heritage is indelibly bound with the struggle of the Church of Jesus Christ of Latter-day Saints to establish itself in Utah. The Thorups' ancestors, church converts who immigrated from Denmark and England to Utah in the early days of settlement by the Saints, include survivors of the Martin Handcart Company, the fifth handcart company to travel to Salt Lake in 1856. Because the cost of a covered wagon and team was beyond the means of most converts coming from Europe, handcarts were proposed as the means of getting more Saints to Zion (Utah). Members of the Martin Company arrived in Boston Harbor from Liverpool, England, on June 28, 1856, but because they had to build their own hand-carts in Iowa City, they did not begin their trek across the desert until a month later. Although it was late in the year, they continued on their journey, arriving in Salt Lake on November 30 of that year. The Thorups' great-grandfather, Herman F.F. Thorup, was a master millwright who built the doors on the east and west side of the great Salt Lake City Temple.

Prior to establishing their own business 30 years ago, the Thorups had worked together as concrete subcontractors. They started Thorup Brothers Construction to fill a niche that the local commercial construction industry lacked — a company that offered one-on-one consulting from beginning to end in a construction project. The idea of top management solving challenges on a construction site was a new one, but one which Thorup Brothers has continued to this day. Today, the company has six full-time employees. It works hand in hand with Pasker Gould Ames & Weaver, Inc. (PGA&W), a Salt Lake City-based architectural firm that has in-house electrical and civil engineering. PGA&W does design work and all the engineering required for Thorup and provides consultants for a project's design team.

The company has built 38 schools, several military projects, numerous projects for the state of Utah such as prisons and university projects, courthouses and many retail sales stores. It has also built facilities for R.C. Willey, a Salt Lake City-based furniture retailer, and Office Depot, a nationwide purveyor of office supplies, furniture and technology. Thorup Brothers razed the old Bennett's Paint Facility in Salt Lake City to build the largest Office Depot supply store in the West in a phenomenal 77 days.

Among Thorup Brothers' noteworthy projects is the new $4 million Box Elder Court Facility in Brigham City and a $3.5 million project for Gunnison Regional Prison. The company carried out all the site development work at Gunnison; prepared secure communications and all building pads; built the kitchen, laundry and

Rose Creek Elementary School, one of 38 schools built by Thorup Brothers Construction

Thorup Brothers built the largest Office Depot supply store in the West in a phenomenal 77 days.

carpentry shop as well as the maintenance facilities; and built all the roads. The construction company also built the $2.8 million medical training facility for the Utah National Guard.

For the College of Eastern Utah, a rapidly growing community college in Price, Thorup Brothers converted a former state hospital building on campus into the Computer Business Building. The $3 million conversion included a total renovation from footings to the roof.

Thorup Brothers' demolition of the existing Cyprus High School in Magna and unique reconstruction of the structure was particularly significant to the Thorups, as all three Thorup brothers attended school at Cyprus. Another project on Salt Lake City's west side involved Monroe Elementary School, which all the Thorups had also attended. This project involved demolition of the old school and building a new showroom for Gus Paulos Chevrolet. The Thorup and Paulos families have been lifelong friends, dating to their school days at Cyprus High School.

The unique design of Utah's Workforce Services Office in South Valley, one of the first buildings totally designed to address Utah citizens' unemployment needs, proved to be a real challenge for Thorup Brothers — the semicircle building is built around the Highway 215 South belt route. Another unique project was building the Utah High School Activity Association's building in Midvale. The association coordinates all the sporting activities of the high schools statewide.

Over three decades Thorup Brothers Construction has evidenced a continuous growth pattern, and within the past five to six years it has

been able to pick and choose the projects it desires to undertake. The company is totally bonded and insured, and attributes its success to several key factors. One is its unique approach to establishing a good working relationship with its clients, for it must be one of the few companies that is still willing to do business by a handshake or phone call. Thorup Brothers considers it a milestone that it is still able to do business in this way, negotiating all its contracts in a low-key manner. A second ingredient to success is the fact that it's based on personalized service, not layered management. And finally, in keeping with its belief that its word is its bond, the company ensures that subcontractors are all paid in a timely manner, well within the time limit established by law.

The second generation of Thorups has been groomed to run the company. Marcus Thorup, son of Kenneth, is scheduled to take over the presidency in 2004, and Michael Thorup, son of Douglas, is scheduled to become the company's chief financial officer. Both young men will assume their places experienced in all phases of the construction business, each having more than 20 years experience with the family firm.

Thorup Brothers Construction believes its business will continue to grow from 10 to 15 percent per year, will stay competitive because the company has found its place in the market, and remain profitable in good times or bad times. Its goal is not to become a super-giant contractor, but to be the base of ethics and standards in the construction industry. "Our good name is more valuable than the money," states Kenneth Thorup, a statement worthy of the ethical pioneer stock from whom the Thorups descend.

Granite Mill

DATING back to 1907, Granite Mill is one of the oldest architectural woodwork companies in the Intermountain West.

Though longevity makes this Salt Lake City company remarkable, it is quality that makes it successful. In every area of its operations — furnishing new commercial, institutional and residential buildings and renovating historic sites as well as contemporary landmarks — customers know that the products made by Granite Mill will meet the highest standards.

It is because of this well-earned reputation that Granite Mill has been asked to create the woodwork for 22 temples of the Church of Jesus Christ of Latter-day Saints, Abravanel Hall, several top Las Vegas resort-hotels, the Scott M. Matheson Federal Courthouse, the new Salt Lake City Library, the Delta Center, the L.D.S. Church's Conference Center, Stein Erikson Lodge and Cliff Lodge in Snowbird, numerous hospitals and schools, Eccles Genetics Laboratories and a number of major hotels, including Marriott, Little America and Little America Grand, Hilton and Weston.

The curved executive staircase at the American Stores tower

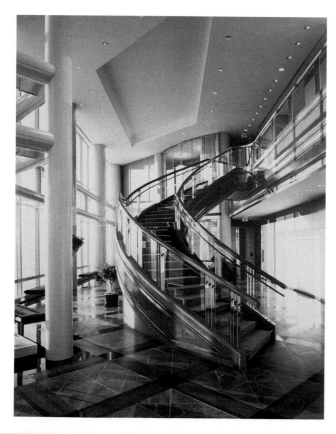

Among Granite Mills' restoration projects are the Cathedral of the Madeline, the Salt Lake City & County Building, the restored Governor's Mansion, the First Presbyterian Church, the Utah State Capitol and the Nevada State Capitol — to name just a few.

When F.R. Sandberg opened his millwork shop in Sugarhouse just after the turn of the century, he would have been pleased to know that his modest enterprise would still be around in the next century. His surprise would certainly turn to pride to see what Granite Mill would become: a prosperous and highly respected company with two affiliates and production facilities that would employ hundreds of people and occupy a quarter of a million square feet of shop and office space.

It took generations of hard work, integrity and customer-oriented service for the company to evolve from the small shop it was in the beginning to what it is today. In the early years, F.R. Sandberg and his associates generated their own power and got their lumber in horse-drawn wagons, often traveling as far as 80 miles to get it. Today, in contrast to the Carlos steam engine that drove the shop's original line shaft, Granite Mill now uses the latest technology in computerized machinery and equipment. Located in its current home at on South Main Street in Salt Lake City, Granite has pushed the boundaries of its service area, expanding outward to include all the western states and occasional shipments destined for jobs around the world.

In 1942 F.R. Sandberg passed the day-to-day responsibilities of the business to his son, Wayne, who would provide sound, forward-thinking leadership for the next three and a half decades. Wayne's son, W. Gary Sandberg, began working in the plant as a young boy, sweeping up wood shavings and doing odd jobs. He assumed the position of president in 1977.

Each successive generation of Sandbergs has overseen an expansion of the business, increasing sales and production by staying on the cutting edge of technology while jealously maintaining the quality standards that have been a trademark of Granite Mill since its inception. Today, a fourth generation of the Sandberg family is working in the business.

Sandberg is not the only family name that figures heavily into the history of Granite Mill. Several other families — the Allingtons, Jensens and Auerbachs — have had a multigenerational impact on the company, fathers passing on the secrets of their trade to sons for two, three and even four generations. Next to the quality of their products, it is this family-orientation of the business that gives its leaders the most pride.

Along the same lines, Granite Mill can boast of a remarkably high worker retention record. Currently, the average length of time an employee stays with the company is 18 years. In other words, when people go to work for Granite Mill, they tend to stay. That means the company's customers are ensured that their work will be done by experienced hands that know how to do what the job requires.

Underlying all this is a high level of worker satisfaction that springs from an atmosphere of camaraderie and mutual respect — a feeling that permeates the plant like sawdust, giving it its own special feel. It is an ambiance that makes Granite's team feel like a large, friendly family — not just a group of individuals who happen to work at the same plant.

Another reason for the notable level of worker satisfaction at Granite Mill is the work itself. It is, as one employee said, "fun." Many of the projects are anything but standard, run-of-the-mill jobs. They involve the kinds of challenges that Granite's craftspeople love to tackle — work they can sink their teeth into; challenges worthy of their considerable skills.

At Granite Mill, old-world craftsmanship meets new-world technology. Using traditional machinery and tools, plus advanced technology such as automated, point-to-point computerized equipment, the Granite team converts raw materials into a wide spectrum of finished products, installed and ready to use. The company's services also include drafting, design, factory finishing, domestic and international delivery and installation.

The restored stairway at the historical Utah State Governor's Mansion

While the majority of Granite Mill's work is in the institutional, monumental and commercial arenas, the company's involvement in residential projects is substantial. For the residential market, the mill manufactures and stocks wood moldings and custom doors and paneling. Crafting fine wood products for the residential marketplace is an increasingly important niche for the company. Roughly three-fourths of Granite's work involves new construction. The rest of its projects fall into the restoration category.

Anderson Mill and Fieldcrest are affiliates of Granite Mill. Anderson Mill complements Granite's product offering by manufacturing high-pressure laminate furniture and fixtures for schools, hospitals and other commercial, institutional and industrial projects. Fieldcrest builds kitchen cabinets primarily for single-family homes and multifamily residential buildings.

The ability to design and produce creative yet practical solutions to meet its customers' needs is one of the reasons why Granite Mill has been able to maintain long-term customer relationships, many of which span decades. The mill's skilled, artistic team is adept at working with architects, interior designers and owners to produce finished millwork that not only supports but enhances a project's desired look and feel.

With a long tradition of quality work behind it and a bright future ahead, Granite Mill is perfectly positioned for continued growth. In a city that has seen a number of mills come and go, Granite Mill is here to stay.

Wall panels at the L.D.S. Church Conference Center

Standard Builders Supply, Inc.

THE leaders of large, successful businesses tend to enjoy pointing back to their companies' humble beginnings. These roots can often be traced back to a tiny store, an old garage where first products were produced by hand, or a cramped office space in a dingy downtown building.

Standard Builders Supply, Inc. — Salt Lake City's veteran building materials seller — takes a back seat to no one in the "humble beginnings" category. Its owners and employees can point back to corporate origins that began in a 10-by-10-foot rented shack that served both as an office and living quarters for the two founders.

O.V. and Evan Hansen launched the Hansen Lime Company (the forerunner of Standard Builders Supply Company) in 1935. They acquired a lime deposit, built the lime kilns themselves and began processing their product.

The country was in the grip of the Great Depression at the time — a precarious time to launch a new venture. In fact, businesses were failing in droves. But the Hansen brothers kept their belts tight and did what they had to do to survive and move ahead. Back then, a load of coal to burn the lime cost $1. Heat for the small shack, which they rented for $10 a month, came from cinders they scavenged along the railroad tracks. Another $10 each month went toward the purchase of a truck.

As the devastating effects of the Great Depression wound down and the economy began to revive, Hansen Lime had proved its worth by surviving and was well on its way to success. Because competitors of the young company had gone out of

(Left to right)
Original owners
Evan Hansen and
O.V. Hansen

Standard Builders
Supply's home

business during the carnage of the Depression, new opportunities arose in 1938 to introduce stucco colors and all plaster and plaster tools.

The ensuing years were marked by rapid yet controlled change and expansion. Evan Hansen left to pursue other business ventures. His brother, O.V., continued building the company and brought Leon Miller in as a partner in 1942. They purchased property on South West Temple for the company's future headquarters. At the end of 1948 they added lumber to their line of supplies.

The following year Beehive Building Supply was opened. Three years later Hansen Lime moved to its new headquarters on West Temple, the property Hansen and Miller had purchased a decade earlier.

In 1957 Hansen Lime Company and Beehive Building Supply merged to become Standard Builders Supply, Inc. — a wholesale and retail builders supply center. The partners decided to move their headquarters to the original Beehive Building Supply site, enlarging it to accommodate a 7,500-square-foot showroom with an additional 45,000 square feet of warehouse space.

As a result of the merger, Standard Builders Supply began operating a Hansen affiliate, Lakeside Lime and Stone Company, and manufacturing DryMix packaged concrete products, packaging the cement sand and gravel near the Point of the Mountain at the south tip of the Salt Lake Valley.

Mike Hansen, son of O.V. Hansen, and Dale Ridd acquired the Salt Lake-based business in 1970, and Standard Builders Supply continued to grow. By 1980 the company employed more than 100 workers and was generating millions of dollars in sales annually. It had come a long way since the days when the two founders lived and worked out of an outhouse-sized shack.

After almost another decade of growth, Dale Ridd sold his share of the business to his sons, Vern and Jim Ridd, in 1989. Vern Ridd retired from the business in 1996. Mike Hansen and Jim Ridd purchased his share of the company. By the end of the 1990s Standard Builders Supply's sales had jumped from millions of dollars to tens of millions of dollars annually.

One of the fastest-growing segments of their business was their packaged concrete operation. This highly successful operation attracted the attention of a national cement company, which made Hansen and Ridd an attractive purchase offer and acquired the packaged concrete operation in July 2001. The sale, according to the owners, was a smart business decision. It also allowed them to concentrate their attention on their company's core business of selling products to home builders (about 95 percent of their business comes from contractors).

Despite national discount builders supply stores popping up in the Salt Lake Valley, Standard Builders Supply continues to thrive as a locally owned, independent supplier. It does not do this by trying to beat the large chains at their price-chopping game. Instead, it focuses on earning and maintaining customer loyalty by offering superior service and high-quality products at competitive prices.

The key to the level of service that brings customers back again and again to Standard Builders Supply is its sales people. They know their products. They know the industry. They know what builders want. They are trained to go the extra mile to be attentive to their customers' needs and satisfy them. Customers are typically assigned a specific sales person who makes sure that they are well taken care of.

Whether they are buying nails, studs or selecting styles for a compete package of doors for a new home, contractors and homebuilders enjoy having a personal contact at Standard Builders Supply — someone they know — and someone who knows them. In today's large and impersonal retail/wholesale environment, this venerable local business has found a niche that promises to remain popular for decades to come.

The Door Shop offers complete door packages for new homes.

A large fleet delivers a full line of materials and supplies to construction sites.

New Star General Contractors

A RISING STAR IN THE CONSTRUCTION WORLD

It makes a difference when people have a passion for what they do.

According to Dave Love, president and co-founder of New Star General Contractors, that's what has propelled the rapid growth and success of this relatively young company. Building high-end projects mainly in Utah's affluent Park City and Deer Valley ski resort areas is what Love loves, and he surrounds himself with people who share his enthusiasm.

Headquartered in Salt Lake City, Utah, New Star General Contractors is big for its age. It was founded in 1986 by Dave Love and Steve Williams. Both had been working for years for Cannon Construction, a major player on the Park City building scene. Love and Williams were top supervisors for Cannon when its owner decided to get out of the contracting business. Their boss asked them to take over a final project they had been supervising.

This forced them to form their own construction company — New Star — in a hurry, which they did in 1986 with only $10,000. Although the market was in the doldrums at the time, thanks to their contacts in the area and the good reputation they had earned as Cannon Construction's supervisors, they soon found themselves filling the niche left vacant by their former boss's abdication. When Williams passed away in 1993, Love assumed full control of the fast-growing company, which today does an average of about $30 million a year in business.

New Star maintains the high-end niche to this day. Almost all the company's projects are designed and built to cater to the wealthy — the very best properties to attract the financially elite. The majority of New Star's jobs involve top-end resort properties — multi-unit residential buildings, including condominiums and hotels. These often feature some ground-floor commercial space for restaurants, shops, or offices. The company also fills a niche (though a smaller one) in the high-end medical area. Although New Star builds all along Utah's Wasatch Front, most of its projects are located in the Summit County mountain resorts east of Salt Lake City, home of many of the 2002 Winter Olympics venues.

New Star also builds a few individual houses — but not just any houses. The homes it builds definitely push the upper limits of price and opulence. The least expensive home it has constructed in the past 10 years cost close to $2 million dollars. The most expensive home it has built to date — a 40,000-square-foot mansion in Montana — cost $60 million. A few years ago Dave and his team built a home in the Park City area for a well-known film and television star. The actor would fly in and out on weekends to check the home's progress. He had specified a number of unique and cutting-edge features for the home, and he liked to check to see how they all looked and worked while it was still relatively easy to change them. If he didn't like them, or if he thought of something different that he wanted to try, he would simply take a sledgehammer or crowbar and tear them out. When the crew came to work on Monday mornings, they knew exactly what he wanted to change.

Most of New Star's work comes from repeat clients. One such client is the Stein Eriksen Lodge in Deer Valley. New Star is currently building the lodge's third phase of expansion. Love and Williams were superintendents for the lodge's first and second phases of construction years ago when they worked for Cannon Construction. This is just one of the many long-term client relationships that Love has built through quality work, responsive customer service and "as-promised" performance.

New Star's mission is to give its clients what they want, when they want it, for the cost they want. This

Caledonian, residential condominiums and retail space, Park City, Utah

philosophy is instilled in all of the company's employees, which number between 80 and 140 depending on the current work-load. Love takes pride in the fact that his core employees tend to stay with New Star — even when they are recruited by other companies that make highly attractive offers. The secret: find the "best of the best" people, give them interesting projects, and treat them right. That includes giving them not only responsibilities but also the freedom and authority to do the best job they can. Because of this, most problems or mistakes are caught and changed by New Star's employees rather than by its clients.

An in-house woodworking mill plays a key role in enabling New Star to take an uncompromising stance on quality. By being able to control the millwork that goes into its projects, the company has been able to meet the unique quality and design requirements for the cabinetry, hardwood flooring and other woodwork that goes into its upscale buildings — and to meet deadlines that are often brutal. The mill also takes on outside projects and has become so busy that it was recently necessary to expand its floor space from 6,000 square feet to 20,000 square feet. Characteristically, Love has staffed the mill with exceptionally skilled craftsmen and equipped it with state-of-the-art equipment.

Sterling Lodge, Deer Valley, Utah

Another key to New Star's success is Teresa Love, Dave's wife. Teresa handles the company's human resource tasks — from maintaining a high level of morale to overseeing payroll. She visits the workers at all the company's job sites at least once a week, finding out what they need and enhancing the feeling of "family" that pervades New Star.

Respect for the employee, respect for the client, commitment to quality, and above all else, love for the work — with qualities like that, New Star will continue to be a rising star in the area's construction constellation for years to come.

Lakota Restaurant, Salt Lake City, Utah

Ralph L. Wadsworth Construction Co., Inc.

RALPH L. Wadsworth received a bachelor's degree in civil engineering from the University of Utah in 1957. After receiving his structural engineering license in 1961, he started a consulting structural engineering firm in Salt Lake City in 1962. Working on such projects as the Valley Music Hall, American Plaza Towers and the Red Lion Hotel in downtown Salt Lake City, and the Latter-day Saints' temple in Washington, D.C., Wadsworth also performed all the structural engineering for the 12-story Spencer W. Kimball Building, the first high-rise structure on the Brigham Young University campus, the high-rise Science Lab Building at Weber State University and the College of Nursing building at the University of Utah.

Golden Wadsworth, Ralph's brother, moved to Utah from Idaho and the brothers founded a construction company in January 1975. They started bidding bridgework, but the brother soon left the business, leaving Ralph Wadsworth with both the engineering and construction work. However, Wadsworth had a ready-made work force at home — seven ambitious, hard-working sons who all helped with projects after school and during the summers. Eventually, all seven boys joined the family firm and worked their way up through the ranks. The two eldest brothers, Guy and Cal, now own their own construction companies; Con, Nic, Kip, Ty and Tod remain with Ralph L. Wadsworth Construction Co., Inc.

The Ralph L. Wadsworth Construction Co. has enjoyed continuous growth in the construction industry since its inception by applying sound, up-to-date construction principles and practices. The company started by bidding on park pavilion jobs that no one else seemed to want and taking on other jobs such

A challenging project for Wadsworth was building the new Eagle Canyon Bridge on Interstate-70 where structural pieces had to be placed by cables over the massive steel arch.

as curbs, gutters and landscaping before starting to build small bridges. Today, the company specializes in the construction of bridges, overpasses, pre-cast concrete bridges, bridge demolition, heavy industrial facilities, water and sewer treatment plants, pile driving, concrete paving, structural steel erection, flood control, parks and recreation grounds, sports facilities, parking garages, pothole and slab repair, and other concrete-oriented construction.

The company's experience in the structural design and construction of bridges, buildings and many other facilities gives it a strong advantage over competitors. Wadsworth built its business reputation on bridge building — it has built more than 120 bridges and overpasses — and its name is linked with some of the most challenging bridges ever built in the Intermountain area. One such bridge crosses Eagle Canyon in Utah's "Canyon Country" between Salina and Green River. Wadsworth created a massive steel arch bridge for the westbound lanes. This required anchoring the bridge with abutments on the face of both canyon walls and erecting two 200-foot-high Sky Horse Cranes on either side of the canyon from which the steel structural pieces were hung using support cables, with the pieces meeting in the middle. Wadsworth then refurbished the deck and replaced the girders for the existing bridge, which carried eastbound traffic. The 400-foot-long bridges rise 300 feet above the canyon floor. Because of its reputation succeeding at risky projects, Wadsworth received contracts for similar bridge projects at Alpine and Green River, Wyoming. In 1994 *Intermountain Contractor Magazine* recognized Wadsworth as the No. 1 bridge builder in volume in the intermountain region.

Wadsworth's most challenging and labor-intensive project, building the bobsled/luge run for the 2002 Winter Olympic Games, resulted in one of the smoothest luge surfaces officials have ever seen.

Wadsworth's work is found throughout the Salt Lake City region. Wadsworth started the original construction of the Jazz Arena (Delta Center), handling all the engineering and footings work. Wadsworth also built ski jumps in Winter Sports Park, but by far the most challenging and labor-intensive project Wadsworth has ever undertaken was creating the bobsled/luge run for the 2002 Winter Olympic Games. Wadsworth crews installed 2,000 cubic yards of shotcrete along the 6,000-foot-long track, which drops almost 400 feet vertically. Every inch had to be hand-finished to within a 3/16-inch tolerance. During the two-year project more than 3,000 4-inch-by-4-inch beams and 500 sheets of plywood were used for the forms, and the project took more than 240,000 pounds of structural 2-inch piping steel for the forms and supporting jig bars. The refrigeration system is composed of 50 miles of 1-inch pipe. Winter Olympic officials have called the surface "one of the smoothest we've ever seen."

In 1991 Ralph Wadsworth sold his structural engineering firm after 30 years of consulting work and concentrated on the construction phase only. In 1992 the company created Wadsworth Design Group, a design-build division formed to more effectively meet the broad and dynamic needs of building owners and developers. With the expertise and backing of more than 40 years of construction, engineering and architectural

experience, this division specializes in the design and building of office, retail and warehouse facilities, bridges, water tanks and other concrete-related projects. Wadsworth Design Group integrates a project's process from initial design to final building, resulting in significant savings for the client.

One of Wadsworth Design Group's first projects was building a new headquarters building for Wadsworth in Draper. The company later built three lease/own buildings, thus creating the four-building Wadsworth Business Park. Wadsworth Design Group's work on Cache Valley Electric's Salt Lake City office earned Wadsworth the Best Small Project of 1996 award from *Intermountain Contractor Magazine*. A unique relationship between the Wadsworth companies and the South Mountain Project, one of Utah's largest residential and multiuse developments, led Wadsworth to incorporate the use of artwork in a railroad bridge. This sparked the attention of the industry and

allowed Tod Wadsworth to use his art background in incorporating artwork and concrete sculptures in future design projects. These include the intricate concrete detailing and finish work found in the single point urban exchange (SPUI) connecting Bangerter Highway and Interstate-15, as well as the Kimball Junction interchange that features 2002 Winter Olympic Games' images cast into bridge abutments. Tod has designed and cast as many as 100 different images throughout the Salt Lake Valley.

Ralph L. Wadsworth Construction Co. has 65 to 150 employees, depending on the season. The company literally thrives on the unusual, complicated and difficult projects that require engineering expertise, from bridges and overpasses to water tanks, street paving, pile driving and bobsled runs. Whether it's contracted for a $100,000 or $30 million job, Wadsworth is committed to the continuous pursuit of excellence in the field of construction.

Wadsworth Construction handled all the engineering work and footings construction for the Jazz Arena (Delta Center) in downtown Salt Lake City.

One of Wadsworth's largest projects was completion of Bangerter Highway, including the single point urban exchange (SPUI) with Interstate-15 that lets traffic flow with minimal use of traffic signs.

The Sandy city wall incorporates artwork — Wadsworth was one of the first construction companies to introduce artwork in construction projects.

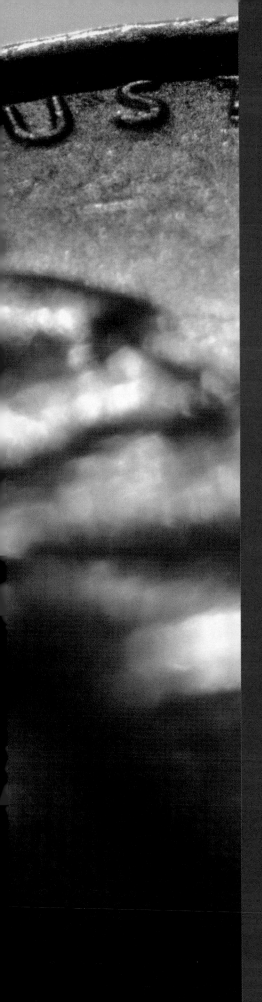

Business & Finance

Financial institutions and insurance companies
offer support for a host of Salt Lake City organizations.

Beehive Credit Union 142

Grant-Hatch & Associates, Inc. 144

Zions Bank 146

Zions Insurance Agency 148

Salt Lake City Credit Union 149

Beehive Credit Union

ONE hour each day, one day each week, Grace Hamal sat at a desk behind a pillar in the Utah State Capitol signing up and serving Department of Public Welfare Credit Union members. From this humble beginning in 1954, what is known today as the Beehive Credit Union was born.

Founded by the Department of Public Welfare as a not-for-profit Utah corporation, the credit union's service-oriented credo attracted members quickly. With the change of its name to Beehive Credit Union in 1971, the burgeoning credit union opened two offices. One was located in a small house on 438 East 200 South, which is reputed to have offered the first drive-up window in Utah: a string attached to a box which the teller pulleyed back and forth between the car and the window.

Irene Himmelberger, who was appointed president of the credit union in 1996, has witnessed Beehive grow and prosper

since she became one of its three employees in 1969. Back then, the triumvirate of employees did everything from managing the savings and loan activities to vacuuming the floors and cleaning the bathrooms. When Himmelberger signed on, Beehive Credit Union had 1,500 members and approximately $500,000 in assets. By the time she became president in 1996, assets had skyrocketed to about $100 million. As of 2001, the credit union's assets had escalated to $125 million, and its membership roster had growth to 22,000.

Growth has been both internal and external. Internal growth was the natural result of excellent service and conservative fiscal and management practices. Growth from the outside has come through a series of mergers — some of which involved smaller credit unions that were facing financial troubles. Other mergers were with credit unions that were too small to cost-effectively offer their customers the expanded range of services credit unions were allowed to provide thanks to the 1981 changes in credit union regulations. These changes gave credit unions the freedom to offer most of the services and capabilities banks could provide to individual depositors.

Already growing rapidly, Beehive Credit Union enjoyed yet another boost in 1983, when the Department of Financial Institutions gave it the go-ahead to serve the public in all 29 Utah counties.

With its current configuration of eight branches in Salt Lake County, one in Provo and one in St. George, Beehive is one of the top credit unions in the state in terms of relative size. But in terms of importance to the managers and employees of this financial institution, size takes a back seat to the quality of customer service. Firmly entrenched in an ethic of friendly, personalized service, the Beehive Credit Union team consistently looks for ways to become more efficient in order to give its members what they need and want.

Technology is one of their key tools in achieving this goal. When Scott Jorgensen came to work for Beehive Credit Union in 1984, so did the corporation's first computer. Jorgensen, who became CFO and vice president, has kept Beehive on the leading edge of computer technology through the whirlwind of cyber-evolution that has taken place over the past two decades. 1999 was a hallmark year for the credit union's customer services, when Jorgensen engineered the launch of a corporate

Web site, complete with rates, applications, contact information and Internet account access with bill payment options. With its many high-tech improvements, Beehive Credit Union's members now have the option of a wide range of Internet-based banking services and other electronic conveniences.

In the midst of ongoing progress on other fronts, Beehive Credit Union experienced one of the worst setbacks in its history on November 5, 1998, with the loss of a 10-year lawsuit to the Utah Bankers Association. For 15 years the financial institution had been able to serve the residents of all 29 counties. The lawsuit restricted membership to residents of only two counties: Salt Lake County and Utah County. With 27

counties cut out of its market area, Beehive Credit Union found itself having to compete with 78 other credit unions in the much-restricted area.

Though Beehive suffered a loss of potential members as a result of the ruling, the backbone of this corporation remains strong as it focuses on growth of capital and surplus profits while continuing to offer customer-pleasing service. The credit union's volunteer board of directors is composed of seven people who are elected by the institution's members and serve rotating terms. A supervisory committee consists of five volunteers selected by the board of directors. Members of this committee serve non-expiring terms and work independently with the board. The supervisory committee serves as a "watch dog" for members.

From top to bottom, the people who form the credit union's team adhere to a strict standard of responsible management and high ethics. The corporation's operating philosophy is grounded in the belief that success requires a healthy corporate environment, which in turn demands a high standard of ethics, integrity and go-the-extra-mile customer service. These standards, according to Beehive's leaders and staff, have enabled them to maintain a winning edge in an extremely competitive market.

Several awards and recognitions from community organizations have substantiated Beehive's excellence. For example, Granite Education Foundation named Beehive Credit

Union "Business Coordinator of the Year" in 1999 — a high accomplishment considering the number of businesses that sponsor community schools.

Beehive has adopted the theme "Working with People" to reflect the importance its people attach to serving their members and the community. This is more than a mere attitude. It has concrete ramifications. For instance, branch sizes have been purposely kept smaller than the norm in order to maintain the personal feel. The credit union team takes pride in being perceived as a small, friendly and helpful financial institution — one that has distinguished itself for decades by establishing personalized relationships with its members, especially in today's depersonalized banking environment.

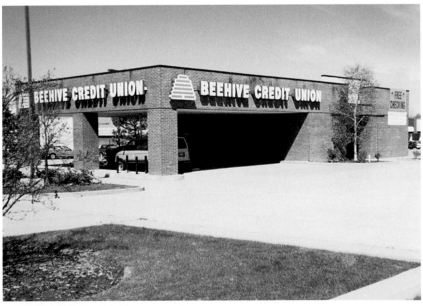

Grant-Hatch & Associates, Inc.

FOR well over a century, Grant-Hatch & Associates, Inc. has enjoyed an illustrious career in the spotlight of the beautiful Salt Lake Valley. As a premier leader in the insurance industry since 1886, Grant-Hatch has safeguarded some of the most magnificent and historic properties in downtown Salt Lake City and beyond. In short, the oldest and betimes largest agency in the history of the state has had a significant impact on the growth and development of the Utah community.

In 1886, Heber J. Grant, prophet and presiding leader of the Church of Jesus Christ of Latter-day Saints, started a general insurance agency to provide for the needs of the people who had settled in the valley. Grant was an unusual prophet by the simple fact that beyond his notable ecclesiastical skills, he was also an extremely competent business leader. Once Grant identified specific needs of the Saints in the area, he took appropriate steps to ensure that those needs were met. One issue he was extremely concerned about was the fact that Utah residents lacked essential fire protection. House fires were common in those days and quite devastating to the families they affected. For that reason, Grant organized an insurance company called the Utah Home Fire Company and subsequently formed a general agency to sell the products of Utah Home Fire and other insurance companies.

Staff at Heber J. Grant Company surely rejoiced over typewriters, when policies written in longhand became a thing of the past.

The agency was named Heber J. Grant & Company. It specialized in personal and commercial insurance. Grant used his business sense to build a solid foundation on loyalty, integrity and service of the highest quality. Three generations of the Grant family went on to continue his principles of representing the interests of Utah residents by protecting their homes, autos and businesses. Many of these entities are of unique interest to the history of the area, such as The Hotel Utah, Beneficial Life Insurance Company and Utah-Idaho Sugar.

Then in 1928, J. Eastman Hatch founded a commercial insurance agency called Eastman Hatch & Company. Hatch adhered to many of the same principles of integrity and service as Grant's agency. He also believed in understanding the client fully before offering coverage on exposures. In other words, Hatch never wrote a policy until he fully understood what coverage would truly help his clients succeed. Eastman Hatch began to enjoy an enviable reputation in the realm of commercial insurance. Grant's agency and Eastman Hatch became friendly competitors.

For almost 90 years the Grant office was located in downtown Salt Lake City. Although it had begun as a general agency, the Grant Company had developed both personal and commercial lines of insurance and was represented by more than 500 agents. Then in 1975,

Grant-Hatch & Associates as it stands today, with 18 employees, state-of-the-art equipment, a global mentality but old-world values

the principals of the organization sold the general agency portion of the business and retained the retail operation. Eastman Hatch was contemplating changes of its own, and the two companies met to see if a mutually beneficial arrangement could be developed.

And so it was that the Heber J. Grant Company and Eastman Hatch & Company decided to integrate. The reasons were many; convenience and continuity were perhaps the primary determining factors, particularly since Mr. Hatch was in his 80s and ready to retire. He was delighted to merge with an organization of similar reputation and standards. It was a natural fit. The two companies already shared comparable books of business, had comparable associations and had at times worked jointly on the same accounts. These two recent yet friendly competitors now brought their best to the table, forging individual strengths into a larger, more effective agency than ever before.

In honor of the original founders, the new agency's name became Grant-Hatch & Associates, Inc. The traditions and principles that had served the community so well for nearly a century were successfully passed to another generation. Grant-Hatch continued to enjoy long-term affiliations with clients and the companies they represented. Grant-Hatch had the pleasure of continuing to protect some of Salt Lake City's most historic properties and ensuring the success of many projects along the Wasatch front and elsewhere in the state.

Today, the legacy of Grant-Hatch lives on. The agency has become fully modernized with 18 employees and offices overlooking downtown Salt Lake City. Between the current principals and the employees, the agency has more than 250 years combined experience. Grant-Hatch's key focus has become industrial, commercial and surety bonds. Like its predecessors, the company carefully reviews its clients' individual needs. However, the new leaders perceive themselves as much more than simply agents; they are planners, advisors, originators and problem solvers who take great pride in constant contact with customers as well as constant personal attention to detail. In fact, this matchless customer service has propelled Grant-Hatch to the forefront of the global marketplace where it now insures and protects properties worldwide, and where new and old clients alike appreciate the company's integrity, stability and strength.

Zions Bank

ON July 1, 1873, in the midst of a financial crisis back east, Mormon leader Brigham Young called together a group of 12 of Salt Lake's leading citizens to consider a matter that had been on his mind for a long time, that of organizing a savings bank. Such a venture was born out of the pioneering spirit that had allowed the Mormons to establish new industries in this desert country where none had been three decades before. The bank was incorporated five days later under Utah Territorial laws with a capital stock of $200,000 and given the name Brigham Young had suggested — Zion's Savings Bank and Trust Company.

For more than 127 years Zions Bank has played an integral role in the development of Salt Lake City. There are few long-established businesses in the community that didn't have the help of Zions Bank in getting off the ground. And today Zions

Bank is still a pioneering institution, for it is in the forefront in utilizing electronic technology to serve its customers.

HISTORIC DOWNTOWN PRESENCE

The bank was opened on October 1, 1873, in the middle of the block on the east side of Main Street, between South Temple and 100 South. One of Zions Bank's early homes still stands today at First South and Main, at what became known as "the Old Clock Corner," named for the clock in front of the building. Made in Philadelphia by Robert Wood & Co., the beautiful timepiece on a pedestal of bronze and iron was brought to Salt Lake by ox team and wagon. Generations of citizens have used the clock to meet streetcar and bus schedules — it is one of the landmarks residents and business people still rely on.

As the bank expanded it required larger quarters. In 1889 Zions Bank constructed the six-story Templeton Building, whose lower-floor housing was made of granite and its upper stories of brick. It occupied space there until the building was demolished in 1959. Zions Bank moved into the Kennecott Building in 1965.

PASSING SAFELY THROUGH TROUBLED WATERS

The panic of 1893 provided anxious moments at Zions Bank. The panic was linked to the bitter battle over silver coinage, so it was naturally felt sharply in Utah, but the faith and integrity of Zion's Savings Bank officials met the test. Zions president Wilford Woodruff sent Heber J. Grant to New York to attempt to raise badly needed cash by selling $100,000 of 6 percent notes held by a sister bank. Bankers whom Grant encountered en route to New York assured him it could not be done, yet he sold $88,000 worth of the notes in New York in 48 hours and the bank withstood the panic.

On February 15, 1932, the day after Deseret Savings Bank failed, many worried depositors showed up at Zion's Savings Bank's office, passbooks in hand. A run on the bank began. Within three days more than $1.5 million was withdrawn. President Orval Adams managed to get $1 million sent from New York, brought it to the bank in a Federal Reserve armored car, laid it on the counter in great stacks of greenbacks and said loudly: "Now here is $1 million and there is plenty more to

Zions Bank's first account was opened by Brigham Young (photo inset).

come. Everybody will get his money. Just stand in line and wait your turn." When depositors were assured that the LDS Church was the largest stockholder in Zions Bank, the run quickly ended. Within a few days more money had been redeposited than had been withdrawn.

THIRTY YEARS OF GROWTH

Because the early Mormon pioneers founded Zions Bank, there is a perception that the bank is owned by the LDS Church today. However, in 1960 the LDS Church sold its 57.5 percent interest in Zions First National Bank — created by a merger of First National Bank of Salt Lake City, Utah Savings and Trust Company, and Zion's Savings Bank and Trust Company in 1957 — to Roy Simmons and others. The holding company, Zions Bancorporation (ZBC) was created in 1966.

Due to profitable expansion Zions Bank now has nearly 150 branches in Utah and Idaho, 47 located in the Salt Lake Valley alone. Roy Simmons is now chair of ZBC. His son, Harris Simmons, who became Zions Bank president in 1986, is now chair of Zions Bank and president and CEO of ZBC. Scott Anderson has been president of Zions Bank since 1998.

MANY "FIRSTS"

Zions Bank was the first chartered savings bank in Utah, the first to develop a trust department and the first to establish a presence in a shopping mall. In 1997, the Zions Bank Women's Financial Group, was established to meet the unique financial needs of women in business and women in general. It was the first of its kind in Utah and perhaps in the nation. In December 1997 it became the first U.S. bank to receive approval to underwrite municipal revenue bonds. In January 1998 it became the first U.S. bank to win approval to offer digital signature repository service. (A digital signature is a string of numbers that identifies a particular customer and sends a secure encrypted message electronically.) Zions Bank provided the digital signature President Bill Clinton used in enacting the Electronic Signature Bill, which makes digital signatures legally binding. Online banking allows customers to access information at any time.

The old clock at First South and Main is a landmark residents and businesspeople still rely on.

PIONEERING SPIRIT CONTINUES

Zions Bank continually looks for new ways to provide customer-friendly, secure banking choices and for innovative, unique ways to provide funding for projects that benefit entire communities. Zions Bank recognizes the significant role its employees play in ZBC being named the "nation's top performing bank" by U.S. Banker (1997). ZBC was ranked by *The Wall Street Journal* and *Fortune* in 2000 as the top bank in the country in terms of return to stockholders, based on a 10-year average return. Noted for its trust and stability through 127 years, Zions Bank has every expectation that it will serve the needs of Utahans for another 127 years.

Zions Insurance Agency

TRUST and tradition are vital elements for success in the insurance industry, and few — if any — agencies rate higher in those areas than Zions Insurance Agency. With a history stretching back more than a century (one of the company's parent entities was founded in 1874), Zions is one of the oldest, most respected and largest personal insurance agencies in Utah.

Through the years, Zions has built a solid reputation for offering outstanding service to its more than 17,000 clients. Although the agency provides services for an impressive number of large businesses and corporations, it focuses on small-business owners and individual consumers, a target audience that allows Zions to capitalize on its ability to write custom-designed insurance coverage.

The sheer number and types of insurance coverage available is staggering. The business specialists at Zions thoroughly understand the many facets of insurance coverage. They also recognize that most insurance companies offer the same products; it's how those products are delivered that sets an organization apart.

Though Zions is part of a large corporation (the agency is a wholly owned subsidiary of Zions Bancorporation), it maintains an individualized, one-on-one way of doing business. Zions prides itself on offering all the resources of large agencies while providing the intimate, "home-town" touch of smaller agencies. Its independent status allows its business specialists to offer competitive alternatives from more than 50 different insurance

companies and broker to hundreds more. This approach practically guarantees that Zions agents can custom build the right insurance package for the right price for almost any client.

The approach works. The company, which has offices in Salt Lake City and Layton as well as business specialists who work out of bank branches in Idaho, Nevada and other parts of Utah, has steadily increased its profitability and clientele through the years. In addition, future plans call for expansion into Arizona and California. With its steady growth, Zions has become a silent partner behind numerous successful companies, providing products and services necessary for growth while confidently managing the accompanying risks of building a successful business.

> Zions prides itself on offering all the resources of large agencies while providing the intimate, "home-town" touch of smaller agencies.

Each client brings different needs to the table. Business owners, whether small or large, might be looking for anything from real property, pollution and equipment breakdown coverage to bonding and professional liability. Zions offers all of these and much more. The individual consumer can select anything from homeowners and auto insurance to private risk management and term, universal or whole life insurance. In a world where cookie-cutter insurance is no longer adequate, the choices provided by Zions bring peace of mind and security to its growing number of satisfied clients.

Zions is committed to utilizing the latest insurance and industry technology, as well as its vast resources and experience, to meet the specific insurance needs of each of its clients — a commitment that ensures the agency will continue to be regarded by its clients as a trusted partner and friend.

Salt Lake City Credit Union

THE five-story, Richardson Romanesque-style City and County Building completed in 1894 is Salt Lake City's most regal municipal building. This elegant building was also the place where Salt Lake City Credit Union had its humble beginnings on January 13, 1941.

Organized by a dedicated group of city employees who pooled together $90 as a start, the Credit Union was designed to benefit members by offering reasonable rates for loans and savings as well as a sense of belonging. The concept of owner-ship and control in their financial future held a special interest to workers coming out of the Great Depression years.

As Salt Lake City welcomes the world for the 2002 Olympic Games, Salt Lake City Credit Union continues to welcome new members to become part of a vibrant, growing and successful organization of people helping people. With a membership exceeding 20,000 and assets approaching $115 million, SLCCU offers the products, services and convenience of a large institution combined with one-to-one service and attention to detail.

The valuable services include the Free Checking, Money Market accounts, Certificates of Deposit, IRAs and many other savings options. Access to account information is available 24 hours a day through Web Teller, the Credit Union's online banking product. Reviewing accounts, paying bills, transferring funds or printing out copies of paid checks are just a mouse-click away, all from the privacy of home.

Salt Lake City Credit Union is the place for loans to meet member's needs. Automobile loans are a specialty with attractive rates and flexible terms. The Credit Union also provides loans for mortgages including a premier home equity loan called "Prime Equity." A no annual fee, low interest rate Visa Platinum Credit Card offers tremendous savings and worldwide acceptance.

Because caring about people and seeking mutual benefit are watchwords at the Salt Lake City Credit Union, community service plays an integral role in day-to-day operations. Credit Union employees donate their time in service that includes fundraising for Ronald McDonald House and collecting stuffed animals for the Teddy Bear

Patrol, which is a program of the Salt Lake Police Department. Employees have also helped at charitable telethons, walks for the American Heart Association, and have participated in the Festival of Trees and making quilts for Primary Children's Hospital.

Another vital community service performed by SLCCU is the partnership that has been formed to help the youngsters at the Edison and South Kearns Elementary Schools.

Salt Lake City Credit Union employees work alongside a committed volunteer board of directors who are elected from among the credit union's membership to serve the needs of the membership. Times have changed with convenience, services and options that the founders could not have dreamed of in 1941. One thing that hasn't changed, though, is the philosophy and commitment to service. Salt Lake City Credit Union is truly an organization where people mean more than profits.

Community Commitment

Many Salt Lake City area companies provide community support through their business activities, charitable work and philanthropic foundations.

Larry Miller Group 152

Deseret Management Corporation 158

Huntsman Corporation 162

Larry H. Miller Group

Larry H. Miller

DOES an individual shape history, or does history shape an individual? The story of Larry Miller, founder of the enormously successful Larry H. Miller Group, may offer an answer to that question. Did he create his success, or did his success create him? Is it one or the other, or a combination of both?

It all started with a realization. Larry Miller was the parts manager at Stevenson Toyota in Denver when he thought about how tenuous life can be. What if he lost his job? What would he do to provide for his family? The questions frightened him enough to force him to make a decision. Miller decided to become the best Toyota parts manager possible.

Working 90 hours a week, Miller did become the best parts manager, then the best store manager, then the best general manager, setting new records in sales as he went along. Then, in 1979, Larry Miller applied his work ethic and determination to the realization of a dream.

It was April of that year, and Miller was in Utah visiting friends and family from his home in Colorado. He sat down to lunch with a friend of his who was the owner of a dealership in the area: Toyota of Murray. Miller asked his friend when he planned to sell his store. Miller had asked him this question many times before, but this time the answer was different. His friend was ready to sell, and Miller was ready to buy. Miller and his friend wrote out the terms of Miller's purchase agreement on the bottom of Miller's earnest money check while at lunch.

Miller took over Toyota of Murray on May 1, 1979. That dealership is still in Murray, but it is now Larry H. Miller Toyota. Of course, the dealership is not the only one that Miller now owns. He has progressed from owning one dealership to owning close to 40, along with the Utah Jazz, the Delta Center, Jordan Commons, a TV station, an insurance company, a real estate company, an advertising agency, a number of Fanzz retail stores in several western states and more.

Looking just at the auto sales side of Larry Miller's business, what has been accomplished is nothing short of amazing. In 1996 the Larry H. Miller Group moved into the top 10 list of automotive groups in the country. Within four years, the company reached another milestone by selling its 500,000th automobile. "We knew this day was coming," Miller said at the celebration. "When you stop and think that it doesn't include fleet or wholesale sales, it's staggering. I have a deep sense of gratitude that this many people would do business with us. It has also brought to mind the value of the hard work that all our employees consistently deliver."

The Larry H. Miller Group celebrated 20 years in business in April 1999. Before reaching that milestone, Miller and his wife, Gail, took the time to reflect back on all that had happened through the years they had been in business. They decided to make a list of all the things they had

Larry & Gail Miller during early Delta Center Construction

Jordan Commons theaters

done professionally. When they finished, they were amazed. The list covered several pages.

"On day one, we had no idea what to prepare for," Miller said when he celebrated his company's 20th anniversary. "Had anyone tried to tell me we would be where we are now, I could not have comprehended it. I truly believe the best is yet to come. We have found many times that hard work has a way of bringing with it interesting results. This has been a pretty remarkable ride, and we're not done."

Miller was right in making that prediction. The months following the anniversary were big ones. Jordan Commons — located in Sandy — became a part of the Miller Empire in November of that year with the opening of the movie MegaPlex. This complex features 16 inviting 35mm theaters and one 70mm theater.

Moviegoers are coming to Jordan Commons because of what Larry Miller offers his customers in every aspect of his business:

doing whatever it takes to make them happy. The MegaPlex's plush and roomy stadium seating and advanced audio-visual technology are one-of-a-kind. As customers enter the movie complex, they become aware of a wide spectrum of uncommon features that have been implemented to make attending movies an unforgettable event. For example, Miller wanted to avoid long ticket lines. The solution was to build 10 separate ticket

One of the many treehouse settings inside the Mayan restaurant

John Stockton drives around one of the famous Malone picks.

Winding their way into the restaurant, customers experience a rain forest, complete with giant Banyan trees, thatched roof huts, waterfalls and even an occasional flood with mist. There is also a waterfall with cliff divers. Animated animals and birds are perched throughout the restaurant for entertainment.

Jordan Commons also includes a 10-story office building that houses the Larry H. Miller Management Company, including Larry Miller's own office.

In traditional Larry Miller fashion, all aspects of the Jordan Commons project have experienced success. Larry Miller's achievements with Jordan Commons and his other businesses in Sandy shed some light on the question, "Which comes first, the success or Larry Miller?" He started business in Murray and is still a big part of that city. However, the Larry H. Miller Group opened a used car supermarket in 1995 in the auto mall in Sandy. At that time, there wasn't much in that area — just a few businesses were starting to develop there. There was some speculation as to whether opening a dealership "out there" was a good idea on Miller's part. Would that business

windows. Also, a food court in the lobby offers a wide variety of meals and snacks. Whether guests are in the mood for pizza, pretzels, ice cream or just plain old popcorn, hot dogs and soda, the MegaPlex has it. While enjoying the food in the lobby, guests are entertained with two huge video walls that run a variety of entertainment, including Jazz games, CNN broadcasts and previews for upcoming movies.

In an effort to create a complete night out for its customers, Jordan Commons offers five dining options, including the Mayan. The Mayan is Miller's effort to recreate what it would have been like to have visited a Mayan community almost 1,500 years ago.

community continue to grow, or would it stagnate? Larry Miller believed — or knew — that it would grow. In fact, he moved two of his dealerships from Murray to the auto mall the following year. Those dealerships have been successful in Sandy, and they have been joined by additional Miller businesses. The city of Sandy has grown around those businesses. Miller was correct in his prediction. But it could be argued that much of the success of that area is due to the fact that Larry Miller is a part of it.

Part of Larry Miller's involvement in Sandy has nothing to do with Jordan Commons or even his dealerships. In 1998 he teamed up with Salt Lake Community College to build the Larry H. Miller Entrepreneurship Training Center in Sandy.

The training center is part of a master-planned campus that includes nine buildings. The training center provides entrepreneurship training for those in the area who want assistance in establishing their own businesses, along with those who currently own businesses and want additional training.

"Larry Miller is well known for his success as an entrepreneur," explained Frank Budd, president of Salt Lake Community College. "He is one of the greatest success stories in the state, if not the country. It seemed logical to form a partnership with Larry. This center will be a beacon of light for all entrepreneurs who come seeking help and want to succeed in establishing their own business."

When it comes to entrepreneurship, Larry Miller is a beacon. In June 1997 he was named Utah's Master Entrepreneur and was honored as a man with a strong commitment to his family and community. The recognition also noted his commitment to his employees. The Larry H. Miller Group employs close to 5,000 people in Utah, Idaho, New Mexico, Arizona, Colorado and Oregon.

The Larry H. Miller Education Foundation is just one example of the many ways Miller has shown his appreciation to the employees that make his company successful. Through the Education Foundation, employees' dependents can receive funding for their college education.

"This program is one we have worked on for a few years to be able to get launched," Miller said when he formed the Education Foundation. "One of the most important objectives of our organization is to improve the quality of people's lives, both our employees and customers. I believe education is one of the best ways we can achieve this goal."

Employees and their families have felt and been a part of the success of the Larry H. Miller Group through its founder's dedication to the true spirit of entrepreneurship. Miller has said that entrepreneurs take risks. That is definitely true for Miller. Many advisers told him not to build the Delta Center — a megastructure that has become the epicenter of sports and entertainment in the heart of Salt Lake City. But Miller said he knew that the Delta Center had to be built to keep his world-famous NBA franchise — the Utah Jazz — from moving to another city.

The Delta Center, which was built in 1991, is still the home of the Utah Jazz, and

Karl Malone making a power move to the basket

Natalie Williams, power forward for the Utah Starzz

The Delta Center opened on October 9, 1991.

Professional ice-skating is one of the many family shows held at the Delta Center each year.

the team, along with the building, has been a part of Miller's success.

The Utah Jazz began as the New Orleans Jazz in 1974. The team announced plans to move from New Orleans to Salt Lake City at the end of the 1978-1979 season because of new ownership. The young franchise struggled for a decade, maintaining a low-profile position at the bottom of the league. It was during the team's hard times when Miller saw an opportunity and decided to purchase the first half and later the second half of the Jazz franchise.

Under Miller's new direction the team began to mature and evolve. The franchise took major steps to ensure that it would become one of the top teams in the league. Among the many initiatives that were taken, it focused on retaining the vital services of key players, talented coaches and a skilled front office staff. Miller's new line-up for the Jazz featured on-court powerhouses who have since become legends, including Adrian Dantley, Darrel Griffith, John Stockton and Karl Malone.

Miller's golden touch for business proved to be just as golden when applied to his sports franchise. Through the late 1980s and early 1990s, the Utah Jazz rose steadily through the ranks of the NBA to become a consistent contender in the league.

By 1993 Miller had a professional basketball team on the rise and a beautiful new arena. Now he wanted to give the Jazz a stronger connection with their fans. Not every Jazz fan can fit in the Delta Center, and not enough games were being broadcast to keep them happy. Miller felt this was a problem that had a solution. Miller purchased KXIV in February 1993, which had been transmitting as an independent television station. The station resumed airing programs that fall and soon began operating under new call letters: KJZZ.

KJZZ-TV has become one of the fastest-growing television stations in the country and the fifth-largest station in its market area. More than 60 translator stations relay KJZZ-TV signals to viewers throughout Utah, southwestern Wyoming, southeastern Idaho, southern and western Nevada, southwestern Colorado and northern Arizona. In the relatively short time Miller has owned the station, he has helped transform it from a station in debt to one that turns a healthy profit. Fans can now see the Jazz, even if they can't get a seat in the Delta Center.

In addition to serving as the home court for the Utah Jazz, the Delta Center now sees basketball action in the summer as the home of the WNBA's Utah Starzz. Miller's Delta Center is also a part of Utah's Olympic dream, hosting figure skating and short-track speed skating competitions for the 2002 Winter Olympics. Miller took a risk in building the Delta Center and keeping the Jazz in Utah. Once again, his entrepreneurial risk paid off.

Larry Miller is a true entrepreneur. As such, he is an expert in his own right. He has taken the opportunity to share his expertise by teaching a course on entrepreneurism at Brigham Young University in Provo, Utah.

Miller has used his success not only to help his employees and future entrepreneurs, but also to better the communities in which he does business. In November 1995, he formed Larry H. Miller Charities. The mission statement of this philanthropic organization is: "We give back to our communities by focusing our united service and corporate giving on youth and children with an emphasis on health and education."

Since its inception, Larry H. Miller Charities has raised more than $1 million, distributing the funds to charitable organizations in the communities where the Larry H. Miller Group does business.

The mission of Larry H. Miller Charities involves every employee of the company. Not only are employees given the opportunity to make financial contributions, but they are encouraged to donate their time and become personally involved in these charitable organizations as well.

Larry Miller. Did he create his success, or did his success create him? Through his amazing success in the business arena and his work in the community, it may be impossible to arrive at a definitive answer to that question. But no matter what the answer, the name Larry Miller is synonymous with success.

Tim McGraw entertains nearly 15,000 fans at the Delta Center.

Deseret Management Corporation

DESERET Management Corporation (DMC) is a for-profit business holding company affiliated with The Church of Jesus Christ of Latter-day Saints (Church). DMC oversees the commercial companies affiliated with the Church, including Beneficial Life Insurance Company, Bonneville International Corporation, Deseret Book Company, Deseret News Publishing Company, Hawaii Reserves Inc., Hotel Temple Square Corporation and Zions Securities Corporation.

DMC was organized in 1966. It provides valuable services to its commercial companies, including coordination of planning and budgeting, accounting, administration, taxation, auditing, information technology, cash management and coordination of charitable contributions. These services have proven important to the growth and development of the companies. Since DMC came into being, the commercial companies have grown, overall, in size, profitability, service and economic benefit to local, national and international communities.

Following are brief descriptions of the DMC companies headquartered in Salt Lake City.

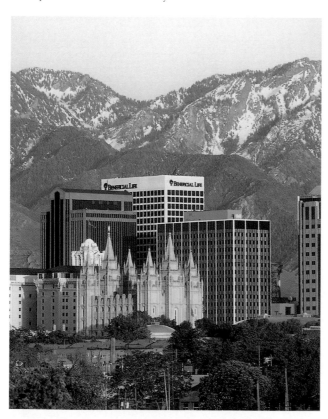

Beneficial Life Insurance Company is headquartered in downtown Salt Lake City.

BENEFICIAL LIFE INSURANCE COMPANY

Beneficial Life Insurance Company (Beneficial Life) was established in 1905. Although it began as a local company serving local needs, it has expanded to serve the entire western United States and parts of the Midwest and the East Coast. It is among the top 10 percent of American insurance companies. During its long history, Beneficial Life has never resorted to a moratorium or a deferral of cash payments, even in the worst of economic times.

The company's mission is "to help people attain financial security...to protect widows, children, and retirees...to help people accumulate and protect wealth...[and] to enhance and protect business profitability and value." Beneficial Life carefully manages its resources in order to protect and safeguard its policyholders. It helps clients develop and maintain "peace of mind" through well-considered financial planning.

In response to changing times and changing economic needs, Beneficial Life has formed several strategic alliances which make it possible to offer a broader array of products to policyholders, including mutual funds, annuities, long-term-care insurance and disability income insurance.

BONNEVILLE INTERNATIONAL CORPORATION

Bonneville International Corporation (BIC) was organized in 1964, but its roots go back to 1922, when the first commercial radio station in Utah (KZN) began broadcasting from a tin shack atop a downtown Salt Lake City building. In 1925, KZN became KSL, which grew to be the strongest radio station in the Intermountain West. KSL Television was added in 1949.

BIC is now a major national broadcasting group. The company owns and operates radio stations in Chicago (WTMX-FM, WTNX-FM, WNND-FM, WLUP-FM, WDRV-FM); San Francisco (KOIT-FM/AM, KDFC-FM, KZQZ-FM); Washington D.C. (WTOP-AM/FM, WGMS-FM, WWZZ-FM, WWVZ-FM, WXTR-AM); St. Louis (WSSM-FM, WIL-FM, WVRV-FM, WRTH-AM); and Salt Lake City (KSL-AM); plus KSL-TV in Salt Lake City, KCSG-TV in Cedar City, Bonneville Communications, Bonneville Satellite Company and Video West Productions.

The company is headquartered at Broadcast House in Salt Lake City. Its stated mission is "making a difference through mass communications."

DESERET BOOK COMPANY

Deseret Book Company traces its beginnings back to 1866, when a Utah pioneer established a small bookstore and publishing venture at the same location where Deseret Book's headquarters building is located today. That original enterprise went through several iterations before being incorporated in 1932 as Deseret Book Company.

The company has three divisions: publishing, wholesale and retail. The publishing division produces books, audio tapes, compact discs (both music and data discs), electronic products and online publications.

The wholesale division distributes Deseret Book products to bookstores and dealers throughout the world.

The retail division operates bookstores in Utah and other states, manages a worldwide book club, distributes mail-order catalogs, conducts an online Internet bookstore and operates Mormon Handicraft, a consignment store for mostly local arts and crafts.

The retail stores — now located in 11 states — carry general trade books of fiction and nonfiction, plus values-oriented products designed to strengthen families and individuals.

DESERET NEWS PUBLISHING COMPANY

The *Deseret News* was first published on June 15, 1850. The first edition carried the motto "Truth and Liberty" in recognition of the multiple challenges facing a frontier newspaper in those days. The first editor wrote: "We hold ourselves responsible to the highest Court of truth for our intentions, and the highest Court of equity for our execution."

In keeping with that pledge, for more than 150 years, the *Deseret News* has been a credible source of local, national and international news for thousands of readers. Its pages are considered by academics to be one of the most reliable and important sources of information about Utah history.

The newspaper and its staff have been honored many times by professional organizations. Its honors and awards include a Pulitzer Prize for "local reporting under deadline."

This long tradition of timely, accurate and fair reporting continues in the Internet age. The *Deseret News* Web site is one of the most active newspaper Web sites in America.

Broadcast House is the home of Bonneville International Corporation.

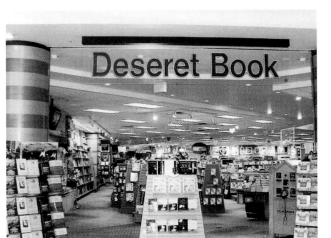

Deseret Book Company's flagship retail store is centrally located in a major downtown mall.

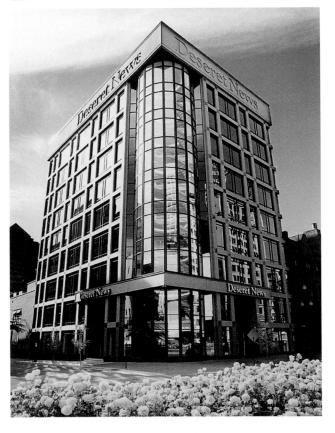

The Deseret News Building architecture resembles a newspaper, with columns and a masthead.

The Inn at Temple Square welcomes visitors from around the world.

places. The spectacular lobby greets visitors. Twelve individually decorated banquet rooms seat 1,700. The 10th-floor Garden Restaurant has a retractable roof so diners can view the stars when weather permits. And the Roof Restaurant offers elegant food, an outstanding buffet and a spectacular view.

The Inn at Temple Square is a landmark building constructed in 1930. It, too, was totally rebuilt inside, providing 90 individually appointed guestrooms, which combine the comfort of earlier times with the luxurious amenities of today. The Inn, conveniently located across from both Temple Square and Abravanel Hall (home of the Utah Symphony), also offers one of the city's finest restaurants — Passages.

In 1997 the *Deseret News* opened a new headquarters building in downtown Salt Lake City, a building with striking architecture designed to reflect the appearance of the printed newspaper, featuring "columns" and a "masthead." The building's state-of-the-art construction facilitates ease of communication and technological adaptability. Whatever changes may come to news and information transmittal in the 21st century, the *Deseret News* is ready to respond.

HOTEL TEMPLE SQUARE CORPORATION

Food and hotel services at three historic downtown Salt Lake City buildings are managed by the Hotel Temple Square Corporation — Lion House, Joseph Smith Memorial Building and The Inn at Temple Square.

The Lion House was built by Brigham Young in 1856. It is now a gathering place for wedding receptions, group dinners, club meetings and other events. The rooms are decorated with photographs and antiques from the Brigham Young era. Food service is abundant and delicious, featuring standard American fare and homestyle rolls, pies and desserts made fresh every day. On the lower level, the Pantry restaurant serves drop-in diners with famous Lion House hospitality.

The Joseph Smith Memorial Building was constructed in 1911 as a luxury hotel. It was totally refurbished and expanded in the 1990s for other uses, but the beauty and historical value of the original structure remain, as do many of the public

ZIONS SECURITIES CORPORATION

Zions Securities Corporation (ZSC) was organized in 1922 as a real estate company. It currently manages land and/or buildings in several states. In downtown Salt Lake City, the company manages approximately 1,750,000 square feet of office space and 600,000 square feet of retail space. In addition, ZSC leases more than 1,100 apartment units, and it maintains and manages 6,200 parking stalls.

Zions Securities Corporation's Gateway West office building is located at the heart of Salt Lake City.

Zions Securities Corporation played a major role in creating Salt Lake City's new skyline. ZSC was involved in the development, construction, rebuilding and leasing of the ZCMI Center, The Inn at Temple Square, Beneficial Life Tower, Eagle Gate Tower, Gateway Tower East, Gateway Tower West, Social Hall Plaza and others. The company also helped stimulate additional growth by "packaging" properties for other downtown developments, including the Crossroads Mall and the Matheson Courthouse complex.

ZSC apartment developments include the Garden Apartments, West Temple Apartments, Deseret Apartments, Eagle Gate Apartments, Gateway Condominiums, Gordon Place Homes, and the 336-unit Brigham Apartments.

One important role filled by ZSC is to anticipate future growth needs and patterns. The company can then seek to acquire land and property in order to facilitate vital developments by itself or other organizations. In this role, ZSC works closely with business and government organizations to provide support, planning and coordination.

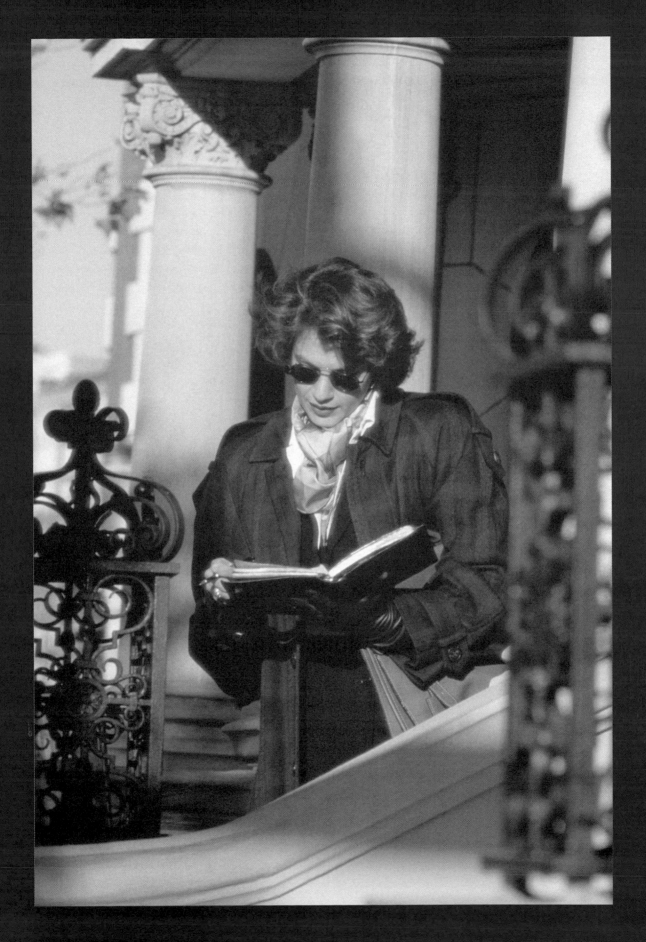

Huntsman Corporation

OUTSIDE of Utah, it's been said that Huntsman Corporation is the biggest company in the world that no one has heard of. While this may be true, it is also a fact that this "anonymous" chemical company has touched innumerable lives in Utah and around the world. And although Huntsman now grosses in excess of $8 billion a year, it's not the company's revenues but its gentle and generous heart that makes it undeniably unique among its peers.

Jon and Karen Huntsman have committed to giving at least 50 percent of their charitable donations to nonprofit causes, education, culture and arts in Utah.

It all began when a poor young man by the name of Jon M. Huntsman worked three jobs to enable his father to earn a Ph.D. at Stanford University. Not only did he learn to work hard, but he also learned to give unselfishly. When he founded Huntsman Container Corporation, young Huntsman had no realization of the magnitude of the company it would become. From modest beginnings in 1970 in pioneering innovative foam packaging products, the company grew rapidly through acquisitions, joint ventures and internal expansion. Huntsman now manufactures more than 32 billion pounds of chemical products per year. Every modern home in the industrialized

world carries many products featuring Huntsman chemicals in one form or another. From carpets to cabinets, paint to perfume, soft drinks to shoes, virtually every product has been manufactured in some way using materials from one of Huntsman's production facilities located in 44 countries worldwide. Stretching out across the Americas to Europe, Africa, the Middle East, Asia and Australia, Huntsman has emerged as the world's largest privately held chemical company.

Jon Huntsman and his wife, Karen, both have a rich pioneer heritage, which they have honored by building their corporate headquarters in Utah. This heritage has given them a rather unusual perspective about business. For example, the company has been built upon three important principles. The first two include providing high-quality products and paying down debt. The third is to lift others out of human suffering and offer them hope of a brighter future. Jon Huntsman has always felt a powerful obligation to give back to his "worldwide" community, and he encourages his 14,000 employees to do the same. Since Huntsman Corporation is not encumbered by the expectations of shareholders, it has more resources at its disposal than most companies. Jon and Karen have therefore found tremendous opportunities to give time and have gone to extraordinary means to care for others in need.

To date, Huntsman has contributed over $350 million to humanitarian causes. Whereas some corporations basically contribute lip service for the sake of tax write-offs or consumer appeal, Huntsman has developed a reputation of giving vastly more than expected in order to make a real difference in the lives of others.

Perhaps the most wonderful example of this philanthropic spirit is the Huntsman Cancer Institute at the University of Utah, built in 1993. The Huntsmans have contributed more than $225 million to the Institute, which researches powerful approaches to cancer therapy and prevention. The reason behind such a magnanimous donation is evident. Jon realized that every family in the world has been touched by cancer. It is no discriminator of age, income, race or religion. Even Jon and his wife, Karen, have been affected in a very intimate way. Between personal battles and family tragedies involving cancer, the Huntsmans have

The Huntsman Cancer Institute at the University of Utah boasts a team of world-renowned cancer specialists to assist in the research and cure of the disease.

made it their most enduring goal to help bring a cure to the world — hopefully within their lifetime.

The Institute has three full floors dedicated to researching cancers, an outpatient care center and a state-of-the-art learning center that allows victims and family members to learn about the disease and the newest options for recovery. Just north of the center, a new inpatient hospital that will provide more extensive treatment is now under construction. The Institute also operates the Children's Cancer Specialty Clinics, working in partnership with Primary Children's Medical Center.

The Huntsmans' desire to relieve suffering reaches far beyond the borders of Utah. When the terrible earthquake hit Armenia in 1988, Jon Huntsman felt they should help the

people devastated by the quake. He immediately sent $1 million in aid, but his heart went out to thousands of people still homeless. Over the last 12 years, Huntsman Corporation built a concrete plant and a roofing tile manufacturing plant to enable the people to rebuild homes and lives. To date, Huntsman Corporation has contributed more than $18 million in assistance as well as an additional $10 million in interest-free loans to the redevelopment of this poor nation. Armenia's people and their leaders have been amazed at the generosity of one American family and the people who work for them.

Nonprofit organizations in Utah are also amazed by the generosity of the Huntsmans. It seems no project is too large or too small. The YWCA of Salt Lake City named its domestic violence shelter in honor of Jon's mother, Kathleen Robison Huntsman, and the corporation's $1 million donation given to complete the shelter. St. Vincent De Paul Center and Traveler's Aid Society are two charities that have benefited greatly. The Huntsmans regularly give to many other service organizations as well as to education, culture and the arts. Since 1997, the educational system in Utah has received more than $12 million in scholarships and support of programs and teachers.

At a commencement address at Weber State University — certainly the most popular address in the spring of 2000 — Jon asked all the graduates to stand, and then he said, "Repeat after me... No exercise is better for the human heart than reaching down and lifting up another." At that point he announced that Huntsman Corporation was giving a very generous gift to the university, wherewith he sat down to the applause of the students whom he had just inspired to be philanthropists (and brief speakers). Jon has always believed that the amount of money you make matters less than what you do with it. Fortunately for Utah, it is evident that Jon Huntsman's business leadership and generosity will continue to grace the community and the world for years to come.

Huntsman was founded in 1970 with three employees and one location. Today, over 14,000 skilled associates in 44 countries worldwide work together to produce the chemical industry's highest-quality products and improve the quality of life for people everywhere.

Manufacturing & Distribution

In addition to producing exceptional goods for individuals and industry, Salt Lake City manufacturing and distribution companies provide employment for area residents.

Associated Food Stores 166

Cummings Studio Chocolates 168

Dynatronics Corporation 170

General Distributing Company 172

Heartland Industries 174

O.C. Tanner 176

A & Z Produce Company, Inc. 178

CCG Quality Office Furniture 179

Colonial Flag & Specialty Co. 180

Dunford Bakers 181

Fetzers' Inc. 182

Hexcel Corporation 183

OGIO International 184

Utah Paperbox 185

Varian Medical Systems 186

Associated Food Stores

FROM the start, the story of Associated Food Stores has been a David and Goliath epic. The saga's roots sink deep — back to the early years of World War II when 34 independent grocers formed a cooperative to secure for themselves the buying power they would need to compete against the invading retail chains that were becoming so common.

They were the Davids — store owners who wanted to remain independent but were tired of paying the "small guy" prices wholesalers would charge them. They told stories about being able to buy cases of products at retail prices from large neighboring chain stores for less than their wholesalers charged them. They complained that wholesalers used multiple secret price lists, quoting their prices from the highest list, while giving their large chain competitors drastically lower quotes from different lists.

In 1940 they took action, forming a cooperative that would allow them to compete and survive. Originally called Reliable Food Stores, the new organization would later become known as Associated Food Stores.

The concept was simple. Each participating grocer, regardless of size, could buy one share of stock for $300, thus becoming a member and partial owner of the new wholesale operation. The owners would then be able to buy directly from the cooperative. There would be only one price list, and any profits made by the cooperative would be distributed to the member grocers in the form of annual rebates. By pooling the buying power of the 34 grocery stores, the cooperative could get and pass on excellent prices that would allow the independent retailers to compete head-to-head with their giant opponents.

Today, Associated Food Stores supplies and serves over 500 stores throughout the Intermountain West from Montana to Arizona, from Colorado to Nevada. Headquartered in Salt Lake City, the growing organization now enjoys annual sales that top the $1 billion mark.

That's a lot of sales. But company spokespeople are quick to point out that while those figures make Associated Food Stores large for a Utah-based company, it is still in the "small and scrappy" category compared to large national competitors.

> Truck drivers for Associated Food Stores operate in some of the most beautiful yet extreme landscapes in the world. They deliver food to Leadville, Colorado, the highest town in the United States at 10,163 feet.

In other words, the cooperative, like the stores that own it, is still in the David category — fighting the super-Goliaths of modern times. Associated Food Stores is frankly proud of that role. It gives the organization a feisty edge that has enabled it to prosper for decades, which has in turn allowed the stores it serves not only to survive, but prosper amid the rising tide of monopolistic retailing.

The organization and its people are also proud of their ability to perform under conditions that are often challenging. Take its delivery area, for example. Truck drivers for Associated Food Stores operate in some of the most beautiful yet extreme landscapes in the world. They deliver food to Leadville, Colorado, the highest town in the United States at 10,163 feet. It is said that the early silver miners used to lose many a mule to altitude sickness there. In Leadville, they say, it's easy to get winded just walking across the street to the grocery store.

The 1-million-square-foot warehouse in Farr West, Utah

Then there's the Mojave Desert that surrounds Laughlin, Nevada. Far from the high, cold air of Leadville, the desert is known for its brutal heat. Associated Food Stores delivers there too. In fact, the cooperative's highly recognizable trucks can be found rolling to and from some of the earth's most scenic destinations, often along the edges of national parks: the Grand Tetons, the Sawtooth Mountains along the Snake River, the Wasatch Mountain front, and forbidding but breathtaking Monument Valley, where the world's most famous Western movies have been filmed.

While it takes toughness and determination to operate effectively in such an environment, Associated Food Stores and its independent grocers have a soft side too. That side is perhaps best seen in the way they become involved in their communities.

Because the individual grocery stores are locally owned and

operated, rather than merely being small dots on large corporate wall maps, they tend to be more attuned to the needs and events in their surrounding communities than larger chain supermarkets. Many of these grocery retailers have served for decades as ad hoc city halls, meeting places and local civic centers. Associated Food Stores itself follows the lead of its member retailers in its commitment to community service and involvement, participating in a diverse range of charitable causes and philanthropic initiatives.

Though firmly rooted in history, today's Associated Food Stores is decidedly progressive, continually looking for ways to improve the quality and economy of its operations and responding to new developments and market trends. Its new warehouse in Farr West, Utah, is an excellent example. The consolidation of its warehousing operations into one huge warehouse facility of close to 1 million square feet significantly improves efficiency.

Though the cooperative's primary role has not changed, it now offers its

grocers more than just wholesale foods. The menu of services it makes available to its member retailers ranges from store design to advertising and marketing programs, from employee benefit plans to assistance with new site selection and construction.

Another illustration of Associated Food Stores' ability to respond to trends and opportunities was its decision at the end of the millennium to purchase Lin's, Macey's and Dan's stores — which had grown into larger chain operations over

Today, Associated Food Stores supplies and serves over 500 stores throughout the Intermountain West from Montana to Arizona, from Colorado to Nevada. Headquartered in Salt Lake City, the growing organization now enjoys annual sales that top the $1 billion mark.

Humble beginnings: a warehouse facility from the 1940s

the years — rather than lose them to the competition. In addition to preserving important volume, this decision has resulted in a better retail-warehouse relationship, increased capital and the heightened value of Associated for all its member grocers.

These and other initiatives have enabled Associated Food Stores to grow and prosper. What does the future hold? Corporate spokespeople point out that the cooperative plans to continue doing what it was originally created to do: supply independent grocers with competitively priced wholesale products and services that will help them compete successfully with the Goliaths of the retail grocery world.

Associated Food Stores trucks are the cooperative's most recognizable icons.

Cummings Studio Chocolates

WHOEVER coined the term "sweet nothings" never tasted anything so tangible, so delectable as Cummings Studio Chocolates: white Boston opera creams, rum Victoria pecan nut creams, amaretto truffles and fresh chocolate-covered California strawberries. The names alone are enough to make the mouth water, but it only takes one taste to understand why these chocolates are in high demand in such faraway places as France and Hong Kong, even as business flourishes in Salt Lake City. Cummings offers over 60 original pieces that are perhaps for chocolate lovers the closest thing to heaven on earth.

For more than 75 years, Cummings Studio Chocolates has been a benchmark of world excellence in candy making. Founder Clyde Cummings began his adventures with candy at the young age of 15 when he attended a home economics class to win the attentions of a girl. Although he never married that particular young lady, he found he had a natural affinity for candy making and the taste acuity of a genius, which would prove priceless in the industry. Continuing to produce delicious concoctions in his mother's basement for friends and church bazaars, the demand for his chocolates increased as his skills became more refined. His favorite challenge was working on the candy centers, creating superbly soft and smooth or delightfully chewy pieces. He continued to experiment with a larger assortment of ingredients and ways to mix them until he developed his "secret process" for producing award-winning chocolates.

Clyde dreamed of opening his own candy studio, but he had no means of purchasing one. He went to see Walter Cosgriff, the president of Continental Bank. Cosgriff had a reputation for granting loans to promising ventures — even those with little or no collateral. The only thing Clyde brought to the meeting was several pounds of his homemade chocolates. According to Clyde's son, Paul, "Fortunately for Dad, Mr. Cosgriff was a chocolate connoisseur. He loved Dad's chocolates and agreed to finance him in his new business."

In 1924 Clyde opened Cummings Studio Candies on the busy corner of 9th South and 7th East. From the beginning, his business was successful. Even in hard times, people couldn't resist his tempting treats. Clyde was able to buy and pay for a home during the Great Depression and continued to reinvest in his company. He even generously though quietly contributed to the local community. Throughout his career, Clyde never lost the vision of his ultimate dream: matchlessly delicious candies. Years later he would tell his son, "I'm a poor businessman, but I have the ability to make the finest chocolates in the country. I will spend whatever time and money it takes to find and buy the finest ingredients available, and expend

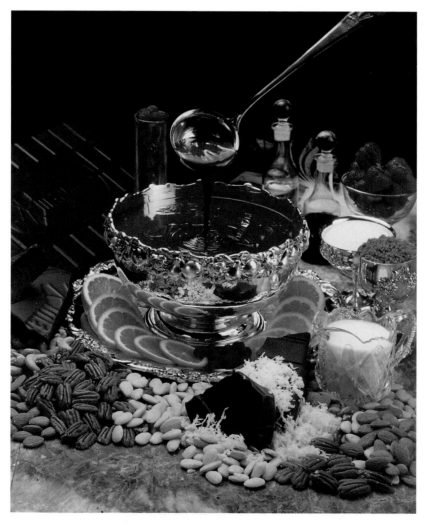

Artistry in chocolate — Cummings Studio Chocolates creates delicacies for those with sophisticated taste. Using only the freshest and finest ingredients available for its secret recipes, Cummings is considered one of the finest confectioners in the world.

whatever effort it takes to make them into the finest candies possible. Then I will decide how much I have to charge for them."

Clyde created the candy centers exclusively under carefully controlled conditions, allowing seasoned apprentices to help only in the cutting and dipping processes. He handed down his "secret process" as a legacy directly to his son, Paul, who continued the candy making tradition when his father died unexpectedly in 1959. Although Paul had not planned to go into his father's business, he never regretted carrying on the tradition, and indeed, brought the company to new heights and a golden age of marketing and production. The original building was renovated to allow advanced machinery for cutting, shaping and

It's a small wonder that Utah has the highest consumption of chocolate per capita when a company like Cummings has featured award-winning chocolates for more than 75 years and produces up to a thousand pounds of fine chocolates per day.

dipping chocolates. This made greater numbers of production easier, although some of the work is still done by hand. Serving as president of Retail Confectioners International (RCI), Paul brought the RCI convention to Salt Lake City in 1988 and instituted a "people-to-people" program that helped members access top professionals in the industry. He also helped implement an industrywide nutritional label program for confectionery.

originators, concentrating on unsurpassed quality and artistry in chocolate. Marion, like her late husband and father-in-law before her, refuses to freeze the candies or add preservatives that could compromise flavor.

Instead, Marion is proactively meeting the increased demand for Cummings' popular chocolates by opening a sister store at The Gateway shopping center in Salt Lake City. For those who don't enjoy crowds, Marion suggests customers order in advance of holidays to make pickup fast and easy. In addition, many customers use mail order to ship Cummings' international, award-winning chocolate truffles, rich raspberry creams and luscious chocolate almond caramels directly to the doorstep of delighted friends and family around the world, as well as being able to easily indulge in their own chocolate fantasies year round.

Paul and Marion Cummings managed the store for over 40 years. Since Paul's recent passing, Marion now oversees all operations including production, to ensure the legacy of quality remains unchanged. Paul handed down his father's "secret processes," and those special recipes continue to win numerous local, national and international awards. *Utah Holiday* magazine rated the store's chocolates the best in the state, while a national publication, *Food Finds*, listed them as best in the nation and recently filmed a segment featuring the store on The Food Network to be shown throughout 2002. Even top European confectioners go so far as to rate Cummings in the top three candy makers in the world.

Unlike commercial producers, Cummings uses only the finest ingredients — the freshest creams and butter, the finest flavorings and nuts. For example, instead of common chocolate, Cummings exclusively uses a rare South American chocolate called Tehuantepec. It is so expensive, only a handful of chocolatiers in the entire world use it in their recipes. Cummings also understands that hand-dipped chocolates, like fine wine, improve their flavor when stored for a few weeks, allowing the creamy centers to mellow and blend with the rich chocolate coating. Cummings has continued the traditions of its meticulous

The secret to success lies in the Cummings family recipes, superb quality and customer satisfaction. The week of Valentine's Day, Cummings sells more than 30,000 large and juicy chocolate-covered strawberries.

Dynatronics Corporation

KELVYN H. Cullimore and Kelvyn H. Cullimore Jr. — father and son — were heavily invested in the food industry and other businesses in Salt Lake City in 1979 when someone brought an idea to their attention that changed the direction of their business interests. They learned of a small company in Pittsburg, Kansas, that had developed a laser product to heal wounds and manage pain. Quintessential entrepreneurs, the Cullimores realized that no comparable medical or health device was then available in the United States. The Cullimores saw potential in this start-up company, named Dynatronics, and bought it for $50,000.

Kelvyn H. Cullimore, chairman of the board (seated) and Kelvyn H. Cullimore Jr., president and CEO, whose acquisition of an idea in 1979 has turned into a $16 million-a-year business

For seven years they wrestled with the FDA to gain approval for the laser, but to no avail. In 1983 Dynatronics went public to raise funds for laser research. By 1986 the company could see that FDA approval seemed unattainable and began to engineer and develop other products for the physical therapy market. Between 1986 and 1991 the company developed a rapid succession of successful products, and in 1991 *Inc.* magazine recognized Dynatronics (NASDAQ:DYNT) as the 43rd-fastest-growing small public company in the United States.

The medical market underwent a transformation in the early 90s requiring Dynatronics to reinvent its products to respond to the changing market. Sales grew from $4.9 million in 1994 to $16 million in 2001. In May 1996 Dynatronics acquired Superior Orthopedic Supply, complete with a manufacturing facility and warehouse in Chattanooga, Tennessee. This acquisition helped boost the company's overall growth.

In little more than two decades Dynatronics has evolved into a company servicing two demand markets, rehabilitation and aesthetics, and has become a major supplier of electrotherapy and ultrasound devices to medical and athletic markets including the U.S. Ski Team, the U.S. Snowboard Association (USSA), the U.S. Speed Skating team, most U.S.

professional sports franchises and many other athletic and rehabilitation organizations.

Dynatronics is a technological leader in developing equipment. It was the first company to create microprocessor-based electrotherapy equipment. Today, Dynatronics designs, manufactures and sells advanced technology medical devices, therapeutic products and medical supplies for the rehabilitation market, a line of products for the aesthetics market, and most recently, a patented process for treating chronic pain.

Dynatronics' core business centers around creating and providing rehabilitation products to physical therapists, chiropractors, athletic trainers, podiatrists and medical doctors. The company's high-tech electrotherapy and therapeutic ultrasound products are the centerpiece of the rehab product line. Having a broad line of more than 1,000 rehab products sets Dynatronics apart as an innovator among competing companies. Dynatronics' rehabilitation products include therapeutic ultrasound, electrotherapy devices, orthopedic supplies and soft goods, wood and metal treatment tables, hot and cold therapy products, braces, belts and other similar products used in physical medicine applications.

The rehabilitation products business is booming. During the two decades Dynatronics has been in the business, the domestic rehabilitation market has grown from $1.5 billion in 1980 to more than $3.3 billion. In the United States there are more than 100,000 practitioners who specialize in physical medicine, with an additional 100,000 in the combined European rehabilitation market.

In July 1998 Dynatronics expanded its product line into the aesthetic market by introducing the Synergie™ Aesthetic Massage System, a vacuum massage therapy device that temporarily reduces the appearance of cellulite. Dynatronics followed the successful deployment of the Synergie AMS with the Synergie

Peel™ microdermabrasion device. Microdermabrasion is quickly becoming the new standard of care in the aesthetics industry because of its distinct advantages over traditional chemical or laser peels. Synergie Peel treatments reduce fine lines, wrinkles and other superficial skin damage by gently peeling away the top layers of skin, exposing softer, smoother skin. In addition, Dynatronics has introduced Calisse™, a unique line of skin care products specifically designed to enhance the effects of the Synergie Peel treatments.

Another focus of Dynatronics' business is the manufacture and marketing of devices that offer effective treatment of chronic pain. This is another growing market since it is estimated that more than 70 million Americans suffer from some type of moderate-to-severe chronic pain. In addition to the direct cost to American businesses of lost workdays, chronic pain diminishes quality of life and exacts a tremendous physical and emotional toll on patients and their caregivers.

Dynatronics has addressed this market by introducing the Dynatron® STS™, a revolutionary advancement in the

Dynatronics corporate headquarters in Salt Lake City

treatment of chronic intractable pain that was approved by the FDA in 2001. In 2000 Dynatronics signed a landmark agreement with Alan Neuromedical Technology to grant Dynatronics the exclusive manufacturing and marketing license to this patented technology for the treatment of chronic pain. The Dynatron STS has proved to be remarkably effective in treating chronic pain associated with numerous neuropathic conditions. Patients who have for years been frustrated by little success from conventional therapies are finally finding relief. Using non-invasive electrical current therapy, the Dynatron STS has proven to safely provide symptomatic relief to a high percentage of patients suffering from chronic intractable pain.

Dynatronics remains committed to being a major long-term player in the rehabilitation and aesthetic markets it serves. In 1999 Kelvyn Cullimore Jr. was a Utah Finalist in the Ernst & Young LLP Entrepreneur of the Year award, although the honor, he states, really recognized the more than 150 employees who have helped create Dynatronics' success.

Dynatronics is a proud supplier of physical therapy devices and products for the 2002 Winter Olympics. Proud to be a Utah-based company, its goal is to be the dominant company in the physical medicine marketplace.

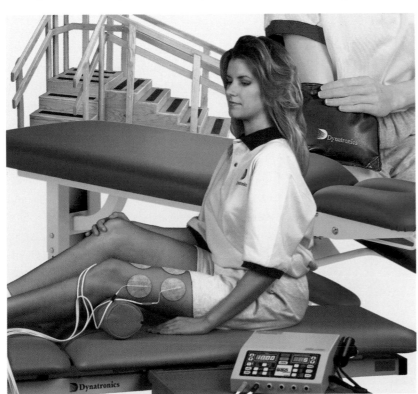

Dynatronics' broad line of medical products includes advanced-technology therapy devices, medical supplies and soft goods, treatment tables to the physical medicine market and a line of aesthetic products for the beauty market.

General Distributing Company

CONVENTIONAL wisdom might have argued against Robert Avery ever thinking he could establish one of the most successful beer distributing businesses in the country in Salt Lake City, Utah. But Avery stuck by his hunch and today, he and his children have not only been recognized multiple times as one of the top wholesalers in the nation for Anheuser-Busch Brewing Company, but have accomplished these remarkable milestones with an unflinching loyalty to three bedrock principles: honesty, hard work and superior customer service.

Avery's daughter, Becky Brennan, whose husband, Mike, now runs Avery's company — General Distributing of Salt Lake City — says family was always important to her father. He

Michael P. Brennan and Becky Brennan are shown here with their son, Michael S. Brennan.

believed Salt Lake's enormous market potential would lead to greater financial security for the family despite the conservative culture, and in 1967 he sold Southern Idaho Distributing Company in Boise, Idaho, and bought the licenses of Lucky Lager and Fisher beer brands in Salt Lake. Two years later he became the exclusive distributor in Salt Lake City of Anheuser-Busch's Budweiser brand, which then had only a 3-percent market share in Utah, and set his sights on becoming the market leader.

Avery, who learned the business as a teen-ager at his father's bottling and beer distribution company, A.H. Avery & Sons, in Pasco, Washington, immediately noticed that his Salt Lake City competitors rarely serviced their products properly. Believing customer service was the key to success, Avery took a personal interest in each customer. He focused on fundamentals, making sure coolers were always filled, working tirelessly on in-store promotions and displays, and giving each customer a timely delivery schedule. For years Avery worked weekends to stock store coolers — no job was too inconsequential. Avery's attention to detail paid off and General Distributing's market share began to soar.

General Distributing not only earned a reputation for stellar customer service, but it also was the first beer wholesaler to modernize the industry in Salt Lake. The entire operation was computerized in the 1970s and sales personnel and truck drivers were outfitted with hand-held palm computers in the late 1980s. General Distributing also introduced the concept of a hybrid sales-and-delivery service devoting its teams to on-premises (restaurants and bars) or off-premises (grocery and convenience stores) customers, bringing more specialization to the market. The operation has become so sophisticated that every day sales data from each store are collected and analyzed by computer, enabling General Distributing to determine how much cooler space should be allocated to beer brands based on volume. Today, as the wholesale distributor for a stable of Anheuser-Busch products (Budweiser, Natural Light, Busch and Michelob), as well as

Heineken, General Distributing commands 69 percent of Salt Lake City's market share.

Avery continually kept a sharp eye on the bottom line but always reinvested most of his profits back into the business, making sure General Distributing had the best, safest fleet of trucks and happy, well-motivated employees. Mike and Becky Brennan, who with Becky's sister, Bobbie Tyacke, now own General Distributing, say Avery led by example, treating his employees like family and offering generous pay and benefit packages, including a 401K plan and vacation incentives. Jobs at General Distributing are so revered that the company has stacks of job applications from workers in the wholesale industry. Today, the company employs 122 full-time and 24 part-time workers. Seven employees have been at General Distributing more than 25 years.

Robert Avery started his business from a rented warehouse in 1971, distributing 10,000 cases of Budweiser that year. A permanent facility near downtown Salt Lake, purchased in 1976, was eventually expanded to 109,000 square feet. In November 2001 General Distributing moved into a new 257,000-square-foot warehouse near the Salt Lake Airport. Besides needing new space, accessibility to rail lines and the interstate were dominating factors in the relocation. Every day the company unloads four rail cars of beer, each containing 5,000 to 6,000 cases. Work that was once outsourced, such as equipment maintenance, printing and signage, is now all done on premises. Although a delivery truck averages about 12,000 miles a year, each is thoroughly inspected every 30 days. Avery's work ethic and traditions still prevail throughout General Distributing. Mike Brennan's day starts around 6:30 a.m. and ends about 6 p.m. Each month Brennan personally visits 50 to 60 customers. Like Avery, Brennan has adopted the approach that by making a friend first, one creates a customer.

Future growth for beer sales in Salt Lake is focused primarily in the off-premises market — at convenience and grocery stores — and in recognition of that, General Distributing has invested in larger trucks that can pull up to a dock and unload beer in pallets from the back, further simplifying the process for customers.

Three bronze eagle statuettes, an expensive hand-blown glass globe from Italy, and shelves full of certificates and awards from Anheuser-Busch and other organizations attest to General Distributing's dominance and customer excellence in the marketplace. More than 800 wholesalers sell Anheuser-Busch beer throughout the United States, but few have ever achieved the recognition of General Distributing, which is located in a small beer market. General Distributing won so many awards from Anheuser-Busch, the world's leading brewer of beer, that it gave Robert Avery the honorary title of ambassador, something the company reserves for a select few.

As General Distributing continues to set ambitious goals in the Salt Lake market, Mike Brennan is passing along his know-how to son Michael, a brand manager at the company. As Mike Brennan and Robert Avery had done, Michael started at the bottom and worked his way up. General Distributing must not only serve a thirsty population in Salt Lake City, but also play a key role in assisting Budweiser get the most bang for its buck as a $50 million sponsor of the 2002 Winter Olympic Games. From Mike Brennan's perspective, the Games won't be any more challenging than that which the company faced when it first entered the Salt Lake market. He thinks honesty, hard work and superior customer service will see them through the biggest worldwide event ever staged in Salt Lake City, Utah.

Barbara Tyacke, who with Michael and Becky purchased the company from Robert Avery in 1998

One of the delivery trucks in the General Distributing fleet

General Distributing headquarters

Heartland Industries

HEARTLAND Industries, America's #1 Backyard Builder®, a Playcore Company subsidiary, was founded in 1975. The nationwide chain, with headquarters in Indianapolis, Indiana, now has 58 branches across the United States. The Salt Lake City franchise, which serves the entire state of Utah, was established in 1995.

Heartland is in the business of selling storage buildings, which it offers in a variety of shapes and sizes to meet customers' individual lifestyles, and the models bear names such as Tackroom, Statesman and Deluxe Estate. A basic Heartland storage building — or yard barn, as a Heartland structure is sometimes referred to within the industry — comes with a floor,

Heartland attributes its success in the Salt Lake valley to its customer service-oriented approach to business.

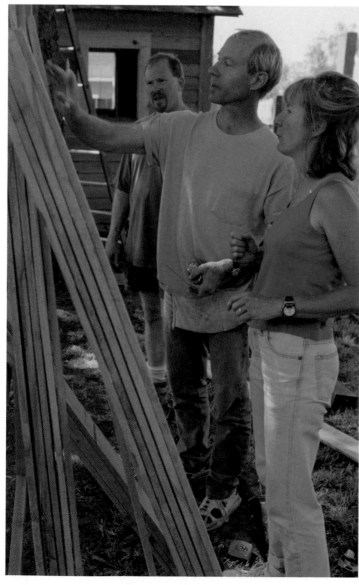

walls and a roof. When a customer purchases a Heartland storage building, the customer is required to provide an unobstructed clearance area around the desired building site. Heartland does the rest, for the purchase price includes professional on-site construction (placing the floor system atop leveled, 4-inch-by-4-inch treated runners), free delivery within limited distances, leveling of the building up to 6 inches using decay-resistant material, a standard floor system, shingles, moisture area-prone caulking, a pair of 8-inch-by-16-inch vents, an aluminum door threshold, door wind restraints and a complete top-to-bottom five-year warranty.

Because customers may desire a completed building to fit in aesthetically with the family home or to meet specific needs, Heartland offers a variety of options and accessories to help provide customers with a personal touch. For example, for an additional cost, Heartland will add treated floor joists and decking to resist moisture and wood-destroying insects. Heartland's features and options can be incorporated individually or in any combination for a storage shed, regardless of its intended use — as a storage facility, workshop or even a children's playhouse. In addition to treated flooring, options and accessories include sturdier doors, windows and skylights, shelving, loft sections for efficient use of overhead space and stairs for the heavy loft models. Surprisingly, a wrap-around loft adds two-thirds additional square footage to the Deluxe Estate (barn) model.

There are several factors that set Heartland storage buildings apart from those competitors offer. Foremost among these is the floor system, which is superior to all other systems, with floor joists built 12 inches on center. Additionally, Heartland's door system is patented, providing a door such as one finds in a residence, and the siding, because it's made for the modular industry, is more durable and water-resistant than that of competitors. Because Heartland is a national company it can contain lumber costs — it uses fir up to 10 inches wide for 2-inch-by-4-inch floor construction and 12 inches wide for 2-inch-by-6-inch construction — well below that of other companies. Heartland also uses only rot-resistant materials and asphalt three-tab residential shingles on all models, and the models come primed, ready to paint. Due to all these factors, Heartland offers consumers good value for their money.

Although storage buildings are Heartland's bread and butter, the company expanded its operation about three years ago to include a premium line of redwood modular playground systems. Families may choose from a variety of designs in bright, attractive color accents to meet their own particular aesthetic needs. Playground Systems are constructed entirely from sturdy, durable heart redwood construction. As with its storage buildings, Heartland offers a wide variety of optional accessories and the industry's largest selection of action slides to complete the perfect playground.

Because a child's safety is a No. 1 priority to all parents, every Heartland unit is engineered, designed and built to meet or exceed all applicable American Society for Testing and Materials (ASTM) safety regulations. For example, all Heartland Playground Systems have rounded corners, recessed hardware and vinyl safety sleeves on the swing chain and are designed with 4-inch-by-4-inch or 4-inch-by-6-inch beam construction to ensure a rock-solid, safe and dependable structure. Heartland is so confident in the quality of its product that it offers a full lifetime warranty on every Heartland Playground System. And because Heartland believes it's important to ensure that natural resources flourish for generations to come, the company purchases redwood only from lumber companies that participate in the Sustained Yield Program and practice proven reforestation methods.

Although Heartland has been in Salt Lake City only six years, it expects to be doing $2 million in business by the end of 2002.

The company ascribes its growth to increased population and economics. In situations where families have outgrown the space in their homes, rather than upgrade to a larger or more expensive home, many are electing to stay in their existing home but adding a storage unit such as those Heartland offers. The Salt Lake City franchise also finds that it sells a lot of storage buildings to schools and governmental agencies. However, more than anything else, Heartland attributes its success in the Salt Lake Valley to its customer service-oriented approach to business. A lot of good shed companies have gone by the wayside but Heartland embraces a customer's need and tries to apply the proper solution to it.

In addition to its office and outdoor showroom, Heartland's Salt Lake City branch also has a sales office in Clearfield. Lowe's Home Improvement Stores, IFA Stores and Home Depot are among the 1,800 dealers nationwide who represent Heartland products, and Heartland is looking at adding two more chain stores to its list of dealers. With its sales in the Salt Lake Valley alone doubling in one year, it is clear Heartland has found an important niche and is continuing to serve a growing list of satisfied customers.

O.C. Tanner

WHEN visitors walk into employee recognition company O.C. Tanner, the first thing they notice is that the factory is made almost completely from glass. A person can look from one end of the building to the other without seeing a wall. Founder Obert Tanner began his career 75 years ago working in the basement of a downtown Salt Lake City building. When he designed his own offices years later, he vowed to keep things bright and open.

That bright and open philosophy influenced more than the groundbreaking design of the building. In fact, O.C. Tanner became renowned for his cutting-edge thinking, and that pattern has continued through seven decades of business. Most recently the company was honored with a 2001 Ernst & Young Entrepreneur of the Year award.

Originally a manufacturer of class pins, Tanner recognized early the importance recognition played in the workplace and actually invented the employee recognition business. Today, O.C. Tanner is the largest company in the industry, shipping some 3 million awards every year and working with more than 10,000 companies around the world, including the majority of the Fortune 100. The company has 60 sales offices spread throughout the United States and Canada; it also operates a small manufacturing facility in Canada.

The company based its business on the fact that workers have many career options. Employee recognition is a proven tool that dramatically improves workplace satisfaction and commitment and helps companies retain valuable staff. Furthermore, employees who are satisfied with their jobs produce significantly higher results and achievements.

Tanner introduced this concept more than 60 years ago, and research has proven this idea correct. Through the years, O.C. Tanner has developed a variety of ideas and programs, and today the business offers the most comprehensive employee recognition options available.

Clients can choose a custom or prepackaged program that includes service, performance, and sales and/or safety recognition, as well as other methods of praise and reinforcement that strengthen employee commitment. Experience shows that when a symbolic, tangible award is given, it has lasting impact and helps bond an employee to an organization. O.C. Tanner offers thousands of award choices covering a wide range of products to fit any lifestyle, from fine jewelry to home electronics to sports accessories. Print and Web communication tools outline the company's goals and recipient's award choices. Awards can be enhanced with the client's logo in gold.

O.C. Tanner also provides unmatched service and support and trains managers to make powerful employee recognition presentations. Recognizing that there is no more powerful moment than the actual award presentation, O.C. Tanner has developed key information to help every manager make a meaningful recognition presentation. This training comes in a variety of forms, including interactive telephone and online options and award-winning videos.

Finally, O.C. Tanner anticipated Internet/intranet use for employee benefits, services and recognition by creating the first fully integrated award program Web site for Apple Computer. Since that time, hundreds of other clients have added cyber recognition to their programs. Recent developments include

Founded in 1927, O.C. Tanner is a premier Utah company. Its world headquarters in Salt Lake City, Utah, employs more than 2,000 people who craft millions of recognition awards for recipients in 166 countries.

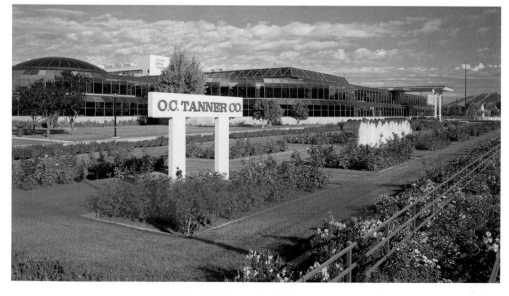

a prepackaged Internet option, making the service affordable for more companies. This option allows recipients to be notified of their upcoming award, view their choices online and make their recognition selection with the click of a mouse.

O.C. Tanner's services are especially valuable in today's workplace, where companies ask their employees to produce more results, often with fewer resources. The role of appreciation and recognition becomes vital in establishing a work environment that is motivating and rewarding for valued employees, many of whom have other job options available.

Since the company has long been recognized as the world's leading resource for recognizing outstanding employees, O.C. Tanner executives felt the jump to recognizing the world's outstanding athletes was only natural. Consequently, when Salt Lake City won the bid for the 2002 Winter Olympics, O.C. Tanner began its own bid to become the "Maker of the Medals." Competing with more than 100 other companies, O.C. Tanner was thrilled to be selected for the honor and, once again, set a precedent for leading the way. The company spent a full year developing the process to create the most complex medals ever made. The medals are designed to appear part river rock, part technological and are customized for each of the 78 Winter Olympic events. Each of the 861 medals takes about 20 hours to complete, and much of the work is done by hand. The entire project was donated as the company's contribution to athletes of the Olympic Winter Games.

This interest in the community is not new for O.C. Tanner. From the very beginning, Obert Tanner insisted that his company donate at least 10 percent of its profits to charitable causes. That tradition continued after Tanner died in 1993. Company representatives are often involved in community service projects and events, including building homes for the needy and providing other volunteer work. The arts are of particular interest to the company. Several Utah arts organizations are regular recipients of O.C. Tanner's legendary philanthropic contributions.

Another tradition continued from Obert Tanner's days is the company's attitude toward its employees. All 2,000 employees, from managers and executives to press operators and designers, work side by side in the all-glass factory. Tanner believed that every person contributed to the company's overall success and every employee deserved to be heard and appreciated.

O.C. Tanner partners with companies, including the majority of the Fortune 100, to create meaningful recognition experiences for employees and build lasting employee-employer relationships.

Still family-owned today, O.C. Tanner remains a company committed to its customers, the community and its employees. When businesses partner with O.C. Tanner, they can rest assured that they are working with the leader in employee recognition, ideas, products and services.

O.C. Tanner, the world's leading manufacturer of corporate recognition products, is providing the highest symbols of achievement — the gold, silver and bronze medals for the 2002 Olympic Winter Games.

A&Z Produce Company

IN the high-tech world of the 21st century, A&Z Produce Company, a father-and-sons operation that relies primarily on verbal agreements rather than signed contracts, stands out as an anomaly — a monument, perhaps, to the old-fashioned values the business was built upon.

One of Salt Lake City's oldest wholesale produce suppliers, A&Z opened its doors for business more than 60 years ago. However, the company truly began growing when Cliff Clark became a partner after World War II. The driving force behind the company during the last half-century, Cliff brought an impressive work ethic with him.

One of 13 children in a family raised during the Depression, Cliff got his first job at age 5 harvesting pickling onions. He's been working nonstop ever since. By the age of 12, he was driving a truck for a local farmer, delivering produce to market. Even then, his career path in produce seemed clearly marked.

Extremely resourceful and incredibly creative, Cliff spent the years after high school graduation making a variety of runs to neighboring states for loads of whatever produce he could find. He built a network of contacts along the way and always found willing buyers when he returned.

After almost four years in the Army during World War II, Cliff returned to A&Z. His reputation still alive with suppliers and customers alike, Cliff established A&Z as one of the largest wholesale produce suppliers in Utah.

A&Z relies on suppliers from all over the world, but it works primarily with contacts in California, Washington, Idaho, Arizona and Mexico. Trucks roll into the downtown Salt Lake A&Z warehouse daily carrying tons of fresh fruits and vegetables. A vast majority of the loads are arranged for over the phone with no written deals.

For decades the company has earned the highest ratings for integrity and credit, and its suppliers see no need for signed contracts. Rather, a phone call alerts A&Z that a load — anything from bananas or strawberries to corn on the cob or zucchini — is ready, and A&Z sends out a truck.

The company conducts business with its customers the same way. A phone call made to evaluate what produce is needed, a promise made to deliver the items and then the promise kept. That's A&Z Produce's simple, unchanging business strategy. After all, as Cliff reminds his employees, it's a lot easier to keep your current customers than it is to find new ones.

In the early 1970s, Cliff's three sons, Jay Dee, Steve and Scott, joined him in the family business, and the four Clark men have continued to run A&Z in much the same manner that Cliff has run it since coming aboard the second time in 1946. They don't really have much of a choice, since even at age 83, Cliff comes in every day to ensure that things are running smoothly. But even if Cliff's sons could change things, they wouldn't. After all, why mess with success?

(Left to right) Steve, Jay Dee, Cliff and Scott Clark

Commercial Contract Group

As the exclusive dealership in Utah to offer Haworth Furniture, Commercial Contract Group (CCG) might have been content to rest on its laurels. After all, representing one of the world's largest furniture manufacturers is clearly an honor, and CCG had worked hard to become one of Haworth's top dealers worldwide.

However, CCG's commitment to superior customer and employee satisfaction prompts constant improvement. Consequently CCG has become a full-service office solutions company, offering warehouse facilities, a state-of-the-art showroom, the latest technology, alliances with other premium manufacturers and a consistent investment in employee training.

From its inception in 1987, CCG has operated on a principal concept, intent on forming a partnership with every client. CCG clients work with a team of employees, thus guaranteeing that they will always be able to communicate with CCG. Since most companies offer only a single account representative, this team approach sets CCG apart from the competition.

The company's first priority, according to owner Carmelle Jensen, is to understand a client's needs. Then company representatives commit to doing whatever is necessary to meet those needs. Handling this task encompasses numerous functions, ranging from simply supplying furniture and identifying budget parameters to product selection, installation and warehousing of inventory. The company employs a staff of five fully trained interior designers who specialize in design and space planning.

Careful consideration goes into each of CCG's recommendations. Having acquired a thorough understanding of space requirements and client needs, company designers use high-tech computer-design software to fuse function with design and determine the most attractive and efficient solution.

CCG also understands the pivotal role that installation plays in completing projects to a client's satisfaction. CCG offers a veteran staff of installers for each project. Installation services are only part of a full range of services that CCG provides, including receiving, delivery, refurbishment, warehousing, stocking programs and asset management.

CCG's unwavering commitment to create and maintain a family feeling among its employees ultimately contributes to its end goal of customer satisfaction. Jensen notes that while customers are important, employees are equally important because when employees are happy, they make sure customers are happy. CCG policy is aimed at creating a cohesive environment where departments feel that they can interface with each other and where respect for employees is encouraged and nurtured.

The company's "open communication" system enables its employees to be aware of the company's status and future goals, as well as participate in formulating processes and controls that make a difference in CCG's performance. This communication occurs in quarterly "Open Forums," weekly department meetings, quarterly individual reviews and numerous other avenues that symbolize CCG's resolve to listen to and respect its employees.

According to Jensen, CCG's sensitivity to customers and employees make CCG the leader it is — a company where clients know that regardless of whether their needs are simple or complex, the ideal solution can be found.

President
Carmelle Jensen

Colonial Flag

ON any given national or state flag-flying holiday, an array of American flags waves across the country. Chances are excellent that many of those flags come from one place — Colonial Flag, a leading supplier of flags and flagpoles not just for Utah but for the entire nation.

With its inventory stored in a garage and an office located in a basement, Colonial opened its doors in 1979, offering flags and flagpoles. From its inception Colonial focused on providing friendly service, the highest-quality product and reasonable prices. That philosophy paid off as Colonial's reputation began to grow. Today, the company has shipped flags and flagpoles to every state, as well as numerous countries, including China, Guam, Germany and Sweden.

Colonial has many claims to fame, including the installation of the tallest-known flagpole (over 200 feet) in the country,

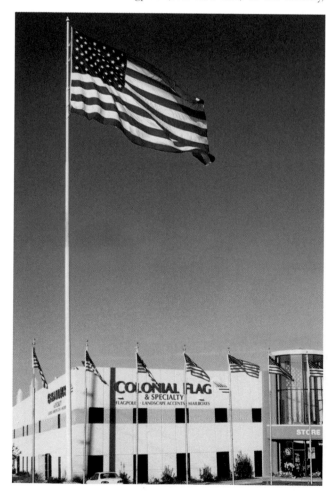

Located west of I-15, Colonial Flag's new facility is a patriotic landmark in Sandy, Utah, made notable by its breathtaking giant flag.

located in Dorris, California. In addition Colonial supplied all the flagpoles in the Carolina Panthers' NFL stadium, Pac Bell Park (Giants Stadium) in San Francisco and Lavell Edwards Stadium in Provo, Utah, to name a few. Colonial also actively supported the 2002 Winter Olympics by supplying most venues with permanent flagpoles prior to the Games.

It would be hard to find a flagpole company with more technical experience. Colonial is famous nationwide for its delicate installations on office buildings (the company uses helicopters) as well as its pole climbing and repair expertise.

Finally, during the patriotic fervor that gripped the nation after the September 11, 2001, terrorist attacks, Colonial became a central source for flags. The company provided more than 1 million hand-held American flags distributed during a variety of prominent sports events, including the World Series.

But while Colonial maintains a huge inventory of U.S. flags, the company also boasts a substantial variety of other flags, including national, state, territorial, military, historic, holiday and festive flags. In 1995 Colonial added its popular line of Landscape Accents, which include mailboxes, garden art, weathervanes, sundials, birdbaths, birdhouses and wind chimes, as well as an "Americana" line of décor items and crafts. The company also recently introduced its own line of custom flags and banners for businesses, fairs, expos and other special events.

In 2001 Colonial introduced "Betsy's Garden" stores, small boutiques located in malls that make it convenient and easy for customers to obtain flags and flagpoles. The shops also carry an array of garden accents and decorations.

In its ongoing commitment to the Utah community, Colonial regularly participates with the National Exchange Club and has supplied hundreds of thousands of flags that are handed out at various parades. Colonial also actively supports Eagle projects and flag fundraisers for the Boy Scouts of America. Colonial is a proud ongoing sponsor of the Freedom Festival in Utah County.

Clearly Colonial contributes in many ways to the growing wave of patriotism sweeping the nation, an attitude that is often best exemplified by Old Glory flying freely from homes and businesses around the country, and even around the world.

Dunford Bakers

DUNFORD Bakers began in the late 1920s with the purpose of creating an avenue to generate an income to provide food on the table, a roof overhead and the necessities to sustain a single mother and her three sons. Hazel Love Dunford, losing her husband to sudden heart failure, became a widow. The school at which she taught Home Economics closed because of hard times. The challenge became greater than ever as the country was facing the Great Depression. She never imagined that what she was about to embark on would become a lucrative business and a bakery dynasty to carry into the next century.

She began baking and selling bread in her own little home. A line of bakery products was created starting with home-baked bread such as many made in their own kitchens. Hazel had the help of her sons, who delivered her products to Salt Lake City homes on their bicycles. Just as Mrs. Dunford had expected, customers did prefer home-style bread.

They were so successful that they could no longer keep up with the increasing demand for the Dunford bread. As the boys continued to grow, so did the business. Steve, Clayton and Burns opened Dunford Bakers. In the mid-1940s Paul Stevens joined them, and shortly after he became a full partner.

Dunford Bakers continued to grow. Eventually it had three locations and also bakeries in some of the local grocery stores. Although sales of the other quality products were constantly increasing, the Dunford family believed that bread was the backbone of any bakery. Their bread was especially important because it was the original baked by their mother.

Through the years the bakery has gone through some transitions but still remains today — offering the same quality products. Hazel Love Dunford had the courage, strength and wisdom to find a way for her family to survive. Through the love of her family she took her energy, abilities and faith to work in a most industrious way. Hazel was their hero and bread was their "staff of life " in more ways than one.

Dunford Bakers today is located in a beautiful new 50,000-square-foot building with plans to double the size in 2002.

President and co-owner John Stevens says, "We have become one of the largest independently owned full-line bakeries in the Intermountain West." Stevens, who became president in 1981, learned the trade from his father, Paul Stevens. Paul brought his experience as a wholesale baker with Royal Baking Co. to the retail business when he joined the Dunfords.

Gary Gottfredson, John's partner and vice-president, expresses admiration and respect for the Dunford family and the road traveled by Hazel Dunford. In 1981 Ron Stevens, John's brother, brought his expertise in bread production to the company, which helped to round out the product line.

In the memory of Hazel Love Dunford, Dunford will strive to carry on her legacy and wishes to serve its customers with the Dunford tradition of quality, value and service.

To achieve progress one must bring time-honored values along the way. Dunford honors those who have gone before.

Fetzers' Inc.

IN the fall of 1909 three young German immigrants set out to start their own woodworking and cabinet business with only several hundred dollars in capital, not knowing it would one day become one of the nation's premier woodworking firms. On Thanksgiving Day of 1909, the three skilled craftsmen and confident businessmen secured a lease at 810 South State Street, Salt Lake City, in a 3,000-square-foot building and soon after bought several pieces of used woodworking machinery including a ripsaw, a planer and a jointer. They began doing small cabinet and remodel jobs, sometimes struggling to find work. Not too long had passed before one of the partners wanted out of the business for fear it would fail. Kaspar J. Fetzer secured a loan and bought out the partner, becoming the majority owner of the company. The third partner stayed on as a foreman for several years but ultimately sold his shares to Fetzer as well. In 1913 the business was incorporated and named the Salt Lake Cabinet and Fixture Company.

Kaspar Fetzer fostered relationships with many people in the growing community of Salt Lake City, and the quality of craftsmanship and skill of its employees quickly elevated Salt Lake Cabinet and Fixture to a place as one of the best woodworking shops in the Salt Lake Valley. The Church of Jesus Christ of Latter-day Saints hired the company to build the organ surround for the extension wings of the famous Mormon Tabernacle organ and also hired it to build the architectural woodwork in several temples during that time, including the Alberta, Canada; Hawaii; and Mesa, Arizona, temples. It was also contracted to build store fixtures for several department stores and restaurants in town, such as ZCMI and the Paris Company.

The Great Depression brought hard times for the young company, which spent time learning as much as it could about suppliers and competitors. Kaspar sent his two sons across the country to gain knowledge and experience in the industry. With the arrival of World War II the factory was full of everything from fuse trays to toboggans and lockers for Remington Arms Co. The Salt Lake Cabinet and Fixture Co. had quickly expanded to out-of-state contracts where to this day most of its business lies. In 1973 the company changed its name to reflect this expansion, and from then on would be known as Fetzers' Inc.

Today, Fetzers' Inc. operates a state-of-the-art manufacturing facility covering nearly three acres of floor space. Fetzers' Inc. manufactures its own veneer panels with custom matching faces. It has the most modern computer-controlled production machinery and its finishing department is among the finest in the industry. It is involved in projects from Manhattan to San Francisco, performing work for retail clients such as Nordstrom, Gap, Banana Republic and Brooks Brothers, as well as numerous university and civic libraries including work done for Stanford University, U.C. Berkley, University of Miami and the University of Arizona. After 90 years in business and with nearly 140 employees, Fetzers' Inc. produces architectural woodwork, library furniture and store fixtures that are seldom matched in quality and craftsmanship.

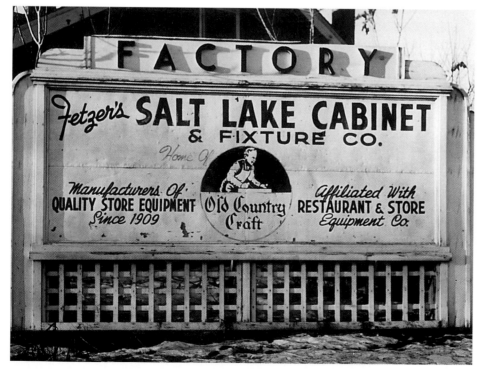

Hexcel Corporation

HEXCEL Corporation, the world's leading advanced structural materials company, a global enterprise with more than $1 billion in annual sales, has had a presence in Salt Lake City since 1913 when it was known as the Hercules Powder Company. Founded in 1948, Hexcel is today the largest U.S. producer of carbon fiber; the world's largest manufacturer of structural fabrics; the leading global producer of fiberglass electronic materials; the premier producer of composite materials such as honeycomb, prepregs, film adhesives and sandwich panels; and a leading manufacturer of composite parts and structures.

Hexcel markets its products to customers in commercial aerospace, space and defense, electronics, recreation and general industrial markets. Hexcel materials are used on virtually every commercial and military aircraft produced in the Western world and in thousands of other products, from satellites and launch vehicles, to high-speed trains and ferries, cars, trucks, cellular telephones, laptop computers, skis and golf clubs, and construction materials.

In 1913 Hercules constructed its plant in West Valley City as a black powder/dynamite production facility. Hercules began producing carbon fiber in 1970 and manufacturing prepreg tape in 1971. Alliant Technology Systems purchased Hercules' Aerospace and Composite Structures businesses in 1995. In 1996 Hexcel acquired Hercules' Composite Products Division and began consolidating its Anaheim operation with the Salt Lake City plant. Through this acquisition Hexcel gained a work force composed of dedicated, knowledgeable, experienced employees and a manufacturing facility that became a valued part of a dynamic corporation.

Today, with 330 employees, Hexcel's Salt Lake City plant has the capacity to produce 5 million pounds of carbon fiber and 22 million square feet of prepreg annually. Hexcel carbon fibers are produced in a continuous operation in which polyacrylonitrile (PAN) precursor fiber undergoes a series of precisely controlled processes to burn off all but the carbon molecules, chemically changing the precursor to yield high strength-to-weight and high stiffness-to-weight properties. The resulting crystalline carbon fiber structure is stronger than steel, lighter than aluminum and as stiff as titanium, making it ideal for use in laptop cases, aircraft primary structure and stowage bins, floor panels and sidewalls, machine parts, gears and chemical valves. Hexcel is a major supplier of carbon fiber used on the C-17 military transport, V-22 tilt-rotor aircraft, and F-18 and F-22 joint strike fighters.

Due to considerable expansion, the 128,000-square-foot West Valley City prepreg plant comprises five buildings, including a raw-material receiving warehouse and material-testing laboratory. The plant produces epoxy resins, adhesives, resin and adhesive films, unidirectional tapes, hot-melt fabrics, solvated fabrics and prepreg tow. Reinforced with carbon, S&E glass, Kevlar, quartz or nickel-coated carbon, prepregs are used in engine fan blades, nacelles, primary and secondary aircraft structures, rocket motor cases, aircraft floor panels and helicopter components for Boeing, Lockheed Martin, Northrop-Grumman and other aerospace companies. Hexcel prepregs are also used in golf club shafts, tennis racquets and arrows.

New aerospace applications, along with buildups in military and space programs, will require increased Hexcel production of prepreg and carbon fiber. Hexcel-Salt Lake City, with 30 years of experience, will easily meet these production demands.

Hexcel's Salt Lake City plant has the capacity to produce 5 million pounds of carbon fiber and 22 million square feet of prepreg annually.

OGIO International

OGIO president and founder Mike Pratt has the bloodline of a Mountain West pioneer: he is a descendant of Orson Pratt, one of Utah's original settlers, a renowned scientist and an apostle in the LDS Church. But Pratt's unorthodox business style has much more in common with Orrin Porter Rockwell, rebel namesake of the business park where OGIO is situated.

Like Rockwell — the desperado bodyguard for Brigham Young — Pratt defies convention. Rather than brandishing an 1851 Colt revolver as Rockwell did, Pratt has blazed his own trail in establishing a multimillion-dollar sports bag empire with a renegade reputation.

As a brash 20-year-old, Pratt had the chutzpah to think he could fix his gym bag, which, on the surface, wasn't broken. Starting with duct tape and cardboard, Pratt created a gym bag that would "carry like a duffle and work like a locker." The "Original Locker Bag" sold like Ace bandages to the U.S. ski team, and a year later in 1988, financial partner Dick McGillis upped the ante, making Pratt free to create an impressive line of daypacks and duffle bags.

Ten years later Pratt took on the golfing industry. No longer just an "old man" sport, golf was attracting the athlete who cared as much about image as quality. OGIO broke paradigms — and competitors' decades-long winning streaks — with the introduction of extreme-sport-inspired golf bags. By 1999 many of these one-time competitors began contracting with Pratt's crew to create their own buzz-worthy product lines. Case-in-point: more than 80 percent of Callaway golf bags today bear the "OGIO Engineered" logo.

Four years after introducing the golf bag line, OGIO has charted 100-percent growth annually, now manufacturing and distributing close to 1 million golf bags per year. Its products are currently sold through U.S. golf specialty, Internet and sporting goods retailers. Overseas, sales are equally impressive, with

OGIO taking market share in a number of countries including Germany, the United Kingdom and Japan.

Recently OGIO opened a new 90,000-plus-square-foot facility just minutes from downtown Salt Lake. Not unintentionally, it is also near an internationally acclaimed hang-gliding center, where OGIO's executive team has become flight certified. They also charge their adrenaline — and their visitors' — with rides in OGIO's sand rails at one of Utah's many sand dunes.

In addition to its OGIO-branded products, the company also co-brands bags through its advertising specialty division with the likes of Gatorade, Microsoft, Dr. Pepper, General Motors and Pfizer. It has also crossed over into the two-wheeled world, creating unusual but effective marketing associations with Yamaha Motor Sports, Mongoose bikes and Ducati.

Most recently, ingenuity has earned Pratt a coveted 2001 Ernst & Young Entrepreneur of the Year award. Sharing credit with more than 1,200 individuals in-house and world-wide who have made the company possible, Pratt also acknowledges his longtime partner Dick McGillis, noting that "every young man should have a mentor like Mr. McGillis." On the other hand, Pratt's design and marketing skills have made him a mentor's dream, too.

Utah Paperbox

UTAH Paperbox, a Salt Lake City-based company that produces both traditional and custom-designed boxes in the Intermountain and West Coast markets, was started in 1910 as Union Label and Box Company. The Keyser family bought the small business in 1922 and changed its name to Utah Paperbox. The company's manufacturing output comprised 85 percent rigid boxes and 15 percent folding boxes. The majority of the rigid boxes were manufactured for the candy trade — Salt Lake City's low-humidity climate was conducive to candy making and its large Mormon population favored candy over alcohol. The city became known for its locally produced quality chocolates and other candies.

As the company has grown, its manufacturing scope has been nearly reversed, with nearly 80 percent of the business now being in folding boxes and 20 percent in rigid boxes. The candy trade is still the largest consumer of rigid boxes, which are boxes that come in two pieces and consist of cardboard covered with printed paper. The company also makes two kinds of folding boxes — one, where a carton is directly printed on the cardboard, and then die-cut and glued in several tuck-end styles, and the other, a box with a lid and/or internal separators. Utah Paperbox has the latest in equipment and computerized operations and a full prepress department that allows for direct-to-plate printing. In addition to box manufacturing, the company offers printing and die-cutting for a variety of uses, such as inserts for plastic trays used for windshield wiper blades and "clam packs" with printed cards that accompany household products.

The confection business is the largest part of Utah Paperbox's business, but the company also produces packaging for pharmaceutical, software, coffee, awards and plaques, as well as a wide variety of household products. The company can manufacture virtually any kind of box that customers need.

Utah Paperbox Company has a reputation within the industry as being an "innovator of paperboard packaging," one of the only companies in North America capable of running in-house folding, rigid and litho-laminated corrugated packaging. The National Paperbox Association named Utah Paperbox a packaging award winner in 2001. The company received excellence awards for its innovative design and manufacture of deluxe assortment chocolate boxes, Sundance boxes and boxes that hold an adjustable shower massage showerhead.

Today, Utah Paperbox is still owned and managed by the Keyser family, with Paul Keyser, CEO, and Stephen Keyser, sales manager, representing the 3rd and 4th generations respectively. With more than 200 regular employees, people have always been and still are the company's greatest strength, with one employee, Wayne Sanford, going on his 59th year of service. In the office alone there are two married couples, three father-son duos and countless generations of fellow workers in the plant. The Keysers believe that Utah Paperbox Company is part of Salt Lake City's heritage and want to keep it that way. Utah Paperbox has a broad customer base and is not tied to any one industry, so it fully expects to continue "full steam ahead" for years to come.

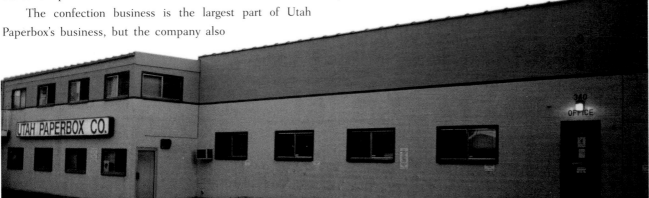

Utah Paperbox operates from three downtown locations.

Varian Medical Systems

FOR more than half a century, Varian Associates has played a vital role in the creation of breakthrough technology that continues to dramatically impact the world. The Varian division in Salt Lake City has not only aided U.S. defense systems and supplied essential elements for communications, it has saved countless lives through specialized X-ray technology. Few businesses can claim more diverse, innovative advances.

The company's history is one punctuated by discovery and transformation. In a Stanford University lab in early 1937, Russell and Sigurd Varian invented an extraordinary vacuum tube that would revolutionize radar. The klystron tube was unequaled in power and accuracy and helped the Allied forces triumph in World War II. After the war, the brothers founded Varian Associates with a mere $22,000 at a small facility in San Carlos, California. The tiny company pioneered technologies that revolutionized many industries, including physics, chemistry, electronics and health care.

In 1967 Varian merged with Eitel-McCullough (Eimac), a manufacturer of radio and microwave tubes. During World War II, Eimac had supplied radar and military radio tubes from facilities in San Carlos and in Salt Lake City on the site of an old Remington arms factory. The later merger with Varian proved a success, and the Utah division focused on black-and-white,

then color television tubes. As makers such as RCA began manufacturing their own tubes, Varian entered the small but rapidly expanding market of X-ray tubes.

X-ray became so successful that the parent company consolidated all of its transmitting business in California in 1995. In 1999 Varian Associates split into three companies, leaving Varian Medical Systems to focus on health care. Located in a sprawling plant on a 20-acre site in Salt Lake City, Varian has become the creator of the world's most powerful X-ray tube as well as the largest independent X-ray tube manufacturer. Sales of CT scanning, oncology, mammography and other diagnostic tubes bring in over $150 million yearly. In addition, Varian discovered that its industrial tubes could be used for analyzing data in the chemical, mining, steel and aircraft industries. Today, 85 percent of Varian customers lie outside U.S. borders, including Asia and Europe. These countries — particularly China — are making headway in improving health care systems and are demanding better, more accurate equipment.

An exciting development in health care is the concept of direct digital imaging. For every tube on the market, there is a receptor to capture images. Digital receptors will likely replace conventional film, allowing greater accuracy and flexibility of transmission between clinics and doctors. Varian is

Against the backdrop of majestic mountains, this sprawling, 300,000-square-foot facility represents an enormous capacity for innovation and production. Varian Associates is the third-largest patent holder in the world — just behind National Semiconductor and Hewlett-Packard. Varian Medical Systems claims a number of these in advanced X-ray technology and health care.

working on a collaborative project with the radiology department at the University of Utah on recent advances in digital imaging that will benefit health care in Utah and the world over.

"The significant thing about our business is that we are in the business of saving lives," says Steve Clark, vice president of sales and marketing. "It's vitally important to each of us to do our best every day."

Associates at Varian enjoy the fact that every tube that goes out on the market saves countless lives through diagnostic treatment and early detection of cancer and other life-threatening diseases. Continuing efforts to bring further advancements in this and other fields promise to make Varian a major world player for years to come.

Marketplace

Area retail establishments and service industries offer an impressive
variety of choices for Salt Lake City residents and visitors.

Hilton Salt Lake City Center 190

Harman Management Corporation 194

Meier & Frank/ZCMI 196

R.C. Willey Home Furnishings 198

ABSOLUTE! Restaurant & Brasserie 200

Anton Boxrud Bed & Breakfast 201

Culinary Crafts 202

Dave Strong Porsche, Audi and Volkswagen 203

Daynes Music 204

Greenbacks/All a Dollar 205

Historic Trolley Square 206

Mr. Mac 207

Winder Dairy 208

Hilton Salt Lake City Center

THE Hilton Salt Lake City Center, as its name implies, is in the heart of downtown Salt Lake City, just one-half block from the Salt Palace Convention Center and near historic Temple Square, Abavranel Hall and The Delta Center. The hotel has been rebranded several times. It opened as The Sheraton in 1983, at a terrible time for the overbuilt hotel market in Salt Lake, and was purchased by Red Lion. When Doubletree bought Red Lion in 1997, the hotel became part of the Doubletree chain. In 1998 Promus Hotels merged with Doubletree and in 1999 Hilton bought Promus.

LUXURIOUS ROOMS AND AMENITIES

The name Hilton is an incredibly well-known brand name that conjures up the image of a hotel that will meet every guest's highest expectations of comfort. The Hilton Salt Lake City Center meets its guests' expectations, for besides the latest rebranding efforts, a significant monetary investment has been made in the Hilton Salt Lake City Center. In June 2000 it became the first former Doubletree hotel to be reflagged by the Hilton chain. Nearly $4 million was spent in renovating the Hilton's two eateries, entertainment lounge, conference center and a portion of the guestrooms. The hotel's 20 suites were all renovated in 2000 at a cost of $450,000. Renovation of the remaining 480 guestrooms began in the fourth quarter of 2000.

By the end of 2001 the Hilton was completely renewed. Each suite and guest room has two dual-line telephones with voice mail and data port, high-speed Internet access, cable TV with on-command video, an in-room safe and the usual complimentary amenities such as a coffee maker, iron and ironing board and a hairdryer. Executive-level accommodations include a private lounge complete with complimentary continental breakfast and evening hors d'oeuvres.

The Hilton is in the heart of Salt Lake's business and entertainment districts.

Other amenities include valet dry cleaning and laundry; car rental on-site; a business center with computers, fax and photocopy machine, secretarial assistance and shipping capabilities; a heated indoor pool and sun deck. A guest services

> By the end of 2001 the Hilton was completely renovated at a toal cost of 15.9 million.

manager and bell staff are available to assist hotel guests in arranging dinner reservations, tickets to any sporting event or theatrical production, ski and golf rentals or any other needs guests may have.

A fitness center, equipped with state-of-the-art cardiovascular and aerobic equipment, whirlpool and dry sauna, caters to travelers who want to keep fit while away from home. The Hilton also has licensed male and female massage therapists who specialize in therapeutic massage, stress reduction, sports massage, acupressure, deep tissue massage and relaxation in a luxurious, relaxed setting.

Frequent guests of Hilton hotels may enroll in Hilton HHonors®, a guest reward program that lets them enjoy a variety of services and amenities tailored especially for members. More than 2,000 hotels participate in HHonors family and let enrollees earn both points for free nights and miles for free flights as well as room upgrades, complimentary health club access during Hilton stays and other rewards. Hilton is the only major hotel company to offer both points and miles for each stay.

CLOSE TO EVERYTHING IMPORTANT

Covered underground and valet parking are available and a local transportation company provides airport transportation. Guests may easily walk from the Hilton to Temple Square, the Capitol Theater, The Delta Center, Crossroads Mall and the State Capitol. Shopping, restaurants, nightlife and entertainment activities are all within walking distance. The Hilton also has car rental services on site for guests who want to visit any of the nine nearby world-class ski resorts or visit sites outside of the downtown area.

In all, the Hilton Salt Lake City Center has 24,000 square feet of meeting space with 19 meeting rooms. The 8,000-square-foot Grand Ballroom can also hold up to 1,100 people.

The Hilton's outstanding indoor pool and exercise facility

whimsical Western flair décor resplendent with bright colors and petroglyph designs on the floor. A extensive menu allows guests a choice of a continental buffet or complete executive buffet for breakfast; fresh roasted turkey; aged beef or daily specialty roast hot lunch sandwiches, with a complete variety of fresh breads, vegetables and sauces; and home-style specialties for dinner.

FINE FOOD, COMFORTABLE SURROUNDINGS

Dining at the Hilton is a memorable experience whether it's a simple continental breakfast, hot beef sandwich for lunch or a Prime Steak dinner. The Hilton Salt Lake City Center proudly boasts of two fine eating establishments. Spencer's for Steak and Chops, the Hilton's fine dining restaurant/bar, has recently undergone a $700,000 renovation. Spencer's sets the standard for steaks in Salt Lake City as the only place in the valley where one can find USDA Prime-Grade Black Angus beef. As one of the country's finest steakhouses, Spencer's is a special place for the best in prime beef or succulent chops served in a stately yet comfortable atmosphere. Spencer's, which is open for lunch and dinner, was voted "Best Steakhouse in Utah" by *Salt Lake City Magazine* in 1999 and 2001.

Following a $750,000 renovation, the Canyon Ridge Café, the Hilton's informal eating establishment noted for its comfort foods, reopened on June 15, 2000. The café has a decidedly

THE ULTIMATE IN DOWNTOWN MEETING SPACE

The Hilton Salt Lake City Center is poised to provide the ultimate in downtown meeting space. This is no ordinary conference center! The Granite Conference Center, which underwent a $780,000 renovation in 2000, provides the most outstanding training space in the area. It is furnished with built-in audiovisual and conference equipment; individual temperature controls, remote lighting and a Bose surround sound audio system; and it provides the most technologically supported fiber-optic Internet connection in Salt Lake City. Standard audiovisual equipment includes plasma screens, DVD, VHS, VCR, LCD video projectors with computer graphics capability, surround-sound multiroom projection capability, a flip chart and standing podium with podium microphone.

In addition, the Granite Conference Center features two state-of-the-art meeting rooms. The Center has 1,218 square

The Granite Conference Center is the most high-tech meeting space in the Salt Lake Valley.

feet of theater-style seating for 52 persons. This area is ideal for training sessions and is always in high demand. The Granite Boardroom has 672 square feet with seating for 16 persons in conference style and features padded executive leather chairs for 12-hour comfort and a computer table. There is a complete all-day break area that is continually stocked for attendees' break needs.

Other services offered by the hotel include a dedicated convention services manager who helps clients coordinate all of their needs from room setup to dinner service, as well as guest room arrangements. Audiovisual technical support is also available to assist clients with equipment and data connections.

In all, the Hilton Salt Lake City Center has 24,000 square feet of meeting space with 19 meeting rooms. The 8,000-square-foot Grand Ballroom can also hold up to 1,100 people.

This is particularly important, not only to the Hilton, but also to the Salt Lake Convention & Visitors Bureau in its efforts to attract convention business to Salt Lake. A strong, stable economy has driven new business start-ups, relocations of existing businesses such as biomedical, high-tech and software companies, and employment growth. Thriving convention business and anticipation of the 2002 Olympic Winter Games has sparked robust growth in Salt Lake's hotel industry, and the Salt Palace Convention Center has recently once again significantly expanded its available

meeting space by 100,000 square feet. The Hilton is positioned to work with the Visitors Bureau to meet the demand for meeting spaces.

The Hilton donated significantly to the successful efforts of the Salt Lake Bid Committee to bring the Olympic games to town.

GEARING UP FOR THE OLYMPICS 2002

The Hilton donated significantly to the successful efforts of the Salt Lake Bid Committee to bring the Olympic games to town. The Hilton has long since been fully booked for the Olympics. NBC, which will be sponsoring and broadcasting the games, and Zerox, which will be supporting its corporate clients, will be the Hilton's guests and will occupy 90 percent of the hotel's rooms.

GIVING BACK TO THE LOCAL COMMUNITY

The Hilton continues to meet its goal of supporting the local community that began when the hotel was a Red Lion property. The Hilton has adopted Washington Elementary School, an inner-city school, as part of its local philanthropy. It backs the fund-raising efforts of the Karl Malone Foundation for Kids, which consists of an annual gala attended by celebrities and friends — country/western singer Neil McCoy was the main attraction in 2000 — and a sports challenge. Proceeds go directly to help underprivileged and chronically ill youth. The Hilton also contributes to the Make-A-Wish Foundation.

In addition to its charitable contributions for children, the Hilton — as befits a hotel in a city center location — greatly supports performing arts groups such as Ballet West, considered one of America's leading ballet companies with a repertoire that includes classical and contemporary ballets; Hale Centre Theatre, Utah's premier family theatre, which provides excellent year-round live stage play comedies and musicals; and the Utah Symphony, which performs in Maurice Abravanel Hall, one of the world's finest concert halls.

A PLACE WHERE CAREERS ARE LAUNCHED

The hotel trade is normally a very transient one with employees soon moving on to other ventures. However, the longevity of employment of the Hilton Salt Lake Center's staff is phenomenal. Many of the key executive and management positions are filled with people who have been with the hotel for

Guests may easily walk from the Hilton to Temple Square, the Capitol Theater, The Delta Center, Crossroads Mall and the State Capitol. Shopping, restaurants, nightlife and entertainment activities are all within walking distance.

many years and through many changes. Since the mid-90s, when the hotel business took off like a rocket in Salt Lake City, the Hilton has experienced double-digit revenue growth. It has re-examined the way it does business and has placed part of this income — $200,000 to be exact — into training programs. By focusing on training that gives team members the tools to do their jobs better, customer service also rises.

Frequent guests of Hilton hotels may enroll in Hilton HHonors®, a guest reward program that lets them enjoy a variety of services and amenities tailored especially for members.

The Hilton's goal is to be seen as a training center, a place that helps launch people's careers by giving entry-level personnel a chance to grow in their careers. In order to be the employer of

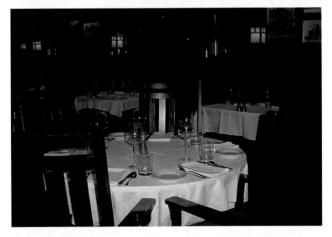

Spencer's has been voted "Best Steakhouse in Utah" in 1999 and 2001 by *Salt Lake City Magazine.*

choice in the hospitality business, the Hilton has looked at its benefit package to be certain that it will not only attract but also retain the people it hires. At a time when people can easily move from job to job and name their salaries, the Hilton Salt Lake City Center has experienced very little turnover. That speaks well of both the community and what's going on inside the hotel operation. It also explains why so many guests decide to stay at the Hilton while visiting Salt Lake City.

Harman Management Corporation

THE name Harman may not ring too many bells with fried chicken lovers, but Harman Management Corporation, known as Harman's, is the driving force behind the original and most successful KFC restaurant franchise. The familiar face is Colonel Sanders, but the man who managed the expansion of a "finger licking good" recipe from a root-beer-stand special to the forefront of American popular food culture is Pete Harman. In 1941 Pete and his wife, Arline, began their career in Salt Lake City when they bought the Do Drop Inn, a 16-seat restaurant at 39th South and State Street. Sixty years later, Harman's empire of KFC restaurants has expanded throughout the West to include 300 restaurants in Utah, California, Colorado and Washington.

Pete Harman's story is an all-American tale of humble beginnings, good ideas and good-old-fashioned hard work. He was born in 1919 in Granger, Utah, and shortly after his birth, his mother died. Not long after, he lost his father, too. The orphan boy was raised by his loving Aunt Carrie, a deeply caring and giving woman, whom he generously credits with molding his character.

As a young man Pete migrated to San Francisco and worked odd jobs. One day he found himself in a steak house, and when he asked for a job, the waitress called the union hall, through which he found work as a dishwasher. It was his introduction to the restaurant business. In 1937 Pete met Arline at a dance hall. He'd paid $5 for dance lessons, which was a steal since he found his true love as well. They proved to be perfect partners, first on the dance floor and soon after in life. After they were married, they returned to Salt Lake City.

Pete and Arline paid $700 for the Do Drop Inn and found it was more than they bargained for. One morning Pete found the kitchen crawling with cockroaches. Dismayed, he asked the iceman if it were possible to make a go of such a mess. The iceman gave Pete this advice: "Clean it up and you'll do

Pete Harman and Colonel Sanders pose in front of the very first Kentucky Fried Chicken restaurant, located on South State Street in Salt Lake City, Utah.

just fine." The restaurant had an all-American wholesome look, topped with a large Coca-Cola logo. Signs offered "delicious coffee, root beer on tap, plate lunches, hamburgers and hot dogs." Hamburgers were two for 15 cents, and draft beer sold for a dime. First day sales totaled $14.

Ten years later, Pete attended a convention of the National Restaurant Association. There he met the jovial Colonel Harland Sanders. The following year Colonel Sanders passed through Salt Lake City on his way to Australia, and he looked up Pete. Declining an invitation to go out to dinner, the Colonel offered to cook. With four chickens and his special mix of 11 herbs and spices, Sanders borrowed a pressure cooker and presented Pete and Arline with a delicious dinner they'd never forget. The pressure cooker was important. It reduced cooking time from 30 minutes to fewer than 12. For the first time, chicken could be a fast food, and hungry customers wouldn't have to wait too long for a good meal.

The very next day, on August 4, 1952, Pete and Colonel Sanders sealed a deal with a handshake. Colonel Sanders agreed to share his secret recipe with the Harmans, and Pete lost no time putting up a sign for his restaurant's new special. Coming up with a name was the work of a conversation between Pete and the sign painter. Colonel Sanders was from Kentucky, which to Pete and the painter meant Southern hospitality and good food. Thus "Kentucky Fried Chicken" went on the new sign, and a fast food empire was born.

Pete Harman likes to say that his business was built on a lot of little ideas, and some of them came in small packages. Takeout was a new concept in the 50s. The Harmans' KFC restaurants were the first to put lunches in a box. The famous bucket came about because a Colorado supplier had 500 too many. Pete bought them, put in 14 pieces of fried chicken, five rolls and some gravy. He charged $3.50, and dinner-to-go became an American institution. Pete recognized that takeout appealed to a huge, untapped market, and before long, takeout equaled half his profits.

> The familiar face is Colonel Sanders, but the man who managed the expansion of a "finger licking good" recipe from a root-beer-stand special to the forefront of American popular food culture is Pete Harman.

> Pete always believed that by treating people well, giving them a stake in their work and promoting them from within, his employees would return his generosity with loyalty and hard work.

Pete was on the move. By the early 1960s, his original restaurant had grown to 11, with a distribution center and more than 400 employees. Throughout the decade he opened a new restaurant a month until Harman's had grown to 100. This focus on growth, volume and people continued, and in June 2001 Harman's opened its 300th restaurant in Maple Valley, Washington. The newest restaurant is a co-branded KFC/Taco Bell. In the last few years, co-branding has become very important in Harman's development of new restaurants and the re-imaging of former ones. Harman's also owns four distribution centers that serve its restaurants.

Much of Pete's strategy had to do with his philosophy. He always believed in people, that they were the key to the growth of his company, and the concept of ownership drives the Harman's culture. Pete based his expansion plans on employee ownership as the cornerstone of success. A manager may own up to 30 percent in a KFC restaurant, or if a couple, a husband and wife may own 40 percent. Pete also pioneered the idea of profit sharing, and Harman's was one of the first companies in the country to implement the practice. Pete always believed that by treating people well, giving them a stake in their work and promoting them from within, his employees would return his generosity with loyalty and hard work. Harman's management turnover is just 11 percent, and many of his employees have worked for the company 30 years or more.

Today, many of the Harman's managers started their KFC careers as cooks, and Pete still visits the kitchens to shake hands with the crew. In return his employees pay tribute to the outstanding financial opportunities, the family atmosphere and the overall caring that characterize the company's culture. Harman's started with Pete and Arline, and it will always be a privately held company. Instead of an annual report issued to shareholders, the company publishes an annual yearbook filled with photographs of the hundreds of employees whom Pete and Arline Harman call family.

Meier & Frank/ZCMI

IN April 2001 when ZCMI, Salt Lake City's historic department store, changed its name to Meier & Frank, it marked the unification of two of the West's oldest and most successful merchandising institutions. ZCMI was founded by Brigham Young and other distinguished Mormon leaders in 1868, while Meier & Frank opened its doors in Portland, Oregon, in 1857. As the West grew and prospered, so did the two retailers who are now part of the American merchandising giant, The May Department Stores Company.

The history of ZCMI is almost as old as the history of the Mormon settlement of Utah. By the late 1860s Salt Lake City

ZCMI, around the year 1870

ZCMI in the late 1870s

was a bustling frontier city of 20,000 inhabitants, dependent for goods on slow-moving wagon trains trekking overland from the Missouri River. Tired of paying high prices for scarce goods, Brigham Young and his fellow leaders recognized the need for Utah to be more self-sufficient, and on October 15, 1868, they organized Zion's Cooperative Mercantile Institution. ZCMI was the parent company for a number of stores that began lining up along Main Street. From those humble beginnings, the merchandising venture soon spread far afield to serve Mormon communities in Utah, Nevada, Idaho, Wyoming and South Dakota.

It didn't take long for the fledgling organization to launch America's first department store, which opened for business on March 31, 1869, at the corner of First South and Main streets. ZCMI's new store was described as "a veritable mercantile palace" and carried clothing and dry goods. It soon added footwear manufactured by ZCMI's shoe and boot factory, and it wasn't long before the store was carrying men's and women's clothing manufactured by ZCMI.

Despite the remoteness of their frontier life, ZCMI's female customers were as fashion-conscious as women back east. During the 1880s ZCMI offered paisley shawls, plain and braided dolman coats, bright colors and a full line of laces, beads, ribbons, feathers, flowers and sashes. One store advertisement invited shoppers to view its "vast varieties of seasonal goods from the ugly and commonplace to the comely and aesthetic."

Fashion continued to be the hallmark of ZCMI as it grew throughout the 20th century, and over the years the store was the final word in style for Salt Lake City shoppers. As far back as 1950, national fashion magazines such as *Vogue, Mademoiselle, Glamour* and *Seventeen* were affiliated with the store, staging seminars and fashion shows. Today, the store is proud to place particular emphasis on American fashion designers in both its men's and women's collections.

ZCMI boasts many firsts. Because Brigham Young believed women were better traders than men, the store was among the first in the West to hire female sales clerks. The store was among the first buildings in Utah to be wired for electric light, and in 1884 the first hydraulic elevators in any American store were installed at ZCMI. In 1920 the first intermountain motorized delivery fleet began distribution in Utah and Idaho, following decades of deliveries by wheelbarrow, pushcart and horse-drawn wagon. The first escalators in a western store were installed in 1946.

Meanwhile, in Portland, Meier & Frank followed a similar trajectory of growth and success. In 1857 an enterprising 26-year-old German immigrant named Aaron Meier opened his first store, a small shop measuring 35 by 50 feet on the corner of Yamhill and First streets. Portland was a fledgling town with a population of just 1,300, and the new venture was a general store catering to everyone from housewives to miners. Goods came from the east via the Oregon Trail and from San Francisco on board steamers.

Building his business on customer service, plenty of credit and a generous return policy, the young man was able to open his second store two years later. However, he was nearly ruined five years later when he returned to Germany for a visit, leaving his new business in the hands of his partner who drove it into bankruptcy. Undaunted, on his return Meier started up another store with a new partner, Sigmund Frank, and the venture was named Meier & Frank. It was a smart move, and the new store flourished as Portland's population exploded. Business was so good that between 1885 and 1891 the store moved to a larger new building which was subsequently expanded.

Growth continued as Meier & Frank built a five-story building on 5th Avenue that included two elevators, a first on the Pacific Coast. It marked a new era in the store's history as it moved from a country-store operation to a huge department store with 120,000 square feet of selling space. Eleven years later it was time to expand again, this time with a 10-story annex, Portland's first skyscraper and the tallest building in the Pacific Northwest. In 1915, Meier & Frank built a new 16-story showpiece store that still stands today. Half a century later, Meier & Frank was bought by The May Department Stores Company. Today, May is a $14 billion retailing corporation that operates eight regional department stores across the country.

Over the years, service above and beyond the ordinary has been the centerpiece of the

ZCMI interior in 1915

Meier & Frank tradition, especially during times of disaster and stress. During a severe flood in 1894 the store stayed open, offering a rowboat service to its customers who walked through the flooded first floor on raised walkways. During World War II, Meier & Frank served its country with great patriotism. In 1945 the store was cited as the country's most outstanding department store because it suspended its merchandise advertising and ran more than 1,000 pages of newspaper ads devoted to the war effort.

Today, commitment to community and customer service are as important as ever. Both are long-standing traditions at ZCMI and Meier & Frank, and uniting the stores brings two great traditions together. With the merger of Meier & Frank's original eight stores and the seven ZCMI stores in Utah, The May Department Stores Company will bring these traditional strengths, plus its exceptional merchandise selection at a great price, to even more customers in the West.

ZCMI horse and buggy

R.C. Willey Home Furnishings

RECOGNIZED today as the largest furniture retailer west of the Mississippi, with a firm grasp on over 50 percent of the greater Salt Lake City furniture market, R.C. Willey Home Furnishings has not always been the retail juggernaut it is today. Fifteen years ago, the company was just one of the several furniture stores vying for dominance in the furniture industry. But since 1990, R.C. Willey has emerged as the state's dominant retailer because of its commitment to customer service and innovative marketing strategies.

The saga of R.C. Willey Home Furnishings began in 1932, when Rufus Call Willey, a full-time power company employee, started driving his little pick-up truck door-to-door selling Hotpoint appliances as a part-time job. With his garage as his warehouse and his pick-up as his storefront, he was ready for success.

Willey's part-time job soon became a full-time career, thanks to his innovative sales and financing techniques. His sales strategy was to put a refrigerator or electric range into a home that didn't have one and tell them to try it out for a week. He told them that if they didn't want to keep it, he would come back in a week and pick it up. He never had to pick one up.

His financing strategy was just as innovative at the time. He would write a "farm contract" and set up a payment plan

The start of something big — Rufus Call Willey (right) in front of his original store in Syracuse, Utah

In 1995 Warren Buffet (right), chairman of Berkshire Hathaway Corporation, concluded a purchase agreement with Bill Child (left) and his management team.

that called for one-third payment each of the following three falls after harvest time. This was the beginning of the extended financing program that has been a key factor in R.C. Willey's success ever since.

Due to wartime shortages during World War II, Willey had a difficult time keeping new refrigerators, ranges and other appliances in stock to satisfy his customers. So he began visiting garbage dumps, where he would collect discarded appliances, ranges and refrigerators, buy parts and refurbish them so they were as good as new. His determination to satisfy the needs of his customers regardless of circumstances increased his popularity and his reputation began to bloom. With the end of the war, both supply and demand escalated and Willey's business grew. Then the Korean War came along. Afraid that there would be appliance shortages as there had been during World War II, people stocked up and Willey's annual volume escalated from $40,000 to $50,000 to over $100,000.

Rufus Call Willey was becoming a force to be reckoned with. His presence was noticed by conventional store-based furniture retailers in the area, who complained that his mobile operations gave him a price advantage. Responding to pressure, one of his distributors threatened to stop supplying him unless he had a regular store.

In 1950 Willey built a store — a small, 600-square-foot cinderblock structure with a cement floor right next to his home

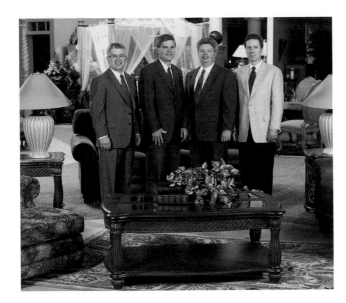

A new generation of R.C. Willey executives — (left to right) Curtis Child, Scott Hymas, Jeff Child and Steve Child

company to billionaire Warren Buffet, chairman of Berkshire Hathaway Corporation. The offer was not only rewarding from a financial perspective, but provided a number of other pluses, such as keeping the existing management team in place.

Growth continues, proving that superior customer service and low prices on excellent products is an enduring formula for retail success. New stores have been added, including locations in Boise, Idaho, and Las Vegas, Nevada.

Under the management of Bill Child, with the help of his brother Sheldon, R.C. Willey grew for over four decades from two employees to over 2,000 employees, from a 600-square-foot store to a highly successful network of 11 large retail locations offering a vast array of home furnishings, appliances and electronics. Sales volume skyrocketed from $100,000 when Bill Child took over in 1954 to well over $400 million by the new millennium.

The company's day-to-day management is now in the hands of a capable new generation of leaders. Yet R.C. Willey remains a family-oriented organization that prizes the values that made it prosper from the beginning: value, hard work and taking good care of the customer.

The key to the company's relentless growth — which has averaged a 17 percent sales increase every year since 1954 — is the integrity of its people at all levels of the organization. All employees are trained to be scrupulously honest with the people they serve. If a mistake is made or a problem occurs, the company and its employees have a longstanding policy of going to all ends to rectify the situation and satisfy the customer. Not surprisingly, R.C. Willey has won numerous awards, including being named the National Home Furnishings Retailer of the Year.

Since its birth in the back of a pickup truck seven decades ago, R.C. Willey's reputation remains its most prized asset.

in Syracuse, Utah. Most of the refrigerators, televisions and other products he sold remained in stacked crates, sometimes with one side of the crate removed so customers could see the contents. With his ongoing emphasis on customer service, his business continued to grow.

But as his business grew, his health failed. Willey passed away in 1954 and left his company, which was still small as retail operations go, to his son-in-law, William H. (Bill) Child. Having just graduated from the University of Utah, Child was ready to accept the challenge of following his father-in-law's footsteps. But it soon became clear that Child would do much more than just follow footsteps. Under his leadership, sales volume increased to $390,000 that year.

Three years later Child asked his brother, Sheldon, to help out. In 1956 they doubled sales after adding a small selection of furniture to their product offering. With the Child brothers living across the street from the store and treating each customer like a friend and neighbor, the business grew steadily. So did the store, which they expanded about every two years.

By 1969 the store had grown to 85,000 square feet and volume now topped the $5 million mark. That was also the year the Child brothers opened their second store in Murray, Utah. Child's reply to their success was simple: "Satisfied customers have always been the key to R.C. Willey's success. The way we got most of our customers was by word of mouth, and that's still the best form of advertising. At first, we had no other choice because we didn't have money to advertise. We had to rely on the people we sold to, to get us more people."

Continued expansion included new stores, outlets and an 860,000-square-foot Intermountain Distribution Center. In 1995 Child and his management team decided to sell the

R.C. Willey Home Furnishings' largest volume store, in Murray, Utah

ABSOLUTE!
Restaurant & Brasserie

In a world of franchise dining, ABSOLUTE! Restaurant & Brasserie and its sibling, Dijon Provencale Bistro, stand out as one-of-a-kind culinary experiences.

Located just west of Salt Lake City's landmark Capitol Theater, these unique restaurants are owned and operated by Staffan and Kimberley Eklund.

Staffan, from Smögen, Sweden, met Michigan-born Kimberley in the early 1980s on a ski trip to Alta, Utah. They returned to Sweden together to run and eventually own a large Swedish summer resort. In 1992 the Eklunds decided to move to the United States, settling in Salt Lake City after touring the nation and parts of Canada because they wanted to live in a clean, attractive city with either mountains or water, a good economy, a low crime rate and a high standard of living (without being too expensive).

Once here, Staffan and Kimberley did not immediately launch their restaurant. They decided to first find the right location and create a network of potential customers. To this end they became real estate agents. They did so well at this that their restaurant plans began to take a back seat. But when a location next door to the Capitol Theater became available, they couldn't refuse. ABSOLUTE! Restaurant & Brasserie was born in September 1996.

The Eklunds are hands-on people, and their high-end Scandinavian restaurant reflects it. From the start, both Staffan and Kimberley have made a point of being there for their guests whenever the doors are open — Mondays through Saturdays and the majority of Sundays — to make sure everything is just right

and to add a personal touch. They make a point of talking to guests and are good at remembering them. Kimberley has an uncanny ability to remember guests' faces and what they ordered — even out-of-state patrons who come in only once a year for conventions. This personal-touch attitude is shared by their waiters and staff.

Ultimately, of course, it is food that brings people to a restaurant, and ABSOLUTE!'s food is absolutely delicious. The menu has an unmistakable Swedish/Scandinavian flavor with a bit of northern-European influence. Entrees feature fresh fish and other seafood, steak, lamb and even some occasional wild meats like boar and bison. A smorgasbord that includes 60 Swedish dishes regales diners each December, and outdoor weekend barbecues with live music make the hot summer months cool. There is even a traditional Swedish crayfish party in August.

When a restaurant space immediately to the west of ABSOLUTE! became available, the Eklunds grabbed it and opened the Dijon Provencale Bistro in October 2000. Like ABSOLUTE!, the Dijon quickly became an icon of fine dining, superlative service and inviting décor — right down to the wood-burning copper stove.

Staffan and Kimberley have further added to their business by offering catering services, making their distinct dishes available to outside business dinners, special events and parties.

Though relative newcomers to the Salt Lake scene, the Eklunds and their restaurants have earned a remarkable reputation for quality and friendliness. Whatever the future holds for them, it will be delicious.

Outside and in, the Eklunds' restaurants make a statement of class.

Anton Boxrud Bed & Breakfast

IT is clear that Anton Boxrud, a Scandinavian emigrant, appreciated quality. When he brought his wife, Minnie, and daughter, Helen, from Pennsylvania to open a men's shirt and ladies' dress goods store in Salt Lake City, he engaged the celebrated architect Walter Ware to design the three-story Boxrud home, which was completed in 1901. After the elder Boxruds died in the 1940s, their daughter sold the house to a Mrs. Draper, who operated a men's boarding-house for several years. Draper removed the front porch, covered the floors with red felt carpet squares, took out the beautiful Tiffany stained-glass and beveled-glass windows, painted some woodwork with white enamel and removed other woodwork entirely. Fortunately, Mrs. Krause, the next owner, stored these treasures in the attic and basement.

The Anton Boxrud home had deteriorated by the early 80s. It was slated to be razed so that a senior citizen center could be built on its site when Margaret and Ray Fuller bought the house to restore it. The Fullers put back the pillared porch, replaced the windows, found the pocket doors of waterfall burl inside the drawing-room walls, stripped the white paint from the fir wood-work and removed the carpeting to reveal the natural maple floors. The Fullers opened the Anton Boxrud Bed & Breakfast for guests in 1985 and operated it until 1993, when they sold it to Mark Brown and Keith Lewis. Jane Johnson had been interested in purchasing the Boxrud house, having felt a rare affinity with it, but, as she told Brown and Lewis, who added many beautiful touches, they had "beaten her to the punch." In 1995, when they were ready to sell, she was ready to buy it.

Located near the governor's mansion in the city's historic area, the 100-year-old, seven-room inn is ideally located for guests who want to explore great restaurants, entertainment and shopping by foot or drive to nearby world-class ski resorts. Off-street parking is available behind the inn.

Johnson operates the inn with the help of her daughter, Jennifer, and her mother, Gladys ("Oma"), who is responsible for all the baking and Pennsylvania Dutch cooking. This warm, inviting home provides the comforts of a Victorian-style home without its stuffiness. Every room boasts signature chocolates, fresh flowers, soap and shampoo, and terrycloth robes. Guests may relax in the hot tub under the grape gazebo or on the grand front porch with its faux-marble pillars. Full homemade breakfasts include sticky buns, cream-filled French toast with raspberry sauce, blackberry cobbler and a special freshly ground roast coffee. In the evening the inn provides complimentary cheese and cracker snacks, wine and other beverages.

In addition to amenities such as private guest business office fax, computer modem, phone and TV, the Anton Boxrud's extensive concierge services range from scheduling carriage rides to acquiring tickets for sporting events, the symphony and ski packages. The inn will also handle specialty wedding brunches, business meetings and family dinners. The Anton Boxrud is a member of Professional Association of Innkeepers International and Bed & Breakfast Inns of Utah.

A Tiffany glass window (upper) and beveled-glass windows in the Anton Boxrud's foyer

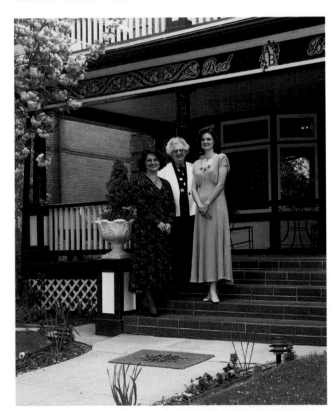

Jane, Gladys "Oma" and Jennifer, Anton Boxrud Bed & Breakfast operators

Culinary Crafts

THIS morning will start like any other for Ron and Mary Crafts. However unlike many people, by day's end they will have fed some 7,642 hungry souls. That's 27 gallons of Vichyssoise, a veritable farmer's field of baby carrots, a bakery full of warm breads, 21,000 petit fours and 40 pounds of Belgian chocolate made into enough exquisite, velvety smooth ganache to float away to chocolate heaven.

The Crafts don't run a Beverly Hills soup kitchen. They own Culinary Crafts, and they figure that in their 16 years of business together they've made enough food to feed every man, woman and child on the planet — and judging from their open-hearted generosity, this would be something they would love to do. "We're not the largest caterer in Utah, nor have we ever

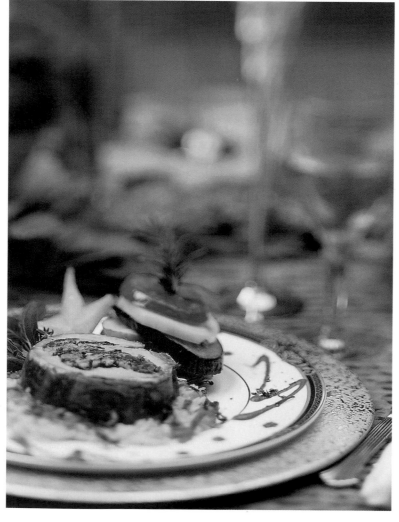

aspired to be," notes Mary. "We just have always wanted to do our best and have people feel truly special."

Of course, many institutions feed that many folks, and even more, all the time. So how do Ron, Mary and their team steer clear of all the "food in volume" pitfalls and set themselves apart?

It could be love.

When the Crafts started their business, there were times when things didn't look so promising. Ron had been in finance, and Mary had been doing social work. While they didn't necessarily know a lot about catering, they shared a passion for hospitality. "We love what we do," says Mary, "so we can do it well, sometimes in spite of ourselves." By combining a flair for good food with a knack for beautiful presentations — almost too good to eat, but not quite — and a gift for hiring skilled professionals, the kind everyone would love to have at home waiting on them hand and foot, Culinary Crafts has evolved into the catering equivalent of Shangri La — a place that's mythic and hard to reach, but once there, feels so good.

And that feeling has been experienced by many of Utah's most prestigious organizations. Culinary Crafts' client lists reads like a "Who's Who" roster, including the Sundance Film Festival, the Salt Lake Olympic Committee, The Office of the Governor of Utah and the Olympic Dream Team. *The New York Times* raved about Culinary Crafts' desserts as the "unquestionable favorite" in a recent taste test.

What does all this good food and perfection mean to Culinary Crafts' clients? It means that for once they can feel like a guest at their own party, a rare treat for anyone planning and hosting an event; the chance to stop worrying about everything and relax because the right people are handling all the little details.

And for Ron and Mary, who have devoted their careers to becoming those "right people," it means that at the end of the day, in addition to feeding more than 7,500 now-satisfied guests, they have once again made a client feel special while doing what they love.

Dave Strong Porsche, Audi and Volkswagen

DAVE Strong was only 20 years old in 1955 when he took over the automobile dealership his father, L.H. "Roy" Strong, had founded 20 years earlier. The elder Strong began business with a Studebaker franchise in Logan in the 1930s; moved to Ogden, where he operated a Packard dealership; and in 1940 moved to Salt Lake City, where he purchased downtown property, built a showroom and began selling Hudson automobiles.

Dave Strong started working for his father at age 14 and learned the car business from the ground up — from detailing and washing used cars to sweeping floors, selling parts and working the lube rack. At 18 he enrolled in the University of Utah, where he was in the basketball program, and married his high school sweetheart, Merle Jackson. Strong postponed his schooling when his father was forced to retire due to health reasons. It was a difficult time for the company, but one filled with opportunity as well. Hudsons, Packards and Studebakers were no longer being manufactured, but shortly before he retired Roy Strong had had the foresight to acquire a Volkswagen franchise. Volkswagen's economical little "Bug" or "Beetle," as the car was affectionately nicknamed, became an instant hit in this country and customers often waited months for their cars to arrive from Germany.

America's love affair with Volkswagen continued, and in 1960 Dave Strong added the Porsche sports car franchise to his growing company. In 1969 Strong and his wife, Merle, who has been a partner in building the business, purchased and remodeled a laundry building on South State and moved the Porsche franchise and the newly acquired Audi franchise there. The auto dealerships grew and prospered, and Dave Strong was able to resume studying selected business classes at the University of Utah and Brigham Young University. Dave and Merle Strong raised five children and have 17 grandchildren.

The company has received many regional and national awards for sales excellence. In 1997 Dave Strong was awarded *Time* magazine's prestigious Quality Dealer Award for "outstanding performance as an automobile dealer and as a valued citizen in the community." Audi Inc. has ranked Dave Strong in Salt Lake City No. 1 in customer loyalty among all U.S. Audi dealerships.

Dave Strong (center) with sons Brad and Blake, who are assuming management of the Dave Strong dealerships

In 1999 and 2000, nearly 60 percent of automobile purchases at the Dave Strong dealership were made by people who already had purchased one or more vehicles there.

Today, the Dave Strong dealerships — the Volkswagen franchise operated on South Main and the Porsche-Audi franchises on South State Street — are owned by Dave and Merle Strong and their sons, Brad and Blake, who are assuming management responsibilities. Dave and Merle Strong's son-in-law, Mike Baich, three grandsons and a granddaughter also work in the business.

Over the past 70 years the company has grown from 10 employees to 75, and the future looks increasingly bright for the Strong family operation. Porsche, Audi and Volkswagen are all enjoying tremendous sales increases and continue to innovate and add exciting new models, and the dealerships are well positioned on the fringe of Salt Lake's central business district.

Dave Strong's dealership has been a downtown mainstay business since 1940.

Daynes Music Company

DAYNES Music Company, the West's oldest music store and Utah's oldest retailer, is also the 76th-oldest family-owned company in America according to *American Family Magazine*. Established in the frontier settlement of Salt Lake City in 1862, Daynes Music turned 34 when Utah became a state in 1896.

Daynes Music and successive generations of the Daynes family have played an important role in the state's artistic history. Their leadership and generosity helped lay the foundations for the three major art institutions in Utah.

In 1940, Royal Daynes, then president of Daynes Music, assisted in the creation of the Utah Philharmonic Symphony, which later became the Utah Symphony. His role as the financial facilitator for the organization made it possible for a relatively small city to enjoy a large and prestigious symphony orchestra.

Royal's son, Gerald, was a primary founder in 1963 of the Utah Civic Ballet, now known as Ballet West. Daynes Music's store on Main Street was the ballet company's first home. For years Gerald Daynes made the entire top floor and basement available for rehearsals, choreography work, costume making and storage. The ticket office was also given space on the main floor.

In 1976 Gerald's son, Gerald Jr. ("Skip"), continued the family tradition by making room in his store for a new artistic entity. The Utah Opera Company was originally based in the Daynes Music store until it could go out on its own years later.

Through the years, Daynes Music has maintained a high degree of youthful energy. Its people are passionate about its products. Though the store once carried a variety of musical instruments, it now focuses on piano sales and is Utah's exclusive Steinway dealer. Daynes' new store, located in the southern part of the Salt Lake Valley, has been designated a model store by Steinway and Sons.

Daynes Music continues to have a strong commitment to the arts. The company provides prizes, including Steinway grand pianos, for winners of the Gina Bachauer International Piano Competition, which Skip helped initiate in 1976. Daynes also provides performance instruments and financial support to the Grand Teton Music Festival in Jackson, Wyoming, and the University of Utah Summer Arts Piano Festival. Currently, Skip Daynes is working to meet the challenge issued by Utah Gov. Mike Leavitt to find ways to restore music education to the prominent position it once held in the public schools.

With a strong commitment to customer service and to carrying only fine merchandise, Daynes Music has become a permanent fixture in the community. Building on this legacy and its continued commitment to the arts, Daynes is sure to remain a positive force for promoting the arts in Utah.

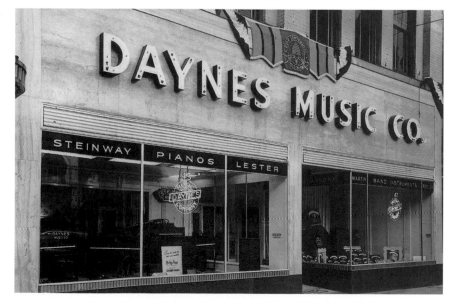

Greenbacks®/All a Dollar℠

BRENT L. Bishop's entrepreneurial abilities were obvious early in his life, and he dreamed of one day owning a successful business that would make a difference in the world. After starting a property management company and later co-founding the Franklin Institute, Bishop became intrigued with the concept of a "$1 price point store" while traveling in New Orleans in 1989. After much thought and research he and Paul Jensen, a real estate developer, opened their first such store, All a Dollar, in Sandy, Utah, in 1991.

Despite the fact that both partners had little retail experience, no knowledge of retail operations or merchandise management, and no supplier relationships, they were committed to creating stores that were bright, clean, professionally merchandised, fun and offered great value. Furthermore, Bishop established the company's values at the onset — ethical business conduct, an associate-oriented environment, a learning organization and giving back to the community. Since its inception, the company has demonstrated consistent growth in both sales and profits, enabling the organization to accomplish its strategic plans. The company changed its name to Greenbacks®/All a Dollar℠ in 1997 to distinguish itself further from competition as the company expanded and new markets were opened.

Greenbacks/All a Dollar creates a fresh approach to retail, mixing the best elements of a party store, variety store, convenience store and discount store into one easy-to-shop neighborhood location with everything priced at $1 or less everyday. Emphasis is placed on name-brand merchandise, exceptional value, first quality, extreme value, service and convenience in clean, spacious, contemporary, attractively merchandised stores. With an upscale approach to the single-price format and the careful development of unique and compelling products, customers feel positive about their shopping experience. Greenbacks has experienced steady, impressive growth with preferred locations in neighborhood or power centers and has been successful in both small and large markets. The company's greatest strength is its people and the senior management team's professionalism, which has grown and refined the company into what it has become.

Greenbacks' mission is to give definitive meaning to the phrase "customer focused," and in keeping with its mission statement, Bishop created the Greenbacks Bringing Hope Foundation. The foundation assists single mothers in achieving self-reliance and increasing self-esteem through mentoring, education and accessing available resources. Bringing Hope has been extremely successful in reaching out to the community and demonstrates the scope and depth of the company's commitment to and concern for others.

Greenbacks/All A Dollar Stores, with headquarters based in Salt Lake City, operated 65 stores as of November 2001 in Utah, Idaho, Nevada, Arizona, New Mexico, Texas and Colorado with plans to add an additional 20 to 30 stores per year. Greenbacks has received numerous awards including the World Trade Association of Utah's 2001 International Company of the Year award; inclusion in PricewaterhouseCoopers' "Utah One Hundred" Fastest Growing Companies for four years; recognition of CEO Brent Bishop as Ernst & Young's 2001 Entrepreneur of the Year; and the Coalition for Utah Families "Agency" Governor's Family Award to Greenbacks' Bringing Hope to Single Moms Foundation.

With a recently redesigned look and layout, a Greenbacks/All a Dollar neighborhood variety store stocks more than 4,000 quality items — and everything sells for $1 or less.

Greenbacks/All a Dollar operates 21 stores in Utah, located primarily between Price and Logan.

Historic Trolley Square

TROLLEY Square has been part of Utah's heritage since 1847 when Mormon leader Brigham Young designated the area as the Tenth Ward. The 10-acre block later served as fairgrounds until Union Pacific railroad magnate E.H. Harriman chose the site for his state-of-the-art trolley car system. He invested $3.5 million to construct the mission-style carbarn complex in 1908. Within six years, over 144 trolleys served the valley from this site.

The old and decaying carbarns were saved from demolition in 1972 when they were transformed into Utah's favorite marketplace. Relics from the turn-of-the-century were rescued and used in constructing its unique stores.

Trolley Square was registered as a historic site by Utah in 1973 and added to the National Register of Historic Places in 1996. The Square quickly became and remains one of the state's most popular attractions, offering unique shopping, dining and entertainment in a charming, historic atmosphere.

The Water Tower, serving as Trolley Square's landmark, is the original 97-foot-high water tower. It was designed to hold 50,000 gallons of water in case of fire. Now it is a colorful neon welcome sign.

Parts from two 510-series trolley cars were saved to re-create the Trolley Car that sits on the original tracks outside the east entrance of the main building which now houses Trolley Wing Co. Visitors can take a peek inside the Old Spaghetti Factory to see the oldest trolley car in Utah. The 300-series car was built in 1919 and now serves as a dining area for the restaurant.

Just inside the east entrance is an original Salt Lake City Gooseneck Street Lamp dating from 1885. Salt Lake City was the fifth city in the nation to have electrical power.

Located on the upper level of the main building is the Attic of the Culmer mansion, which now houses The Original Way Gallery. Just outside the north entrance is the Gazebo, the cupola from the famed Dinwoody mansion that once stood among the mansions on South Temple. Many of the hand-carved doors in Trolley Square originate from this stately home, as well as the staircase in The Spectacle.

The Spectacle's facade is copied from Ameila's Palace, which stood across from Brigham Young's house and was built for his last wife. Its most famous owner was the Silver Queen, Suzanna Bransford Holmes, who made her fortune in the Park City silver mines.

The building that houses Pottery Barn was the machine shop. The blacksmith shop on the west end is occupied by Green Street Social Club.

The building at the northwest corner was the paint and carpenter shop. It is now home to Hard Rock Café, Restoration Hardware and Tony Roma's. The Wells Fargo Bank building was the sand shop.

At the west entrance to the main building visitors will find stained glass from the First Methodist Church in Long Beach, California, in The Old Spaghetti Factory and Pub's Desert Edge Brewery.

The skybridge that connects Trolley Square with its parking lot didn't start out that way. It was a Mining Trestle from the Anaconda Mines near Tooele, Utah.

This is just a sampling of the historical features built into Trolley Square. Other interesting pieces are tucked away in its unique stores.

Visitors are invited to take a moment and relive the Old West by strolling through the historical highlights of Trolley Square.

Mr. Mac

WALK through the door of any of the nine Mr. Mac stores scattered throughout Utah, and the effect is the same — a huge array of smart-looking, durable men's suits, shirts and business accessories. Although the stores carry casual clothing items, Mr. Mac's emphasis is, and always has been, selling suits.

"No one buys the way we do; no one sells the way we do. No one." This Mr. Mac motto is familiar to anyone who has ever watched television in Utah for more than five minutes, and the man who makes the claim has become something of a Utah legend.

Fred MacRay Christensen (known as Mr. Mac to thousands of suit buyers throughout Utah) started building his legacy in the late 1950s. Newly married and barely 20, he found a job selling men's accessories in the bargain basement of ZCMI, one of America's oldest department stores. Mac had a knack for selling and quickly became one of the youngest managers ever in ZCMI history. Within a few years, he'd become the store's menswear buyer, then moved up to become menswear buyer for a chain of department stores.

It didn't take Mac long, however, to realize what he really wanted. A hands-on manager, he knew his talents would best be served in his own store. By 1966, Mac had opened Mac's Clothes Tree in Bountiful, Utah. Initially he drummed up business by loading suits into his old wood-paneled van and driving office to office. "Come out and see what I've got in the car," he'd say.

Another key to Mac's success was his personal way of conducting business. Mac was in his stores from open to close, six days a week, and he waited on every customer he could. Mac also focused on innovation. Because he bought in bulk, he got unbeatable prices, but he had to have huge sales to move the merchandise.

Consequently, he opened satellite stores and outlet stores; he rented fairground space and organized tent sales. Once he even set up shop in a football field for a weeklong sale.

Thus the birth of the Mr. Mac store motto. At first, Mac was reluctant to do his own advertising, but he quickly became quite recognizable. Although he's been semi-retired for the past few years (all stores are still owned by family members), Mac still utters those famous words in every Mr. Mac commercial, and his work ethic lives on in every store. Every owner waits on customers and places a high priority on personal interactions. Buyers also purchase inventory in the legendary Mr. Mac fashion — finding high-quality suits to buy in bulk so stores can sell the clothing at incredibly affordable prices.

"Mr. Mac's has a reputation," observes Mac's son, Stuart, owner of one of the stores. "We all work hard to protect and maintain that reputation. The name Mr. Mac is representative of one man's drive and ambition, one man who saw what he could do and devoted himself to it. I think people recognize that and respect it, and that's why the stores are what they are today."

Mac Christensen welcomes World Heavyweight Champion Muhammad Ali and United States Senator Orrin Hatch to one of his Mr. Mac stores.

Winder Dairy

In an era when personalized service and unwavering commitment to quality are on the decline, Winder Dairy stands out as an exception. In fact, the core of the company's business — door-to-door milk delivery — means that Winder must keep its customers satisfied in order to succeed. And as one of the oldest companies in Utah, Winder is doing exactly that.

A Winder Dairy truck

John R. Winder, an immigrant from England, pioneered Winder Dairy, a family-owned business that started out selling rich, creamy butter to neighbors. In 1880 the family began concentrating on milk delivery. A single contract with a downtown hotel quickly grew into a commitment to deliver the dairy's rich, pure Jersey milk to numerous hotels, lodging houses and individual homes throughout the valley.

John R. Winder

Originally, the business required only one horse, one milk-wagon and one delivery man; today the Winder delivery force includes two full-time tanker drivers and 34 delivery drivers to bring Winder products to nearly 20,000 customers. Back then, the milk was not processed but delivered directly to customers, who often received it within hours of milking. Today, the milk goes through rigorous pasteurization and homogenization processes, and Winder remains absolutely committed to quality, following a rigid "72 hours from the cow to your door" philosophy.

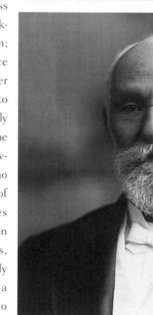

In fact, one of the defining differences between Winder and other dairies is the company's ability to identify what produces superior milk and then protect that process every step of the way. Winder milk comes from Winder cows, and the dairy pasteurizes its milk higher than regulations require and avoids exposing its products to UV lights (UV lighting can diminish Vitamin D values and levels). Consequently, Winder Dairy enjoys a solid reputation for producing what many consider to be the best-tasting milk on the market.

Certainly an ever-growing number of home delivery customers scattered throughout Utah feel that way. In addition to providing outstanding milk, Winder Dairy also offers more than 100 other products, and its customers can place orders 24 hours a day, seven days a week. Offering so many options has helped Winder achieve steady growth. In the past two years, the company has extended its home delivery service to Wasatch, Summit, Iron and Washington counties. Winder products are now delivered along the entire Wasatch front and Tooele, Park City, Heber, Cedar City and St. George areas.

While Winder's core competency is home delivery, it has also been an industry leader in breaking new ground. Winder was first in Utah to offer flavored milk, and in 2001 the company partnered with Cutler Cookies to open several country market-type stores where customers can buy fresh-baked cookies, tasty sandwiches and cold, refreshing milk. In addition, Winder has branched into the vending business, placing several cow-decorated machines filled with milk, fresh cookies and cold cereal in schools and businesses.

From its inception, Winder has stood for quality, creativity and taste. Today the century-old company continues to deliver these principles — along with great-tasting milk — right to the front door.

Networks

Salt Lake City utilities, media and business-support organizations promote economic growth.

KSL 212

Central Utah Water Conservancy District 216

Utah Film Commission 218

The Economic Development Corporation of Utah 220

Salt Lake Chamber 221

Utah Power 222

KSL

KSL has been an integral part of Salt Lake City's history and identity for generations. It began in the early years of the Roaring Twenties, when KZN Radio went on the air with only 250 watts of power. Today, KSL's television station and AM radio station are the award-winning flagships of Bonneville International Corporation, which is owned by the Church of Jesus Christ of Latter-day Saints.

KZN Radio began as an offshoot of *The Deseret News*. The radio station's first broadcast emanated from a tin shack atop the Deseret News building in downtown Salt Lake City on May 6, 1922. LDS Church President Heber J. Grant was the featured speaker. He promised that the radio entity would be the source of community service and reliable information.

For the first few months, occasional talks and songs were aired between the hours of 8 a.m. and 8:30 p.m. Airtime soon expanded when the ZCMI department store sponsored the station's first commercial messages. Even with the weak signal, letters of appreciation were sent that first year from listeners in 18 states, Canada, Hawaii and Mexico.

Two years later the radio station broke away from *The Deseret News* and changed its call letters to KSL in 1925. By then the station had begun broadcasting the LDS General Conferences throughout Utah. KSL aired its first Mormon Tabernacle Choir network broadcast in 1929. Today, the weekly choir performance is the longest-running network broadcast program in the world.

KSL Radio evolved rapidly as an AM station. Its transmitting power jumped from the initial 250 watts to 5,000 watts in 1929 and to 50,000 watts in 1932, making it one of the first 50,000-watt, clear-channel stations in the nation and one of the few to be allowed the FCC's most powerful radio designation.

It also grew in terms of programming diversity, providing visitors throughout a far-reaching area with entertainment, sports and regularly scheduled news programs. In fact, KSL was one of the first stations in the West to use the United Press and Associated Press wire services. An NBC affiliate since 1928, KSL switched to the new CBS radio Network in 1932 because it agreed to carry the weekly Mormon Tabernacle Choir broadcasts to the entire nation.

Today, KSL Radio and other Bonneville radio stations are acknowledged leaders in the industry. The National Association of Broadcasters bestows 10 Crystal Awards annually on radio stations that exemplify the best in public service. In the 10-year period from 1991 to 2000, Bonneville's radio stations won nine of the 100 Crystal Awards given to stations throughout the country.

The history of KSL Television, like the history of its older radio sibling, is intimately entwined with the story of the city, state and nation in which it has matured.

The owners of KSL Radio began investigating the possibilities of television as early as 1934. But World War II and congressional bottlenecks slowed the progress of commercial television. It was not until June 1, 1949, that KSL Television celebrated its entry into this science fiction-like arena with its first broadcast.

Cramped production facilities in what had been KSL Radio's Studio A in the Union Pacific Building at South Temple and Main Street became KSL

LDS Church President Heber J. Grant delivers initial radio broadcast.

Television's first home. A hole had to be cut in the building's roof because the new equipment was too large for the doors and elevator. In a little more than a year, the station would move to a new home on Social Hall Avenue called the Broadcast House.

A promise was made on the first day of broadcasting that has guided the station's operations ever since. KSL President J. Reuben Clark Jr. went on the air and said, "We pledge to you we shall do our best not to injure, but to uphold your family life." There were few television sets in the community to hear that promise, however — so few that engineers were able to go from house to house helping people adjust their sets to tune into the KSL signal.

The fledgling television station drew much from the experience and resources of KSL Radio, from which it sprang. The radio station's affiliation with CBS led to the TV station's early relationship with CBS Television Network. KSL Television also signed short-term agreements with DuMont and ABC networks until other stations in the area became operational.

Even though the station was launched on a tight budget of only $100,000, the first half-year of television broadcasting operations was a financial disaster. KSL lost close to $70,000, with an average of only three broadcasting hours per day. Within just 18 months the situation had turned around drastically, however. Annual revenues shot from $20,000 to $400,000, and the station was providing 11 hours of programming each day. Television had become a fact of life throughout the nation and the community.

The broadcast coverage of early KSL Television was relatively small. The construction of a 370-foot transmission tower on 9,245-foot Coon Peak (now Farnsworth Peak) in the Oquirrh Mountains rectified that limitation. The new tower facility pushed the television signals as far as parts of Wyoming, Nevada and Idaho, and covered the entire Wasatch Front with remarkable clarity. For a time it was the highest television tower in the United States. When a severe windstorm destroyed it in late 1952, crews raced to rebuild it. A taller and more stable tower emerged. Later, a network of microwave translators boosted transmission capabilities yet further, resulting in clear transmissions to even the most remote areas within the station's expanding reach.

When the tower was initially built, KSL employees put on their hard hats and bulldozed and blasted a road up the mountainside to it. Because the road was impassible during the long winter months, supplies had to be trucked in and

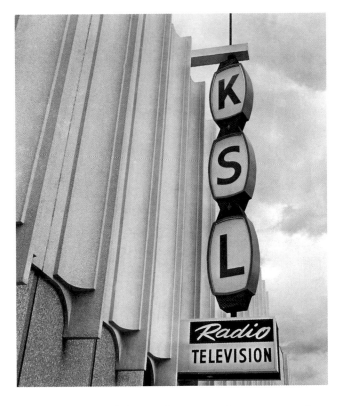

The Broadcast House on Salt Lake City's Social Hall Avenue was home to KSL Radio and Television for over three decades.

stored to last from fall through spring, and operators, working shifts of one week on and two weeks off, had to ski or snowshoe in. In 1954 an aerial tramway to the tower was built but was later abandoned as unsafe for carrying personnel. Helicopters now carry supplies, equipment and personnel back and forth to the tower facility.

Color television emerged in the 1960s, making KSL's existing equipment suddenly obsolete. The costs of re-engineering and re-equipping the station were staggering. New cameras, tape

Mobile TV broadcasting has come a long way since the delivery van days.

214

machines, even a new transmitter had to be acquired. The station's decision-makers, committed to maintaining front-runner status in the industry, dove into the new technology. In 1964 "Channel Five" produced the first color broadcast in Utah.

The advance of technology made KSL increasingly mobile. The station went on the road in the late 1960s in a converted bread delivery van. A series of "trade-ups" moved KSL's mobile operations through a succession of vehicles, from a remodeled school bus to a Lake Shore Lines bus to a fully equipped remote production truck. Then came Mini-Cam Five, the microwave technology that took viewers live to the scene, revolutionizing the way news was gathered. Chopper Five began flying in 1979. It was the Intermountain West's first full-time news helicopter. In the 1980s the station brought StarWest Five online — a mobile satellite uplink truck that gave live access to any geographic area in the United States.

KSL Video Production was formed in 1977 as a professional production facility to serve the region's advertising agencies and independent producers. Two years later the concern evolved into Video West Productions. Today, Video West Productions is its own operating division and ranks as Utah's largest and leading production, post-production and duplication facility.

Channel Five continued to grow, as did KSL Radio. By the early 1980s they had outgrown their 34-year home on Social Hall Avenue. It was time for a new Broadcast House. This time — for the first time — their home would be engineered and built from the ground up. The new facility at the Triad Center facility in downtown Salt Lake City was specifically designed for their operations.

KSL Television's longstanding affiliation with CBS came to an end in 1995 when CBS purchased a competing television station in the Salt Lake area. While KSL Radio continued with CBS, its television counterpart — one of the strongest stations in America — was successfully courted by the NBC Television Network. That relationship continues to be mutually beneficial today.

Channel Five has maintained its edge in technology and audience service. The station's leadership role in preparing the area for the new era of High Definition Television (HDTV) is just one example. KSL led a consortium of eight Salt Lake City-based broadcasters in the construction of a multimillion-dollar digital television facility on Farnsworth Peak. The DTV-Utah facility was one of the first multistation sites built in the United States. To ensure that its Southern Utah viewers would have access to the new digital television technology, KSL began operating station KSCG in Cedar City in 1999, to which it transmits its programming via fiber optics.

From the beginning, KSL Television's broadcasters have been among the most visible and popular personalities in the viewing area. The famous Dick Nourse, Bob Welti and Paul James triumvirate stayed together for 26 years, becoming the longest-running anchor team in the history of American television. They dominated the region's news, weather and sports coverage, setting a high ratings benchmark for other stations throughout the nation.

Today, both KSL Television and KSL AM Radio are award-winning icons of broadcasting excellence — known not only locally but nationally for their leadership in a rapidly evolving industry.

KSL pioneered commercial television broadcasting in Utah.

KSL sponsored the 2002 Olympic announcement party in 1995.

214

A word about corporate genealogy is in order. KSL is part of Bonneville International Corporation, which in turn falls under the umbrella of Deseret Management Corporation — the holding company for all the for-profit companies associated with the Church of Jesus Christ of Latter-day Saints. Bonneville has a number of operating divisions. At center stage is the Salt Lake broadcasting group, which includes KSL Television, KSL Radio and Video West Productions.

Bonneville International Corporation also owns a number of radio stations in San Francisco, Chicago, St. Louis and the Washington D.C. area, plus a television station that serves the southern Utah area around Cedar City and St. George.

In addition to its broadcasting divisions, Bonneville International Corporation operates two non-broadcasting operations: Bonneville Communications and Bonneville Satellite. Bonneville Communications is an advertising agency. It has produced the now-famous "Home Front" television and radio public service campaigns for the church since the early 1970s, winning every award there is to win in the advertising industry. The other division, Bonneville Satellite, owns and resells satellite communication capacity. The largest client of both divisions is the LDS Church, although many other top national and international companies and organizations can be found on their client rosters.

A commitment to community service pervades KSL and its parent company. When the Children's Miracle Network was established by the Osmond Foundation in 1983, KSL Television and Video West Productions were instrumental in the launch of the annual broadcast that raises funds for children's hospitals throughout North America. Since that first CMN broadcast, over $1.5 billion has been donated. Video West Productions and KSL continue to support this effort.

KSL Radio has donated its resources for over two decades to an annual radio-thon to raise money for charity care at Primary Children's Hospital in Salt Lake City. This effort raises hundreds of thousands of dollars each year. Another example of the community service-oriented attitude at KSL and Bonneville is their sponsorship of the "Family Now" program — an umbrella of initiatives that focus on strengthening the family and helping children. In recent years, they also

Salt Lake City's Triad Center has been the headquarters for KSL Television and Radio since 1984.

began co-sponsoring the Service to America symposium with the National Association of Broadcasters Education Foundation. The symposium recognizes the public service efforts of individuals and broadcasters.

KSL has long been recognized as a national leader in public service and broadcasting. In the future, the men and women of KSL plan to continue advancing the tradition of professional excellence, technological leadership and community service that has set their organization apart for so many decades. Their motto is simple yet powerful: "Do good and do well."

Central Utah Water Conservancy District

THE struggle to ensure adequate water resources has been a major thread through Utah's history from the time Brigham Young led the first vanguard of pioneers to the Salt Lake Valley. Arriving in the hot summer of 1847, they knew that water would be the key to growing a city in the dry, high-desert climate. They responded by launching the first large-scale irrigation initiative in the United States.

The Central Utah Water Conservancy District is a direct descendant of Utah's early fight for water. At the root of its existence and mission is the fact that Utah was granted the right to 22 percent of the Colorado River drainage. Having the right to all that water, however, is like being given a banana that happens to be in a gorilla's cage. It's nice knowing it's yours, but it won't do you a bit of good until you go get it.

Getting the water allotment out of the Colorado River drainage to where it can do Utah some good is the challenge that gave life to the Central Utah Water Conservancy District (CUWCD). The district was formally established in 1964. But the roots of its creation go all the way back to 1902 when farmers began investigating the feasibility of diverting water from the Colorado River to the Bonneville Basin in central Utah. Over the ensuing years studies were conducted and projects were undertaken to explore this issue. The U.S. Bureau of Reclamation began its own investigations of the "Central Utah Project" (CUP) in 1945 and authorized portions of the CUP in 1956 and 1968.

The state of Utah established the Central Utah Water Conservancy District in 1964 to serve as the local entity to contract with the federal government for the construction, operation and financing of the CUP. The district is governed by a board of 18 trustees representing 10 central Utah counties.

The CUP's final construction was reauthorized in 1992 with the Central Utah Project Completion Act. The act designated the district as the "lead agency" for bringing the work to completion. In that role, the district works closely with the

> Since its creation the Central Utah Water Conservancy District has been more than a match for its challenging mission.

U.S. Department of the Interior and other key agencies to plan and build the pipelines and other features that bring water to the various counties.

The CUP is the largest water resource development project ever undertaken in Utah. It involves five specific units, each consisting of a series of dams, pipelines, reservoirs, tunnels and aqueducts designed to help meet the water needs of each of the 10 counties — either directly or through exchanges — through approximately the year 2020.

This makes CUWCD a major water wholesaler. In this role, the district captures water as it flows from high mountain areas — primarily the Uintah Mountains — and conveys it to storage facilities and treatment plants. This water is then sold and distributed to the various municipal and irrigation water user companies in the district. It is used for municipal, industrial, irrigation, hydroelectric power, fish and wildlife, conservation and recreation purposes. In the early years, most of the district's water was used for agriculture. But the complexion of many of the areas within the district has changed, and today more water is used for municipal and industrial purposes than for agriculture.

The Jordanelle Reservoir has been called the "jewel" of the Central Utah Project.

Construction of the Olmsted Pipeline, which now brings Provo River water into the Salt Lake Valley

The district is already advancing in these directions. Case in point: it has been taking an expanding role in promoting and facilitating water conservation efforts. Sixty-five percent of the water used in the district's geographic domain goes to outdoor use, primarily to water lawns and gardens in the summertime. With the area's rapid growth, increasing numbers of yards are demanding more water. Conservation, once an option, is now a necessity — a cause that the district has adopted with characteristic zeal.

The district is currently involved with a number of initiatives, including the statewide "Slow the Flow" water conservation radio and television campaign, a water audit program, demonstration gardens that show the attractiveness and feasibility of drought-resistant plants and grasses, and experimentation with new PC-based water-sensor systems that measure the moisture content of the soil and automatically turn on sprinklers only when water is needed. These systems are designed to eliminate the waste of over-watering, enabling home and business owners to conserve water and cut water bills significantly.

CUWCD's role has expanded over the years. For example, the district has become involved in water treatment and in fact operates the only water treatment facility in Utah Valley.

The district is proud of its financial record. The CUP is not completely federally funded. Although the federal government put up all the money at first, the district is responsible for repaying all of the costs of developing municipal water; and since the passage of the Completion Act, the district must have approximately 35 percent of the cost of a project in hand before construction begins.

CUWCD's leaders have managed its revenues wisely, not only living within the district's financial means, but going the extra mile to reduce the cost of its debt to the federal government. This has been accomplished by negotiating to pre-pay the district's obligations at a discount and then borrowing the repayment money on the open market for a net savings. Because of this, the district is making the same approximate overall payments but is paying the debt off faster. The savings: a whopping $100 million (more or less) over the repayment period.

In the coming years, as work for the CUP progresses to completion, the district's role and responsibilities will change. One change is financial. Without the federal CUP funding, the district will become completely locally funded, similar to other water districts in the state. Other changes will be mission-oriented. No longer will the CUP be the district's reason for existence. That reason will shift to other missions focusing on water conservation, the use and re-use of water and the continued development of water supplies beyond federal projects.

The CUWCD board of directors examines a tunnel-boring machine at the launch of a major tunnel project.

Since its creation the Central Utah Water Conservancy District has been more than a match for its challenging mission. In future years this resourceful organization promises to continue to serve the people of central Utah with the same responsible leadership for which it has earned a sterling reputation.

Utah Film Commission

UTAH'S picturesque, natural beauty did not escape the attention of the burgeoning film industry a century ago. From water-etched desert canyons and the unmatched, awesome majesty of Monument Valley's monoliths to snow-capped mountains, blue streams and majestic lakes, including the Great Salt Lake itself, Utah has long been favored by film producers over other Western locales. In fact, outside of California, more films are currently produced in Utah than in any other neighboring Western state.

"Ain't it beautiful?!"
Thelma and Louise
Sunset at
Dead Horse Point
Photo by Tom Till/
©Tom Till

Utah's rugged canyon lands, deserts and mountains provided an irresistible allure to early film producers, and it was one of the first states that film producers traveled to outside of Hollywood, where studios began to proliferate in the 1910s. Many silent movies, such as Paramount Pictures' *The Covered Wagon* (1923), were made in Utah. Utah's diverse beauty has doubled for Africa, New York City, the Atlantic Ocean and even, in the case of the movie *Galaxy Quest*, an alien planet.

Charlie Chaplin, whose creation of "The Little Tramp" made him famous, is said to have hidden out in Utah when he was going through an infamous divorce. Kanab, on the Utah-Arizona border, became known as Utah's "little Hollywood" as more Westerns were made here than in any other place. Metro-Goldwyn-Mayer (MGM) even had a makeshift studio at Kanab. Kanab was the setting for such classic films as *Westward the Women, Sergeants 3* and *The Outlaw Josey Wales*, and two television series, "Gunsmoke" and "Death Valley Days."

In 1948 Moab visionaries established the Moab Film Commission in recognition of the impact the film industry had on the Moab-Kanab-Monument Valley triangle, where so many films were continuing to be made. Moab is known in local parlance as "John Ford country," since the award-winning film director, who introduced the world to Monument Valley and filmed such memorable movies as *Stagecoach, My Darling Clementine* and *Rio Grande*, got his start there.

The Moab Film Commission was actually a precursor to the Utah Film Commission, which was created in 1974 as part of the Utah Department of Business and Economic Development. Utah was one of the first states, after Colorado, to create a state-sponsored film commission, and its mission is to promote Utah as an attractive and viable on-location production center to the expanding global visual industry. In addition, the Utah Film Commission works to facilitate and maintain business development by promoting the creation of jobs for local Utah support services and professionals in the motion picture, television, commercial, corporate and print advertising/production industries.

There is never any time for slacking off at the Utah Film Commission. To market the state of Utah it must consistently produce innovative and alternative media campaigns ranging from interactive CD-ROMs, Web-based promotions and display advertising in trade magazines, to promotional items such as tee shirts, hats, mugs, photo books and calendars. The commission also visits prospective clients in industry centers and hosts events that are creative, relevant and appealing to the production industry.

In addition to marketing, the Utah Film Commission prepares and updates materials for prospective clients, including photo presentations and digitally delivered information that promote maximum use of Utah locations, hard-working crews, equipment, quality support services, and, of course, local talent. The commission can assist movie producers with professional script development, breakdown and post-production facilities, and it is available to help resolve complaints or problems with locations.

Della Reese, Roma Downey, John Dye and Valerie Bertinelli play celestial beings in human form in the perennially popular "Touched by an Angel" TV series. *Courtesy of CBS, Photo by Tony Esparza*

The Utah Film Commission is charged with promoting a public-private industry awareness of the positive economic impact the motion picture industry has on Utah; the role of the state film commission programs to facilitate on-location filming; and building strategic alliances with agencies and nonprofit organizations that promote Utah to the film industry.

The state investment in the Utah Film Commission has paid off in a number of ways. Economically, $1 billion has been spent on filmmaking in Utah since 1990. In 1999 $146 million was spent in Utah on filmmaking, a figure that includes monies spent on crews, support services and lodging, among other things. Filmmaking is a viable industry in Utah, which attracts independent filmmakers — many movie-of-the-week productions are made here because of the beauty of the state — and producers who come to Utah to film simply because of the talented, efficient crew base available to them locally.

Celluloid aficionados can doubtless name dozens of the several hundred movies, television shows and documentaries shot in Utah. In addition to Westerns already named, such a list ranges from children's classics such as *Lassie Come Home* and *My Friend Flicka* to perennial favorites such as *Drums Along the Mohawk, Jeremiah Johnson* and *Forrest Gump*, and other classics such as *Butch Cassidy and the Sundance Kid, Easy Rider, Indiana Jones and the Last Crusade,* and *Shepherd of the Hills*. Besides the directors of memorable films made here, names such as John Wayne, Robert Redford, Clint Eastwood, Roy Rogers and Dale Robertson will always be linked with Utah.

The award-winning "Touched by an Angel" TV series, with Martha Williamson as executive producer, has been based in Utah since its inception in 1994. Some of the stellar cast of the show, including Roma Downey, Della Reese, John Dye and Valerie Bertinelli, maintain homes in Utah, as do many crewmembers. The popular "Touched by an Angel" shows are filmed in Salt Lake City, the Wasatch Front and other regions of the state.

During fiscal year 2000-2001, 21 feature films/independent/cable features, two complete network series, 10 made-for-television movies or portions of other network series, and 153 commercials, print ads, documentaries or videos were produced in Utah. The Utah Film Commission has been and continues to be an official sponsor of the internationally renowned Sundance Film Festival. Robert Redford's Sundance Institute, celebrating its 20th anniversary, has created theater, writer, composer, producer and filmmaking programs, workshops, labs and conferences to advance the independent filmmaker and other artists. The Utah Film Commission has recently begun expanding and accelerating marketing efforts to target new feature and television production, as well as take advantage of Utah's heightened profile with the 2002 Olympic Winter Games.

John Ford on the set of *Wagon Master* (1950), RKO Radio Pictures *Brigham Young University HBLL Photographic Archives*

Back to the Future III (1990), Universal Pictures *Brigham Young University HBLL Photographic Archives*

The Economic Development Corporation of Utah

FOR decades, Utah's bumper crop of highly educated and motivated workers grabbed their diplomas and started looking for jobs — out of state.

No longer could the promise of cradle-to-grave jobs in steel production or copper mining keep this economic treasure in the Beehive State. By the 1980s Utah's business and community leaders faced a crisis with the state's burgeoning out-migration. To be sure, there were 10 chambers of commerce and 13 municipalities attempting to attract new business to Utah. But not only were their efforts needlessly duplicated, they simply were not working.

In August 1987 a group of business leaders in Salt Lake City took a long, hard look at the problem and decided to join forces. The Economic Development Corporation of Utah fused public and private sectors into one cohesive force. EDCU quickly amassed an impressive database enabling the organization to offer grants, contacts and research to prospective clients.

Today, the EDCU has clearly influenced a business shift in Utah. The Wasatch Front's thriving high-tech industry proudly claims Intel, Gateway, Novell, WordPerfect, Iomega and a host of dot-com start-ups. The 225-plus investors of EDCU have formed partnerships to recruit targeted industries for relocation or expansion in Utah.

Driving Utah's economic boom is the Utah Technology Alliance, a group organized by the EDCU, state economic developers and business leaders to seek expanding high-tech firms. Utah's Delta Air Lines hub, lower real estate costs, an educated work force and access to three first-rate research universities have also made the state an attractive location. The infamous Silicon Valley traffic jams and out-of-sight real estate prices further helped EDCU lure six high-tech companies to Utah in 1999 alone.

The EDCU's CEO, Chris Roybal, has also witnessed an expansion in business services in the past decade. Marketing efforts have succeeded in landing regional centers for such companies as Goldman Sachs and Dean Witter. Roybal says that Utah's young, educated work force and competitive operating costs are tipping the scales for Utah being the location for business expansion. The online brokerage firm of DLJ*direct* recently announced plans for an investor service center in Utah with immediate jobs for 300 to 400 employees and plans to expand to 1,000.

The speed with which the EDCU can operate in smoothing the way for an incoming business is illustrated by a report from the Internet weekly magazine, *The Industry Standard*. The auction house, eBay, met with representatives on a Tuesday, "decided to come to Salt Lake City on Thursday, began hiring immediately and moved into a renovated facility five weeks later."

With Utah on the nation's radar screen because of the 2002 Winter Olympics, Roybal sees the EDCU capitalizing on the publicity. Attracting venture capital to the state is high on his list of goals. Utah Gov. Mike Leavitt upped the ante at a recent EDCU annual meeting citing the need for 350,000 new jobs in the next decade. The Economic Development Corporation of Utah is prepared to meet that challenge.

Salt Lake Chamber

THE nearly century-old Salt Lake Chamber is a dynamic organization that represents more than 2,000 businesses with 340,000 employees. The Chamber's members throughout Utah represent a good mix of various-sized businesses, but nearly 80 percent are small businesses. The Chamber takes a leadership role in the community and state as the voice of business. It supports programs that improve economic vitality and quality of life, initiates actions that enhance business, cultural and social environments, and builds coalitions that unify and strengthen the Chamber's voice in the community.

The Chamber was created in 1902 as the Salt Lake Commercial Club when 100 business leaders united to settle differences that had cropped up in the commercial business district. Today, the Chamber still addresses critical community issues. Throughout the past century it has spurred thousands of improvements along the Wasatch Front, including downtown growth and development, the birth of a transit system, the creation of an international airport, economic expansion, and effective government and public affairs work.

The Chamber makes great strides because of the strength of many dedicated volunteers and a professional staff who work well together to produce effective results. Chamber members have plenty of opportunities from which to choose. Monthly Business After Hours and quarterly Breakfast Clubs provide members with important networking opportunities. The Chamber also provides numerous seminars and workshops annually on such topics as technology, management, employment law, and violence in the workplace. Recently the Chamber presented the annual Business to Business Expo; honored businesses at the annual Giant Step Small Business Awards dinner; organized the American Express Women & Business Conference; and the Women's Business Center hosted the annual Women's Business Luncheon.

As growth in the Salt Lake Valley causes the face of business to change, the Chamber is adjusting, too. In order to truly fulfill its leadership role as the voice of business, it has undergone a rebranding effort to define that role. The Chamber is not a branch of government, as is often thought, but it is the largest business association in the state. As the Chamber prepares to enter its second century, it will be stepping up its government advocacy, becoming more involved with lobbying for a proactive business agenda and even taking a stance on political candidates. It will also be developing a more extensive networking program, providing more educational programs and looking to expand in both numbers and diversity through active recruitment and retention efforts.

The Chamber is proud of its involvement in recruiting the 2002 Olympic Winter Games to come to Salt Lake, as well as significant achievements in establishing a Multi-ethnic Business Committee to promote diversity; lobbying legislation; establishing a public policy agenda; and partnering with education on work force development issues. Although all the Chamber's accomplishments may not always be visible from the outside, its members are constantly at work to create a more vibrant Chamber and a better community for all.

The Salt Lake Chamber celebrates a century of business in 2002. *Photo ©1998 by Steve Greenwood*

Utah Power

THE history of Utah Power is in large measure the history of electricity in America. True to its pioneering origins, Salt Lake City was also a pioneer in the development of electric power. Despite being still very much a dusty frontier town in 1881, on March 31 of that year Salt Lake City became the fifth city in the world to install central station electric street lighting, following New York, London, San Francisco and Cleveland.

The city of Ogden, Utah, followed on May 10, 1881, with central station street lighting of its own, continuing a series of "firsts" in the American West's electric power industry, resulting from a combination of necessity and nerve.

A predecessor company of Utah Power in 1889 was the first in the world to make commercial use of alternating current (AC) electricity. Until this time, direct current (DC) electricity was used exclusively. AC was considered a laboratory curiosity — too dangerous for any commercial use. However, DC electricity at that time could only be transmitted about a mile from the generator. Lucien L. Nunn's Gold King Mine in southwestern Colorado's San Juan Mountains was about three miles from the San Miguel River.

Nunn consulted George Westinghouse on the design of a hydroelectric generator to supply electricity to his mine. Despite having to adapt, improvise and invent nearly everything they used, engineers built a new AC hydroelectric generator that ran steadily for 30 days once it was started. Nunn's Telluride Power Company expanded in the Intermountain West and became home, at the mouth of Provo Canyon just south of Salt Lake City, to a unique training school for electrical engineers and line workers. Practical education in electricity was not available anywhere else.

While the mining industry drove the development of the electric utilities, the use of electricity for other businesses and homes grew steadily. Dozens of small, less-efficient electric companies were consolidated into Utah Power & Light Co. in 1912. Still, only 30 percent of American industry was run by electricity. By 1929 that figure had increased to 70 percent. Residential electric service took hold more slowly, with many rural areas still without electric utility service well into the 1930s. Today, however, it's hard to imagine modern life without the convenience and efficiency of electricity.

Utah Power continued to grow in the West, and in 1989 merged with Portland, Oregon-based PacifiCorp, which now serves 1.5 million customers in six states. In 1999 PacifiCorp merged with ScottishPower to join a growing list of international energy companies.

Recently, during a time of unprecedented challenge and rapid changes in the electric utility industry, Utah Power made substantial strides in fulfilling commitments to improve an already excellent record of customer service and reliability.

Utah Power is proud to be an Official Sponsor of the 2002 Olympic Winter Games in Salt Lake City. Supplying reliable electric service to 12 of 14 official Olympic venue sites is a continuation of the company's longstanding support of the communities it serves.

J. Harry Carson, March 11, 1904, at the original Ames power station on the San Miguel River in Southwestern Colorado

Quality of Life

A variety of religious, educational, medical, cultural and entertainment organizations contribute to the quality of life enjoyed by Salt Lake City residents and visitors.

Episcopal Diocese and Friends 226

LDS Hospital 230

Oasis Stage Werks 233

ARUP Laboratories 234

NPS Pharmaceuticals, Inc. 236

Plaza Cycle 238

The Church of Jesus Christ of Latter-day Saints 240

The University of Utah 242

University of Utah Health Sciences Center 244

Utah State Historical Society 246

VA Salt Lake City Health Care System 248

Episcopal Diocese and Friends

ALTHOUGH Salt Lake City is widely known as the headquarters of the Church of Jesus Christ of Latter-day Saints, it is also the home of a number of other churches with robust memberships and deep roots in the valley's historical soil. Among the most progressive and prosperous of these congregations is the Episcopal Diocese of Utah. Its long history in the Salt Lake area, combined with its many humanitarian initiatives, makes it an essential and highly respected member of the city's religious fabric.

Episcopal Bishop Daniel Tuttle arrived in Utah in 1867.

The Episcopal saga in the area began in May 1867 when two missionaries — George W. Foote and T. W. Haskins — arrived in Utah. A few months later, Episcopal Bishop Daniel Tuttle and two more missionaries arrived in Utah. They represented the first Protestant church to come to the state with a definite plan to organize itself and become an enduring presence in the Mormon community.

The cornerstone of the Cathedral Church of St. Mark was laid in 1870.

Officially, Tuttle was the first Episcopal Missionary Bishop of Montana, with jurisdiction over Utah and Idaho — a vast mission field. But instead of going first to Montana, he decided to begin his new ministry in Salt Lake City, in response to Salt Lake banker Warren Hussey. The banker asked Tuttle to come to Utah first because there were no other non-Mormon churches in the state. He assured Tuttle that there would be no resistance from the Mormons or their leader, Brigham Young, whom he knew personally.

According to one account, Bishop Tuttle's first service in Salt Lake City, held in Independence Hall, was held for a congregation of three women. The missionaries had opened St. Mark's School in a rented building on Main Street three days before Tuttle's arrival.

After Bishop Tuttle became familiar with the situation in Utah, he left Foote and Haskins in charge and went to Montana, returning with his family in 1869 to stay until 1886.

During the bishop's absence, the local congregation and the enrollment of St. Mark's School grew. Soon the school expanded beyond the adobe schoolhouse into the two adjoining storerooms. By 1873, donations helped to establish the school in its own building at 141 East 100 South. In 1880, Bishop Tuttle oversaw the creation of a boarding and day school for girls named Rowland Hall. When public education was finally established at the turn of the century, St. Mark's School was closed, but opened again in 1959 as a boy's school. In 1964 the two schools combined to form Rowland Hall-St. Mark's — one of the top private schools in the area.

The cornerstone of the Cathedral Church of St. Mark was laid in 1870. The structure would become one of the city's most beautiful architectural landmarks. Today, the cathedral has the distinction of being Utah's oldest church building in continuous use. Later that year the parish was formally organized. Bishop Tuttle was appointed rector.

Utah's Episcopal community established St. Mark's Hospital in 1872 — the first hospital between Denver and the West Coast. There had been no hospital to care for injured miners or railroad workers, nor to offer the area's sick the latest medical treatments. The hospital's first location was at 500 East and 400 South. But the demand for medical care increased quickly, precipitating moves to larger facilities in 1879 and again in 1893. St. Mark's Hospital is currently located at 1200 East and 3900 South.

The Rt. Reverend Abiel Leonard succeeded Bishop Tuttle as Missionary Bishop of Utah in 1888 and served in that position until 1903. He furthered Bishop Tuttle's work and was passionate about establishing churches in mining towns and other outlying communities. Subsequent bishops continued building on the firm foundation established by Bishops Tuttle and Leonard, starting new programs, establishing new churches and parishes and addressing relevant issues. But throughout the decades, they have all focused first and foremost on meeting the spiritual needs of the members of what is now the Episcopal Diocese of Utah and providing services for the betterment of the communities in which they ministered.

The years after World War II were financially challenging for the expanding Diocese. By the early 1980s, the church's financial problems had become serious. One solution to the growing problem was to sell St. Mark's Hospital. This was an emotionally difficult and controversial course of action. But escalating health care costs and increasing challenges related to running a hospital made the decision easier. On the last day of 1987, the hospital was sold to Hospital Corporation of America.

The then Bishop George E. Bates, echoing the sentiments of the Diocesan leaders and members, insisted that the proceeds from the sale be handled in a sound, conservative way that would provide ongoing financial stability and allow the Diocese to achieve many of its long-held goals. This strategy has allowed the organization to take great strides forward in recent years in the form of Diocesan growth as well as new and expanded community service programs.

These initiatives include charitable and educational grants, youth and student ministries, work with the elderly and disabled, soup kitchens, indigent medical care, hospital ministries, scouting and programs addressing alcohol and drugs, domestic violence, AIDS, homelessness, latchkey kids and other critical issues. The Jubilee Center, located near the cathedral, is the headquarters of Episcopal Community Services. It houses a major food bank, health clinics, legal services for the poor, ecumenical offices for churches in Utah and other humanitarian programs.

The Jubilee Center in downtown Salt Lake City is home to a variety of Episcopal community outreach services.

The Episcopal Church has always maintained friendly relationships with the Church of Jesus Christ of Latter-day Saints. One of Bishop Tuttle's first acts upon arriving in the Salt Lake Valley was to pay a courtesy call on Brigham Young and establish cordial ties. Mutual respect and helpfulness has marked the relationship between the two organizations ever since.

The friendly attitude of the Diocese extends to all churches. Salt Lake City's Episcopal population has earned a reputation for its ecumenical outlook. According to Bishop Carolyn Tanner Irish, "We're not an either/or church, but a both/and church." In fact, the Diocese helped to establish and continues to support the organization of the Community of Churches in Utah in order to promote mutual support rather than competition.

Today, the Episcopal Diocese of Utah is a dynamic, positive presence in communities throughout Utah, with fingers of involvement reaching into surrounding states. From its humble beginnings in 1867, this community-minded organization has exemplified the twin Christian ideals of faith and good works.

THE CATHOLIC CHURCH

A mural decorating the dome of the Utah State Capitol portrays the expedition of two Franciscan missionaries into Utah in 1776. The unprecedented journey of Francisco Dominguez and Velez de Escalante set the stage for future exploration and inscribed Catholicism indelibly into Utah's pre-settlement history.

The discovery of mineral ores in 1863 and the transcontinental railroad brought many Catholic pioneers to Utah.

A youth group enjoys the outdoors in an excursion sponsored by the Episcopal Diocese's Camp Tuttle.

UNITARIANISM IN SALT LAKE CITY

In November 1890 the minister to a Unitarian congregation in Denver journeyed west across the mountains to address an audience of 300 in the Salt Lake Theatre. His name was Reverend Samuel Atkins Eliot, and he warned that although the Unitarian faith offered "no fire insurance against the future," it provided a place where the "heterodox" could "protest against dogmatic tests of fellowship."

Inspired by Eliot's remarks and drawing on a recent influx of prominent Easterners in the mining and railroad industries, 46 Utahans affixed their signatures to a constitution creating the First Unitarian Society of Salt Lake City on February 24, 1891. In less than a year membership had grown to 187.

The early years of the church were sometimes turbulent due to financial woes, a husband-wife ministerial team in the late 1890s and a decade later, an avowed socialist at the pulpit. But the congregation held together as it continued to seek a church building appropriate to its religious tradition.

Under the leadership of Father (later Bishop) Lawrence Scanlan and the Sisters of the Holy Cross, the settlers built churches, schools, and a hospital and orphanage in Salt Lake City. In 1891 the 8,000-member Catholic community became a full-fledged diocese.

The Cathedral of the Madeleine is an elegant symbol of Catholicism in Salt Lake City.

The Cathedral of the Madeleine, dedicated in 1909 in the heart of Salt Lake City and renovated in 1993, symbolizes a Catholic spirit marked by both struggle and success. During World War II Bishop Duane G. Hunt established 14 new parishes and organized Catholic Community Services for the poor. Shortly after the war he welcomed the opening of Christus-St. Joseph Villa in Salt Lake, and later, the arrival of the cloistered Carmelite Sisters in Holladay.

Bishop Joseph Lennox Federal guided the diocese gently when the Second Vatican Council of 1962 through 1965 ushered in renewal and ecumenism. In the 1980s Bishop William K. Weigand expanded the ministry to ethnic immigrants whose numbers helped raise the current census to 110,000 Catholics worshipping in 47 parishes throughout Utah. At the opening of the millennium, Bishop George H. Niederauer dedicated the Skaggs Catholic Center, a landmark 57-acre complex in Draper for education and worship.

That structure was finally built in 1927 (currently the New England Georgian church at the corner of 6th South and 13th East.) A series of dynamic ministers from the 1930s to the present has maintained a robust membership. By the mid-1980s, the South Valley Unitarian Universalist Society had spun off of the mother church to be joined later by congregations in Ogden and Logan. Today, the Unitarian church has a earned a reputation for serving the larger community as a "church for the unchurched."

THE GREEK ORTHODOX CHURCH

Depressed economic conditions in Greece triggered the migration of predominantly young Greek males to the United States during the late 1800s. By 1900 Utah's industrialization made the state a destination of opportunity for many immigrating Greeks.

Despite discrimination and prejudice, the Greek immigrants made plans for the formation of a Greek Orthodox Church in Salt Lake City. On January 22, 1905, they organized the Greek Community. Salt Lake City's first Holy Trinity Greek Orthodox Church was built at 439 West 400 South and dedicated in October that same year.

By World War I, the Greek Orthodox congregation had outgrown the church and began making plans to erect a larger new building. The stately new Holy Trinity Church at 300 West and 300 South was consecrated in August 1925 and was elevated to the status of cathedral six decades later, in 1986.

"Greek Town" developed in the section of Salt Lake City between the Union Pacific and Denver Rio Grande railroad depots during the early years of the 20th century. By 1910 the area boasted over 100 Greek-owned businesses. Greek Town became the home for thousands of Greek immigrants. But by the end of World War II, Greek Town no longer existed. The assimilation of the Greek immigrants, their progeny and their businesses into the American landscape had been achieved.

Today, the 1,200-families of the Greek Orthodox Church Community of Greater Salt Lake City worship at the Holy Trinity Cathedral and Holladay's Prophet Elias Church.

THE JEWISH COMMUNITY

Members of the Jewish faith came to Utah as early as 1826 as trappers, traders and explorers. Later they came as pioneers and entrepreneurs. According to Eileen Hallet Stone, author of *A Homeland in the West: Utah Jews Remember* (University of Utah Press, 2001), these newcomers comprised a resourceful, individualistic Germanic Jewish population. In 1864 they formed the Hebrew Benevolent Society and two years later built the region's first Jewish cemetery.

Though few in number, Salt Lake City's early Jews incorporated Congregation B'nai Israel in 1878, built a schoolhouse in 1881 and added a synagogue. After a year of orthodox rituals, the services became more liberal (Reform). In 1889 its members sold the building and in 1891 built a new synagogue at 249 South 400 East. B'nai Israel's membership grew to 82 families.

In 1903, amid the heavy immigration of Orthodox Russian and Polish Jews to the city, Congregation Montefiore was built at 355 South 300 East. Deeming Montefiore too conservative, some members then organized a third synagogue in 1918: the orthodox Shaarey Tzedek, which did not survive the Great Depression.

In time, Salt Lake's traditional and liberal Jews interacted socially and religiously in an attempt to overcome differences. In 1972 B'nai Israel and Montefiore merged to form Congregation Kol Ami (All of My People).

In 1987 Chavurah B'Yachad, a modern-day, Reconstructionist-affiliated congregation, was established. The orthodox Chabad Lubavitch Synagogue, Bais Menachem, settled in the city in 1994 as an outreach Jewish organization designed to educate Jews. Today, Salt Lake City continues to be home to a growing and diverse Jewish population.

The First Unitarian Church was built in 1927.

The stately Holy Trinity Church was elevated to the status of cathedral in 1986.

LDS Hospital

THE dedication ceremony was reported to be "simple, impressive and brief." Joseph F. Smith, president of the Church of Jesus Christ of Latter-day Saints offered the dedicatory prayer. Franklin S. Richards, general attorney for the church and executor of the Groves estate, addressed the invited guests, church officials and medical staff who had gathered in the dining room of Salt Lake City's new hospital to commemorate its opening.

Dr. William H. Groves, 1834-1895, Founder of LDS Hospital, originally called, "Dr. W.H. Groves Latter-day Saints Hospital"

At its opening in 1905 the hospital was a magnificent structure with its cream colored brick, white stone trim and red sandstone base. The edifice measured 175 feet by 40 feet and was located on a 2.5 acre block surrounded by a neatly cemented stone wall.

With that solemn yet unpretentious ceremony just four days into the new year and five years into the new 20th century (January 4, 1905), the Dr. W. H. Groves Latter-day Saints Hospital was established.

Paradoxically, it was a dentist — not a physician — who bequeathed the money that triggered the creation of the hospital. William H. Groves was born in Nottingham, England, and studied dentistry as a young man. He eventually traveled to California and joined a whaling ship's crew for a long voyage in the Pacific. Groves joined the L.D.S. Church in 1862 and moved to Salt Lake City where he opened a dental practice. The well-dressed dentist-adventurer drove the finest horses and became a social figurehead in his new community. He had accumulated a fortune of $85,000 when he suddenly closed his practice, withdrew from his friends and moved into a poorly furnished room above an undertaking parlor. His reclusion was shrouded in mystery.

In 1895 Dr. Groves suffered a heart attack. Dr. Joseph S. Richards was called to attend him. As they drove to St. Mark's Hospital, Dr. Groves told his physician that he had been saving his money to endow a library. Dr. Richards told him that there was more need for a new hospital than for a new library. After 18 days in the hospital, Dr. Groves died. But during his stay he rallied long enough to change his will. The new will directed that his fortune would be used to build a new hospital: the Dr. W. H. Groves Latter-day Saints Hospital.

The land and construction of the new five-story, 80-bed hospital cost $175,000. Dr. Groves' $85,000 estate had decreased in value to $50,000 by the time it was finally sold. To cover the additional funds that were needed, the L.D.S. Church donated $115,000 and the Fifteenth Ecclesiastical Ward Stake of Zion contributed $10,000. Area citizens also responded by donating equipment, furniture and money.

According to the *Deseret News*, the new medical facility, located on 8th Avenue between C and D Streets, was "modern in every sense of the term ... not surpassed in all the world." Almost 1,000 patients were admitted that first year.

As Salt Lake City and the region surrounding it grew, so did the demands placed on the hospital. To meet those demands, east and west wings were added in 1913 and 1929, followed by periodic expansion and remodeling projects, including a $10 million project in 1959 that added six new operating rooms and a seven-story center wing, raising the bed capacity to over 500. The hospital also grew in terms of equipment and technology, staff and research, earning a reputation for excellence throughout the region.

In 1975, after deciding that the operation of health care facilities was no longer critical to its religious mission, The Church of Jesus Christ of Latter-day Saints donated its 15 hospitals, including the Dr. W. H. Groves Latter-day Saints Hospital (which was formally renamed "LDS Hospital") to the communities in which they were located.

Intermountain Health Care (IHC) was formed to own and operate the hospitals on behalf of the communities. This charitable, nonprofit, community-owned organization is based in Salt Lake City and serves the residents of Utah and Idaho. The IHC system includes dozens of hospitals, clinics, home health agencies, women's centers and drug dependency units, plus physicians and health insurance plans. IHC is committed to providing quality medical care to all people, regardless of their ability to pay.

In the January 31, 2000, issue of *Modern Healthcare* magazine, IHC was ranked as the leading integrated health care system in the nation.

Traditionally, LDS Hospital — like its sister medical facilities and most health care centers in the country — focused on caring for the sick and injured. While the hospital continually strives to improve this aspect of its mission, it has also become intensely involved in preventing illness and improving health in the past several decades.

From its humble beginnings in 1905, LDS Hospital has become a beacon of leading-edge, compassionate health care that has earned a worldwide reputation for its clinical services and research in cardiology, organ transplantation, pulmonology, oncology, trauma and medical informatics.

It has also become the largest hospital in the Intermountain West. With 520 beds, LDS Hospital is the major referral center for six states and more than 75 regional health care institutions. The educational initiative it sponsors reaches out to the populations of surrounding communities, providing much-needed, up-to-date health care information and programs.

In cardiology, LDS Hospital is considered a world-class facility in terms of volume and outcome of procedures. The hospital is a leader in open heart surgeries, tallying over 5,000 heart catheterizations each year. It is one of the few medical centers in the nation that has been licensed to implant mechanical assist devices and complete artificial hearts into patients awaiting heart transplants. LDS Hospital

"Luxurious" is the best way to describe transportation to LDS Hospital in the 1920s.

is one of four Utah hospitals involved in the UTAH-Cardiac heart transplant program — a program that has achieved one of the highest survival rates in the world.

The hospital doesn't limit itself to heart transplants. Kidney, liver, pancreas, bone marrow, tissue, skin, heart valve, cornea and tendon transplants are routinely performed at LDS Hospital. Many of these transplant techniques and procedures were pioneered at LDS Hospital.

In a world where computerization is improving the delivery of services and information, LDS Hospital has long been recognized as a world leader in health care computing. In fact, it was the first hospital in America to have a fully operational computerized patient care system at patients' bedsides. Researchers at the hospital have pioneered and refined computer-enhanced clinical decision-making systems since the 1950s. This has resulted in improved medical outcomes, reduced costs and the more effective use of medications.

LDS Hospital also shines when it comes to medical services that have been designed specifically for the needs of women. The hospital's highly respected perinatal facility provides obstetricians and family practitioners throughout the West with high-risk maternal/fetal medicine consultation services. Its advanced, attractive birthing center is home to an average of nearly 5,000 births per year. A mammography center is easily accessible, private and comfortable. Women-oriented services also include educational programs for breast cancer and osteoporosis, as well as hysterectomy and breast cancer support groups.

State-of-the-art cancer care is provided at LDS Hospital. Patients are followed from diagnosis through treatment and follow-up with many research protocols available. LDS Hospital Oncology is a pioneer of surgical intervention techniques including intra-operative radiation therapy, isolation perfusion therapy and sentinel node biopsies. Marrow transplants are also performed.

Today, LDS Hospital is widely acknowledged as a leader in kidney, pancreas, heart, liver, bone, bone marrow, tissue, heart valve, eye tendon and skin transplants.

LDS Hospital is the largest hospital in the Intermountain West and serves as a major adult referral center for six states and more than 75 regional health care institutions.

oxygen therapy and dialysis. Short-stay and outpatient surgeries are performed at the hospital's surgical center.

It is difficult to isolate individual areas of excellence at LDS Hospital simply because all the departments, programs, specialties and services at the hospital have been developed and refined to meet the uncompromising standards that have set this institution apart since the beginning.

Whatever the future holds for LDS Hospital, the people it serves today and will serve in years to come can be certain that they will receive the most advanced and compassionate health care services available in the Intermountain West.

Medical diagnosis is one of the fastest-paced arenas in modern medicine, thanks to rapidly advancing technology. LDS Hospital has maintained a front-running position in this important field with the latest equipment and capabilities for magnetic resonance imaging, ultrasonography, angiography, computed tomography (CT) scanning, PET scanning, fluoroscopy, electron microscope and breast cancer detection.

Only two hospitals in Utah have earned the Level I adult trauma center designation: LDS Hospital and the University of Utah Medical Center. LDS Hospital is the largest of the two and treats a high percentage of the area's most critically injured and ill patients. The hospital's intensive care units include the well-respected Shock/Trauma/Respiratory ICU and an emergency department with 22 beds that treats approximately 34,000 patients each year. LDS Hospital is also home base for IHC's Life Flight air ambulance service, featuring both helicopter and fixed-wing aircraft, with highly trained pilot/medical crew teams.

Neuro-musculoskeletal services at LDS Hospital have also earned widespread acclaim. Neurological and orthopedic specialty teams provide advanced assessment and treatment, major joint replacement, and limb reattachment and reconstruction. A broad offering of highly specialized services is available at the hospital, including a sleep disorder clinic, comprehensive physical exams at the LDS Hospital Fitness Institute, hyperbaric

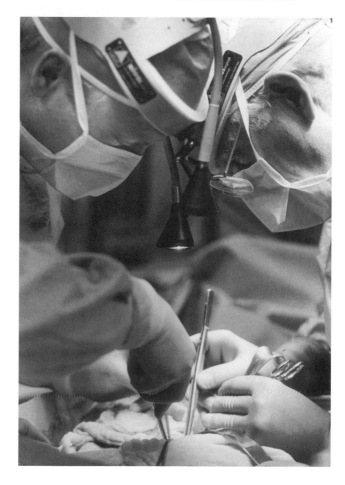

Oasis Stage Werks

PASSION. Romance. Drama. Technical Perfection? While audience members enjoy an inspiring ballet or a magnificent Broadway play, few realize the complexity behind the scenes of modern-day productions. From timed curtains to intricate lighting and sound, a plethora of props, floors and technical equipment is critical for superb performances. Beyond stage directors, perhaps no one understands this as perfectly as Oasis Stage Werks. Headquartered in Salt Lake City, Oasis supports performers with everything needed to delight audiences. From a pop concert in the Delta Center to special events worldwide, Oasis has a hand in bringing beautiful performances to light.

Oasis began modestly in the 1970s, the dream of Gary Justesen, a traveling technician in the entertainment industry. Justesen saw the need for production supplies and equipment. He partnered with Howard Neslen to form Oasis Productions. Beginning with a personal investment of $500 each, they built scenery for clients such as the Utah Opera Company and the San Francisco Ballet. Occasionally, Oasis created tradeshow exhibits for local organizations. In those early years the partners discovered variable cycles that predominated their profession.

After five years, Neslen sold out his half of the partnership and Rebekah Justesen became a part of Gary's team. Together the Justesens envisioned Oasis Stage Werks: a multi-faceted organization to provide a broad spectrum of services while weathering the ups and downs of the industry. The company designed ingenious ways to meet the needs of its clients. This explains how Oasis naturally developed into four divisions. The first consists of retail sales of theatrical products and lighting systems for colleges and theatrical institutions nationwide. The second is a rental service division providing equipment, crew services and production management services for a wide range of entertainment events. The third offers industrialized product sales and installation of permanent theatrical equipment. The fourth division manufactures unique products such as stage draperies, protective equipment and a resilient basket-weave floor that guards against injury and increases the career of professional dancers by several years.

The Justesens' persistence paid off. As society renewed emphasis in the arts, city festivals and promotional affairs became popular. Catering to the Utah Arts Festival, Sundance Film Festival and celebrations across the nation, Oasis tapped into this flourishing industry. Meanwhile, the company's reputation for excellence grew. For its magnificent yearlong sesquicentennial event, the Church of Jesus Christ of Latter-day Saints selected Oasis to assist with multiple performances; from the prairies to a culminating event at BYU. Cougar Stadium was dressed like a theater, including four stages and two sets of dancing waters, accommodating a cast of 4,500 members performing for crowds of 65,000.

Oasis Stage Werks now provides equipment and services for Olympic games, big-name concerts, Disney and some of the most illustrious theater and dance companies in the world. Yet one of Justesen's greatest joys is strong contribution to local arts. Besides providing jobs for 50 individuals, Oasis donates yearly scholarships to young performers in Utah. This once-struggling company guarantees someone else a little less drama outside the theater, and a little more showmanship among the footlights. In short, Oasis has set the stage for continued growth and preservation of the arts in Utah.

Gary Justesen, owner of Oasis Stage Werks working on NuSkin's elaborate new setup.

ARUP Laboratories

WHEN Salt Lake City-based ARUP Laboratories surveyed its top 200 clients, the results were impressive. Clients rated the full-service reference laboratory very highly and when asked if they would recommend ARUP to other organizations, clients answered with an overwhelming "yes."

Of course, ARUP executives, administrators and employees weren't surprised at the survey results. ARUP Laboratories is recognized in the health care field as an outstanding esoteric reference laboratory. The laboratory works in partnership with hospitals and their physicians to improve patient care and contributes to accurate medical diagnoses. ARUP's vision is to be the most responsive source for laboratory testing and quality information to improve health care and disease management. Survey results simply indicate that the company's vision is a reality.

ARUP's success began almost 20 years ago in 1984, when the company was created to support the University of Utah's academic mission. One of the first-ever university-owned laboratories venturing into private enterprise, ARUP began as a trend-setting organization for the School of Medicine's Department of Pathology. The academic department benefited from access to state-of-the-art laboratory facilities in which to perform research and development, and ARUP benefited from this continuous source of leading-edge scientific knowledge.

ARUP Laboratories processes more than 15,000 specimens of blood, body fluids and tissue biopsies every day for testing. With a staff of 1,300, ARUP provides services for clients throughout the United States and some foreign countries.

Requiring an expansion almost every five years, today's laboratory facilities encompass a 270,000-square-foot building.

ARUP offers more than 2,000 laboratory tests and test combinations to more than 3,000 hospitals and other clients located in all 50 states and some foreign countries. ARUP offers access to a broad spectrum of testing capability. The laboratory processes more than 15,000 specimens of blood, body fluids and tissue biopsies every day, and 98 percent of all testing is conducted onsite. Testing is performed 24 hours a day, seven days a week, and the laboratory boasts some of the best turnaround times available in the industry, thanks in part to the advanced instrumentation and automated systems used for specimen receiving, tracking and retrieval. Test results are also rapidly delivered to clients through customized information systems.

While ARUP is recognized as an outstanding esoteric reference laboratory, which services more than 50 percent of the nation's university medical centers, including Stanford University, the University of Pennsylvania and Emory University, it is also a hospital laboratory. A separate onsite laboratory and transfusion service continues to handle the diagnostic needs of the 490-bed hospital and clinics owned and operated by the University of Utah Health Sciences Center.

While ARUP has earned a national reputation for excellence, it also places a high priority on local community involvement and service as well. The laboratory operates an onsite blood donor center and organizes blood drives throughout the greater Salt Lake area. The center provides life-saving blood donations for the Primary Children's Medical Center, the University of Utah Hospital and the Shriner's Hospital and also serves as a resource for other area hospitals when needed.

Given that its beginnings are deeply rooted in education — the University of Utah's Department of Pathology remains the sole owner of the laboratory — ARUP's high priority on education seems only natural. Most recently, ARUP founded its Institute for Learning, an entity dedicated to providing clients and employees with a diverse range of educational options. ARUP ensures that its employees stay updated and educated, offering more than 500 different in-house presentations and a generous employee tuition package that encourages employees to pursue academic degrees.

In 1996, ARUP coordinated its research efforts by forming the ARUP Institute for Clinical and Experimental Pathology, LLC. The formation of the Institute places ARUP squarely on the forefront of innovative research and development in clinical and experimental laboratory medicine. ARUP's relationship with the Department of Pathology at the University of Utah's Health Sciences Center provides additional momentum for the Institute's success. In one recent 18-month period, Department of Pathology faculty produced 360 research articles and medical textbooks; faculty members also regularly log more than 23,000 hours per year teaching. In addition, department faculty are nationally recognized for their ability to obtain research and grant funding; the Association of American Medical Colleges rates the department in the top 80th percentile in obtaining research funding.

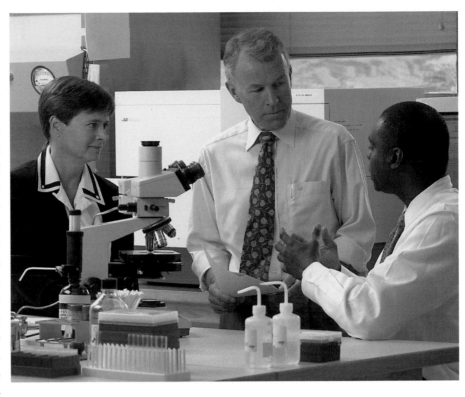

Carl R. Kjeldsberg, M.D., ARUP President/CEO and Chairman of the Department of Pathology at the University of Utah School of Medicine (center), confers with colleagues. ARUP's pathologists hold faculty appointments at the University of Utah School of Medicine.

While ARUP's vision and organization are certainly key to its sterling reputation, the real core of the laboratory's success is its services — and the people behind those services. The goal of ARUP's Client Services team and other ARUP employees is to provide unparalleled customer service, ensuring client satisfaction and, ultimately, quality patient care.

The company also prides itself on creating a work-friendly atmosphere and placing a high priority on keeping its employees happy with an extensive list of internal "morale-building" events and activities. Employees receive quarterly bonuses when the company performs well, and regular employee gatherings and interdepartmental recognition programs are ARUP hallmarks. In 2000, the Utah Department of Workforce Services presented ARUP with a Utah Worklife Award, an honor that recognizes companies that provide an exemplary work atmosphere.

Finally, a leading-edge company is only complete with a leading-edge Internet presence. Updated regularly and with more than 3,000 pages, ARUP's Web Site is the perfect complement to the laboratory's services, offering not only its complete printed User's Guide online but also secure access to test status and results.

Small wonder that ARUP clients report such satisfaction with this outstanding laboratory. With such a broad array of customized services and a strong emphasis on customer satisfaction, no doubt future customer surveys will continue to prove that ARUP is, indeed, the reference laboratory of choice.

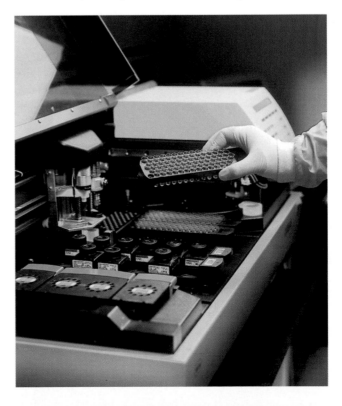

Skilled technologists perform laboratory testing that supports ARUP's clients, including hospitals, other laboratories, major clinics and major pharmaceutical firms.

NPS Pharmaceuticals, Inc.

NPS Pharmaceuticals, Inc. discovers and develops drugs to treat a number of important diseases. NPS was founded in 1986 by two professors from the University of Utah, and the Company's headquarters is still located near the University in Research Park. Early work at NPS was based on the extraction and exploration of venom from spiders, scorpions and centipedes and the effects of these toxins on the central nervous system. Based on this early research, the company's original name was Natural Product Sciences. As the research focus shifted and expanded, the name was changed to simply, "NPS Pharmaceuticals, Inc."

NPS building
*Photo by
Michael Schoenfeld*

*Photo by
Noel Barnhurst*

NPS established collaborative relationships with Pfizer, Inc. in 1987 and with FMC Corporation in 1988 to provide support for its expanded research. In 1992 the company completed two rounds of venture capital funding followed by an initial public offering of stock in 1994. Additional funding was provided by collaborative agreements with Glaxo-SmithKline in 1993, the Pharmaceutical Division of Kirin Brewery Company, Ltd. of Tokyo in 1995 and Amgen, Inc. in 1996. In addition to these collaborations, agreements with companies such as Eli Lilly, Abbott Laboratories, Janssen Pharmaceutica, AstraZeneca, and Forest Laboratories have added cash and drug development support to the company into the present.

In December 1999, NPS acquired Allelix Biopharmaceuticals of Toronto, Canada, and now has offices in the United States and Canada. The merger was an exciting development in the history of NPS, both in terms of broadening the company's base of operations and in enriching its pipeline of potential drug candidates. NPS now has several drug candidates in late-stage human clinical trials and several programs with promising compounds in preclinical studies. Current areas of research and development include treatments for osteoporosis, hyperparathyroidism, gastrointestinal diseases, and neurological and psychiatric disorders.

The company's Purpose and Principles statement begins, "The commitment of the people of NPS Pharmaceuticals is to build an enduring, worldwide company, the purpose of which is to develop innovative drugs to maintain human health and relieve suffering. This commitment is founded on principles of honesty, hard work, respect, the constant quest for knowledge, and the realization of marketplace success." Throughout the company's history, the people of NPS have dedicated themselves to integrity and innovation in their business practices and in their scientific endeavors. As the company has expanded from a one-room office with three employees to facilities in two countries and 140 employees, it has maintained its focus on these ideals.

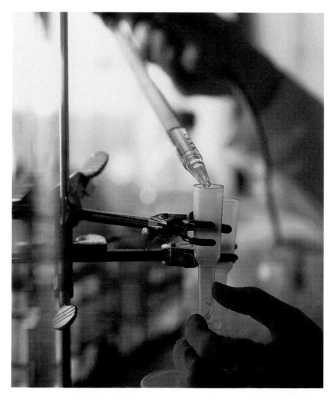

Members of the pharmaceutical industry have the exciting potential to develop drugs that can improve the quality of, and even save, lives. They also find themselves in a highly competitive industry, in which the companies that survive must couple cutting-edge research in discovering drugs with sound business acumen to benefit patients and create solid shareholder value, which, in turn, ultimately leads to success. As NPS continues to grow, it strives to wisely manage its resources, promote the advancement of its employees, and develop drugs that address unmet, or poorly met, medical needs.

Photo by Michael Schoenfeld

Research at NPS is enhanced by collaborations with leading academic institutions such as Brigham & Women's Hospital and the University of Toronto. In addition, NPS has close, ongoing ties with the University of Utah. These ties are bolstered by a summer internship program in which undergraduate students have the opportunity to work under the tutelage of scientists who are experts in their disciplines; support for the College of Science's ACCESS program, which sustains young women involved in science throughout their college careers; financial contributions to and participation in the College of Science's "Science at Breakfast" lecture series; and collaborations with university faculty.

The company's ongoing commitment to community and industry strength is reflected in the conclusion of its Purpose and Principles statement, which says, "Finally, we dedicate ourselves to serve, in order of priority, the patients who use our drugs, our employees, and the communities in which we live and work." In the area of commitment to its employees, NPS has been recognized by two awards: the 1997 Arthur Anderson Utah Best Business Practices Award in the category of Motivating and Retaining Employees, and the 1998 Most "Family Friendly" Business award in the category of middle-sized companies, which was sponsored by the Utah Department of Workforce Services, Office of Child Care.

The support NPS lends to the community in which its employees live and work is epitomized by its enthusiastic participation in Utah's Promise program. NPS provides financial contributions and encourages the volunteer efforts of its employees in the community, including paying for time away from work that is spent on volunteer activities. Contributions of both time and money support the Transitional Housing Program of the Travelers Aid Society, the University of Utah Medical School and Hospital, and the Utah Food Bank. Other organizations to which NPS and its employees contribute include the United Way, the Ronald McDonald House, the American Society of Pediatric Nephrology, the Muscular Dystrophy Association, and the National Ability Center.

The people of NPS Pharmaceuticals look forward to continued scientific progress and commercial success through their drug development efforts. As the Purpose and Principles statement concludes: "Building the enduring company that we envision will be our most lasting legacy."

Photo by Michael Schoenfeld

Plaza Cycle

WHEN it comes to having motorized fun in Utah's great outdoors, Plaza Cycle is the No. 1 source for everything from motorcycles and all-terrain vehicles (ATVs) to snowmobiles and watercraft. This Salt Lake City-based company is also one of the nation's largest dealers for Yamaha, Honda, Polaris, Kawasaki and Cannondale products. In addition, Plaza Cycle manufactures recreational vehicle trailers.

Plaza Cycle is the No. 1 source for power sports vehicles, accessories, apparel, parts and service in Utah.

Plaza Cycle was established in 1964. Since its formation, the power sports company has moved several times to accommodate its expanding business operations. Today, Plaza Cycle is located a few miles southwest of downtown Salt Lake City. Plaza Cycle features an expansive sales area, a large, well-equipped service department with a dynamometer and a personal water craft indoor water test tank, a well-stocked parts and accessory department, and plenty of storage space.

A fun, festive atmosphere pervades Plaza Cycle's showroom.

The company's forward progress has not been without its challenges, however. It faced hard times in the early 1980s, when interest rates for flooring new products skyrocketed as high as 21 percent, making survival almost impossible. In July 1982, when Plaza Cycle was three weeks away from filing for bankruptcy, one of the owners approached the dealership's service manager, Delyle Billings. "Why don't you buy the company?" he asked. "I think you could make it work." Billings discussed the opportunity with his wife and two sons and decided to buy Plaza Cycle.

It took a lot of work in a tough economic environment, but the Billings' family – along with the "right people" who came with them – dug in and pulled Plaza Cycle from the brink of failure to new heights of success. Whereas gross sales in 1982 had been a dismal 670 units, by 1983 the number of units sold had shot to 2,600. By the end of 1984, Plaza Cycle was ranked fourth in the nation in Yamaha sales and was among the top 10 Honda dealers in the country.

In 1986 Delyle Billings and his son, Chris, decided they could build a better trailer than they were buying. Chris took over the trailer department and they began building trailers for motorcycles, snowmobiles, ATVs and personal watercraft. The trailers proved to be popular products that enhanced Plaza Cycle's sales.

In 1998 the Billings family decided to sell the business. Claude Hicken, a successful businessman from Wasatch County, Utah, purchased Plaza Cycle in April 2000. Under his direction the company continues to grow, building on the solid foundation established by the previous owners. Hicken remodeled and expanded the existing facility and moved the trailer manufacturing operation to a separate nearby facility. His team further improved their trailer line (now, Royal Trailers) and

significantly expanded sales from this separate division of the company to other Utah dealerships between St. George and Logan, but predominantly along the Wasatch Front.

Hicken's management style is characterized by delegating responsibility and accountability to trusted employees and giving them the authority and incentive to excel. This form of management has worked well, resulting in high levels of employee accountability and participation. Hicken believes that the company's success is the result of the efforts of his entire 60-plus member team — from his department heads to the newest employee.

All the recent improvements have made the business, which was already highly successful, even more prosperous. Sales were strong when Hicken purchased Plaza Cycle. They are now even stronger.

Today, Plaza Cycle offers Utah's most extensive selection of power sport products, including new and used motorcycles, snowmobiles, ATVs, watercraft, trailers and generators, plus accessories, parts and sport-specific apparel. Already a major dealer for Yamaha, Honda, Kawasaki and Polaris and Cannondale, the company is moving in the direction of further expansion by becoming a dealer for other top lines. The Royal Trailer division adds additional steam to its upward trajectory.

Plaza Cycle also maintains a top-quality service department with certified, factory-trained mechanics and the latest equipment and tools. This department can handle any repair or maintenance task for the wide spectrum of power products it sells, from minor tune-ups to major overhauls.

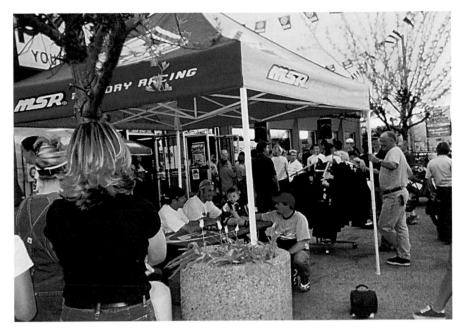

Plaza Cycle sponsors numerous events for its customers' enjoyment.

In addition, Plaza Cycle sponsors a variety of events in the power sports industry in an effort to better serve its customer base.

Hicken's team has made even a visit to Plaza Cycle something of an event. He and his people are aware that they are not, after all, selling groceries or some other product that people have to have in order to survive. They know that their customers don't have to come to their store. Consequently, they have tried to make Plaza Cycle a uniquely friendly and fun destination where people can enjoy themselves — where they will want to come. At Plaza Cycle, products are accessible. "Kids" of all ages can come and hang out, placing themselves in the driver's seat of any number of different models and makes of power sports products in the showroom. Salespeople are there to give information and advice, not to pressure people to buy. It's even fun to negotiate for prices at Plaza Cycle, largely because Hicken's philosophy is to keep the store's new and used product inventories turning quickly, even if prices have to be lowered. This, of course, results in better buys for customers.

Hicken, like his predecessor, is a family man. His wife, June, a former college-level teacher who has played a major role in the success of his other businesses — including a dairy farm — is a key player in Plaza Cycle's day-to-day operations and long-term planning. Several other members of his family are also a part of the company's success.

Plaza Cycle has always been about having a good time, and the smiles of the people who work there — from the owner on down — confirm that they have not forgotten it. Sure, business is business. But Plaza Cycle proves that good business can also be great fun.

Plaza Cycle supplies everything for the power sports enthusiast — right down to the smallest accessories.

The Church of Jesus Christ of Latter-day Saints

PERSECUTED for their beliefs and driven from their homes, pioneering members of The Church of Jesus Christ of Latter-day Saints who first arrived in the Salt Lake Valley in 1847 were "a ragged and impoverished band, stripped of virtually all their earthly goods." Here the Saints laid the foundation for what would become a thriving city. Once a group of religious refugees struggling to survive on the edge of a barren frontier, they now provide aid to impoverished people around the globe.

From its headquarters in Salt Lake City, the Church operates one of the most effective welfare and humanitarian programs in the world. Church efforts to aid the needy are built upon a timeless principle: the admonition of Jesus Christ to feed the hungry, take in the stranger, clothe the naked and visit the sick and imprisoned (Matthew 25:35-36). Latter-day Saints' fundamental desire to follow the Savior manifests itself in a spirit of giving that blesses others in many nations.

In the earliest years of the Church, helping one another was a matter of survival. Saints banded together to ward off persecution, then sustained fellow pioneers through the difficult trek west and helped one another settle the wild areas that would become the Utah Territory. New arrivals, who sacrificed everything to come to "Zion," were gently sheltered by those already established here. A revolving credit source, the Perpetual Emigrating Fund, was instituted to help over 30,000 poor converts move their families to Utah. Donations of tithes and fast offerings filled bishops' storehouses for the care of the poor and needy.

During the Great Depression, President Heber J. Grant instituted a centrally directed welfare program to meet the needs of struggling members. Food, clothing, employment and education as well as spiritual sustenance were provided. So that no one felt ashamed for accepting aid, the program provided for recipients to give back through work, thus enabling and ennobling individuals and families. Today, Church Welfare Services is supported through Church members' volunteer labor and donations. Latter-day Saints fast one day each month and contribute the value of the meals missed or more if their means allow. Also, more than 1,600 Church members volunteer full time, serving as welfare missionaries worldwide to teach basic living skills such as nutrition, sanitation, literacy and career development.

Members of the Church are taught to provide for themselves. However, if they cannot meet basic needs, they may turn to their bishop for temporary assistance. The bishop, a local lay minister, can best determine the nature and quantity of help needed and is assisted by volunteer leaders within each ward (congregation). He meets needs using resources available from bishops' storehouses, canneries, employment resource centers, Deseret Industries thrift stores and LDS Family Services counseling agencies. As in the early days of the program, recipients work in return for assistance.

To encourage self-reliance among Latter-day Saints in less-developed areas, the Church has established the Perpetual Education Fund. Modeled after the pioneer emigrating fund, it utilizes resources from Welfare Services and the Church Educational System to provide low-interest loans, counseling and mentoring to help ambitious, worthy young members reach their education and employment goals.

Resources from Welfare Services enable the Church to render humanitarian assistance around the world. In recent years, the Church

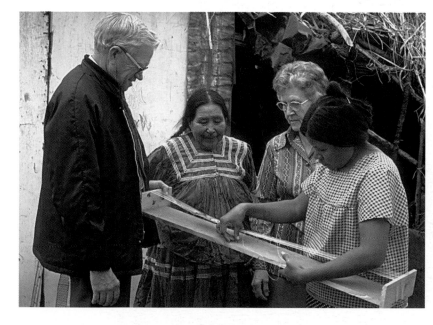

More than 1,600 welfare missionaries serving throughout the world teach life skills that enable individuals to successfully care for themselves and their families.

has shipped more than $61 million in cash donations and $291 million in material assistance to areas of urgent and ongoing need. Goods helped refugees in the Bosnian/Croatian/Serbian crisis and aided victims of flooding in Mozambique and those devastated by earthquakes on several continents. The Church has provided humanitarian aid to 147 countries, shipping more than 76,000 tons of materials, including medical supplies and equipment, educational supplies, food and clothing.

Every year, the Humanitarian Center processes, transports and distributes to needy people around the world thousands of tons of clothing, educational materials, and medical equipment and supplies.

While the Church helps those abroad, it also partners with many human service agencies in Utah to meet needs close to home. The Church makes regular donations to the Utah Food Bank, the Utah Boys Ranch, the Salvation Army and St. Vincent de Paul's kitchen and shelter. Members of the Church volunteer as mentors and counselors in underprivileged, inner-city neighborhoods. The success of Welfare Services attracts business and government leaders to Salt Lake City to learn more about how the program lifts and blesses people.

"The generosity of Church members makes food, clothing and essential help available to millions of our Heavenly Father's most needy children the world over," says Harold Brown, managing director of Welfare Services. "These humanitarian efforts provide literacy training, home production skills, medical care and vital knowledge to liberate those who might otherwise remain enslaved by indigent circumstances."

While much of Church aid is given quietly, news of humanitarian efforts is sometimes shared to encourage others to serve. After reading about a Church humanitarian project,

an employee of Delta Air Lines called to say that Delta was re-covering its passenger seats and planned to throw away the old seatcovers. The sturdy cloth was salvaged and sewn by Church volunteers into toys and bags for educational supply kits for needy children. When a Church member in California learned that several hundred thousand syringes were for sale from a financially distressed medical supply company, he contacted two Utah physicians who bought the syringes and donated them to the Latter-day Saint Humanitarian Center.

The Humanitarian Center helps people develop employable skills through a unique, paid training program designed to promote self-reliance. Trainees from 26 countries speaking 17 different languages work at the Center, including refugees and recently arrived immigrants. As workers sort clothing destined to respond to human needs across the world, they benefit

through job skills training, including computer and language fluency classes. Additionally, the Center works with the Salt Lake Community College to provide other on-site classes.

As visitors tour the Center and observe the work that both relieves suffering abroad and meets needs close to home they ask, "Why? Why do you do this?" Their curiosity is further piqued when they learn that over 90 percent of the aid shipped from the Center goes to people not of the Mormon faith. Harold Brown explains, "If we truly believe in being followers of Jesus Christ, then every person on this earth is our brother or sister, regardless of faith. How can we not help others when we have the means and resources to do it?"

Many of the trainees at the Humanitarian Center are immigrants from other countries. Working within a unique system of training and education, they are paid for their work, while at the same time studying English and developing job-related skills to assist them in finding permanent employment.

The University of Utah

NESTLED in the foothills of the Wasatch Mountains and minutes from downtown Salt Lake City, the University of Utah, the state's flagship institution of higher education, is a comprehensive research university that offers a full range of undergraduate, graduate and professional degrees. The University has been an integral part of the state's history — existing long before statehood was granted — and its diverse student body, faculty and staff pride themselves on working with communities throughout the state to meet the University's educational mission.

In the 2001-02 academic year, the University has taken on a new role as the site of the Olympic Village and Rice-Eccles Olympic Stadium for the 2002 Olympic and Paralympic Winter Games. The University welcomes thousands of international visitors, athletes and officials who will participate in the Opening and Closing Ceremonies, stay in the University's residential living complex, Heritage Commons, and take

advantage of University programs, cultural events and expertise associated with the Games.

Founded in 1850, the U, as Utahns refer to it, is the oldest university west of the Mississippi River. It currently has more than 27,000 enrolled students (2001-02) who come from all 29 Utah counties, all 50 states, and 102 countries. The U offers 75 undergraduate degree programs, along with more than 50 teaching majors and minors, and 96 graduate majors.

The University offers opportunities for undergraduate students in every discipline to access the faculty and programs at the U through integrated programs. Because academic excellence is the top priority of the University, students are encouraged to avail themselves of these remarkable programs that facilitate learning at all levels.

- LEAP, a nationally recognized, yearlong program for students just starting college, offers an environment of cooperative learning and mutual support, with personal attention from a faculty member.
- Honors Program — the third-oldest in the nation — offers an honors baccalaureate degree to selected students within their majors.
- Undergraduate Research Opportunities Program (UROP) offers semester grants to undergraduates who join faculty in scholarly activity.
- Bachelor of University Studies (B.U.S.) enables students to design interdisciplinary majors.
- Transfer Interest Group (TIG) informs first-year transfer students about resources and opportunities available in their major.

For graduate students, the U is a center for scholarship and creativity in science, humanities and fine arts. According to the most recent survey, students choose the University because of the quality of its faculty, its unique research opportunities, its great location, the opportunities to teach and its affordability. In fact, the U is ranked among the top 35 research institutions in the nation, according to the National Science Foundation, with particular distinction in medicine, genetics and engineering. The University was awarded more than $255 million in research and student-aid funding from all external sources in 2000-01. Patents brought in $4.6 million.

Opportunities for students are not limited to traditional classroom- and discipline-based instruction, however. The University's Academic Outreach and Continuing Education department offers continuing education, distance education, professional development and academic outreach programs at the U campus and at off-campus sites to meet a range of educational needs. Enrollment for the 2000-01 academic year totaled almost 31,000 students.

The University is an integral part of the communities it serves, and perhaps nowhere is this better exhibited than in its role in the arts and culture of the region, in stimulating and representing imaginative capacities. On campus, the new Utah Museum of Fine Arts, housed in the Marcia and John Price Museum Building, is the only general art museum in Utah, with a permanent collection of more than 17,000 objects. The Utah Museum of Natural History explores the natural systems and cultures of the earth and

serves as the state's natural history museum. Red Butte Garden offers 150 acres of gardens, walking paths and hiking trails on the eastern edge of campus, and Pioneer Theatre Company, a fully professional, not-for-profit theatre in residence on campus, offers seven productions annually. Kingsbury Hall, the U's historic performing arts center, is home to more than 200 performances — ballet, opera, comedy and concerts — every year. In addition, the Babcock Theatre, the main stage space of the Department of Theatre, and the modern dance, ballet and music departments offer cutting-edge performances year-round.

For many, the University of Utah is a locus of health care. The U's Health Sciences Center is a major patient care, research and health professions training center for the six-state intermountain region. Students are educated in a number of health professions, including medicine, pharmacy, nursing, public health and the physician assistant program. Roughly 786,000 inpatient and outpatient visits are logged annually at University of Utah Hospitals & Clinics, which includes the University Hospital, the University Neuropsychiatric Institute, the Huntsman Cancer Institute, the John A. Moran Eye Center, and a number of neighborhood health centers in the Salt Lake valley and nearby towns. In addition, the Eccles Institute of Human Genetics combines scientific expertise from the Department of Human Genetics and the Eccles Program in Human Molecular Biology and Genetics to create its own interdisciplinary research community.

Befitting its location in a recreation-oriented state, the University comes alive with Saturday football games and evening basketball games, as well as gymnastics meets, skiing competitions, volleyball games and a slew of other athletic activities. The U sponsors 11 women's and eight men's sports at the NCAA Division 1 level. University of Utah teams have won 24 national championships and 112 conference championships.

From its 180,000 alumni worldwide to its distance-education students at home in rural Utah towns, members of the University of Utah community share a sense of pride in the U's diverse peoples and offerings, its commitment to excellence and its strong Western heritage. These traditions continue to motivate the University to seek the very best ways to fulfill its mission of serving the public through teaching, research and service.

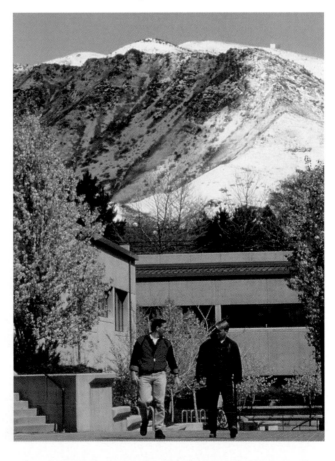

University of Utah Health Sciences Center

THE sprawling University of Utah Health Sciences Center campus that anchors the northeastern foothills of Salt Lake City is a major patient-care, research and health professions training center for the entire Intermountain West.

Chances are good that the physicians, nurses, pharmacists and other health-care professionals Salt Lakers have counted on throughout their lives completed all or part of their education in one of the center's academic components: the School of Medicine and the colleges of Pharmacy, Nursing and Health. Public health officials, physician assistants, physical and occupational therapists, laboratory technicians, speech pathologists, and nutritionists and dietitians are among the specialists educated at the center.

There are nearly 3,000 students enrolled in health-related disciplines, including the basic biomedical sciences, who are mentored by a dedicated, nationally recognized faculty more than 1,000 strong.

The work of student and faculty scholars and health professionals throughout the region is enhanced by the collections of the Spencer S. Eccles Health Sciences Library, designated by the National Library of Medicine as a regional medical library in the National Network of Libraries of Medicine.

Students in the health sciences, along with more than 500 physicians completing residency programs, receive clinical training at University of Utah Hospitals & Clinics, which includes University Hospital, the University Neuropsychiatric Institute, Huntsman Cancer Institute, the John A. Moran Eye Center and a number of community health centers.

Thousands of residents in the six-state Intermountain region — from burn victims to critically ill newborns to persons needing organ transplants to cancer patients — owe their lives to the high-quality patient care available here. Countless others depend on the center's clinical programs for help with everything from routine illness and injury to care for complex orthopedic, ophthalmic, fertility and cardiac problems, as well as genetic-related diseases.

University Hospitals & Clinics logs roughly 786,000 inpatient and outpatient visits annually. It is the state's largest hospital-based provider of ambulatory care services, with 80 general and specialty clinics for outpatients.

In 2001, for the third straight year, University Hospitals & Clinics was named the Consumer Choice Award winner in the Salt Lake City metropolitan area, receiving top honors for best doctors, best overall quality, best image and reputation, and a tie for best nurses. The polling group, National Research Corporation, said Salt Lakers judged University Hospital the most preferred hospital overall, the most preferred for cancer care and orthopedic care, and said it has the latest technology and equipment, widest range of services and best community health programs. The center's academic program in public health has been ranked third in the nation for the past two years by *U.S. News & World Report*.

In 2001 construction began on the George S. and Dolores Doré Eccles Critical Care Pavilion, a $43 million expansion project that will house a new emergency services department, 26 surgical intensive-care beds, six operating rooms, a short-stay surgery center, and post-anesthesia care unit.

The Health Sciences Center is a city within a city, with a combined student, faculty and employee population totaling more than 11,000.

The U of U Health Sciences Center is a thriving city within Salt Lake City, with a substantial population and a healthy economic impact. When considered separately from the U of U, the center ranked as the ninth-largest employer in Utah last year, with a full-time equivalent of 7,581 persons and a payroll of $429.5 million.

Research is a top priority at the center — its projects represent 66 percent of the $242.3 million in research awards received by the university in 2000-2001. Since 1974 the College of Pharmacy has ranked among the top five in the nation for peer-reviewed research funded by the National Institutes of Health (NIH), and in the year 2000 the College of Nursing ranked 25th among the nation's nursing schools in NIH grants, nearly doubling its funding from the previous year.

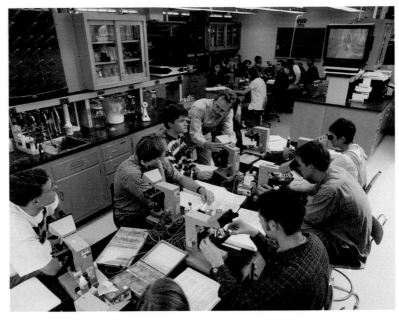

The highly competitive U of U medical school offers the majority of its positions — 75 percent, on average — to Utah residents.

Some of the center's most well-known and noteworthy programs are a blend of sophisticated patient care and cutting-edge research. The Huntsman Cancer Institute (HCI) conducts genetic cancer research, utilizing the largest genetic database in the world, composed of more than 3 million people. HCI offers patients and the public genetic counseling; high-risk breast cancer, colon cancer and melanoma clinics; and a cancer learning center staffed by specialized health educators. HCI conducts medical clinical trials and houses outpatient clinics, infusion suite facilities, and a pain and palliative care program for cancer patients. Ground was broken in 2001 for the six-story, 50-bed Huntsman Cancer Research Hospital to be located adjacent to the institute.

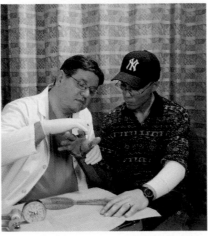

The John A. Moran Eye Center is the largest eye-care and vision-research center between the Mississippi River and the West Coast and is known internationally for its comprehensive approach to vision research. Researchers at the center are focused on areas such as artificial vision, ophthalmic genetics, vision rescue and restoration, and understanding of the retina. The Moran Eye Center's graduate physician training program was ranked 8th in the nation — tied with Harvard — in 2001 by *Ophthalmology Times*. Construction is expected to begin in spring 2002 on a new, expanded Moran Eye Center.

At the George and Dolores Doré Eccles Institute of Human Genetics, scientific expertise from the Department of Human Genetics and the Eccles Program in Human Molecular Biology and Genetics combine to create a broad interdisciplinary research community. Specialties include RNA translation and editing, developmental genetics, genomics, population genetics and human evolution, and disease genetics. Gene targeting was originally developed here and is currently a major focus of study. Using the knockout mouse technology developed at Utah, scientists around the world have created thousands of mouse models for studying the role of specific genes in a living organism.

Over the past century, what began as a two-room, two-year, pre-clinical medical education program in the early 1900s has evolved to encompass education, clinical care, research and community service in a full spectrum of health-care disciplines. The University of Utah Health Sciences Center has become an indispensable part of the quality of life and health in Salt Lake City, the state of Utah and the Intermountain region.

The Health Sciences Center has a proud history of research innovations and a culture that encourages interdisciplinary research collaboration and entrepreneurship.

University Hospital's Intermountain Burn Trauma Center, the only burn facility in the region, treats 325 critically ill inpatients and some 3,000 outpatients annually.

Utah State Historical Society

It was July 22, 1897 — exactly 50 years after the vanguard of Mormon pioneers entered the Great Salt Lake Valley and just more than 18 months after Utah won its long struggle for statehood. Responding to the request of Gov. Heber M. Wells, 27 community leaders met in the Templeton Hotel in the heart of Salt Lake City to found an historical society for the young state.

Franklin D. Richards was named president of the new Utah State Historical Society. It was a logical fit: Richards was the historian for the Church of Jesus Christ of Latter-day Saints, and the history of the church and the territory-turned-state were tightly interwoven. Non-Mormon attorney Jerrold R. Letcher, who had suggested that the society be formed, was appointed recording secretary and enthusiastically filled that post for the next 18 years.

The Society evolved slowly during its first decades. It was housed in a small office at the state capitol and hampered by scanty funding. Although the Utah State Legislature made the historical organization an official state agency in 1917, its operations remained largely dependent on membership fees.

J. Cecil Alter, the state's meteorologist and an avid historian, donated his time and energy to bring these lackluster years to an end during his 1926-1937 reign as secretary/treasurer. Other dynamic volunteers, including prominent merchant Herbert S. Auerbach (president, 1936-1945) and Marguerite L. Sinclair

The Historical Society has occupied the Rio Grande Depot since 1980. Shown here in a c. 1910 photo is the front of the newly built Denver & Rio Grande Depot. *Photo by Shipler Commercial Photographers, used by permission of the Utah State Historical Society; all rights reserved.*

(executive secretary/manager, 1937-1949), also played pivotal roles in the growth of the maturing Society during this era.

One of their initiatives was the launch of the *Utah Historical Quarterly* in 1928. Alter served as editor. The publication gave the Society much needed visibility as well as an ongoing purpose and scholarly credibility. It has been published continuously since its first issue except for a hiatus during the Great Depression.

In 1957 the Society moved into a new home: the majestic Kearns Mansion on historic South Temple Street. When the governor decided to return to the mansion, the organization eventually took residence in the impressive 1910-vintage Denver & Rio Grande Railroad Depot, where it has been since 1980.

Visitors to today's Utah State Historical Society can expect to be impressed. Its home is a spacious icon of architectural grandeur, giving visitors the impression that they are stepping back into history. But what it holds is even more impressive. The Society's main exhibit provides a fascinating glimpse into Utah's history. Other exhibits are available for public viewing in other rooms in the depot.

What is not on display is even more impressive. The organization's library and archives represent a treasure trove of history. The constantly growing archival collection includes over 25,000 published volumes, more than 20,000 published pamphlets, about 1 million photographs, selected issues of close to 900 different periodicals, approximately 30,000 published and unpublished maps, and hundreds of oral histories. It also contains over 900 manuscript collections of varying sizes. These include records of organizations and companies, as well as personal records consisting of individuals' diaries and journals, correspondence, financial records, photographs, films, videos and other remembrances.

Gathering these archives is a never-ending task. Some items are donated, part of a rigorous collection program responsible for the majority of its holdings. The Society often mounts theme-oriented collecting campaigns. It has, for example, collected extensive archives relating to water issues, which have always been extremely important in the high desert state. This led to the gathering of a large collection on the Colorado River, which includes written and filmed accounts of river-runners through the years. One is a 16-millimeter "home movie" that documents trips down the river in the 1930s and 1950s. It includes scenes of Glen Canyon, now hidden under Lake Powell. The same man who shot this film was the physician for Admiral Richard Byrd's exploration of Antarctica. He captured that expedition on 16-millimeter film, which is also found in the Society's archives.

Some collecting efforts are geographically oriented. An example of this is the Society's campaign to collect oral histories of ranchers, farmers, miners and other long-time residents in the relatively isolated communities around the Grand Staircase-Escalante National Monument in Southern Utah.

All of these archives are available to the public. Interested parties can visit the Society's research area — the Utah History Information Center — sign in and search for the desired information or items aided by research staff members. A catalog for the entire collection is available in the research area. (The catalog, as well as a wealth of other historical resources, is also available on the Society's Web site.) Once the desired archives are identified, staff members can bring them out into the research area for perusal.

As impressive as the library and archives are, they represent only one of the many services the Utah State Historical Society provides to individuals and organizations statewide. Another important function involves the official designation of sites and buildings that are of prehistoric and historic significance, including locations worthy of being listed on the National Register.

The Society is involved in archaeology, issuing permits and consulting with archaeological groups and individuals. It helps local community and historical organizations do field work. Educators and students alike can depend on the organization to supply a wide variety of educational resources and opportunities, including an on-site book-and-gift shop and an

Utah at the Crossroads exhibit, Rio Grande Depot. *Photo by Dave Jonsson, used by permission of the Utah State Historical Society; all rights reserved.*

informative Web site where visitors can drill deep into the roots of the past. The Society also provides historians with grants and technical assistance. Plus, it has membership and affiliates programs involving thousands of individuals, libraries, and local historical organizations.

The leaders and staff of the Utah State Historical Society invite all who are interested in the state's rich and unique history to visit its headquarters, enjoy the exhibits and take advantage of the fascinating library and archives, as well as the Web site. Together they are working to continually expand their resources and services to ensure that the future of the Utah State Historical Society is even brighter than its illustrious past.

The Historical Society was founded in 1897 in the Templeton Building, shown here in a 1905 photograph. *Photo by Shipler Commercial Photographers, used by permission of the Utah State Historical Society; all rights reserved.*

VA Salt Lake City Health Care System

FROM high atop Salt Lake City's east bench, the VA Medical Center overlooks the valley from a verdant 86-acre campus. Some 27,000 Utah veterans received health care here in 2001. Utah veterans and their survivors also collected disability compensation or pension payments. GI Bill benefits assisted over 3,000 veterans with their education while nearly 20,000 Utah veterans claimed home ownership with the assistance of VA home loan guarantees.

Veterans from Utah, Idaho, Nevada and Wyoming are served by the Salt Lake City facility — the largest geographic area in the VA system. The modern 106-bed medical center offers specialized cardiology, oncology and amputee care and serves as a training site for the nearby University of Utah School of Medicine. VA researchers have been at the forefront in developing the cardiac pacemaker, the CT scan, magnetic resonance imaging and improving artificial limbs.

Research continues to be a VA priority with the Salt Lake facility sponsoring 220 active investigations to improve the prevention, diagnosis, treatment and control of disease. The VA funds more than $3 million in research-related projects in Utah including conditions related to audiology, pulmonary diseases, cardiology, geriatrics, endocrinology, rheumatology, infectious diseases and neurovirology.

In addition to research and traditional medical care, the VA Medical Center's other specialized services include pathology, radiology, neurology, nuclear medicine, psychiatry and open heart surgery, including cardiac transplantation.

The Salt Lake facility has followed national health care trends that have mandated a change from a hospital-based system to one focused on outpatient care. Over the past seven years, while working with 27,000 fewer employees, the national VA system has provided care for 930,000 more veterans.

For veterans in the western region, this means special outpatient clinics for post-traumatic stress disorder, domestic violence, same-day surgery and ambulatory medicine. The Salt Lake facility offers a 30-bed "hoptel," which is a hospital-based hotel unit for those veterans who need accommodations the night before or immediately following an outpatient procedure. The medical center also offers a recreational vehicle lot for those who have a "home on wheels."

Rural veterans can access medical care at primary care clinics in Ogden, Orem, St. George, Nephi, Fountain Green, Milford and Duchesne. Out-of-state clinics operated by the VA Salt Lake City Health Care System are located in Ely, Nevada; Pocatello, Idaho; and Green River, Wyoming.

The VA mandate includes serving the 25 percent of homeless people who have served in the armed forces and many more who are on the edge of homelessness. As the only federal agency to provide direct, hands-on assistance to homeless veterans, the VA has more than 7,000 transitional and permanent beds available for homeless veterans throughout the states.

The Utah program is called Healthcare for Homeless Veterans (HCHV), and working in conjunction with social service agencies and shelters, it coordinates benefits for veterans. Treatment is available for veterans with chronic mental illness and for alcoholism and drug addiction.

The VA Salt Lake City Health Care System recognizes the needs of America's veterans and is committed to providing quality health care services.

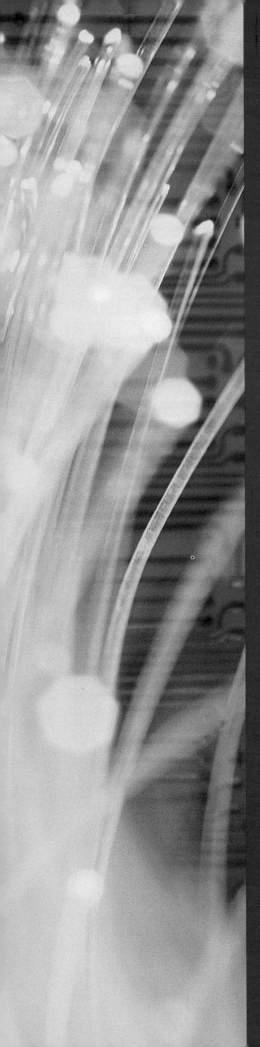

Technology

Diverse businesses have gathered to make Salt Lake City
one of the country's leading centers of technology innovation,
development, manufacturing and employment.

BC Technical Inc. 254

Equis International 256

Evans & Sutherland 258

Novell 260

Fairchild Semiconductor 262

Floppy Copy, Inc. 263

BC Technical Inc.

BC TECHNICAL INC., a West Jordan company that specializes in sales, service and repair of ADAC™ nuclear medicine equipment across the United States and international, was founded by Charles F. "Chuck" and Beverly Hale on December 13, 1995. Prior to starting this business Chuck Hale had gained valuable experience working for 12 years for ADAC Laboratories, the world leader in nuclear medicine equipment and service. While based in California's Bay Area, Hale traveled to 48 states and particularly liked Utah's mountains, people and the family values he found there. When he learned that ADAC had an opening in Salt Lake City, he fought to obtain a position there.

Two years after moving to Salt Lake City, Hale decided it was time to found his own company. Although ADAC's products are excellent, their service and parts are extremely expensive, which drives up health care costs significantly. It also provides opportunity for a business such as BC Technical Inc., to supply superior service and parts at substantial savings from the original equipment manufacturer (OEM). The Hales thought the moment was opportune and BC Technical was started in a bedroom of the Hale home.

From the moment Chuck and Beverly Hale met — Hale had been sent from California to Las Vegas to attend a seminar at the same time his future bride came to Las Vegas from Missouri — it was literally a case of "love at first sight," and they have had a true 50-50 partnership in their lives. Beverly Hale had worked as a legal secretary for 22 years and continued working during BC Technical's first year of operation so that they could pay bills. Chuck Hale began business by providing service for GE Medical. Because many businesses charge

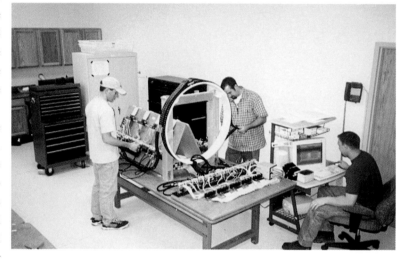

exorbitant rates for parts, Hale focused his business on being able to supply the full line of ADAC parts at substantial savings.

As the saying goes, "Nothing succeeds like success," and after only six months the business had taken over a second bedroom, part of the living room and garage. The Hales rented a 900-square-foot building and only nine months later leased a 1,400-square-foot building, thinking "We'll never fill it up," but they outgrew it within a year. In rapid sequence they bought a 6,000-square-foot building, a second 6,000-square-foot building and the lot behind the second building, where they will soon erect a third building. Chuck Hale was spending so much time flying from client to client that he found they were losing business because no one was able to answer the phone. At that point Beverly Hale came into the business. Although she had no prior experience in accounting or human resources work, she took the bull by the horns and expanded her areas of expertise.

BC Technical cables, manufactured on-site from the highest-quality wire, are thoroughly tested on state-of-the-art, computer-based testing equipment.

Because BC Technical operates in a family-type working environment, employees work harder and take pride in their work.

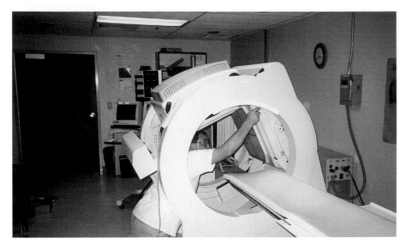

Today, BC Technical is the only independent service organization (ISO) specializing in servicing only ADAC nuclear medicine equipment, and the company has grown from a single service engineer in 1995 into a multimillion-dollar company dedicated to providing the highest-quality and affordable parts, service and refurbished ADAC systems. BC Technical provides parts at an average of 50 to 80 percent below the OEM's list price and an hourly rate that's 48 percent less than the OEM's. BC Technical, the leading third-party provider of quality parts for ADAC equipment, has made strategic alliances with third-party service companies, insurance companies and health care facilities by supplying training, parts and free technical support — all focused at cost-containment of service. This approach has allowed BC Technical to fill a special niche market, but one that does not have to compete directly with ADAC Laboratories.

Service, including free technical support, is a cornerstone of BC Technical's business, based on the company's motto, "Affordable Excellence" and the philosophy that a service organization should give great service. BC Technical's clients include hospitals with full-service or first-pass contracts, hospitals that hire BC Technical on a billable basis, insurance companies, asset management companies and other independent service organizations.

BC Technical also excels in training and has recently expanded its training operation to accommodate the many clients who have requested it. GE Medical, Premier Inc. and many other facilities have requested training on all ADAC equipment, including the powerful new $400,000-to-$600,000 Forte camera.

BC Technical actually does more business in the area of parts, board repair and refurbishment than in service. Refurbishing medical equipment is a very profitable business targeted at health care facilities that must contain costs. For facilities that cannot afford to buy expensive new medical-imaging equipment, purchasing refurbished equipment is an attractive solution. BC Technical buys used ADAC equipment from brokers and hospitals, checks each system thoroughly, installs new parts, rebuilds detectors and performs extensive system tests to ensure years of highly dependable performance. It then sells the equipment to hospitals, doctors and clinics.

BC Technical also offers a full line of parts for ADAC gamma cameras, which are used to detect cancer, cardiac problems and other diseases of the body. Repaired parts are fully tested to ensure proper operation. The company also supplies ring and take-up cables for all ADAC cameras.

BC Technical cables are manufactured from the highest-quality wire, exceed OEM specifications and are thoroughly tested by BC Technical's sophisticated, state-of-the-art computer-based testing equipment.

Three of the Hales' children — Charles L. "Chuck Jr." (and his wife, Tiffani), Jason D. and Heather Latas — are all involved in the business, which operates with a family atmosphere. The senior Hales believe that by treating people "like people" their employees work harder and take pride in their work. They provide flexible schedules to college students who want to work and gain experience while also obtaining a degree.

GE Medical, BC Technical's first customer, constitutes 25 percent of BC Technical's business, with the remaining 75 percent coming from clients such as Premier Inc., a chain of 200 hospitals, for which BC Technical supplies service and solutions, and other major health care providers such as US Counseling, Inc., MediServe, Inc. and Core Master Plan. Business has been growing so rapidly that BC Technical is in an enviable position — the company can hardly keep up with all the growth — but one thing is clear, the quality of its work will never suffer.

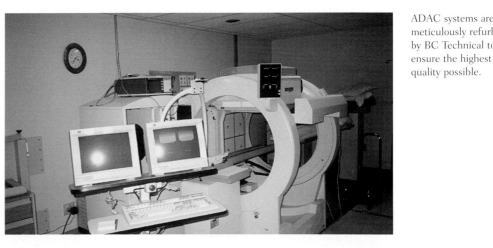

Equis International

EQUIS International is widely considered the world standard in the stock charting and technical analysis tool industry — a position it has held for most of its 18-year existence.

It all began in the early 1980s. Steve Achelis, founder of Equis International, was working in a diesel mechanic shop. While reading a popular investment book, he realized that many of the charts and calculations contained in the book could be translated into personal investor programs.

Risking it all, Achelis quit his job and bought his first computer — the original Apple II. He was actively involved in trading stock index futures at the time. He purchased various computer programs to help perform his technical analysis and charting, but the programs wouldn't do what he wanted them to do. They were also expensive. Worse, they were mainly designed for wealthy professionals and institutional traders — definitely not for the retail individual investor.

MetaStock's razor-sharp graphics provide amazing insight to the markets.

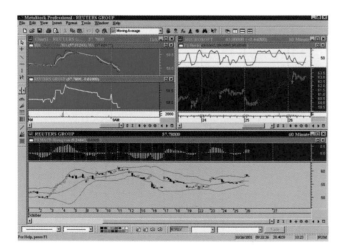

Achelis had a different vision for the future of computerized investment tools: regular investors analyzing their stock charts and calculations from the convenience of their own computers, using reasonably priced software. Determined to see this vision materialize, he taught himself computer programming so he could create his own software.

As a result, Achelis launched a one-man operation, running the business from his home in West Valley City, Utah. He acted as programmer, salesman, technician, mailroom clerk and floor sweeper for his business, Computer Asset Management. Seated in front of his computer, he wrote code day after day, eating all his meals at his desk. He was determined to create software that would provide the average investor with the same information and analysis tools only big-spenders on Wall Street could then afford.

Achelis' first product, The Market Mood Monitor for the Apple II computer, received poor reviews. Undaunted, he

By building a consistent methodology, MetaStock takes the emotion out of trading, creating a foundation for investment success.

kept on working, and in 1983 ported his program from the Apple II to the DOS environment. Achelis renamed this product the Technician, one of the first multiple, moveable windows programs within the DOS environment. These two market timing products let investors focus on broad market analyses, such as depth and breadth indicators of the New York Stock exchange. However, these programs were not yet capable of giving people access to individual stocks.

Affordability was one of Achelis' primary goals. And he did it without sacrificing quality. The program included high-quality packaging, documentation and product support. In contrast, the main competitor's product sold for a staggering $1,900 and came with only a dot-matrix-printed manual.

In 1985 Achelis released MetaStock — an affordable program that permitted investors to finally chart and analyze individual securities, options and futures. In April 1986 MetaStock and Achelis' other product, The Technician, received *PC Magazine's* prestigious Editor's Choice Awards and were featured in an article on investment analysis software. Sales quickly rose from 200 units annually to 200 units per month. As a result, Achelis' business grew quickly. The name of the company also changed, and Computer Asset Management became Equis International.

MetaStock is Equis' flagship product. It offers security charting of all types, explorations to find securities that meet the user's criteria, system back-testing to discover the success of a trading system before risking real money, expert advisories that show how select experts would trade in a particular situation, a high-powered set of systems and exploration tools called Performance Systems, and much more. The software also includes buy/sell alerts to help give each trade the highest profits with the lowest degree of risk. With the click of a mouse, MetaStock can also access up-to-the-minute fundamental information relating to each security.

Equis founder, Steve Achelis, is shown here working on MetaStock in 1988.

Equis currently services 100,000 customers in 70 countries with more than 140 independent user groups.

By building a consistent methodology, MetaStock takes the emotion out of trading, creating a foundation for investment success. Consequently, the company has earned a strong reputation for quality products that are easy to use and have the most in-depth analytical capabilities available, as well as excellent customer service.

Since 1986 MetaStock has gone through 10 different versions and upgrades as Equis works to ensure that its product is current with the ever-evolving demands of advancing technology.

For the past eight years MetaStock has received the "Reader's Choice Award" from *Stocks and Commodities* magazine in its price range. In fact, most people recognize Equis International by its product name, MetaStock, rather than the company name.

In 1996 Equis was purchased by Reuters, the global leader in financial news and information. It was a good fit — the purchase terms allowed Equis to continue doing what it has always done best, with its same management team.

Like other top computer software companies, Equis cannot sit still. Always improving, evolving and progressing, the company was recently selected to take charge of Reuters' graphic works. The company will be providing technical analysis and charting capabilities for Reuters' institutional marketplace, as well as providing for its own retail market.

Equis currently services 100,000 customers in 70 countries with more than 140 independent user groups. Now under new leadership, Equis plans to continue its expansion into the professional community while increasing international sales. But its primary mission remains the same: to provide

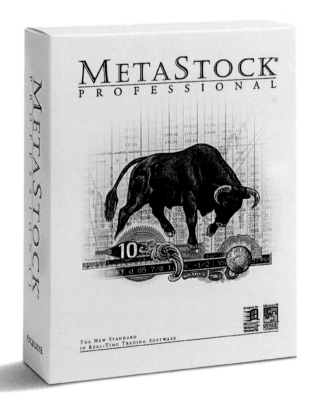

MetaStock helps investors uncover hidden profit-making opportunities in the markets.

investors everywhere with the finest products that guarantee up-to-the-minute, user-friendly technology for investment success.

Evans & Sutherland

FORTY years ago computer-generated virtual reality was just a vision of specialized scientists. Today, virtual reality is everywhere, from families going to movies to soldiers training to defend the country. Much of that transformation is a result of the work of the visionaries who founded Evans & Sutherland (E&S) and the creative team they assembled to break new ground in the field of computer-generated graphics technology. E&S began in 1968, and more than 30 years later it is a leading developer of realistic 3-D synthetic worlds.

Evans & Sutherland dual-dome visual systems are being integrated onto the Boeing WAH-64 Apache Longbow Full Mission Simulator at Boeing facilities in St. Louis, Missouri.

December 1969: Ivan Sutherland (left) and Dave Evans (right) with Line Drawing System 1

These worlds range from planetarium shows where children feel as if they are flying through space to simulated combat training for the U.S. military. Known as the power behind the scenes, E&S produces visual systems hardware and software for commercial airlines, NASA, American and international armed forces, aerospace companies, the shipping industry, the real estate industry, planetariums, science centers, domed theater entertainment venues, laboratories and mechanical designers. E&S has the depth of experience and breadth of technical expertise to create innovative and sophisticated applications that are applicable across a broad spectrum of the marketplace.

Simulated reality has a fun side and a serious side. Entertainment applications enable audiences to experience cutting-edge digital entertainment on the big screen, immersed in adventures that take them to realms beyond their imaginations. Serious applications enter the realms of outer space, flight and combat.

Most of the world's commercial pilots receive their training in simulators that use E&S visual systems. Commercial airline pilots, required to log 5,000 hours of training time, train on flight simulators, saving the airlines up to $20 million a year. These systems create realistic scenarios in which pilots can experience the sights, sounds and motions of flight while still on the ground. In addition to being a cost-effective way to provide quality training, simulation allows students to practice emergency responses and maneuvers in a completely safe environment, without risk to personnel or equipment.

Simulators are essential to every military training program and must be able to create realistic environments. As a military contractor, E&S sets the standard for advanced training solutions, including helicopter and fixed-wing flight and ground warfare training. Combat-training programs teach personnel to operate in all types of battle conditions. These applications include air-to-ground and air-to-air, targeting and tracking, terrain following and calculating target objects.

Taking computers beyond collecting data to simulating reality was the innovative idea that led to the formation of E&S. Back in the early 1960s, Dave Evans and Ivan Sutherland had already established reputations for ground-breaking thinking in the emerging field of computer science. When computers first came on the scene, they were used for routine tasks like billing and storing information. Dr. Evans was among the first to be interested in the idea that people could interact with their computers, in what he described as the man-machine interface. As a visiting professor at UC Berkeley in the mid-60s, he pursued his interest in applying computer graphics to other fields outside traditional computer science.

Harrier jets created using Evans & Sutherland's Harmony® image generator

Meanwhile, Ivan Sutherland had made a name for himself in 1963, when his movie, *Sketchpad: A Man-Machine Graphical Communication System*, documented his doctoral dissertation. Until then, computer graphics had been two-dimensional. Sutherland pioneered the idea of using a data structure based on the topology of three-dimensional objects, an idea that established him as a leading computer science researcher. Sutherland became a professor at Harvard where he continued his research, much of which became the basis for the development of E&S products.

In 1967 the University of Utah invited Evans to establish the college's computer science program, where he continued his research in computer graphics. Today, the university's computer science department is one of the country's best. The following year he recruited Sutherland to join him. While at the university the two performed consulting work for large companies but were frustrated that most of their suggestions were not implemented. In order to develop products from their ideas, they decided to start their own company. Because of the large number of college graduates in Utah and the professors' association with the university, the partners were able to staff their new firm with exceptionally talented people. Many prominent graphics pioneers worked at E&S in the early years of their careers.

Evans and Sutherland were interested in developing technology that would promote the use of computers as tools. Theirs was the unique idea that computers could be simulators, and that simulators would replace reality when a physical model would be prohibitively expensive to build. E&S began as a graphics producer because graphics were the connection that linked the user with the simulation.

As extraordinary as it seems today, the partners' most pressing challenge was not inventing the technology but finding a market for their products. At that time, the concept of the computer as an interactive design tool was so new that E&S was opening an entirely new market. As is the case with most visionary pioneers, Evans and Sutherland led the way, and the market followed.

After more than 30 years in business, E&S is both a uniquely Utah company and a major player in the international market. E&S is rooted in Salt Lake City, home to the company's headquarters, a 36-acre campus in the University of Utah Research Park. Other American offices include Boston, Orlando and Bedford, Texas. Because about one-third of the company's business is generated in Europe, Asia and the Middle East, E&S also has offices in England, Germany, Japan, China and the United Arab Emirates.

E&S is one of the leaders of the Utah high-tech economy and one of the world's foremost producers of visual systems for simulation. In a state that boasts of its pioneer heritage, E&S has helped pioneer the technological revolution, blazing new trails in computer graphics and visual systems technology. The company, in business longer than many computer giants like Microsoft or Intel, flourishes because it has always encouraged innovation, creativity and risk-taking. The E&S culture invites its employees to generate ideas and make decisions and invests extensively in research and development.

Today, E&S continues to deliver the future of simulation technology, providing its customers with a unique product road map that protects their investment for the long term. E&S uses the motto, "When training counts, count on Evans & Sutherland" and is committed to helping its customers provide the most realistic training experiences possible.

Technology

Novell

A LEADING PROVIDER OF NET BUSINESS SOLUTIONS

NOVELL helped invent the corporate network in the early 1980s and continues to drive technology and solutions for the Net today. Networking software began with the sharing of files and printers within local area networks and evolved into the management of wide area networks that enabled enterprise-class computing. Today, Novell is committed to providing solutions for a world in which all types of networks — corporate and public, intranets, extranets, and the Internet — work together as one Net and securely connect employees, customers, suppliers and partners across organizational boundaries. Novell's promise is to give organizations the ability to adapt to — and profit from — the opportunities of the networked world.

A HISTORY OF TECHNOLOGY LEADERSHIP

Novell Data Systems began life in 1979 as a computer manufacturer and maker of disk operating systems. In 1983 Novell Data Systems was reincorporated as Novell, Inc. with a focus on designing and marketing software and hardware for data networks. Novell helped found the corporate network market with the introduction of the local area network, or LAN. In 1983 Novell introduced NetWare, the first LAN software based on file-server technology. Novell developed a PC networking system that designated one machine to manage the network and control access to shared devices, such as disk drives and printers. This marked an important early step in the network revolution that has culminated today in the one Net economy.

Through the 1980s, corporate requirements for networks grew significantly, with LANs being increasingly replaced by Wide Area Networks, which unified large corporate environments. By the early 1990s Novell's NetWare operating system, updated to add key features for distributed enterprises, led this market with nearly a 70-percent share.

In 1996, recognizing that the Internet was beginning to revolutionize the traditional network market, Novell took steps to make the company's products Internet ready. Novell decided to base its products on IP, the Internet communications protocol.

Novell corporate headquarters

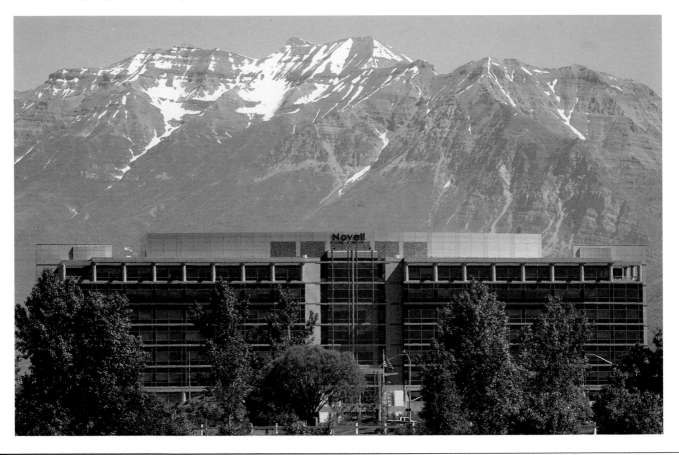

The following year, both NetWare 5, Novell's server operating system, and Novell Directory Services (NDS), an identity and network management technology that had become the basis for Novell's new Net services software, began shipping with native IP support.

With the increased heterogeneity in corporate networks and the need for interoperability across the Internet, Novell began in 1998 to promote its directory as a means to tie diverse platforms together. The company also began shipping the first of its new Net services software products that use information stored in the directory to simplify the management of networks and better secure access based on the identities of users. In late 1999 Novell released NDS eDirectory, a true cross-platform directory service that epitomized Novell's commitment to interoperability and open standards, key Internet requirements.

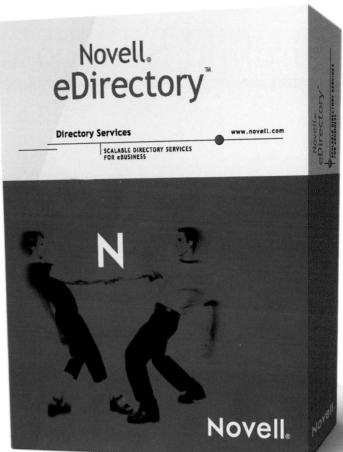

Novell eDirectory™ for identity management

A LEADING I T CONSULTING FIRM

In the summer of 2001 Novell acquired Cambridge Technology Partners, a leading consulting firm, to strengthen its ability to deliver solutions to customers. The advent of eBusiness over the preceding few years had changed the dynamics in the software market. Previously, technology was sold to technologists. With the emergence of the Net, companies moved quickly to open up their corporate networks to partners, suppliers and customers to improve efficiencies and build better relationships. Technology decisions became fundamental business decisions, and technology had to be delivered in business terms as solutions to problems. Companies increasingly sought comprehensive approaches — involving both products and services — to integrate their business processes with their technology to drive growth opportunities. Novell recognized the need to acquire business expertise to match its technology strengths. The combination of Novell's industry-leading technology and Cambridge's eBusiness consulting expertise gives Novell new strength to deliver Net business solutions.

A LEADER IN NET BUSINESS SOLUTIONS

Today, Novell solves real-world business problems by offering industry-leading software and consulting services for solutions that make the Net work. These solutions help companies simplify the complexities of eBusiness, secure their enterprise resources, accelerate their return on investment and extend their business process, applications and networks across organizational boundaries.

Novell provides reliable, high-performance network services as foundations for Net business solutions. With the introduction of premier products such as Novell eDirectory™ for identity management, Novell iChain™ for access and security, Novell iFolder™ for Net storage and DirXML™ for data integration, Novell delivers on its promise of providing services that span all leading operating systems, within and between organizations. Continued improvements in Novell's Net services software products like NetWare®, GroupWise®, and ZENworks® enable corporate IT departments to simplify the complexities of the Net and securely extend and integrate applications and networks between organizations. Cambridge Technology Partners provides customers with best-in-class solutions to help solve complex business challenges. With an impressive track record of proven methodologies, innovative solutions and best-of-breed technology, Cambridge enables its clients to support, extend and transform their businesses to achieve competitive advantage.

Novell today provides solutions that solve complex business and technical challenges that enable people, processes and systems to work together more effectively. At the start of the new millennium, Novell is poised to become a leader in delivering Net business solutions, helping customers around the globe profit from the opportunity of a networked world.

Fairchild Semiconductor

IF the average family were asked to live without semiconductors, most members might believe they couldn't care less. But if that family were forced to survive without alarm clocks, automatic coffee makers, cell phones, CD players, video games, lavish cars and personal computers, however, it would be an entirely different story. As these tiny chips recently evolved into the "backbone" of most new technologies, Fairchild Semiconductor positioned itself as the first multi-market supplier in the world. Today, Fairchild remains one of the top purveyors of these technological "building blocks" that make the modern world go 'round.

A machine operator monitors a robotic equipment cluster in Fairchild Semiconductor's cleanroom manufacturing environment.

What is so remarkable is that by focusing on a part of technology that other companies give only fractional attention to, Fairchild has created the world's largest and most comprehensive portfolio of high-performance products in the power, interface, analog, mixed signal, logic, optoelectronic and configurable markets. Anything plugged in or battery-operated is supported by Fairchild's semiconductors or could be in the future.

Fairchild's devices support the world's desire for high-performance portable devices through the use of small-scale packaging.

Fairchild has played its part from the beginnings of the semiconductor industry. In 1957 Sherman Mills Fairchild had the foresight to sponsor a small group of young scientists in California in their development of a revolutionary process for the manufacture of transistors. This group and their findings became the foundation for Silicon Valley. Since that time, the Fairchild name has continued to mean innovation and excellence. In addition, this multibillion-dollar enterprise has achieved rapid expansion through carefully planned acquisitions and captured market share.

Fairchild's Utah facility has become a hub of technology development for advanced power products. As expectations grow for lighter and longer-lasting battery power for the world's portable appliances, Fairchild's development teams focus on satisfying those needs. The company's power products provide superior power management in all types of transportable devices, such as cell phones, PDAs and notebook computers.

Fairchild's West Jordan facility has played a significant role in the local community for more than 25 years. Besides its enormous contribution to the tax base, Fairchild is working to become an "employer of choice" in the area. The company attracts a skilled work force through nationally competitive salaries and benefits, inside promotion and 100-percent college tuition support. It practices participative management, fostering a work environment conducive to personal and professional growth. With the added attractions of an onsite fitness center, cafeteria and credit union, it's not surprising that Fairchild's turnover is lower than other companies in the same industry.

Fairchild's support of the community extends far beyond the walls of the huge facility. By providing support through contributions and involvement, employees engender excitement about engineering and technical careers at local schools. Educational partnerships, from elementary on up to the university level, are an integral part of the company's strategy to pass along the knowledge and skills of its work force to the academic environment.

Fairchild recently released an advertising campaign with engaging images that suggest a literal truth: "No matter where you go. There we are." As the world continues in its love affair with technology and communication, Fairchild's innovative semiconductors will be a part of the technology shaping the world.

Floppy Copy, Inc.

SALT Lake City's Floppy Copy, Inc. makes the Information Age a reality for many consumers by replicating computer disks and CD-ROMs, packaging materials and printing labels and related items. The company began in 1988 when Steve Smith made a small but significant investment to meet the duplication and packaging needs of his employer, Megahertz. Smith started the firm in a spare bedroom where he used one machine to copy large and small floppy disks. Later he operated in the basement of a house, and then he moved the business to a 1,600-square-foot office.

Floppy Copy's main customers include hardware manufacturers, software developers, Internet service providers, universities and medical products firms.

Originally, Floppy Copy outsourced all its printing needs, but in 1992 it added print services to decrease response time. In 1993 Smith transferred ownership, which ended up with co-owners Shane Argyle, the company president, and Vice President Craig Mortensen.

In 1996 Floppy Copy purchased the 38,000-square-foot building at its current location. With its floor capacity quadrupled, the company added automated packaging machines and more diskette duplicating machines. Later it partnered with other firms that duplicated CD-ROMs.

Floppy Copy's main customers include hardware manufacturers, software developers, Internet service providers, universities and medical products firms. Diversification began in 1998 when it started packaging nonsoftware items such as scrapbooking and craft materials. However, about 95 percent of its integrated packaging services are used to support high-tech customers.

The business community has recognized Floppy Copy's achievements. *Inc.* magazine included the company in its 1997 list of the nation's 500 fastest-growing companies. MountainWest Venture Group included Floppy Copy in the Utah 100 list of the state's fastest-growing companies from 1996 through 1999.

Initially, Floppy Copy recycled obsolete computer disks, but later it decided to donate disks to Utah school districts and Third World hospitals and schools. By 2000 Floppy Copy had reformatted, relabeled and donated more than 200,000 used disks. It plans to continue that program and support other community activities.

In 2000 Floppy Copy employed 32 people full time and utilized up to 60 temporary employees to meet flexible production demands. Floppy Copy has little turnover, averaging just one employee annually. "Once you land a job at Floppy Copy, you're foolish to leave," says Roger Ochocki, head of Floppy Copy's print services.

Floppy Copy's main goals are to diversify its customer base and continue its reputation for quickness and reliability. In the last two years it has reduced its average time of three weeks for complete software duplication and packaging for one of its major customers to eight days. It has fulfilled some requests in just a few hours. Its deliveries in 2000 were an impressive 99.7 percent on time. Floppy Copy's customers appreciate such timely response to their duplicating, packaging and printing orders, especially as more manufacturers use just-in-time production that minimizes inventory and keeps consumer prices low. Floppy Copy's speedy and dependable work bode well for its future growth in the 21st century.

Floppy Copy's software-manufacturing headquarters

BIBLIOGRAPHY

CHAPTER ONE

For the trek of the Mormon pioneers into the Salt Lake Valley see: Orson Pratt, *The Orson Pratt Journals* Elden J. Watson, ed. (Salt Lake City: Privately Printed, 1975); Thomas Bullock, *The Pioneer Camp of the Saints: The 1846 and 1847 Mormon Trail Journals of Thomas Bullock* ed. Will Bagley *Kingdom in the West: The Mormons and the American Frontier*, Vol. 1 (Spokane, WA: Arthur H. Clark, 1997); *Wilford Woodruff, Wilford Woodruff's Journals, 1833-1898 Vol 3, 1 January 1846 to 31 December 1850* ed. Scott G. Kenney (Midvale, UT: Signature Books, 1983). On Colorado Tick Fever see Ronald V. Loge, "Illness at Three Forks: Captain William Clark and the First Recorded Case of Colorado Tick Fever," *Montana: The Magazine of Western History* 50 (Summer 2000): 2-15.

On the geology of the Salt Lake Valley see Lehi F. Hintze, *Geologic History of Utah* (Provo, UT: Brigham Young University Department of Geology, 1988). On the general pre-history of the region see Kimball T. Harper, Larry L. St. Clair, Kaye H. Thorne, and Wilford M. Hess, eds. *Natural History of The Colorado Plateau and Great Basin* (Niwot, Colorado: University Press of Colorado, 1994).

On the native peoples see David B. Madsen, *Exploring the Fremont* (Salt Lake City: Museum of Natural History, 1989). On the Utes see David Rich Lewis, *Neither Wolf Nor Dog: American Indians, Environment, and Agrarian Change* (New York: Oxford University Press, 1994) and Fred A. Conetah, *A History of the Northern Ute People* ed. Kathryn L. MacKay and Floyd A. O'Neil (Salt Lake City: Uintah-Ouray Tribe, 1982). On the Shoshoni see Brigham D. Madsen, *The Northern Shoshoni* (Caldwell, Idaho: Caxton Printers, 1980). On the beliefs of these people see *Stories of Our Ancestors: A Collection of Northern-Ute Indian Tales* ed. Norma Denver, June Lyman, Daisy Jenks, Floyd A. O'Neil, Gregory C. Thompson, Fred Conetah, and Kathryn L. Mackay (Salt Lake City: Uintah-Ouray Tribe, 1974)

On the trappers see LeRoy Hafen, *The Mountain Men and the Fur Trade of the Far West, Biographical Sketches* 10 vols. (Glendale, CA: Arthur H. Clark, 1965-1972); David J. Weber,

The Taos Trappers: The Fur Trade in the Far Southwest, 1540-1846 (Norman: University of Oklahoma Press, 1971). On Frémont see Donald Jackson and Mary Lee Spence, *The Expeditions of John Charles Frémont*, 3 vols. (Urbana: University of Illinois Press, 1970ff). On the overland migrations see John D. Unruh, *The Plains Across: The Overland Emigrants and the Trans-Mississippi West, 1840-1860* (Urbana: University of Illinois Press, 1979).

On the journey to Salt Lake City and the first organizing of the city see the Orson Pratt and Thomas Bullock journals noted earlier. See also Leonard J. Arrington, *Great Basin Kingdom: An Economic History of the Latter-day Saints, 1830-1900* (Cambridge: Harvard University Press, 1958) and Brian Q. Cannon, "Salt Lake City (1847)" *Historic Atlas of Mormonism* eds. S. Kent Brown, Donald Q. Cannon, Richard H. Jackson (New York: Simon and Schuster, 1994).

On the government of Salt Lake City see Dale L. Morgan, *The State of Deseret* (Logan, Utah: Utah State University Press, 1987), which includes verbatim copies of the ordinances of the Salt Lake Stake High Council as a temporary government and of the government of the State of Deseret. On the first years in the valley, the coming of non-Mormon merchants, and the impact of the Gold Rush see Arrington, *Great Basin Kingdom*.

On the various cultural organizations see Joseph Heinerman, "Early Pioneer Cultural Societies," *Utah Historical Quarterly* 47 (Winter 1979): 70-89. On the Reformation of 1856-57 see Paul H. Peterson, "The Mormon Reformation" (Ph. D. Dissertation, Brigham Young University, 1981)

On the Utah War see Donald R. Moorman with Gene A. Sessions, *Camp Floyd and the Mormons: The Utah War* (Salt Lake City: University of Utah Press, 1992) and Norman F. Furniss, *The Mormon Conflict, 1850-1859* (New Haven: Yale University Press, 1960). On Utah during the Civil War see E. B. Long, *The Saints and the Union: Utah Territory during the Civil War* (Urbana: University of Illinois Press, 1981). On ZCMI and the cooperative movement see Arrington, *Great Basin Kingdom* and Martha Sonntag Bradley, *ZCMI: America's First Department Store* (Salt Lake City: ZCMI, 1991). On the Godbeite movement see Ronald W. Walker, *Wayward Saints: The Godbeites and Brigham Young* (Urbana: University of Illinois Press, 1998).

CHAPTER TWO

On the economic history of Utah see: Leonard J. Arrington, *Great Basin Kingdom: An Economic History of the Latter-day Saints, 1830-1900* (Cambridge, Mass.: Harvard University press, 1958); "Measures of Economic Changes in Utah, 184701947," *Utah Economic and Business Review* 7 (December 1947). On mining in Utah see the Summer 1963 issue of the *Utah Historical Quarterly*; Rodman W. Paul, *Mining Frontiers of the Far West* (New York: Holt, Rinehart and Winston, 1963); Clark C. Spence, *British Investments and the American Mining Frontier, 1860-1891* (Ithaca: Cornell University Press, 1958); George A. Thompson and Frazier Buck, *Treasure Mountain Home: Park City Revisited* (Salt Lake City: Dream Garden Press, 1981); and Charles E. Hughes, "An Investigation of Smelting in the Salt Lake Valley Prior to 1900" Timpanogos Research Associates, 1990.

Much work has been done on the non-Mormon churches. On the Catholics see: Robert Joseph Dwyer, *The Gentile Comes to Utah: A Study in Religious and Social Conflict (1862-1890)* (Salt Lake City: Western Epics, 1971), Bernice Maher Mooney, *Salt of the Earth: a History of the Catholic Diocese, 1776-1987* ed. Jerome C. Stoffel (Salt Lake City: Catholic Diocese of Salt Lake City, 1987). On the Episcopalians see Daniel Sylvester Tuttle, *Missionary to the Mountain West: Reminiscences of Episcopal Bishop Daniel S. Tuttle, 1866-1886* (Salt Lake City: University of Utah Press, 1987). On the other churches see Dwyer, Ferenc Morton Szasz, *The Protestant Clergy in the Great Plains and the Mountain West, 1865-1915* (Albuquerque, University of New Mexico Press, 1988); and Thomas Edgar Lyon, "Evangelical Protestant Missionary Activity in Mormon Dominated Areas, 1869-1962" (Ph. D. dissertation, University of Utah, 1962). On the Godbeites see Ronald W. Walker, *Wayward Saints: The Godbeites and Brigham Young* (Urbana: University of Illinois Press, 1998).

On plural marriage see Richard S. Van Wagoner, *Mormon Polygamy: A History* (Salt Lake City: Signature Books, 1986) and Jessie L. Embry, *Mormon Polygamous Families: Life in the Principle* (Salt Lake City: University of Utah press, 1987). On James B. McKean see Thomas G. Alexander, "'Federal Authority vs. Polygamic Theocracy,' James B. McKean and the Mormons, 1970-1875" *Dialogue: A Journal of Mormon Thought* 1 (Autumn 1966): 85-100. On the career of Charles S. Zane see Thomas G. Alexander, "Charles S. Zane: Apostle of the New Era," *Utah Historical Quarterly* 34 (Fall 1966): 290-314. On the Woodruff manifesto see Alexander, *Things in Heaven and Earth* and Davis Bitton, *George Q. Cannon: A Biography* (Salt Lake City: Deseret Book, 1999). On the struggle for statehood see Edward Leo Lyman, *Political Deliverance: The Mormon Struggle for Utah Statehood* (Urbana: University of Illinois Press, 1986).

CHAPTER THREE

For general histories of the period see: Thomas G. Alexander and James B. Allen, *Mormons and Gentiles: A History of Salt Lake City* (Boulder, CO: Pruett, 1984) and John S. McCormick, *Salt Lake City: The Gathering Place* (Woodland Hills, CA: Windsor, 1980). For architecture of downtown Salt Lake City see John S. McCormick, *The Historic Buildings of Downtown Salt Lake City* (Salt Lake City: Utah State Historical Society, 1982). On prostitution in Salt Lake City see Jeffrey Donald Nichols, "Prostitution and Polygamy: The Contest over Morality in Salt Lake City, 1847-1918," (Ph. D. Dissertation, University of Utah, 1998) and John S. McCormick, "Red Lights in Zion: Salt Lake City's Stockade, 1908-11," *Utah Historical Quarterly* 50 (Spring 1982): 168-181. On the national debate over prostitution see David J. Pivar, *Purity Crusade: Sexual Morality and Social Control, 1868-1900* (Westport, Conn.: Greenwood Press, 1973); Ruth Rosen, *The Lost Sisterhood: Prostitution in America, 1900-1918* (Baltimore: Johns Hopkins University Press, 1982); and Anne M. Butler, *Daughters of Joy, Sisters of Misery: Prostitutes in the American West, 1865-1890* (Urbana: University of Illinois press, 1985).

On the development of urban utilities and parks and the battle against air pollution see Thomas G. Alexander, "Cooperation, Conflict, and Compromise: Women, Men, and the Environment in Salt Lake City, 1890-1930," *Brigham Young University Studies* 35 (1995): 6-39 and idem., "Sylvester Q. Cannon and the Revival of Environmental Consciousness in the Mormon Community," *Environmental History* 3 (October 1998): 488-507. On the smoke campaign see also Walter E. Pittman, Jr., "The Smoke Abatement Campaign in Salt Lake City, 1890-1925," *Locus* 1 (Fall 1989): 69-78; and John E. Lamborn and Charles S. Peterson, "The Substance of the Land: Agriculture v. Industry in the Smelter Cases of 1904 and 1906," *Utah Historical Quarterly* 53 (Fall, 1985): 319-21.

On the Salt Lake Theatre see: Ronald W. Walker and Alexander M. Starr, "Shattering the Vase: The Razing of the Old Salt Lake Theatre," *Utah Historical Quarterly* 57 (Winter 1989): 64-88; and Thomas G. Alexander, *Mormonism in Transition: A History of the Latter-day Saints, 1890-1930* (2nd ed.; Urbana: University of Illinois Press, 1996)

On African Americans in Salt Lake City see France Davis, *Light in the Midst of Zion: A History of Black Baptists in Utah* (Salt Lake City: University Publishing, 1997) and Ronald G. Coleman, "Blacks in Utah History: An Unknown Legacy," in *The Peoples of Utah* ed. Helen Papanikolas (Salt Lake City: Utah State Historical Society, 1976), 115-140. On the Japanese of Utah see Helen Z. Papanikolas and Alice Kasai, "Japanese

Life in Utah," in *The People's of Utah*, 333-362; McCormick, *The Historic Buildings of Downtown Salt Lake City*; and Nancy J. Taniguchi, "Japanese Immigrants in Utah," in *Utah History Encyclopedia* ed. A. Kent Powell, pp. 281-283. On the Greeks see Helen Zeese Papanikolas, "Toil and Rage in a New Land: The Greek Immigrants in Utah," *Utah Historical Quarterly* 38 (1970). On the Italians see Philip F. Notarianni, "Italianita in Utah: The Immigrant Experience," in *The Peoples of Utah*, 303-331. On the Joe Hill case see: Gibbs M. Smith, *Joe Hill* (Salt Lake City: University of Utah Press, 1969).

CHAPTER FOUR

For statistics on economic conditions in Salt Lake City and Utah during the 1920s and the Great Depression see "Measures of Economic Changes in Utah 1847-1947," *Utah Economic and Business Review* 7 (December 1847). For a narrative treatment of conditions during the Depression see Wayne K. Hinton, "The New Deal Years: A Political History of Utah, 1932-1940," (M.A. thesis, Utah State University, 1963). For conditions in Salt Lake City see McCormick, *The Gathering Place*, Chapter 8 and Alexander and Allen, *Mormons and Gentiles*, Chapter 7. For an extended discussion of welfare, employment, and other assistance see Garth L. Mangum and Bruce D. Blumell, *The Mormons' War on Poverty* (Salt Lake City: University of Utah Press, 1993). On the work of women during the Depression see Linda Sillitoe, *A History of Salt Lake County* (Salt Lake City: Utah State Historical Society, 1996). On the federal art projects see Vern G. Swanson, Robert S. Olpin, and William C. Seifrit, *Utah Painting and Sculpture* (Salt Lake City: Gibbs Smith, 1997).

On the Provo River Project see Leonard J. Arrington and Thomas G. Alexander, *Water for Urban Reclamation: The Provo River Project* (Logan, UT: Utah Agricultural Experiment Station, 1966).

On the development of winter sports see Alan K. Engen and Gregory C. Thompson, *First Tracks, A Century of Skiing in Utah* (Layton, UT: Gibbs Smith, 2001), Alexis Kelner, *Skiing in Utah: A History* (Salt Lake City: Privately Printed, 1980) and Alan K. Engen, *For the Love of Skiing: A Visual History* (Salt Lake City: Gibbs Smith, 1998). For the role of the Forest Service in developing ski areas see Thomas G. Alexander, *The Rise of Multiple-use Management in the Mountain West: A History of Region 4 of the Forest Service* (Washington, D. C.: U. S. Forest Service, 1987).

On Salt Lake City during World War II and the Erwin and Jenkins scandals, see Alexander and Allen, *Mormons and Gentiles*.

CHAPTER FIVE

On the conversion and changes in the defense plants see Alexander and Allen, *Mormons and Gentiles*. For the change in downtown Salt Lake City see McCormick, *The Gathering Place* and Alexander and Allen, *Mormons and Gentiles*.

On the defense installations see a series of articles by Leonard J. Arrington, Thomas G. Alexander and others. These include: Arrington, Alexander, and Eugene A. Erb, Jr., "Utah's Biggest Business: Ogden Air Materiel Area at Hill Air Force Base, 1938-1965," *Utah Historical Quarterly* 33 (Winter 1965): 8-33; Arrington and Alexander, "Supply Hub of the West: Defense Depot Ogden, 1941-1964," *Utah Historical Quarterly* 32 (Spring 1964): 99-121; Arrington and Alexander, "They Kept 'Em Rolling: The Tooele Army Depot, 1942-1962," *Utah Historical Quarterly* 31 (Winter 1963): 3-24; and Arrington and Alexander, "Utah's Small Arms Ammunition Plant During World War II," *Pacific Historical Review* 34 (May 1965): 185-96; and Arrington and Anthony T. Cluff, *Federally-financed Industrial Plants Constructed in Utah During World War II* (Logan, UT: Utah State University Press, 1969). On the changes at the University of Utah see Paul W. Hodson, *My Several Lives: An Autobiography* (Midvale, UT: Keeban, 2000).

On music and the arts see Lowell M. Durham, Abravanel (Salt Lake City: University of Utah Press, 1989); Trudy McMurrin, ed., *Utah: State of the Arts* (Ogden, UT: Meridian International, 1993).

On the development of skiing see: Engen and Thompson, *First Tracks, A Century of Skiing in Utah*, Engen, *For the Love of Skiing: A Visual History* and Kelner, *Skiing in Utah: A History*.

On African Americans see Ronald Coleman, "Blacks in Utah History: An Unknown Legacy," *The Peoples of Utah* ed. Helen Z. Papanikolas (Salt Lake City: Utah State Historical Society, 1976), 115-140; Linda Sillitoe, *Friendly Fire: The ACLU in Utah* (Salt Lake City: Signature Books, 1996); Sillitoe's History of Salt Lake County (Salt Lake City: Utah State Historical Society, 1996); and Alexander and Allen, *Mormons and Gentiles*.

CHAPTER SIX

The classic study of American suburbanization is Kenneth T. Jackson's *The Crabgrass Frontier: The Suburbanization of the United States* (New York: Oxford University Press, 1985). For information on the Gateway project see the Boyer Company's Web site, the *Deseret News*, October 25, 2000, and the *Salt Lake Tribune*, March 16, 2001. On the city's historic districts see the *Salt Lake Tribune*, February 26, 2001. I obtained information on Mike and Cindy Mitchell from personal interviews, February 26 and 28, 2001. For statistical information I relied on Allen Kent Powell, ed. *Utah History Encyclopedia* (Salt Lake City: University of Utah Press, 1994) and the *Salt Lake Tribune*, March 23, 2001.

On relations between Mormons and non-Mormons, I found most useful Anne-Marie Waddell's "Ways of Accepting Difference: An Ethnographic Study of Modern Non-Mormon Immigrants to Salt Lake City," (Master's Thesis, University of Utah, 2000). This was an attempt to provide a balanced study. News stories and letters to the editor in the *Salt Lake Tribune* which complain about the excessive Mormon influence in the city seem to represent the attitudes of people with axes to grind.

For the 2002 Olympic games, I have relied principally on stories in the *Salt Lake Tribune*, especially December 11, 1998; January 22, 1999; 2000, June 12, July 3, 21, December 19, 2000; and February 9, and March 17 and 18, 2001. On the Olympic venues, I have relied on the *Daily Herald*, January 29

and February 9, 2001 and the *Salt Lake Tribune*, January 29, 2001. On the TRAX line, I got information from the Utah Transit Authority website and the *Salt Lake Tribune*, February 22, 2001.

For the general information on the city and especially information on minorities, I have relied on Linda Sillitoe's *A History of Salt Lake County* (Salt Lake City: Utah State Historical Society, 1996), Alexander and Allen, *Mormons and Gentiles: A History of Salt Lake City* (Boulder, CO: Pruett, 1984), the second edition of John McCormick's *The Gathering Place* (Salt Lake City: Signature Books, 2000), Jorge Iber's *Hispanics in the Mormon Zion, 1912-1999* (College Station, TX: Texas A & M University Press, 2000), Jessie Embry's *"In His Own Language:" Mormon Spanish Speaking Congregations in the United States* (Provo, UT: Charles Redd Center for Western Studies, 1997), Leslie G. Kelen and Eileen Hallet Stone, *Missing Stories: An Oral History of Ethnic and Minority Groups in Utah* (Salt Lake City: University of Utah Press, 1996), France A. Davis, *Light in the Midst of Zion: A History of Black Baptists in Utah* (Salt Lake City: University Publishing, 1997), and Forrest S. Cuch, ed., *A History of Utah's American Indians* (Salt Lake City: Utah State Division of Indian Affairs and Utah State Division of History, 2000). On Karl Malone, I relied on the Utah Jazz Web site. Information on the percentage of Hispanics in the LDS Church came from an interview with Ignacio Garcia.

On changes in the business community see *Salt Lake Tribune*, January 13, 23, 2000 and January 1, 2001. On June Morris see *Utah Spirit* 26 (February 2001): 6-7. On Southwest Airlines, I obtained the information from the company's Web site.

INDEX

Abel, Elijah 38
Abel, Mary Ann 38
Abravanel Hall...........93
Abravanel, Maurice 93,95,97
Adams, Maude 64
African Methodist Episcopal Church ..35
Alcoholics Anonymous 87
Alexander Dumas Literary Society 65
Alexander, Marilyn 119
Allen, Clarence E. 58
Allen, Corinne T. 58
Alpine Loop...........82, 102
Alta Club...........52
Alta Ski School 102
American Civil Liberties
Union, The...........105,114
American Fork Canyon 32
American G. I. Forum 121
AMOCO 90
AMTRAK 113
Anderson, Judge Thomas J. 47
Anderson, Marian 105
Anderson, Ross C. "Rocky" 113
Andreasen, Calmar 80
Andresen, Axel 79
Angell, Truman O. 26
Antelope Island 16
Anthony, Susan B. 38
Armstrong, A. J. 59
Armstrong, Mayor Francis 46,48
Arsenal Hill 52
Art Barn...........77
Arthur, President Chester A. 42
Auerbach, Samuel H. 35
Auerbach, Theodore 35
Backman, Gus P. 73,105
Bamberger, Ida Maas...........56
Bamberger, Simon 56
Baring Brothers 53
Barnett, Alan 110
Barney, Lewis 19
Barrett, Patty 102
Barrett, Robert M. 102
Baskin, Mayor Robert N. 48,57
Bass, Richard D. 102
Bates, George C. 41
Beales, Reginald 76
Bear Hollow 115

Bear River 15
Beaver County...........29
Beaver Mountain 82,103
Becker Hill 79
Becker, Gus...........79
Becker, Sharon 86
Beehive House 26,36
Beers, W. D. 75
Belafonte, Harry 105
Bennett, Senator Wallace F. 105
Bernhardt, Sarah 64
Big Cottonwood Canyon 78,102
Big Cottonwood Creek 32
Bingham 27,32,67
Bingham Canyon 27,32
Bingham, Sanford 27
Bird, George W. 52
Bjorngaard, Halvor 79
Blue Vein Society 67
Bonneville Golf Course 78
Bonneville, Benjamin L. E. 16
Book of Mormon 17
Bosone, Reva Beck 87
Bowman, Mayor John F. 72
Box Elder...........32
Box Elder County 16
Boy Scouts...........64
Boyce, Ronald 117
Boyer Company...........13
Brandebury, Judge Lemuel G. 24
Brannan, Samuel 17,23
Bransford, John S. 34,54
Brewster, Sheldon 103
Brian Head 103
Bridger, James 15,18,
Brigham City 32,96
Brigham Street 52
Brigham Young Monument 114
Brigham Young University 13,78,95
Brighton 13,78,82,102
Brocchus, Judge Perry E. 24
Brooks, Juanita 77
Brown, Hugh B. 105
Brown, Les 77
Browning, Jonathan...........122
Buchanan, President James...........25
Buddhist Association 68
Buddhist Church 68,119

Bullock, Thomas 19
Bureau of Mines 64
Burke, Billie 64
Burleigh, Charles 32
Burnham, Daniel H. 56,57
Burns, Robert 102
Burrows, Julius C. 54
Burton, Harold W. 68
Burton, Sir Richard 29
C. C. Bates Electric Company 52
Cable Act 68
Cache National Forest 82
Cache Valley...........15,32
Calder's Park 39,59
Callister, Dr. A. Cyril...........99
Calvary Baptist Church...........55,67,120
Camelia Arts and Crafts Club...........67
Camp Floyd...........25
Camp Scott 25
Campbell, Andrew...........65
Cannon, Curtis Y. 53
Cannon, George Q. 34
Cannon, Martha Hughes 57
Cannon, Sylvester Q. 58,72, 73
Capital Hill 50,110
Capitol Theater 93
Carlson Hall 74
Carranza, Venustiano 67
Carson City 77,102
Carson, Kit 16,39
Carter, C. W. 14,32
Carvalho, Solomon Nunes 14
Cassidy, Butch...........103
Catherine Pass 78
CBS...........96
Cedar Breaks National Monument 103
Cedar City 35,93
Cedar Valley 25
Center Street...........108
Central City 109
Central City Community Council...........91
Central Pacific 29,32
Central Park 56
Centro Civico Mexicano 121
Chamber of Commerce 56,59,73,92
Chevron...........90
Chicken Creek 32
Chicken Springs 82

Christensen, Willam.....................96,97
Church of Jesus Christ of Latter-day Saints 10,12,52,54,72,73,90,104,113,114
Church of Jesus Christ of Latter-day Saints, First Presidency.............24,48,96
Church of Jesus Christ of Latter-day Saints, General Conference 54,114
Church of Jesus Christ of Latter-day Saints, Museum of Church History and Art 92
Church of Jesus Christ of Latter-day Saints, Relief Society 24,39,73,74
Church of Zion 38
Church Welfare Plan...........................74
City and County Building 39,52,110
City Creek..12
City Creek Canyon 62
Civic Improvement League 56
Civil War 26,41
Civil Works Administration (CWA) 74
Civilian Conservation Corp........75,82,83
Clark, John 54
Clawson, Rudger 42
Clawson, Spencer 47
Clayton, William 18
Clearfield Naval Supply Depot 85
Clift House 39
Clinton, Jeter.....................................41
Clyde, George D. 110
Coalition Mining Company..................34
Cobb, Henry Ives 52
Coconut Grove.............................77,103
Cody, William F. (Buffalo Bill) 64
Cold War 90,122
Coleman, Dr. Ronald...........................120
Collins, Fr. James E. 121,122
Colombian Exposition 56
Colorado Plateau..................................32
Colorado River 75
Columbia Records................................96
Commercial Street 55
Condie, Conductor Richard P. 96
Confederate Army 26
Congregationalist New West Education Commission 37
Connor, Patrick Edward...........27, 26,41
Cooper-Roberts Architects 110
Cornwall, J. Spencer 96
Corradini, Mayor Deedee 110,112,114
Cottonwood Mall 92
Council of Social Agencies 73
Cowles, President LeRoy 99
Crane Building 110

Crimean War...25
Crismon, Charles 22
Crockett, J. Allan................................95
Crosby, Oscar 18
Cross-Country Combined Championship.....................................80
Cugat, Xavier 77
Cumming, Alfred..................................25
Dallin, Cyrus 37
Davis County..108
Davis, Rev., France A. 120
Day, Indian Agent Henry R. 24
Dee, James 41
Deer Creek Dam and Reservoir 75
Deer Valley 80,100,117
Delta Airlines 99,122
Delta Center, The 112
Denver and Rio Grande Western Pacific Railroads 32,68,80
DePaulis, Mayor Palmer.............110,111
Derks Field...................................100,112
Derks, John C. 100
Dern, George H. 34
Deseret Club 40
Deseret Dramatic Association 24
Deseret Employment Bureau 73
Deseret National Bank 34
Deseret News 26,92
Deseret Philharmonic Society.............24
Devereaux House 34,26,53,111
Dillards 122
Dillworth, Mary Jane...........................23
Dixie Land...67
Dokas, N. A. 68
Dominguez, Francisco Atanasio 15
Dominguez-Escalante expedition 15
Donner Lake 17
Donner, Jacob 16
Dooley, John E. 58
Douglas Arms Corporation 86
Doyle, Zane 82
Droubay, S. K. 102
Drummond, Judge William W. 25
Dry Creek Canyon 78
Duchin, Eddy 77
Dugway Proving Grounds 85,90
Dyer, Frank H. 44
Eagle Emporium 34
Eagle Gate..47
Eccles, George 122
Echo Canyon..16
Ecker, Peter...79
Edmunds Act.......................................42

Edmunds-Tucker Act 44
Egan, Howard 18
Egbert, John 27
EIMCO...35
Eitel McCullough 85,90
Eldredge, Horace 27
Electric Alley..55
Emerson, Judge Philip..........................42
Emigration Canyon 10,77,93
Emigration Creek 12
Emma Mine 32
Engen, Alf 79,102
Engen, Corey 79,82
Engen, Sverre 79
Englebrecht, Paul 41
Ensign Peak..18
Episcopal Church...........................36,65
Estin, Hans 103
Fairbanks, J. Leo 58
Farnham Hotel 38
Federal Arts Project 77
Federal Emergency Relief Administration 73,74
Federal Housing Administration 90,91
Ferris, Warren A. 16
Ferry, W. Mont 56, 63
Field House of Natural History 74
Fillmore, President Millard 20
Finch, Harry L. 87
First Interstate Bank 122
First Security Corporation..................122
Fitzpatrick, John F. 105
Fitzpatrick, Thomas.............................16
Fletcher, James C. 99
Floyd, John 25
Folsom, William H. 26
Ford Motor Credit Union 102
Fort Bridger 16
Fort Douglas 26,36,65,74,90,117
Fort Hall 16
Fort Nez Perce 15
Fort Vancouver 15
Foulger, Sidney 92
Fowler, William 64,95
Foy, Eddie 64
Frankfurt, Michael P. 103
Frederick, David 35
Fremont Indian Village 13
Frémont Island 16
Frémont, John C. 16
Frisco 29,32
Fuller, Craig W. 112,118

Gallatin, Albert 16
Gardner, Archibald 27
Gardo House, The..............................35
Gates, Crawford 96
Gates, Susa Young 56
Gila River Valley 17
Gilbert, Cass 57
Glade, Mayor Earl J. 87,90
Glendale Gardens 86
Glendinning, James J. 48,54
Godbe, William S. 28,35
Godbeite 28,29,38
Goldsmith, Stephen 111
Gottschalk, Robert M. 103
Grant, Jedediah M. 24
Grant, Ulysses S. 40
Greater Avenues
Community Council 109
Grice, Frances H. 65
Guadalupana Society 121
Gurr, James E. 80
Hager, Cristl 116
Haggin, James Ben Ali.........................34
Hale, Albert 112
Hale, Frederick Albert.........................52
Hampton, Brigham Y. 43
Hampton, Lionel...............................105
Hancock County 17
Hancock, Joseph 19
Hanks, Lincoln 98
Hansen, James 117
Harding, Richard F. 86
Harmon, Appleton M. 18
Harmony Dancing Club 39
Harriman, Averell 80
Harriman, Edward H. 55
Harris, Broughton D. 24
Harris, Fisher S. 75
Harrison, Conrad B. 92,111
Harrison, Elias L. T. 28
Hashimoto, Edward I. 65,67,85
Hashimoto, Lois Hide Niija 67
Hastings, Lansford W. 16
Hatch, Senator Orrin 117
Haugen, Anders..................................79
Haugen, Lars.....................................79
Hayne, Julia Dean 24
Haywood, William D. 69
Hemingway, Richard 92
Hempstead, Charles H. 26
Henry, Matthew 35
Hill Air Force Base 85
Hill, Emma 78

Hill, Joe 69
Hilton, O. N. 69
Hitler, Adolph...............................83,95
Hogle Zoo 77
Hogle, James A. 77
Hogle, James E. 102
Holding, Earl 117
Holy Trinity Greek Orthodox Church 68
Hooper, William H. 27
Hoover, President Herbert 73
Horne, Alice Merrill.......................56,93
Horticultural Society 24
Hotel Utah 52,77,105,114
Houlihan, Richard 102
Houston Symphony............................95
Houtz Livery Stable............................41
Howell, Martha J. Perkins 38
Howell, Paul Cephas...........................38
Hudsons Bay Company........................15
Humboldt River.................................16
Hunsaker, Paul 102
Hunt, Bishop Duane 122
Hurd, Kate May Erskine 59
Hurst, George 34
Hussey, Warren 36
Hvalstad, Halvor 79
Ickes, Harold.....................................74
Iliff, Thomas Corwin...........................38
Immanuel Baptist Church....................65
Independence Hall 36
Indian Training Education Center 121
Indian Walk-In Center 121
Industrial Workers of the
World (IWW) 69
Intermountain Buddhist Church..........68
Intermountain Republican 57
International Olympic Committee 115
Iroquois 15
J. Willard Marriott Library 116
J.C. Penney 122
Jackson Hole 100
Jackson, Sheldon.................................37
Janssen, Werner 95
Japanese-American Citizen's League....86
Jennings, William 26
Jensen, Vernon 69
Johnson, Dave 115
Johnson, G. Ted 102
Johnston, Albert Sidney 25
Joklik, Frank 115
Jolson, Al 64
Jordan River 14,52,119

Joseph Smith
Memorial Building 35,52,114
Juab Valley..32
Kalunite Alumina Company 85
Kane, Thomas L. 25
Katsanevas, Emmanuel 69
Kearns Army Air Base 85
Kearns Family 33
Kearns Mansion, The 34,93
Kearns, Edmund 33
Kearns, Helen 33
Kearns, Jennie Judge 33
Kearns, Thomas 33,54
Keith, David 34
Kelly, Edward 36
Kennecott Building 92
Kennecott Copper Corporation 122
Kennedy, John F. 104
Kessler, George E. 57
Key Bank 122
Khashoggi, Adnan.........................93,111
Khashoggi, Essam 93,111
Kimball Junction 115
Kimball, Ellen Sanders 18
Kimball, Heber C. 19,93
Kimball, Spencer W. 105,120
Kincaid, Charles A. 23
King, Congressman William H. 56
King, Martin Luther.......................65,120
Kittson, William 16
Kletting, Richard K. A. 53
Knight, Jesse 34
Kobe College 67
Korean War 90
Koziol, Felix C. 80,82
Krupa, Gene 77
KSL-TV 93
Kurumada, Jun 86
Kuwahara, Kenryo 68
Lake Bonneville 13
Lawrence, Henry W. 40
Leatherwood, Elmer O. 57
Leclerc, Francois.................................15
Lee, Ann 17
Lee, J. Bracken 92
Levitt, Anne......................................93
Liberty Park..................39,52,56,77,111
Liberty Stake 73
Lincoln, President Abraham 26
Lindsey, Mark 62
Little Cottonwood Canyon 27,32,78,100
Little Mountain..................................10
Livingston, Charles 23

Logan Canyon 82,103
Louisiana Tech 120
Lunt, Emma 53
Lyman, Amasa 38
Lyman, Amy Brown 73
MacArthur, General Douglas 88
Main Street 21,34,52, 90,91,114
Malone, Karl 119
Mann Act 55
Marcus, Mayor Louis 74,75
Marist Fathers 36
Markham, Stephen 18
Marmalade District 108
Marsh, Benjamin C. 57
Marshall, James............................23
Marysville 36
Massachusetts Institute
of Technology 58
Matheson, J. B. 87
Matheson, Norma Warenski 110
Matheson, Scott M. 110
Matthews, Milton P. 100
Maw, Governor Herbert B. 87
McAlfred, A. D. 65
McAllister, City Marshal John D. T. 41
McBean Gladden, ...85
McCornick, William S. 34
McDowell, General Irvin 27
McGarry, Edward 26
McKay, David O. 104,105
McKean, Judge James B. 40,41
McLeod, Norman 36
Merrill, Emily L. Traub 64
Merrill, Fr. Jerald H. 121
Merrill, Joseph F. 64
Merrill, Marriner W. 44
Metropolitan Hall of Justice 92,112
Metropolitan Opera Company 95
Metropolitan Water District 75
Mexican War, The 17
Midgley, Waldo 75
Miera y Pacheco, Don Bernardo 15
Military Department of Utah 26
Miller, Allie 53
Miller, Larry H. 112,114
Miller, William 17
Miscegenation Law 67
Missouri River.............................12
Monheim, Henry............................52
Monnett, Osborne..........................64
Morgan, Dale 77
Mormon Battalion 17

Mormon Church (See also Church of
Jesus Christ of Latter-day Saints) 105
Mormon Island, California 23
Mormon Pioneers...........................12,53
Mormon Tabernacle Choir.............39,96
Moroni, Angel 37
Morrill Anti-bigamy Act 41, 42
Morris, June 122
Morris, Nephi L. 56
Morrison, John G. 69
Moss, Frank E. 104
Mount Ogden.............................. 82
Mount Timpanogos 75,102
Mountain Meadows Massacre 36
Moyle, James H. 82
Mulvey, Councilman Martin E. 55
Murdock Travel 122
Museum of Utah............................114
National Association for the Advancement
of Colored People (NAACP)..............120
National Association of Home Builders 91
National Register of Historic Places......108
National Ski Association 79
National Ski Hall of Fame..................80
National Youth Administration 75
Nauvoo Legion 25
Nauvoo, Illinois 12
Navajos 121
Newhouse, Samuel 34
Newman, John Philip 37
Nibley Park Golf Course 39,62
Nibley, Charles W. 59
Nieves, Roberto 121
Ninth Army Corps Area......................86
Nixon, Richard M. 105
Nobel, Alfred..............................32
Nordic Valley 83,102
Nordstrom 122
Northern Pacific...........................29,32
Northwest Energy Company 90
Northwestern Shoshone..................14,15
Norwegian Young Folks Society............79
Norwegian-American Athletic Club 79
Notre Dame 36
Obon Festival 119
Office of Public Archaeology................13
Ogden Arsenal 85
Ogden Chamber of Commerce 79
Ogden Valley 79,102
Ogden Winter Sports Committee 79
Ogden, Peter Skene...........................15
Ogilvie, Alex 27
Oglesby, Belle 38

Okland, Jack 92
Olpin, A. Ray..............................95
Olympic Winter Games 115
Olympics 80,114
Oquirrh Mountains 13,32
Oquirrh Park Oval.........................117
Order of Perpetual Adoration 121
Oregon Trail 16
Ormandy, Eugene 96
Oswald, Delmont 93
Ottley, Jerold 96
Pacific Coast League 100,112
Pack, John 18
Paiutes 15,121
Papanikolas, Helen 68
Park City 27,32,56,78,115
Park, John R. 23
Park, Lindsey..............................62
Park, Samuel C. 57
Parsons, C. C. 75
Patterson, D. J. 53
Paul, William 26
Pearce, Elijah 108
Pearce-Browning-Auers Home, The ..108
Pearl Harbor.............................. 85
Perpetual Emigrating Fund Company 23
Philadelphia Symphony....................96
Phillips Petroleum Company 90
Phillips, LaRue 62
Piercy, Frederick 19
Pilot Peak 16
Pioneer League 100
Pioneer Park 19,60,113
Pioneer Stake 72
Pivar, David J. 55
Platte River 12
Plum Alley................................ 39,65
Poland Act................................42
Polk, President James K. 20
Polysophical Society...................... 24
Pope, Hyrum C. 68
Pope, Robert A. 57
Powder Mountain 83,102
Powers, Orlando W. 56
Pratt, Orson 10,37
Pratt, Parley P. 20
Preuss, Charles 16
Princess Alice 77
Progressive Movement 64
Promontory Summit 29
Proudfoot, Willis T. 52
Provo Canyon 82
Provo River Project.........................75

Provost, Etienne 15
Public Works Administration (PWA) 74
Pueblo 18
Radio City Music Hall 95
Rainbow Randevu 103,105
Raleigh, George 54
Rampton, Governor Calvin 110,115
Ramsay, Welcome F. 57
Ransohoff, Nicholas S. 35
Rasmusen, Henry 75
Rasmussen Ranch 79
Rasmussen, Lawrence 79
Rawlings, Calvin W. 95
Reconstruction Finance Corporation ..73
Red Butte Creek 12
Redford, Robert 103
Redman, Don 102
Reed, James....................................16
Rees, A. C. 75
Reichhold Award 95
Remington Arms Plant 85,90
Reynolds, A. E. 65
Reynolds, George 42
Rice, John D. 75
Rice-Eccles Stadium 117
Rich, Maxwell 115
Richards, Franklin D. 19,44
Richards, Lee Greene 75
Richards, Willard............................12
Rio Buenaventura 15
Rio Grande Depot 53,111
Ririe-Woodbury Dance Company 93
Rivera, Orlando 121
Roberts, Bolivar..............................46
Roberts, Jack 102
Robertson, Leroy 95
Rocky Mountain Conference 38
Romney, L. C. 87
Romney, Mitt 115
Roosevelt, President Franklin..........34,73
Rosenblatt, Morris............................95
Roundy, Frederick 18
Rowland Hall 36
Russell, Lillian 64
Salt Lake Chamber of Commerce......105
Salt Lake City
...........12,22,30,40,50,52,72,88,106,108
Salt Lake City Commission 87,103
Salt Lake City Council 114
Salt Lake City Engineer 58
Salt Lake City Gas Company 48
Salt Lake City
International Airport 99

Salt Lake City Library 112
Salt Lake City Mechanical
Inspection Department 64
Salt Lake City Post Office..................67
Salt Lake City School District.............75
Salt Lake Council of Women 56
Salt Lake Country Club 59
Salt Lake County Charity Department....73
Salt Lake County Department
of Public Welfare..............................74
Salt Lake Diocese 121
Salt Lake Federation of Labor.............86
Salt Lake Junior
Chamber of Commerce.......................80
Salt Lake Stake 19
Salt Lake Tabernacle 26,37,54,95
Salt Lake Temple 35,52
Salt Lake Theatre 24,39,64
Salt Lake Tribune...............34,78,92,115
Salt Lake Valley 32,53,93,118
Salt Palace 58,111
Salvation Army Thrift Store...............113
Sam, David 117
San Juan County 121
Saunders, T. 65
Savage, Charles R. 19,35,46,53
Scanlan, Bishop Lawrence 36
Schlachs, Henry 53
Schreiner, Alexander 95
Scott M. Matheson Courthouse, The 112
Scott, George M. 45
Second California Cavalry...................26
Sells, Elijah 48
Sheets, George A. 54
Shenck, Robert C. 34
Sherwood, Henry G. 19
Shipp, Ellis Reynolds 43
Shoshonis 14
Shumway, Charles............................17
Silliman, Benjamin 34
Silver King Coalition Mine 32
Skliris, Leonidas G. 68
Skousen, W. Cleon 92
Smet, Father Pierre Jean De 18
Smith, Allen 65
Smith, Bathsheba W. 43
Smith, Elias....................................17
Smith, George Albert 12,43,93,110
Smith, Gibbs 69
Smith, Hyrum 17
Smith, Jedediah Strong 15
Smith, John 19
Smith, Joseph F. 17,44,54,114

Smith, K. 82
Smoot, Reed 54
Snow Park Lodge 102
Snow Pine Lodge 83
Snow, Eliza R. 24
Snow, George W. 64
Snow, Lorenzo 24,69
Snowbasin 83
Snyderville.....................................102
SOCIO 121
Solitude Fork..................................102
Solitude Resort 102
South Temple 26,34,92,110
Sowles, M. B. 46
Spalding, Franklin S. 56
Spencer, Allen 53
Speyer, Fred H. 80
Spry, William 57
Squaw Valley 100
St. John 121
St. Louis 15,57
St. Marks School 38
St. Vincent....................................113
Staines, William 26
Standard Oil 55
Stanton, Elizabeth Cady 38
Starlight Gardens 77
State of Deseret, Legislature 20
Stavis, Barrie 69
Stegner, Wallace 69
Stenhouse, Thomas B. H. 26
Stevens, Lucinda Flake 38
Stewart, Hilda 102
Stone, Barton 17
Stoney, Charles T. 78
Strand, Mark 79
Suazo, Pete 120
Sugar House................................41,52
Sugar House Park...........................43,69
Sun Valley 80,100
Sundance Kid 103
Sutherland, George 56,121
Tanner, Elder Nathan Eldon 96,105
Tanner, Obert C. 96
Taylor, John 17,20,34
Taylor, Julius F. 67
Taylor, William W. 67
Tedesco, Fred 87
Temple Square 19,38,52,92,114
Thatcher, Moses 44
Thompson, Mayor Ezra 54
Thorpe, Vern R. 83
Timpanogos 102

Tintic Milling Company 34
Tojo, Hideki 83
Tokyo Bay 88
Tomomi, Iwakura 39
Tooele Ordnance Depot 85,90
Topham, Dora B. (Belle London) 55
Toyatome, H. 68
Tracy, Russell Lord 58,77
TRAX 13,118
Treasure Mountains 102
Treaty of Guadalupe Hidalgo 20
Triad Center 93,111
Trinity African Methodist
Episcopal Church 65
Tschaggeny, Judy 102
Tsukada 115
Tuttle, Bishop Daniel S. 36,38
U. S. Army Mountain Troops 84
U. S. Attorney General 41
U. S. Bureau of Reclamation...............75
U. S. Department of Transportation 99
U. S. Forest Service 80,81,102,117
U. S. House of Representatives 20
U. S. Supreme Court 41,56
Ulland, Sigurd 79
Union Pacific Depot 26,34,53,114
Union Pacific Railroad
...................26,32,53,55,80,111
United Air Lines 99,122
United Park City Mines Company 100
United States Olympic Committee......80
Universal Scientific Society.................24
University of Utah
.................23,52,74,90,114,117
Upper Snake River 32
Utah Arts Council, The.....................93
Utah Copper Company.......................67
Utah Court of Appeals 112
Utah Federation of Women 56
Utah Grizzlies Hockey Team.............117
Utah Heritage Foundation 110
Utah History Information Center
...............................55,72,110
Utah House of Representatives..........103
Utah Humanities Council........... 93,110
Utah Jazz...................................112
Utah Magazine 28
Utah Northern Railroad 29
Utah Opera Company........................93
Utah Opportunities
Industrialization Center 120
Utah Power and Light Company 55,98
Utah Ski Club 79

Utah Special Olympics 119
Utah Starzz 112
Utah State Capitol Building 39,75,93
Utah State Historical Society 18,110,113
Utah Statehood Enabling Act 48
Utah Sugar Company 35
Utah Symphony 76,92
Utah Territorial Organic Act 20
Utah Territorial Supreme Court 40
Utah Theater Ballet Company 96
Utah Transit Authority 99,118
Utah War...................................35
Velez de Escalante, Silvestre 15
Vietnam War 119
Waddell, Anne-Marie 114
Wade, J. H. 26
Wadsworth, Nelson 40,59,96
Wagner, I. J. 111
Waite, Morrison R. 42
Waldron, George B. 24
Walker Brothers 35
Walker Opera House.........................39
Walker, Jane 34
Walker, Joseph R. 15
Walker, Samuel Sharpe 35
Wallace, Glenn Walker 95
Wallace, John M. 90
Wallace, M. Walker 100
Wallace, William R. 75
Ward, Jordan 27
Warner, Theodore F. 23
Wasatch Academy 121
Wasatch Mountain Club 78
Wasatch Mountains 10,32,117
Wasatch National Forest 80
Wasatch Oasis 82
Washington Monument 24
Washington Square 39,56
Watson, Mayor George H. 80,81
Weber Canyon..............................16
Weber County 16
Weber State University 117
Weigand, Bishop William K. 121
Welch, Tom 115
Wells Fargo 122
Wells, Daniel H. 40,48
Wells, Heber M. 48,59
West Temple 65,92,111
West Valley City 92,108
West, Territorial Governor Caleb W. 46
Western Airlines 99
Western Federation of Miners 68
Westminster College 121

Whiskey Street 23
White River..............................16
White, James L. 95
Wilkes, Albert 59,74
Wilkinson, Manasseh H. 67
Williams, Kate 58
Williams, Terry 120
Wilson, Mayor Ted 99,110,111
Wilson, President Woodrow 69
Wolf Mountain 102
Woodbury, T. Bowring, ...95
Woodhull Brothers 12,32
Woodruff, Emma Smith 44
Woodruff, Wilford 12,44,93,110
Workman, Nancy............................113
Works Progress Administration 74,75, 86
World War I 72
World War II 64,75,87,99,105,120
Wright, Robert J. 100
Wright, Wallace A. 111
Yerba Buena...............................17
Young Men's Christian
Association (YMCA) 39
Young, Amelia Folsom 49
Young, Ann Eliza Webb Dee 41
Young, Brigham 12,52,24,62,93,114
Young, Clarissa Decker 18
Young, Harriet Decker 13,18
Young, Joseph Don Carlos.................52
Young, Lorenzo Dow 13
Young, Lucy Bigelow 56
Young, Mahonri M. 93
Young, Seraph 44
Young, Willard 58
Zane, Judge Charles S. 42
Zion's Cooperative Mercantile Institution
...................28,34,49,68,73,91,121
Zions Bancorporation 121
Zions Bank 122
Zoological Society 77

See following page for Partners & Web Site Index

PARTNERS &
WEB SITE INDEX

A & Z Produce Company 178
www.AZproduce.net

ABSOLUTE! Restaurant & Brasserie 200

Anton Boxrud Bed & Breakfast 201
www.bbiu.org/antonboxrud/

ARUP Laboratories 234
www.aruplab.com

Associated Food Stores 166
www.afstores.com

BC Technical Inc. 252
www.bctechnical.com

Beehive Credit Union 142
www.beehivecredit.com

Bush & Gudgell, Inc. 128
www.bushandgudgell.com

CCG Quality Office Furniture...................179
www.ccgqof.com

Central Utah Water
Conservancy District...................................216
www.cuwcd.com

Church of Jesus Christ of
Latter-day Saints, The 240
www.lds.org

Colonial Flag 180
www.colonialflag.com

Culinary Crafts 202
www.culinarycrafts.com

Cummings Studio Chocolates 168
www.citysearch.com/slc/cummingscandy

Dave Strong Porsche, Audi and
Volkswagen 203
www.davestrongs.com

Daynes Music Company 204
www.daynesmusic.com

Deseret Management Corporation 158
www.deseretmanagement.com

Dunford Bakers 181

Dynatronics Corporation 170
www.dynatron.com

Economic Development
Corporation of Utah, The..........................220
www.edcutah.org

Episcopal Diocese and Friends...................226
www.episcopal-ut.org

Equis International 254
www.equis.com

Evans & Sutherland 256
www.es.com

Fairchild Semiconductor 260
www.fairchildsemi.com

Fetzers' Inc. 182
www.fetzersinc.com

Floppy Copy, Inc. 263
www.floppycopy.com

General Distributing Company....................172

Granite Mill..132

Grant-Hatch & Associates, Inc. 144

Greenbacks®/All a Dollar℠ 205
www.greenbacks.com

Harman Management Corporation 194

Heartland Industries 174
www.heartlandind.com

Hexcel Corporation....................................183
www.hexcel.com

Hilton Salt Lake City Center 190
www.hilton.com

Historic Trolley Square 206
www.shopsimon.com

Huntsman Corporation 162
www.huntsman.com

KSL 212
www.ksl.com

Larry H. Miller Group 152
www.lhm.com

LDS Hospital 230
www.ihc.com

Meier & Frank/ZCMI 196

Mr. Mac..207
www.mrmac.com

New Star General Contractors 136
www.newstargc.com

Novell 260
www.novell.com

NPS Pharmaceuticals, Inc. 236
www.npsp.com

Oasis Stage Werks 233
www.oasis-stage.com

O.C. Tanner 176
www.octanner.com

OGIO International 184
www.ogio.com

Plaza Cycle 238
www.plazacycle.com

R.C. Willey Home Furnishings 198
www.rcwilley.com

Ralph L. Wadsworth
Construction Co., Inc. 138
www.wadsco.com

Salt Lake Chamber 221
www.saltlakechamber.org

Salt Lake City Credit Union........................149
www.slccu.com

Standard Builders Supply, Inc....................134

Thorup Brothers Construction 130

University of Utah
Health Sciences Center 244
www.hsc.utah.edu

University of Utah, The 242
www.utah.edu

Utah Film Commission 218
www.film.Utah.org

Utah Paperbox 185

Utah Power 222
www.pacificorp.com

Utah State Historical Society 246
www.history.utah.gov.

VA Salt Lake City Health
Care System 250

Varian Medical Systems 186
www.varian.com

Winder Dairy..208
www.winderdairy.com

Zions Bank 146
www.zionsbank.com

Zions Insurance Agency 148
www.zionsbank.com